Diary of the Dark Years, 1940–1944

Collaboration, Resistance, and Daily Life in Occupied Paris

JEAN GUÉHENNO

TRANSLATED AND ANNOTATED
BY DAVID BALL

OXFORD
UNIVERSITY PRESS

OXFORD
UNIVERSITY PRESS

Oxford University Press is a department of the
University of Oxford. It furthers the University's objective
of excellence in research, scholarship, and education
by publishing worldwide.

Oxford   New York

Auckland   Cape Town   Dar es Salaam   Hong Kong   Karachi
Kuala Lumpur   Madrid   Melbourne   Mexico City   Nairobi
New Delhi   Shanghai   Taipei   Toronto

With offices in

Argentina   Austria   Brazil   Chile   Czech Republic   France   Greece
Guatemala   Hungary   Italy   Japan   Poland   Portugal   Singapore
South Korea   Switzerland   Thailand   Turkey   Ukraine   Vietnam

Oxford is a registered trade mark of Oxford University Press
in the UK and certain other countries.

Published in the United States of America by
Oxford University Press
198 Madison Avenue, New York, NY 10016
Originally published as *Journal des années noires, 1940–1944*

© Editions GALLIMARD, Paris, 1947 and 2002
English translation © Oxford University Press 2014

First issued as an Oxford University Press paperback, 2016,

Library of Congress Cataloging-in-Publication Data
Guéhenno, Jean, 1890–1978.
[Journal des années noires, 1940–1944. English]
Diary of the dark years, 1940–1944 : collaboration, resistance, and daily life
in occupied Paris / Jean Guéhenno ; translated and annotated by David Ball.
pages   cm
Originally published as Journal des années noires, 1940–1944
by Gallimard (Paris) in 1947, 1973, and 2002.
ISBN 978-0-19-997086-5 (hardback); 978-0-19-049584-8 (paperback)
1. Guéhenno, Jean, 1890–1978—Diaries.   2. Authors, French—20th century—Diaries.
3. World War, 1939–1945—Personal narratives, French.   4. Paris (France)—History—
1940–1944.   5. France—History—German occupation, 1940–1945.
I. Ball, David, 1937–translator.   II. Title.
PQ2613.U187Z46   2014
848'.91209—dc23   2013050415

1 3 5 7 9 8 6 4 2

Printed in the United States of America
on acid-free paper

Diary of the Dark Years, 1940–1944

CONTENTS

ACKNOWLEDGMENTS

I wish to thank the Andrew W. Mellon Foundation for supporting my research in the Bibliothèque Nationale de France with an Emeritus Fellowship and Smith College, particularly Denise Rodino, for helping me apply. My office in Neilson Library, near many books and a knowledgeable staff, supported my work as well.

For the translation, I owe a great debt of gratitude, as ever, to my frequent co-translator who this time was my best critic: Nicole Ball. Her sharp eye and fine ear for both French and English improved this translation immeasurably.

I wish to thank my colleague Professor Thalia Pandiri for help with quotations from the Latin and Greek. Thalia, Tom Raworth, and my colleague Betsey Harries were all kind enough to lend me their excellent ears to test out different versions of some tricky passages. And thanks to Professor Gertraud Gutzmann, who helped with the German.

Special thanks to Tom for invaluable help with the photos. Without him there would have been no illustrations.

I am grateful for the assistance of Patrick Bachelier and Jean-Kely Paulhan for corrections to the text of the original and for their willingness to share their vast knowledge of Jean Guéhenno and his times. They are the source of a number of annotations in this edition. Among the corrections Patrick Bachelier supplied to the published French text are a few dates revised to conform to Guéhenno's original manuscript. The most important is the entry for May 15, 1941, the day after the first round-up of Jews in Paris, incorrectly added to the May 9, 1941, entry in the 2002 Gallimard edition.

Finally, thanks to my wonderful editor at Oxford University Press, Nancy Toff. I am grateful for her support and persistence in getting the project through, and also for her rapid, smart, and sometimes funny answers to my questions; they made her a pleasure to work with.

NOTE ON THE TEXT

This translation is based on *Journal des années noires, 1940–1944*, Gallimard/ Folio, 2002, but with corrections to the French text—particularly the dates of a few entries—graciously supplied by Patrick Bachelier, who, with Jean-Kely Paulhan, prepared the scholarly edition of the *Journal* from Guéhenno's original manuscript; it appeared a few months after the hardcover edition of this *Diary* was published. Both provided precious information and insights about Guéhenno that contributed to my annotations and *Translator's Introduction* to the present edition.

TRANSLATOR'S INTRODUCTION

Ever since it first appeared in 1947, Jean Guéhenno's *Journal des années noires* (*Diary of the Dark Years*) has been the book French readers have turned to most readily for an account of life under German occupation; its most recent paperback edition can be found in nearly any big bookstore in France. One French novelist and critic, Pierre Assouline, wrote in 2006 that it "has never left [him]," and the British biographer and journalist Catherine Moorehead put it at the top of her "Five Best" books on the French Resistance in the *Wall Street Journal*, calling it "both a portrait of the Occupation and a remarkable essay on courage and cowardice."[1] It is quite a portrait. No one gives us a better feel for daily life in occupied Paris than Guéhenno: the curfews, the increasing lack of food, the lack of heat through two very cold winters, the ever-present German military and bureaucracy, the controlled French radio and press ceaselessly presenting the same twisted version of reality, the feeling of no longer having any control over one's own life, the sense of being cut off from the outside world—in short, to use Guéhenno's word: prison.[2] Because its author was a writer by profession, the diary also gives a picture of the Paris literary world during that time; that is one place where "courage and cowardice" come in, particularly the latter. This is the diary historians quote the most to describe literary life and ordinary life in Paris during the Occupation.[3] Moreover, as the British historian Richard Cobb

---

[1] Pierre Assouline, in his blog in *Le Monde*'s book section, January 9, 2006 (http://passouline. blog.lemonde.fr/2006/01/09/2006_01_pourquoi_la_fra/); Caroline Moorehead in the *Wall Street Journal*, December 3, 2011 (http://online.wsj.com/article/SB10001424052970203802204577065990552888100.html).

[2] Guéhenno uses the words "prison" and "prisoners" 125 times in this diary. Camus employed the same metaphor in *The Plague* (1947), his allegorical novel of the Occupation, which he was writing in the center of France at the same time Guéhenno was keeping his diary in Paris: the people in Camus' plague-struck Oran are "prisoners of the plague." Clearly, that's what it felt like to live in occupied France.

[3] Thus Julian Jackson, in his monumental *France: The Dark Years, 1940–1944* (Oxford: Oxford University Press, 2001) cites Guéhenno ten times, occasionally at some length, and recommends we

says, Guéhenno knows "how to walk through the occupied city... to distinguish between the familiar and the unfamiliar, the reassuring and the alarming (the appearance of a yellow poster in the corridors of the *metro*, shiny and menacing)"—menacing because such posters usually announced German executions of hostages.[4]

Among the "unfamiliar," more striking scenes Guéhenno describes is the sight, on the streets of his neighborhood, of the first arrests of Jews headed for deportation to the concentration camps. "The working people of Paris who saw these heartrending scenes were full of indignation and shame," he concludes (May 15, 1941). A year later, the "unfamiliar" and the horrible have become familiar parts of daily life:

> Toward the end of a meager meal, we turn the dial on the radio. We calmly listen to them say that fifty-five hostages were shot in Lille, two divisions were exterminated in Russia, Malta has just undergone its 2,000th bombing, etc.... Then we savor that drop of wine we had been saving for the end of the dinner, we keep it in our mouths for a long time, dreaming of wine-cellars and barrels; finally we make up our minds to swallow it. And then we talk of the war that's coming, inevitably—civil war... We walk over to the window. The first iris has opened in the garden...
>
> —(May 4, 1942)

Later, he reports hearing French Resistance prisoners locked in a paddy wagon going down the Boulevard Saint-Michel at dusk, no doubt to their death, singing the *Marseillaise*. He notes that "[a] few people on the sidewalk barely stopped to watch them go by. It's true that night was already protecting us, but the black-uniformed police were watching. I hope the people were at least clenching their fists in their pockets" (December 3, 1943). And finally, in August 1944, he records his unforgettable impressions of the liberation of Paris.

Although he had written books that looked back on his life and reflected on his present, Guéhenno had never kept an actual, day-to-day diary before 1940.

---

read the diary. Richard Cobb, in his compelling essay *French and Germans, Germans and French: A Personal Interpretation of France Under Two Occupations, 1914–1918/1940–1944* (Hanover, NH: University Press of New England, 1983), has over twenty citations from the diary, calling it "moving" and "much the most illuminating" of the Occupation diaries (p. 181). Gisèle Sapiro, in *La guerre des écrivains (The Writers' War), 1940–1953* (Paris: Fayard, 1999), cites Guéhenno no fewer than fifty times, sometimes as an actor in the Intellectual Resistance, sometimes as a witness. She highlights his judgments on the responsibility of the writer.

[4] Cobb, op. cit. p. 116. He adds, among other tributes to the diarist's ability to capture the odd but significant details of life under Nazi occupation, "he has an eye for the desolate little groups of field-gray soldiers... as they wander through the sordid, seedy... run-down topography of a declining [amusement park.]" Cobb also pays tribute to Guéhenno's "exceptional imagination and generosity, capable of seeing the German soldier as an *individual*" (p. 117).

What drove him to write this one, and what enabled him to write it so well? The answer lies in the life of the diarist and the dramatic historical events that surrounded the production of this book.

Jean Guéhenno was fifty when, on June 17, 1940, after just six weeks of fighting, Marshal Philippe Pétain, a renowned eighty-four-year-old World War I general and the newly appointed premier of France, announced on the radio that French forces must lay down their arms: he had asked Germany for peace. Never in its long history had France known such a humiliating defeat.

Pétain's delegates signed the armistice on June 22, in direct violation of France's agreement with England but to the delight of Adolf Hitler, who was present for part of the ceremony. After Poland, Belgium, the Netherlands, and Luxembourg, France was going to be occupied by Nazi Germany—directly occupied as far south as the Massif Central (roughly three-fifths of France). However, there would be a "Free Zone" below it governed by the new French regime, whose authority theoretically extended all over what remained of France. Alsace and Lorraine were annexed to Germany, and there were smaller "forbidden zones" along the Atlantic and in the north.[5] Above all—though few saw it at the time— an armistice is a peace agreement that goes well beyond a simple ceasefire, so officially, Germany was no longer France's enemy: the foundations for French collaboration with their Nazi occupiers had been laid.

Despite the mortifying defeat and armistice, most French people were probably relieved that the slaughter had stopped. In those six weeks, the French had lost between 50,000 and 90,000 men, with at least twice that number of wounded.[6] Their army was cut into disorganized pieces, and millions of civilian refugees were clogging the roads, fleeing the German advance. It aroused memories of the more than 1.3 million dead and 4 million wounded France had suffered in the last war, which had ended just twenty-two years before. Nonetheless, for Guéhenno and many French men and women, the main feeling was no doubt one of shame: the humiliation of the crushing military defeat was intensified by witnessing the total capitulation of the new leaders of France and, increasingly, by their collaboration with the Nazi occupiers.[7]

[5] It was also agreed that France would pay Germany "the tidy sum of 400 million French francs [per day]" for the costs of occupying it (Allan Mitchell, *Nazi Paris: The History of an Occupation, 1940–1944* [New York: Berghahn Books, 2008], p. 14, citing German sources). Finally, the armistice signed with Italy two days later stipulated that Italy would occupy a good part of the Côte d'Azur.

[6] Julian Jackson, *The Fall of France: The Nazi Invasion of 1940* (Oxford: Oxford University Press, 2003), p. 180. Estimates of the number vary; some historians put it much higher.

[7] Jacques Debû-Bridel, who played an important role in the Resistance, quotes one of the first underground leaflets to appear in occupied France: "In 1940, France lived through two calamities: defeat and shame" (*La Résistance intellectuelle en France* [Paris: Juillard, 1970], p. 15). Despite appearances, this summed up the sentiments of the majority, he affirms. In 1944, Guéhenno expresses his shame that young Resistance fighters and, after D-Day, young Englishmen and Americans are fighting in his place. He uses the word *honte*—shame—over fifty times in this diary and its opposite,

Roughly two weeks after the armistice was signed, the panicked deputies and senators, meeting in the south-central resort town of Vichy, voted overwhelmingly to invest Pétain with "full powers," and the military defeat turned into the end of the French Republic. The "French State," as Pétain now called it, would have its capital down in Vichy. "An unregulated authoritarian regime was substituted for the structures of parliamentary democracy," as one historian summed it up.[8] Everything Guéhenno believed in had been destroyed—or worse, abandoned.

Jean Guéhenno was a well-known intellectual at the time, the author of four books and many essays and articles. From 1923 on, he had been the main literary critic for *Europe*, a respected left-wing cultural and political monthly, and its editor-in-chief from 1929 until 1936, when it was taken over by the Communist Party and he left to co-edit another journal. He was a *Normalien*—a former student of the prestigious École Normale Supérieure (like Sartre and Beauvoir a few decades later). He taught in Parisian lycées (public secondary schools) but only the highly selective post-graduate secondary school classes (*khâgne*), which prepared students for the nationwide competitive entrance examination to the humanities section of the École Normale, the public institution that has regularly produced the most distinguished intellectuals, researchers, and scientists of France to this day.

None of this would be very different from the profile of many Parisian intellectuals in 1940 were it not for the extraordinary facts of Guéhenno's life. He was born Marcel Guéhenno (but called Jean after his father, Jean-Marie) on March 25, 1890, in Fougères, a newly industrialized town in Brittany, one of the poorest regions of France; his father worked in a shoe factory and his mother was a piece-worker, stitching leather at home for a wage even more wretched than her husband's.[9] "She was at her sewing machine from 5 a.m. to 11 p.m. The poor woman wore out two machines, but the third outlived her," Guéhenno would write years later.[10] He did well in school, but that meant nothing: poor children just got the *Certificat d'études primaires* at the end of elementary school—where they studied reading, writing, arithmetic, and a few fragments of history and science, and that was it. They were not expected to go on to lycée, the

the longed-for *honneur*, over seventy. It is true that for a humanist like him, shame can have many sources. In his *Journal d'une "révolution": Cahiers de vacances, 1937–1938* (Paris: Grasset, 1939), he notes, upon hearing Hitler on the radio: "I was ashamed for Germany, for Europe and for all of us— for humanity" (p. 198).

[8] H.R. Kedward, *Occupied France: Collaboration and Resistance, 1940–1944* (Oxford: Basil Blackwell, 1985), p. 2.

[9] Patrick Bachelier and Alain-Gabriel Monot, *Jean Guéhenno* (Rennes: La Part Commune, 2007), p. 10.

[10] *Journal d'un homme de quarante ans* (Paris: Grasset, 1934, reprinted many times and translated into a number of languages, including German), pp. 63–64. All translations here are my own.

school that taught history, classics, and philosophy and gave students the possibility of entering the French elite.

Getting a higher education seemed still more impossible for Guéhenno: when he was fourteen, his father fell ill, and he had to leave school and work in the shoe factory to help support the family. But he had fallen in love with books, literature, and the world of ideas: at night after work, he would read and study by himself for the Baccalauréat, the examination young people normally take at the end of their studies in lycée: students who pass it enter the university. He passed the exam, got a scholarship, and became a student in *khâgne* and then in the École Normale Supérieure in Paris, where studies and living expenses are paid for by the Republic.

His studies were interrupted by the First World War. As a *Normalien*, he was made a student-officer. At first, he was an enthusiastic supporter of the French cause, but he soon came to see it as an "infernal machine" for producing dead bodies: "By the end of October [1914], almost all my fellow students were dead."[11] Like many intellectuals of his generation, the senseless slaughter turned him into a pacifist: "I am convinced today that the war we waged can only, must only, fill us with shame."[12] Only the rise of aggressive Nazism and the German invasion of France changed his mind: "I will never believe that men are made for war," he writes at the end of the first entry in this diary, precisely on the day Pétain announced his capitulation. "But I know they are not made for servitude, either."[13]

He took up his academic career again after the war, passed the examination called the *Agrégation*[14] in 1920, and taught in lycées in the north of France for the next seven years. In 1916, he married a young historian, Jeanne Maurel, like him an *agrégée*, and in 1922, their daughter Louise was born: he calls her "Louisette" in his diary. Jeanne Guéhenno died in 1933.

He never lost his love for literature, his sense of the beauty of the intellectual life, or his love for teaching. Above all, he never forgot his origins, the importance of education, and the necessity of strengthening the Republic that had provided it for him—particularly the necessity, as we would say today, of leveling the playing field. His first book, *l'Évangile éternel* (*The Eternal Gospel*, 1927), was a study of the historian Jules Michelet,*[15] but far more: it was a plea for educating the common people in scientific and philosophical thought. The next year, his *Caliban parle* (*Caliban Speaks*) created a furor in intellectual circles. In his

---

[11] Ibid., pp. 179, 180.

[12] Ibid., p. 178.

[13] June 17, 1940. He repeats the phrase almost word for word on August 15, 1942.

[14] The *Agrégation* is a national competitive examination that can lead to a university career. The *khâgne* classes Guéhenno taught were considered part of the university.

[15] Names followed by an asterisk can be found in the *Biographical Dictionary* at the end of this book.

"philosophical drama" *Caliban*, Ernest Renan* had used Caliban—Shakespeare's "deformed monster" in *The Tempest* who rebels against his master Prospero, the learned magician—as a symbol for stupid but salvageable democracy.[16] Guéhenno answers him by speaking in the first person as Caliban and producing a tract against social and economic inequality. "Our revolt, after our servitude, is the whole movement of history," we read early on. And later: "To follow the world as it is and use the mind to justify it is, truly, treason.... The hierarchy of humanity is founded only on fear." Denouncing the role of the Church in this unjust social order, he writes: "Prayers seem to me no more than never-ending chatter which has no connection to my fate."[17] From 1940 on, he saw Pétain as the embodiment of the triumph of the reactionary bourgeoisie, which had always resented the Republic with its motto of "liberty-equality-fraternity" and which had occasionally tried to destroy it.

There are many reflections of all this in *Diary of the Dark Years*, including discreet allusions to his late, truly lamented wife, but the driving force of this diary can be understood only by taking a closer look at the world in which Guéhenno suddenly found himself.

First, the swift and total defeat. The reasons for the fall of France are many, but most can be summed up in two words: military incompetence. France had built its Maginot Line, an impressive series of state-of-the-art defenses along its eastern borders, and waited to be attacked; the Germans went around it and attacked from the north, through Belgium. The French high command was stupefied when German forces attacked through the forest of the Ardennes: Pétain had called it "impenetrable" in 1934, and the doctrine did not change until masses of German tanks had actually crashed through it.[18] The inability of military leaders "to grasp the nature and speed of [modern] warfare" and thus to formulate an adequate response to the attack, the gross deficiencies of French military intelligence—all this rendered the efforts of their troops on the ground hopeless.[19]

---

[16] *Caliban, suite de "La Tempête," drame philosophique* (Paris: C. Lévy, 1878), translated as *Caliban: A Philosophical Drama Continuing "The Tempest" of William Shakespeare* (New York: AMS Press, 1971).

[17] All quotations from Jean Guéhenno, *Caliban parle* (Paris: Grasset, 1928), pp. 10, 54, 65, and 68, respectively. (My translation.)

[18] Jackson, op. cit., p. 32. He cites Pétain's testimony before the Senate Army Committee: "[I]f any enemy attacked he would be pincered as he left the forest. This is not a dangerous sector." He also quotes General Gamelin, who said in 1937 that the Ardennes "never favored large operations." While David Chuter claims Pétain is often "selectively quoted" and "was not so obtuse as to imagine [the forest] was 'impenetrable'" (*Humanity's Soldier: France and International Security, 1912–2001* [New York: Berghahn Books, 1996], p. 125), the full quotation shows he thought an enemy going through it would be caught in a very bad position indeed. At any rate, it is absolutely certain that the French generals were not expecting a German tank attack through the forest and were incapable of reacting quickly when it happened.

[19] Jackson, op. cit., p. 221. Jean-Pierre Azéma puts it succinctly: "*Le haut commandement français fut au-dessous de tout.*" Freely translated: "The French high command was absolutely useless" (*Nouvelle*

Although the brilliant medieval historian Marc Bloch, who served as a French army officer in that short war, perceived these factors quite clearly, few saw it at the time; de Gaulle was a great exception.[20] Pétain ascribed the disaster to the lack of military preparedness and the decadence of France under the Third Republic; his propaganda hammered away at those themes constantly. "Too few children, too few weapons, too few allies. These are the causes of our defeat," he said in his speech of June 20. "Our defeat came from our laxity. The spirit of pleasure destroys what the spirit of sacrifice has built," he moralized on June 25.[21]

Today we know that all these "explanations" are myths.[22] For Pétain, they were self-serving myths that justified his political, cultural, and moral program for France: his call for a "National Revolution," a "Moral Order," a "new order," and "regeneration."[23] This reform of French society was, of course, to be accomplished

histoire de la France contemporaine. 14. De Munich à la Libération 1938–1944 [Éditions du Seuil, Paris: 1979, 1992], p. 57). There is ample contemporary evidence for this judgment in Claude Paillat's *Dossiers secrets de la France contemporaine*, Tome V, *Le Désastre de 1940: La Guerre éclair 10 mai–24 juin 1940* (Paris: Robert Laffont, 1985). In Karl-Heinz Frieser's chapter on the decisive German break-through, the German military scholar outlines "The French Army's Six Fatal Mistakes at Sedan," among them "Neglecting the Sedan Sector" and "The Gaulier Gap" ("One is...astonished to find not a single bunker at the most endangered point...[precisely] where the breakthrough was later located!") (Karl-Heinz Frieser with John T. Greenwood, *The Blitzkrieg Legend: The 1940 Campaign in the West* [Annapolis, MD: Naval Institute Press, 2005], Chapter 5, pp. 145–52, quotation p. 148). But these were mistakes in *preparation*; what followed after that was even worse.

[20] Marc Bloch, *L'Étrange défaite* (1940), posthumously published in 1946 with four subsequent re-editions (*Strange Defeat*, translated by Gerald Hopkins [New York: Octagon Books, 1969]). For Charles de Gaulle in June 1940, see "The Call of June 18" in the Appendix: it is a famous piece of rhetoric but also a lucid analysis of the situation. Guéhenno himself essentially takes de Gaulle's position as his own on June 22, the very day the Armistice was being signed: "All resistance may well have been impossible, yet reason and courage demanded that we end our resistance on the ground but say to the enemy: 'Come in. Occupy all of France, but the Empire is standing fast. Go take it. We're ordering our ships and planes to go over to England. We'll endure you as long as we have to.'" Pétain, of course, said no such thing.

[21] Philippe Pétain, *Discours aux Français: 17 juin 1940–20 août 1944*, edited and presented by Jean-Claude Barbas (Paris: Albin Michel, 1989), pp. 60, 66. (My translation.)

[22] The Germans had roughly 3 million men under arms; the French, 5.7 million; the Germans had 2,800 tanks, the Allies, 3,000—and so on (Serge Berstein and Pierre Milza, *Histoire de la France au XXe siècle Tome II: 1930–1945* [Paris: Éditions Complexe, 1991], p. 310). As for "laxity," as Julian Jackson points out, "The defeat of France was first and foremost a military defeat—so rapid and so total that these other factors [like France's supposed "decadence"] did not have time to come into play" (op. cit., p. 213).

[23] "The Moral Order" (*l'Ordre moral*) is one of the terms used to describe the Vichy government's cultural and "moral" program, the values it preached in its effort to control the lives of the French people. It is one aspect of Pétain's "new order" (*ordre nouveau* in French). In his speech of June 25, 1940, Pétain announced that "[a] new order is beginning...I am urging you, first of all, to intellectual and moral regeneration (*redressement*)" (*Discours aux Français*, op. cit. p. 66). In April 1941, four members of Pétain's government sent Hitler a "Plan for a New Order in France," ending "We beg the Führer to trust us" (Henry Rousso, *Un Château en Allemagne: Siegmaringen 1944–1945* [Paris: Fayard/ Pluriel, 2012], pp. 70–71). In August 1941, Pétain deplored the slow pace of "building, or more exactly imposing, a new order" (*Discours*, op. cit., p. 166).

in a country where the real power lay in the hands of Nazi Germany, with its soldiers and Gestapo there to enforce its power if necessary. But France could do
whatever it wanted, as far as the occupiers were concerned, as long as it kept
quiet (sparing them the task of policing the country themselves),[24] turned over
a large part of its economic and agricultural production to Germany, furnished it
with cheap labor, and helped the Nazis to get rid of the Jews.

Not that Pétain's program had anything in it to bother the Nazis, far from it.
It was essentially a program for a hierarchical regime in which all "real Frenchmen"
(but not Jews or Masons) had their assigned place, as in an imagined Middle
Ages: peasants happily tilling the soil, craftsmen plying their age-old trades,
workers at their machines under the unquestioned authority of their bosses (the
fact that the fruit of their toil was going to Germany was, of course, ignored),
families—as large as possible—under the authority of the father... and all under
the benign authority of Marshal Philippe Pétain, the Head of the French State:
"Chef de l'État Français" was his official title. No parliament, none of the
disorderly disagreements that had soiled and weakened the old Republic,
according to Vichy; and none of the individualistic striving for self-fulfillment or
the "individualistic ardor" Guéhenno admires in Montaigne and Walt Whitman[25]:
All that was to be replaced by a vague "community" and absolute submission to
the chief.[26] This is how Guéhenno describes Vichy's propaganda for the New
Order, tirelessly repeated on the radio and in the totally controlled press: "The
same soppy nonsense on the family, the crafts, folklore (there is an overdose of
folklore in Vichy), flowing interminably on like a dribble of dirty water. It seems
that for the past 150 years we had been living in the darkness of sin. This dirty
water, like a new baptism, is supposed to regenerate us" (December 29, 1940).

Day after day, Vichy radio and the Nazi-controlled press told the French they
should be ashamed to have followed the lax ways of the Republic. Guéhenno was
ashamed—and disgusted—for precisely opposite reasons.[27] Yet even Guéhenno,
who loathed Pétain and all he stood for, particularly his "New Order," did not

---

[24] "[T]he manpower of the German police force in all of France probably exceeded no more than
3,000 [in 1940] and was never to become far more numerous" (Mitchell, *Nazi Paris*, op. cit., p. 7).

[25] See the journal entry for October 29, 1940.

[26] There was also a technocratic side to Vichy—the various Metro companies in Paris, for example,
were centralized into the RATP we know today—but this was not part of its cultural program or propaganda. Robert O. Paxton's *Vichy France: Old Guard and New Order, 1940-1944* (New York: Knopf,
1972), which illuminates this dual aspect of Vichy, is still a classic and revolutionized French studies
of the regime.

[27] His feelings would only intensify as time went on. Thus on June 16, 1941, he writes: "I've timed
it. I can't stand Vichy Radio for more than three minutes. Oh, never has a state been more faithfully
represented! Stupidity, sermonizing, and growling in a vulgar accent all day long. Nothing can give
an idea of the voice of those announcers. All have the same unctuous, sing-song voice...The radio
vocalizes on Work, Family, Country, and Collaboration. It says 'the Marshal' as it would say 'my love.'
The miseries of France are bits of sherbet that melt in its mouth."

escape all the prejudices of his time: thus he, too, sometimes deplores the influence of pleasure-seeking writers like André Gide,* who had supposedly sapped the morale of the younger generations.[28]

Mainly, however, he views Pétain's "French State" as the triumph of the old, reactionary Right—which it certainly was—and the revenge of the French bourgeoisie on the common people. In doing away with the Third Republic, which, for all its faults, had enabled him to go to the best schools in France and teach and write freely, the new regime had destroyed a political order—a country, in his mind—that he had often criticized and fought to improve but which, he realized, he treasured. Again and again, he evokes the beauties of the French countryside—and of the values of the Republic. At that time of shock and confusion, when many turned to Pétain as the savior of the country, these feelings isolated him from others: "I've reached the point where I can't talk to anyone I suspect of judging this event in a way that differs from mine. At the first word that reveals his spinelessness, his acceptance, I hate him. I feel a kind of physical horror, I move away. That coward, that craven, cannot belong to the same people as I do...I am going to bury myself in silence. I can't say anything I think out loud" (June 25, 1940).

For an intellectual like Guéhenno, the death of free expression, the sense of isolation, and the ubiquitous propaganda of Vichy and Collaboration could easily lead to despair and paralysis. One of his main reasons for living now seems to him pointless: "How can one still write?" he asks on September 25, 1940. "I can sense the deep connection that links a writer to his era as I had never sensed it before. I suddenly feel eighty years old. All the frameworks of thought in which I thought and lived have, perhaps, been destroyed. I feel completely insecure when I write. My thoughts seem to me those of a madman. It is the world which is mad around me. But the effect is the same. The connection between it and me has been destroyed."

In actual fact, he will continue to write—but only in this diary. As he says in the preface he added after the war, he would "never, ever, play our jailer's game,

---

It is interesting to compare this to Richard Cobb's recollection. The British historian often cites Guéhenno's diary, but he also writes:

> I did not need to read Guéhenno to recall the sniveling vocabulary of cloying hypocrisy and sackcloth-and-ashes *mea culpa, mea culpa*, retribution and atonement poured out nasally from *Radio Vichy*, as if the station had been taken over by battalions of French Uriah Heeps, trained in high-frequency seminary-voice control, whining and shrill clerics...Vichy, a clerical regime, admonished its erring and incorrigible *administrés* in clerical tones of high-pitched lament. (op. cit., p. 133)

[28] See, for example, the third paragraph of the entry for April 19, 1941. For once, Guéhenno is going along here with the prevailing view. Professor Jackson reproduces a 1941 French cartoon in which "two bemused French peasants are being told: 'How can you be surprised [about the defeat]? You gorged yourself on the works of Proust, Gide and Cocteau'" (op. cit., p. 4).

never do what he hoped we'd do: appear in print, for example—appear as if we were still living and enjoying ourselves as we used to, in the time when we were free." He was one of the few intellectuals in occupied France who sensed that what one writes takes on its full meaning only in the context of a historical situation, and that its meaning depends in part on where it is published and the conditions of its publication.[29] For writers, to accept Nazi control of their publications is a fundamental choice—not to publish at all is another—and it is far more important than the choice of words in their writings. When Paul Valéry,* whom Guéhenno admired enormously, publishes a new poem in the most important literary review in France, which is now edited by a fascist,[30] Guéhenno writes in his diary: "I can't help being sorry to see him go along with the ploy of our occupiers, who want everyone to think that everything in France is continuing just as it did before" (January 10, 1941). When he reads the *Journal* of André Gide, which had just come out in the distinguished *Pléiade* series published by France's most important house, Gallimard, he writes: "Is it the circumstances? Never have I been so irritated by that air Gide has, on almost every page, of sucking on a piece of candy. I think I can hear him catching his saliva the better to savor his pleasure. So many delights, so much enchantment—I find it depressing" (April 12, 1941). The essential source of his irritation, which he senses more or less clearly ("Is it the circumstances?"), is not only Gide's perceived frivolousness but his failure to understand the *situation* that has given an unintended import to his practice as a writer: he is refusing to see that as the conditions of publication have changed, the meaning of what he is writing has changed, too. Guéhenno is still harder on most of his fellow writers:

> Men of letters...no longer deserve [the respect they have traditionally enjoyed in France]. All too many of them are merely merchants. But as the respect they were given by other people finally made them excessively vain, they think they are above the miseries and servitude of their country, and beyond responsibility, like gods. Thus one can see them continuing to go about their business—under Goebbels'* surveillance. Their little business, their sacred work. Nothing can interrupt it. Is it their fault if their merchandise must bear a little Hitlerian flag in order to be sold?
>
> —(October 31, 1941)

---

[29] Gisèle Sapiro demonstrates this with extended analyses and masses of examples in her magisterial study *La Guerre des écrivains 1940–1953* (*The Writers' War*), op. cit.

  Much of what follows is borrowed from my own article in *Raison Présente 145, Automne 2003*: "*L'Intime et l'histoire, deux journaux personnels sous l'Occupation*," pp. 103–26.

[30] Pierre Drieu la Rochelle* was the new editor of the *Nouvelle Revue Française*, or *NRF* (see note 37 to the entry for August 17, 1940).

On the other hand, as an eminent member of the Resistance pointed out after the war, for a writer in those times, "silence had its eloquence, by signifying refusal" to collaborate.[31]

This attitude was extremely rare. Even pro-Nazi, fiercely anti-Semitic news-papers and journals like *Le Petit Parisien* and *La Gerbe* could boast of attracting some brilliant non-fascist writers to their pages—Colette, Jean Anouilh, and Marcel Aymé among others. If we read what they wrote at the time, it would seem that most French writers lived through the Occupation without seeing it.[32] Guéhenno was one of the very few who did not merely avoid obviously pro-Nazi venues, as Sartre and Beauvoir did, but who took the "maximum position" expressed in the radical slogan "legal literature means treasonous literature."[33] He refused to contribute a word to a publishing industry under the control of German censors. What he wrote was to appear, if at all, only underground.

But under these conditions, as Guéhenno asks a number of times in this very diary, why write at all? And for whom?

One obvious reason for keeping the diary was the urge to bear witness to the life of the French in Paris under German occupation: as he says at the outset, the diary is "the journal of our common miseries."[34] But Guéhenno also felt the need to record his thoughts and feelings. *Diary of the Dark Years* is a testimony to the inner life of an intellectual, teacher, and scholar resisting intense pressure with all his strength. Many diaries, especially writers' diaries, record the authors' reflections and state of mind as much as events and actions, but Guéhenno's is a special case: his whole intellectual and spiritual life was forced inward by the situation of his country. Three weeks after the fall of France, he quotes the poet Charles Péguy's* warning against "the most dangerous of invasions...the inva-sion of the inner life, infinitely more dangerous than a territorial invasion or occupation" (July 5, 1940). In a sense, Guéhenno is talking to himself in this diary, in order to defend himself against that invasion. It is a necessity for

---

[31] Jacques Debû-Bridel, *La Résistance intellectuelle en France*, op. cit., p. 37.

[32] In *La Littérature occupée* (*Occupied Literature*) (Paris: Hatier, 1995), Francine de Martinon uses a line of Baudelaire's poem called "The Blind" (*Les aveugles*) as the title of her chapter on such writers: "Contemplate them, my soul, they are truly hideous."

[33] In *La Guerre des écrivains* (op. cit., p. 64), Gisèle Sapiro quotes Simone de Beauvoir's description of Occupation etiquette for "writers on our side": to publish in some venues but not in others. The slogan "legal literature means treasonous literature" was not Guéhenno's but that of Communist intellectuals; although Guéhenno was never a Communist, the equation sums up his position. Out of the myriad French novelists, essayists, poets, and critics, Sapiro names only five other writers who took that stance (pp. 60–61). The novelists André Malraux,* Roger Martin du Gard, and the poet René Char are probably the best known; Char later joined the armed Resistance and fought in the maquis in the south of France.

[34] *Preface*, p. xxix. One thinks of the end of Camus' allegorical *The Plague*, where the narrator decides to "testify" in favor of those who had suffered from the plague, "to leave at least a memory of the injustice and violence" that had been inflicted on them.

someone who cannot write publicly, as he had through most of his adult life. After all, he had been a public intellectual, an editor and political writer who energetically defended humanist values and social equality; now he was reduced to silence—voluntary silence, out of fidelity to himself—and thus solitude. In his worst moments, it led to despair, as did the helpless position of France and the barbarity of the war whose echoes reached him daily in his "prison."

But he hangs on. At the beginning of the first year of the Occupation, he tells his students

> that this year's work would have a still more serious meaning, that my job was to teach them France and French thought—that is, something which...seems to me as solid as the Alps or the Pyrenees; this solidity would be our guarantee and nothing and nobody could make France something different from what she was...I told them that Montaigne, Pascal, Voltaire, Michelet, Hugo, and Renan were its guardians, and that consequently, according to the law of my profession and out of simple honesty and faithfulness to myself, to Europe and my country, I would speak to them as I had always spoken. I told them victory would not have changed anything in my way of thinking, so defeat could not change it either.
>
> —(October 10, 1940)

This book is the register of the way in which "defeat could not change [his] way of thinking."

Diary of the Dark Years is the result of a fundamental decision its author made: to remain silent (not to appear in print) and to write. He proclaims this from the start: "I am going to bury myself in silence...I will take refuge in my real country. My country, my France, is a France that cannot be invaded" (June 25, 1940).[35] That France is the country of Montaigne and Rousseau, of Voltaire and the Enlightenment, of the Declaration of the Rights of Man, of Renan and Michelet, of the authors and values Guéhenno loved. He will also hang on, passionately, to the culture of Europe, of which Germany is a part: he reads and re-reads Goethe, for example, and thinks of him often—he is mentioned eleven times in the diary.

It is well known that presenting ourselves to others makes up an important part of our daily lives.[36] But our presentation of ourselves to ourselves is at least equally important, particularly at a time when the self is under considerable pressure from the repressive world around us. We all have a more or less

---

[35] Guéhenno gives this title to the piece he writes for *Marianne*, an important left-wing political and cultural weekly of the 1930s. It means so much to him he copies the whole article into this diary on July 5, 1940, noting: "I am afraid it is my last essay as a free man."

[36] The classic work on this is Erving Goffman's *The Presentation of Self in Everyday Life* (Garden City, NY: Doubleday, 1959, many subsequent editions).

conscious defining narrative of ourselves that begins "I am someone who ..." In this diary, Guéhenno's self-representation is that of a total but solitary resistance, tenacious, heroic in its firmness, but almost completely *interior*. When a well-known French fascist sends him his latest book with a friendly dedication, Guéhenno notes: "We have no means of telling these gentlemen what we think of their activity. At least they might leave us in peace" (January 24, 1941). What can he do "now that everything has been destroyed, now that all ideas are flattened," he asks himself. Later, he answers his own question: "'[T]o have some soul'—words that stirred us into fervor when we were twenty—seem to me to define the only possible revenge. To have some soul, at least to suffer well, if we can do nothing else. To have some soul, to say no" (January 27, 1942).[37]

The "soul" he presents in the diary is indeed that of a person who says "no" to the propaganda around him, preserving—and transmitting to his students, at least—the values of the Enlightenment, of the French Revolution and its offspring the Republic, which Pétain had abolished; here, he will be the defender and guardian of the "France that cannot be invaded." The fact that this is the only place he can express in writing his feelings about the France that really was invaded, and is now officially and actively collaborating with its invader, emphasizes his solitude.[38] But as it causes him to write profusely, and often with passion, it also defines his resistance.

Even his notes on his extensive reading are an expression of resistance. Take this aphorism of Vauvenargues* that he transcribes on May 18, 1943: "Servitude debases men so much they begin to love it": we can sense him thinking of the enthusiastic French collaborators writing in the daily press. He cites Voltaire, that crusader for intellectual freedom, twenty-two times in this diary. He cites Rousseau twenty-nine times and sets to work on his biographical study of the philosophe, which he will finish after the war: "the exemplary life of a man who does not surrender"—like Guéhenno himself.[39] (And Rousseau came from the common people—also like Guéhenno.) He resists, too, by frequently judging the collaborators, especially his fellow writers. This severe judgment, for example, has been widely quoted[40]:

---

[37] "To have some soul" was the phrase of his "old enemy" Maurice Barrès,* whom he is now re-reading, he says in that same entry.

[38] Solitude is a recurrent theme in the diary, especially at the start: "I lived and thought inside a civilization (and much more than I thought). I am going to have to live and think among and against the barbarians. But the time has come, perhaps, for real work, solitude, difficulty, and knowledge" (September 27, 1940).

[39] See the entry for July 17, 1940.

[40] For example, in Robert O. Paxton, Olivier Corpet, Claire Paulhan, eds., *Collaboration and Resistance: French Literary Life Under the Nazi Occupation*, translated by Jeffrey Mehlman et al. (New York: Five Ties Publishing/Imec éditeur, 2009), p. 21 (in a slightly different translation). Gisèle Sapiro quotes it in *La Guerre des écrivains*, op. cit., p. 60.

The man-of-letters species is not one of the greatest species in the human race. The man of letters is unable to live out of public view for any length of time; he would sell his soul to see his name "appear." A few months of silence, of disappearance, have pushed him to the limit. He can't stand it anymore. All he quibbles about now is the size or font of the characters that will print his name, or his place in the table of contents. Of course he's chockfull of edifying reasons: "French literature must go on," he says. He thinks he *is* French literature and French thought, and they would die without him.

—(November 30, 1940)

Thus *Diary of the Dark Years* becomes, with its varied expressions of resistance, a series of public gestures in a private space. Apart from Guéhenno himself, his audience is precisely the "France that cannot be invaded"—an invisible France that also, of course, cannot read him.

That is one reason, perhaps, why the style of *Journal des années noires* is quite different from the style of most diaries. So are the subjects that interest the diarist. There is none of the quotidian detail found in the classic English diary of Samuel Pepys, for example: "This morning sending a packet by Mr. Dunne to London. In the afternoon I played at ninepins with Mr. Pickering. I and Mr. Pett against him and Ted Osgood, and won a crown apiece of him. He had not money enough to pay me. After supper my Lord exceeding merry, and he and I and W. Howe to sing, and so to bed" (Saturday 28 April 1660).[41] The little details of their daily lives are exactly what interest most diarists. They jot them down in a relaxed, shorthand style, and that is what charms us about them. We feel we are getting an uncensored glimpse into real life.

But for someone with eyes and a conscience, real life in occupied Paris forced quite different objects to the diarist's attention. Moreover, for Guéhenno, they deserved to be recorded in a controlled, ordered style, not in the "natural" style of the usual diary. "The self that one relates in a diary is most often only a loose, anecdotal, and chancy self. The only self worth anything is one that is constructed and desired. An elevated style...has its value. Its tension can be the tension of the man himself, not of the author" (May 21, 1941). Guéhenno's French lives up to his goal. His diary is written in literary, tightly controlled French, with no attempt to sound like the spoken language except when dialogues or other people's expressions are reproduced. Slang is almost entirely absent. So are the incomplete sentences so common in diaries, or the shorthand notations of trivia—what Louis Menand calls "the *woke up, got out of bed, dragged a comb across my head* pieces" which seem to him to define the very nature of the genre.[42]

---

[41] http://www.pepysdiary.com/diary/1660/04/28/.

[42] *The New Yorker*, December 10, 2007, p. 107.

But there are many kinds of diaries. By using a consistently distinguished and sometimes eloquent French in his, Guéhenno not only sought to order his inner life but to preserve a certain literary tradition against the reigning vulgarity of Vichy and the Nazis. If there is eloquence in his diary, it will be the opposite of that "eloquence for the masses" he hears when he listens to Hitler ranting on the radio (January 31, 1942). This translation seeks to give the reader an English equivalent of Guéhenno's rather elevated style.[43]

Despite the often lofty language addressed to an invisible audience and frequent expressions of despair and solitude in this diary, it is clear that in his private life, the diarist was not so isolated. He records Sundays spent with friends, some of whom were well-known literary figures, like Jean Paulhan,* or friendly conversations with famous writers like François Mauriac.* Then, as the organized Resistance grows, he receives letters, underground articles, and visits from young people in the Resistance or even fighting in the maquis guerrilla groups in the countryside—some of whom were his former students. (Guéhenno copies out some of these documents in this diary: they are remarkable pieces of testimony in themselves and bear witness to a very different kind of resistance to German occupation.) What came to be known as the Intellectual Resistance is organized, too—clandestine meetings of writers to plan what they could do to further the cause of free French literature and stir the conscience of their fellow citizens. Guéhenno was prominent among them.[44] For obvious reasons, there is no record of those meetings in this diary. Yet as he says in his postwar preface, he "witnessed the birth and growth of *Les Lettres Françaises*," an underground left-wing literary magazine, and he contributed to it, with his friend Jean Blanzat* and François Mauriac—forming an underground "cell." He also saw the birth of Éditions de Minuit (Midnight Editions), the clandestine publishing house that brought out the first part of this diary in 1944 under the title *Dans la prison* (*In the Prison*), signed "Cévennes." He distributed *Les Lettres Françaises* and the forbidden publications of Éditions de Minuit to people he knew in Paris; these activities are, of course, also not mentioned in his diary. All this was punishable by death or deportation.[45]

---

[43] I also wished to give a sense of the period: the kind of literary prose Guéhenno uses in *Journal des années noires* was more common then than it is now, and the author was a man of his times in other ways, too, in some of his attitudes as well as in his vocabulary and usage. Thus he writes *un homme* (a man) when no gender is really intended, usually thinks of his students as "young men" whereas he taught young women as well, etc. I decided to keep these signs of the era rather than tactfully modernize them, just as I preserved his "Annamite" where a modern writer would say Vietnamese or Laotian.

[44] Thus in the fifty-odd references to Guéhenno in Gisèle Sapiro's *La Guerre des écrivains*, he is often quoted as a witness but also cited as an actor in the Intellectual Resistance, a member of the underground Comité National des Écrivains, the CNE.

[45] Guéhenno relates all this in his interview with Jacques Debû-Bridel in the latter's *La Résistance intellectuelle*, op. cit., pp. 35–36. *Les Lettres Françaises* and Éditions de Minuit are still alive and well in

Guéhenno was never a member of what we usually think of as the Resistance, those French men and women who risked their lives daily to help the Allies and undermine German military forces. For one thing, the Resistance was really a youth movement. Guéhenno was over fifty when it got organized: spying, sabotage, and eventually fighting were carried out almost exclusively by young people. A more important reason, no doubt, is that he was simply too well known: as a public figure on the anti-fascist Left who "had written incredible things about Hitler," as he later said, he was under the surveillance of the authorities from the start, and he knew it.[46] It was enough to get him "demoted" to teaching the equivalent of junior high school classes by the Vichy Ministry of Education in 1943 and make him fear increasingly for his safety.[47] But even as early as March 1941, after he indiscreetly "exploded" in a hotel full of Gestapo officers when "Mme X ..." tried to persuade him to found a collaborationist journal, he put a ladder up against the back window of his little house so he could "get the hell out of there," as he said much later, if there was a threatening knock on the door.

On October 1, 1941, he feels it "prudent to put these 'notebooks' in a safe place," and from then on he will "keep this diary on separate sheets of paper." Only when the war is over does his friend Jean Paulhan, now back in charge of publishing books at a free Gallimard, prod Guéhenno to give it to him for publication. At first reluctant to do so ("It's so slight!" he exclaims in a letter),[48] he is

Paris. Éditions de Minuit was also responsible for the first sizeable underground publication: Vercors' novel *Le Silence de la mer* (*The Silence of the Sea*) in 1942. In a note to his preface to this diary, Guéhenno modestly refers to his own clandestine publication with Minuit as "a few fragments," but it is well over sixty pages long. Similarly, after the war, Guéhenno said he was never a member of the Resistance, although he admitted to being one of the founders of that little cell in the "literary resistance" as early as 1941 and to distributing underground literature. Later, he participated in the clandestine meetings of the CNE (see Jacques Debû-Bridel, *La Résistance intellectuelle*, op. cit., pp. 28–35; see also Gisèle Sapiro's chapter on the CNE in *La Guerre des écrivains*, op. cit., especially pp. 543–45).

[46] He speaks of this to Jacques Debû-Bridel, in his interview in *La Résistance intellectuelle*, op. cit., p. 30. I owe this insight to Jean-Kely Paulhan, who (in private correspondence) cites as one example of Guéhenno's exposed position the first page of the August 22, 1940, issue of *La Gerbe*, a pro-fascist weekly with a circulation of 140,000: Abel Bonnard,* who later became Vichy's Minister of Education, has an article on it denouncing left-wing intellectuals, next to a lengthy quotation from Guéhenno's 1939 book *Journal d'une "Révolution"* praising the "bloodless revolution" of the Popular Front for making French workers "the freest in Europe" and also praising the desire proclaimed by "our Communist comrades" to build a free, strong France—subversive literature in the eyes of Vichy, and not without danger for its author.

[47] While such a "demotion" is unthinkable in the educational system of the French Republic, it is not so surprising under Vichy for a teacher who ended every class by crying "... Et la liberté!" (". . And freedom!"). See Jean-Kely Paulhan, Text for DVD: La Résistance en Ile-de-France (Association pour les Études sur la Résistance Intérieure, 2004).

[48] This quotation and what follows are drawn from Jean-Kely Paulhan's account of the diary's publication in his foreword ("*Le Vengeur fraternel*") to *Journal des années noires* (Paris: Gallimard/Folio, 2002), pp. i–iii.

finally persuaded by Paulhan, and by a desire to sound a different note from the ones he heard in some of the botched trials during the postwar purge of collaborationist intellectuals. Furthermore, he was struck by the blind love for France he saw in many of the people he met when he was sent by the new government on a cultural mission to Brazil in 1945–1946: he felt the need to show the truth of what ordinary life under the Occupation was really like in his country. He made big cuts in his manuscript when he got back to Paris and gave it to Paulhan. The result is *Journal des années noires*, which Gallimard published in 1947 and whose first English translation is published in these pages.[49]

—David Ball

---

[49] In the postwar years, Guéhenno was covered with honors. Once "demoted" by Vichy, he was appointed *Inspecteur général de l'Éducation nationale* by the new Ministry of Education. He inspected French schools in Africa and the Americas, chronicling what he saw in the literary supplement to the newspaper *Le Figaro* and reflecting on his experience in two books. In 1946, he married Annie Rospabé, a *Résistante* who was deported by the Nazis and managed to escape. Their son, Jean-Marie Guéhenno, was born in 1949. Just after giving an impassioned lecture on Voltaire and Rousseau at an academic conference in Paris at the age of eighty-eight, Jean Guéhenno was felled by a stroke and died three months later, on September 22, 1978. His ashes were scattered in the sea off the coast of Brittany.

PREFACE

All you will find here is the journal of our common miseries. You will not find the unknown story of any event or the explanation of any secret intrigue. The witness was not privy to the secret of the gods, thank heaven. But you won't find any exceptional tragedy or suffering related here, either. Our French masters (so to speak) and our foreign ones did not honor him with any particular offense. Nor did he merit it. He merely had a few little problems. He lived through these four years like everybody else, any way he could, champing at the bit in the frightful silence imposed on everybody. One of his professions was writing, but he remained silent. He was lucky enough not to be obliged to write for a living. He earned his living from another profession. He had given up the idea of any open publication. He felt that in a time when you had to keep quiet about the one thing you wanted to shout out loud, if you weren't absolutely obliged to "appear" because of the need to earn a living, the least you could do was hide— and also be quiet about everything else that no longer had any importance, or hardly any. Since we were in prison, we had to live like prisoners and at least hold on to a prisoner's honor: fully appreciate our servitude, the better to find an intense, living freedom inside ourselves.

Of course you had to play tricks on the guards if you had the chance—assuming you didn't have the courage for the boldest enterprises—at least, for example, suddenly fall madly in love with blue, white, and red on your tie or dress, or make V's and H's out of Metro tickets.[1] In other words knock on the wall: pass little notes, little newspapers, create, keep up and spread the conspiracy of deliverance through smiles or little words of no importance, and warm the heart of all your companions.

But never, ever, play our jailer's game, never do what he hoped we'd do: appear in print, for example—appear as if we were still living and enjoying ourselves as

---

[1] The colors of the French flag are the same as the American, but their order is different. V for *Victoire* ("victory"); H for *Honneur* ("honor"; see the entry for July 25, 1941).

we used to, in the time when we were free. Paris had to smother its lights, since traitors and enemies had smothered the city. The whole world had to feel that in this place where normally so many lights shone there was now only a black hole, from which no word, no thought, would spring. And the whole world had to feel the shame of this black hole. Perhaps it was the witness' inhuman intransigence—or call it his bad mood (prisoners can sometimes be in a bad mood)—which had this effect on him: he judged it particularly intolerable when writers thought only of making a career out of the disaster, of keeping up their reputation, and thus became the entertainers of our servitude. So he shut himself in, and out of habit still scribbled down what he could not shout out, but for himself alone. That is how he spent the time, and his anger. This diary is composed only of those jottings. The ordinary Frenchman will recognize himself in them, and that is all this witness could wish for: the ordinary Frenchman will find his shame in them, that terrible shame which devoured us, which sometimes even made us lose our taste for life—the feeling of the stain the traitors had inflicted on us—but also, perhaps, all those stirrings of the heart, all those cries of one's own hope and all the reasons to be proud once again.

The diary as you will read it here is somber, too somber. And yet the manuscript is still more somber. I decided not to publish many pages. I crossed out some names. When I happened to meet hacks yearning for an ill-gotten reputation, I do sometimes describe the pathetic act they put on to justify their actions to themselves, but most of the time I thought it better to call them only Monsieur X... Not that they are not well known—too well known. But their vanity is such that the confusion of that X... will no doubt be sufficiently unpleasant for them. Nothing can be more humiliating for them than to see themselves brought down to a base, banal anonymity. And this diary will have gained at least this: treachery, cowardice, stupidity, and vanity will not acquire the ultimate luster a name would give them. Thus the journal is a bit less dark.

Moreover, despite that bad mood to which I was confessing a moment ago, I would be sorry if the reader were to attach too much importance to everything in this book that is merely a footnote to the history of the Republic of Letters. The question of the writer's responsibility is complex. Perhaps men of letters are not so important, and to consider even their misdeeds with so much gravity is to give them too much credit. There are many kinds of men of letters. A great number of them think only of enjoying themselves and of giving us some enjoyment. Clowns have every right to be astonished and open their eyes wide in their whitened faces if we suddenly treat them like directors of public conscience. And then, after all, they never say anything other than what we allow them—or ask them—to say. Our own cowardice and stupidity are their whole source of inspiration.

I must warn the reader that I could not write everything down, and this above all darkens my diary. Such were the times, such is servitude: we did not even have the right to have secrets. However prudent this diary may be, I still had to hide the pages as they were written. But I always had to fear that the ever-present police might discover them. There had to be no trace anywhere of what my comrades and friends were doing. And yet I could have kept track of their failures, after all. I was not absolutely forbidden to note their imprisonment or their death. But I could write nothing about their courage, about all they were daring to do, without running the risk of compromising them. I am not sure that I was not somewhat frightened of writing down the fraternal thoughts I had about them. That prudence distorts the tone of this diary. The reader will not find enough of that which made us live, through all our shame and misery. France was not that sad. It was not in league with its own unhappiness. We endured, but we were durable. As he reads me, I want the reader to remember that hope never stopped running through these pages just as it ran through the streets of Paris: by hiding. Faces in the Metro were morose. But could we know what that seamstress was carrying in her handbag, between her lipstick and her compact? That ordinary-looking package a young student had set down on the floor next to her was a radio transmitter, lists of airdrops, mail from London, or weapons... I witnessed the birth and growth of *Les Lettres Françaises* and Éditions de Minuit.[2] But, my dear friends Blanzat,* Duval,* Paulhan,* Mauriac,* Claude Morgan, and Édith Thomas[3]: quite simply, in this diary, I could not say what you were up to. Oh! I didn't know everything. You didn't tell me everything. It was advisable to be discreet, even with one's friends. But after all I did know enough—enough to get you shot, if I had written it down and my papers were discovered. I knew enough to have confidence and to hope, and if I had been able to say all that, this book would have a different tone. The reader would feel more strongly that liberty never died. The mute, covert, suppressed and yet fervent life of France during those years was wonderfully cunning. This diary does not give a sufficiently good idea of that great cunning, which saved our country.

I was particularly well placed to see the dramatic situation of French youth during those years. On this point above all I regret that the testimony which makes up the substance of this diary is so insufficient, so incomplete—for the same reasons I have already mentioned. I was all too right, in 1940, to fear that servitude would be a still greater ordeal for young people than war. The crime of

---

[2] A few fragments of this diary were published by Éditions de Minuit under the title *Dans la prison* (*In the Prison*) under the pseudonym of Cévennes.—J.G.

Les Lettres Françaises was a left-wing underground literary magazine; Éditions de Minuit ("Midnight Editions"), was an underground publishing house. Both continued after the War.—D.B.

[3] Writers and members of what came to be called the Intellectual Resistance: François Mauriac and Jean Paulhan are the best known; the novelist, scholar, and feminist Édith Thomas (1909–1970) repeatedly crossed Paris with a suitcase full of underground literature and gave it to Guéhenno, who in turn distributed the literature to people he knew.

For names marked with an asterisk, see the *Biographical Dictionary*.

ex-Marshal Pétain was to make dishonor a temptation for a whole people. There is no worse crime against man than to tempt him in the viler, more cowardly part of his nature. But above all there is no worse crime against young men. I saw them struggling with the shame that was offered to them. Sometimes I noted down some of their failings in this journal. What I could not note was their struggle and their victory. I will evoke this briefly here as an homage to their torment.

The drama reached its full grandeur in 1943. At that time, the government had already done all it could for over two years to persuade the young people of France that they were incredibly lucky. Stupid propaganda tried to lead our youth to believe that the other young people in the world were exhausted and dying in the war, while the wisdom of an old soldier had saved them from that fate. It was to him that they owed their safety, able to watch, as if from the sidelines, the fight that others were engaged in. They simply had to keep themselves ready, devoted to their leader, and tomorrow the exhaustion of the countries engaged in the fighting would become the strength of France. It was impossible for a few imbeciles and cowards to resist this temptation. My class, which was preparing the entrance examination to the École Normale in 1942–43,[4] had about sixty students, and for the first time in my life there were two or three informers in it, and around them a kind of swamp. This was the fruit of the Moral Order.[5] You will find traces of these things in this diary. But what I could not write at the time was that in the same class, a Resistance group was at work. It was led by a blind young man, Jacques Lusseyran*; he ended up being deported, along with some of his comrades. One can only imagine the arguments between those who wore the *francisque*[6] and the *Résistants*. In February 1943, about twenty of these young people were drafted into the Compulsory Work Service.[7] Not one of them agreed to leave for Germany. They went into hiding, or joined the first armed groups of maquis in the countryside.

To be able to hold on to one's honor only by breaking the law and agreeing to become a suspect is a difficult undertaking. That was the situation of all the young men in this country. So servitude operated the same selection among them that war does, in reverse. Never had there been so many authentic "volunteers." The most intelligent and the noblest were the most deeply committed, and all became victims. All those who, like me, lived alongside of these young

[4] For the elite École Normale Supérieure and the classes that prepare students for it (*khâgne*), see the *Translator's Introduction*, p. xiv.

[5] A term used to describe one aspect of Vichy's "National Revolution." See the *Translator's Introduction*, particularly note 23, p. xvii.

[6] The double-headed ax used by the ancient Gauls, taken by Vichy as the official emblem of the French State.

[7] The STO (Service du Travail Obligatoire), which obliged young men to go work in German factories. As Germany and Vichy increased their quotas, growing numbers of young men, faced with the choice of either working in Germany or "disappearing," joined the armed Resistance.

people for the past ten years, thanks to their profession, were able to verify that with frightening precision. Was it inevitable that the clearest minds should also have been the freest, and become martyrs to liberty? I dedicate this journal of our miseries to those of my students who helped to give this suffering its meaning and guarantee its greatness. Imprisoned, tortured, deported, executed, or killed in combat, they bore witness, through their suffering or death, that we were not mistaken: that the vague thing we had talked about together, anxiously yet fervently—freedom—exists; and that humanity in the universe and in history is only, after all, a sort of honorable plot to spread that freedom and preserve it.

—Jean Guéhenno

1940

There, it's over. At half past noon an old man who doesn't even have the voice of a man anymore, but talks like an old woman, informed us that last night he had asked for peace.[8]

I think of all our young people. It was cruel to see them leave for the war. But is it less cruel to force them to live in a country that has lost its honor?

I will never believe that men are made for war. But I know they are not made for servitude, either.

June 19

Last night the voice of General de Gaulle on London radio. In the midst of this vile disaster, what a joy to hear a voice with some pride in it at last: "I, General de Gaulle, I am asking... The flame of French resistance cannot go out..."[9] A new adventure of our liberty.

At nightfall, I went up to the plateau by the road that looks out over the city.[10] It was so strange. The Germans are about ten kilometers away.[11] They'll probably be entering the city tomorrow morning. And it was an evening like any other. People were enjoying the fresh air on their doorsteps. The debacle had stopped flowing south and we were alone on the road. At long intervals, cannon fire like a warning. You could still sense the reddish roofs and white facades in the plain,

---

[8] Marshal Philippe Pétain, who was then eighty-four years old, had just asked the French army to lay down its arms and called for a peace agreement. The army had lost between 50,000 and 90,000 men in six weeks. In addition, 150,000 were injured, and over 1.5 million were prisoners of war.

[9] It is not clear how many people actually heard de Gaulle's June 18 radio address that evening. It is now a classic: one version of it is publicly posted all over France every June. It is a short, lucid analysis of the war and an eloquent call for French resistance. See the Appendix for the full text.

[10] Guéhenno had been teaching in a Paris lycée (secondary school), but in October 1939 he and his students in *khâgne* (the highly selective post-graduate secondary school classes) were evacuated to the city of Clermont-Ferrand in Auvergne, in central France, to be out of harm's way. He taught there at Lycée Blaise Pascal, returning to Paris for the next academic year.

[11] One kilometer is about 0.6 miles, so the Germans are roughly 6 miles away.

and the diabolical shape of the cathedral towering over them. The moon was rising behind the towers, and in the distance, the fire from the burning gas depots was glowing. The smoke blocked the whole sky all the way up to the mountain, like a huge black flag.

June 21

The Germans entered Clermont this morning. Place de Jaude, I am told, is full of people watching them. The refugees staying in the building of the École Technique had to be forbidden to come out. These poor people, who traveled 600 kilometers so as not to see the Germans, wanted to run and see them today. God, what idiocy. Yesterday's barbarian is merely today's celebrity: people want to see the circus.

June 22

The situation is the very perfection of everything that cowardice and mental confusion could produce. All resistance may well have been impossible, yet reason and courage demanded that we end our resistance on the ground but say to the enemy: "Come in. Occupy all of France, but the Empire is standing fast. Go take it. We're ordering our ships and planes to go over to England. We'll endure you as long as we have to."

I don't want to say anything here about those gray men I begin to pass in the streets. An invasion of rats.

June 23

"This is France radio news: The Armistice was signed last night between Germany and France." I listen, dismayed, with my arms dangling at my sides, and I realize how utterly stupid I had been. For eight months I've increasingly let myself believe in the illusion that my kingdom was of this world. Let us follow Reverend Father Cruchard's advice and go back to "eternal things."[12]

Glimpsed on the Place de Jaude: the men in Hitler's guard (?) around their cars. They had stretched a rope from tree to tree so they could feel at home and the good people of Clermont could not come and distract them. They work, polish their boots, grease their machines, and clean their weapons. Robots!

---

[12] Reverend Cruchard is a creation of Gustave Flaubert, who facetiously called himself by this name in letters to his friend George Sand in the 1870s and even composed a "biography" of the fictive Jesuit for her. Because an armistice is not just a simple cease-fire but a preliminary peace agreement ending all enmity between two states, it was—as de Gaulle (and Guéhenno) saw at the time—the beginning of Collaboration between Pétain's embryonic government and Hitler's Germany. It was also a direct violation of France's agreement with England: both countries had pledged not to make a separate peace.

June 25

The bells for the "Ceasefire" rang at midnight.

I had not realized that I loved my country so much. I am full of pain, anger, and shame. I've reached the point where I can't talk to anyone I suspect of judging this event in a way that differs from mine. At the first word that reveals his spinelessness, his acceptance, I hate him. I feel a kind of physical horror, I move away. That coward, that craven, cannot belong to the same people as I do. At last I can understand all too well how civil wars can be born.

I am going to bury myself in silence. I can't say anything I think out loud.

Already we're settling into servitude. I heard a few of these noble citizens of Auvergne say: "Oh, well—they won't take our mountains." Never have eggs, cherries, and strawberries sold so well. Few men really need freedom.

I will take refuge in my real country. My country, my France, is a France that cannot be invaded.

June 27

The military philosophy of history. The valor of armies and their generals is what wins battles. But it is, of course, "the fate of arms" that loses them. Cf. General Weygand's* address to the troops.

What silence. No more newspapers. All the French radio stations are silent. We are entering into servitude without knowing exactly what it will be like. It is only by listening to the German radio last night that I was able to learn the twenty-four points of the treaty. All continental Europe was speaking German.

I make an effort to be more reasonable:

1. Once again, my country, that country which is only an idea, has not been invaded and never will be.
2. Pétain is not France. Pétain and Laval* do not speak for us. Their word does not commit us to anything and cannot dishonor us.
3. The only right way to gauge this event must be in terms of the world. In the world, France has not been defeated.

June 28

The Germans left Clermont last night. The Marshal can now make his entry into the city. The Oberkommandant's bed at the prefecture is free. No need to change the sheets.

It's the "6th of February" all over again.[13] They failed on the Place de la Concorde. They had to cross a river, the Seine, and storm the Chamber. To succeed

---

[13] On February 6, 1934, right-wing organizations hostile to parliament demonstrated violently on the Place de la Concorde across from the Chamber of Deputies—in an attempt to bring down the Republic, many felt. Sixteen people died; hundreds were injured. The date became a symbol for the Right and the Left, for diametrically opposed reasons.

this time, all they had to do was flee across five or six rivers: the Meuse, the Marne, the Seine, and the Loire. It all boils down to settling old domestic political scores in the vilest possible way.

July 2

When I got to school this morning, one of my colleagues warned me that there is a rumor going around about me: I'm supposed to be organizing a "Committee of Rebellion against the Government." Already! I burst out laughing, but now I feel a great sense of sorrow. I must be silent. So that's what the distress I've been showing for the past two weeks can become in the mouths of malicious idiots. Upon inquiry, the source of the rumor is my discussion with X... X told Y..., who is a gossip and came up with the slanderous assertions.

Is this the world in which we're going to live? Luckily, I'm getting back to work. I will definitely write a Rousseau.[14]

July 5

Marianne[15] is asking me for an article in which I would define what the reconstruction of France might look like. I am afraid it is my last essay as a free man. Here it is:

THE FRANCE THAT CANNOT BE INVADED

Never have I written so gravely. All the images of the debacle are still in my eyes. I saw it rolling like a dirty river through this city where the war had exiled me. A large part of this people were no more than a wandering, terrified horde, and I'm afraid of all that such a panic might leave in one's soul. The most urgent task is to give this country back its pride. It is on pride alone that this country must be reconstructed. You cannot build fine houses with crumbling stones. It seems to me that today every piece of writing, every word one Frenchman can say to all the other French must be first and foremost a sign of fraternity, and then must mean: "Be proud, whoever you are, my comrade, my brother. All this happened only because we were not proud enough. Be proud. You are not defeated and you never will be."

We all know very well that democracy in this country was not sufficiently real for the conscience of all our citizens to be moved by the scheming, cheating, and intrigues that teams of politicians have indulged in for the past twenty years—teams on different sides, representing opposing

[14] Guéhenno's work on the great 18th-century writer and political philosopher will come up many times in this diary. *Jean-Jacques*, his two-volume biography, was published after the war (1948, 1950) and translated into English.

[15] An important left-wing literary and political weekly of the thirties. Marianne is also the symbol of the French Republic, abolished by Pétain. Town halls have busts of Marianne, and postage stamps bear her image.

interests, but unfortunately all very similar in their presumption, their inconsistency, their fecklessness, and their lack of presence of mind. These politicians were able to jeopardize our happiness and throw us into dangerous ventures. They failed to engage our honor. And then, the psychology of a people is not the psychology of an individual. An individual cheats, lies, and betrays others. The collective conscience is incapable of cheating and scheming. A people never cheats, lies, and betrays others. It never takes the low road. Yes, when we consider the history of these past twenty years, the honor of the French nation is assuredly safe. The severest self-examination will reveal mistakes it has probably committed, but not crimes; and it will enable it to find the way to recovery and salvation.

A reform of the Constitution is absolutely necessary; nothing could be more certain. Anyone who has been paying attention to the political life of this country has sensed this and wanted it for a long time. Our misfortunes have perhaps made it necessary right now. But for it to be durable and not aggravate the confusion and disorder of the country, it must comply with the deep wishes of the French people.

The greatest misfortune that could befall this country would be that out of weariness and disgust—out of a kind of remorse, too, at not having made good use of its liberty for years—the country should rush into moronic servitude or let itself be slowly imprisoned of its own volition.

No doubt each of us needs to reform himself first. "Let us concentrate," Renan* said in 1871, "on the humble work of our inner reformation." Reformation of this kind is only possible if each of us goes back to the deepest sources of his life. Reforming oneself does not mean repudiating oneself. The worst defeat for the French would be for them to be ashamed of France. Péguy,* of whom one cannot think today without great sadness, said it magnificently: there is something worse than "barbarous military invasion which aims to put a country into servitude," and that is: "the most dangerous of invasions, the invasion that enters inside us, the invasion of the inner life, infinitely more dangerous for a people than a territorial invasion or occupation."

The France that cannot be invaded... That was the title of an article I was writing for *Marianne* while the German armies were pouring into Paris and moving south toward the Loire. The article never appeared. But these words have still more meaning today. They represent our impregnable refuge, the fortress into which each of us must retreat. Yes, if each of us deepens his reasons for loving and believing, if he has thoughts that are really his own, by which he "wants to live and die," like Villon's* old mother;[16] if, behind his brow and eyes, his thoughts

---

[16] In his "Ballade (that Villon Wrote at His Mother's Request, to Pray to Our Lady)," each stanza ends with the line "In this faith I want to live and die": *En cette foi je veux vivre et mourir.*

have ripened into their own shape, with their own taste and color, as inevitably as the fruits of our trees on our hillsides; if he remains faithful to a certain idea of man and human dignity which centuries of French history have given him; if he is truly a part of the France that cannot be invaded—if he wants to be part of it—then nothing has been lost: France will be reborn, France will continue.

And the reformation of the state, the revision of the Constitution itself, will mean something only if it is paralleled by this individual reformation. The work of our "constituents"[17] will only be worthwhile if they ignore all those foreign ideologies which have been all too attractive for all too many of us over the past twenty years, and apply themselves to thinking of France. But a France possessed by the feeling of its defeat and discouraged by its misfortune will never be able to find its own way again. It is still the idea of the France that *cannot* be invaded which must direct our national reconstruction. The constitution of the French people, a French constitution, can only be a constitution of men who have their own thought—a constitution of free men.

July 7

Yesterday a big fuss and a Comedy of Virtue. Parade of the 14th Division before the statue of Vercingetorix.* They lay down a wreath with this inscription: "To the chieftain of the Arverni, from the 14th Alsatian Division."

July 10

A disappointing visit. I have reached the point where I don't want to see anyone at all. X . . . descended upon me the day before yesterday. He escaped from Paris on June 10 and, after an incredible trip, landed in Auvergne.[18]

What an enigma. His Catholic mother made him forget that his father was Jewish. He is a nationalist, Péguyist, and Maurrasian. But his homeland, like the homeland of everyone in Action Française,[19] is nothing more than a myth: the France of Louis XIV. It is the France of today that one should love. He hates it. Naturally he acquiesces in everything that has been done for the past two weeks. He himself declares that Pétain's government can only be like Hácha's.[20] But he submits to it, adheres to it and rejoices, taking his revenge: the republic

---

[17] A French reader would think of the Constituent Assembly that gave France its first Constitution in 1791, just after the Revolution.

[18] June 10 was the day the French government fled Paris. The German army entered the city four days later.

[19] A monarchist, nationalist movement, part of the far Right since 1898 and a strong supporter of Vichy, particularly its anti-Semitic measures.

[20] Emil Hácha (1872–1945) was President of Czechoslovakia when Germany invaded in March 1939. Hitler gave him the humiliating choice of accepting the invasion or seeing his country destroyed. He accepted the invasion.

has lost and is lost. That's all he cares about. Talking about Blum,* he says to me with wicked glee, "Seems he's crying a lot these days. He cries everywhere. Of course he's in London." For a minute I throw him off balance by replying that it so happens I spent all morning with Blum the day before yesterday . . . In this man who thinks he's my friend, I detect the terrifying force of hatred. I am exactly everything he hates—an independent man who owes his independence to himself alone, to his effort, to his profession; a Caliban set free,[21] a barbarian who shook up the important people, a scholarship-student with no respect for the heirs of the earth, a free man with no reasons for being free since he is not rich.

July 15

This country is slowly sinking into servitude. For how many weeks, months, years?

There is such a stampede (at least it seems that way when one reads the papers) that I'm beginning to wonder if I'm in my right mind to resist as I do.

But all the cards haven't been played in this game. The English card remains— and the American card, and the Russian card. Let us hope.

Marianne can reappear this week and has asked me to bring my article up to date. I am adding a paragraph. I'm curious to see what the censors will do with it:

"I am writing these lines on July 14, 1940, and I am sure that I am only expressing the deep, ancient faith of my country. A hundred and fifty years ago the Fête des Fédérations was held on the Champ-de-Mars.[22] France was proclaiming its unity. All the men of this country recognized each other as equals and brothers. For all of them—they would not have been able to say how—had come to the conviction that for man and his country, liberty is the source of courage and the means for its greatness. We must be daring, said the young Saint-Just,* the future Jacobin. We must be daring, said the young Chénier* as well, the future Feuillant.[23] This is how France had to reform itself, renew itself. But only free men are daring, or can be daring." [24]

---

[21] For Guéhenno's use of Shakespeare's and Renan's Caliban to represent the common man, see the *Translator's Introduction*, pp. xv–xvi.

[22] The Fête de la Fédération was a celebration of the new constitutional monarchy (which did not live long). It was held July 14, 1790, on a large square (Champ-de-Mars), then just outside Paris, to commemorate the storming of the Bastille in 1789, the beginning of the Revolution. July 14 is still the national holiday of France.

[23] The Club des Feuillants was a moderate political group founded in 1791; it advocated a constitutional monarchy. During the Reign of Terror (1793–1794), most were guillotined by the Jacobins, radicals who wanted a "pure" republic. When they fell from power, Saint-Just, a leader of the Jacobins, was guillotined along with Robespierre. The poet André Chénier had been guillotined as a "royalist" earlier the same year.

[24] The article did appear. *Marianne* was to disappear a few weeks later.—J.G.

July 17

I am thinking about what my work will be in the years ahead. I will have to work well, under this damper. Renan said there was no use demanding freedom all the time. Just begin, he said, by thinking freely. Let us make a virtue out of necessity. The circumstances themselves may help us, who knows. Perhaps we will grow more intelligent. We'll have to use cunning, turn our tongue around in our mouth ten times, and our pen in its inkwell. We will speak better. We will write better. Art will be the better for it. The men of the 18th century would not have been so witty if they had been completely free.

From a more personal point of view, it seems to me that through all these difficulties I have moved closer to myself. Perhaps in time I will know what I can do best. What I have written best, I wrote when I was concentrating, when despair and solitude preserved me from eloquence and kept me far from all "literature." Never, unfortunately! will I write beautiful novels or fine stories. I lack the greatest of all gifts. I will always be clumsy at inventing things. I can only write well with the most intimate part of myself. I stupidly need to believe everything I say. But on this path, could I not some day gather all my experiences together and sing a pure song which, because of its very simplicity, will confront those who read it with their own destiny? That is what the notes I have taken might become, under the title of *Changer la vie* (*Changing Life*).[25]

Other projects: the Rousseau, the exemplary life of a man who does not surrender; a history of ideas in 19th century France; a return to the sources of my faith.

July 24

Things are moving fast. Yesterday, for the first time, as I was discussing a text by Renan, *La poésie de l'exposition* (*The Poetry of Exposition*), I felt these young people already getting away from me. It seemed to me they were avoiding my eyes. That liberty, that idealism, seemed to them from an old world, and they were unconsciously resisting, impermeable already. Already they're afraid of compromising themselves if they approve of me, approve of Renan, and I don't dare blame them. I already feel that I myself am merely the debris of an old, suspect world.

For the few years that remain to me, I can remain faithful to my beliefs. But as for them, they have to try to live. So the pure instinct of self-preservation comes into play: they are adapting. Already they feel that those old thoughts inspired by exemplary honesty would bother them, give them a bad conscience—and they slowly sink into stupidity. In a few months they'll feel comfortable in it. They will be beaming. It's a question of age. All the same, their eyes will be dulled.

[25] Guéhenno would finally publish this autobiographical account of his childhood and youth in 1961.

The fate of the world may be played out this week. Everything depends on the gauntlet Hitler and Churchill are throwing down to each other.

Never have I better understood the strangeness of Montaigne. The most admirable thing about these "Essays"—so reasonable, so moderate—is that they were written during the Wars of Religion, when excess was the rule. Do we realize that the "Apology for Raymond de Sebonde" was published the same year as the St. Bartholomew's Day Massacre?[26] While people were ripping each other's guts out in all good conscience, Montaigne was murmuring: "The cause of truth should be common to each."

Finally, we had paid attention to that murmur: that was the whole progress of the world. No one listens to it anymore today.

I think of what a Montaigne would be like today, caught between the various "leagues" that are drenching the world in blood, but trying to define the order of human thought, as Montaigne defined the order of French thought four centuries ago.

July 26

Saw my students again this morning. Perhaps I was wrong the other day. I want to think well of them.

I would like to think less about these things. My gravity weighs on me; it is silly, and I am at odds with myself. You can't live on disgust and scorn.

August 4

X..., the poet, comes to see me. I ask him about his experience as a soldier. He talks about the army as the most incredible surrealist monster. Which isn't bad. As for what has happened, history doesn't interest him. So he's going to keep at his little investigations, and "work on his poems." In the end, he is certain his freedom is not threatened. He will retire to his nice, cushy, poetic profession... I threw him out. These hedonists disgust me. It would have been ludicrous to argue, to explain that poetry—great poetry, true poetry—is knowledge, and consequently, freedom, freedom itself... Why bother...

Victory would have changed nothing of my thoughts about anything important. Why should defeat change them?

The new masters are organizing the silence, proud of their lost battles. But there is silence, and silence. Everyone remains the sole master in the silence of his heart.

---

[26] Montaigne's *Essais* (*Essays*), published in 1580–1595, have remained classics of world literature. His tolerant "Apology for Raymond de Sebonde" verges on religious skepticism, whereas the St. Bartholomew's Day Massacre of August 24, 1572, when thousands of Protestants were murdered by Catholics led by the "League" (or "Holy League"), is the prime example of murderous fanaticism during France's Wars of Religion.

What efforts to wrench a word of repudiation from us. On that condition, they promise, you will resuscitate. Tricks of soul thieves. They're counting on our lassitude to extort a lie from us. They pressure us to repent. But we have nothing to repent for.

From now on, nobody has a right to do anything but talk about the speeches and celebrate the wisdom of a Marshal from the previous war who can't even count the number of stars above the visor of his kepi very well anymore, a very old man with a military pension, who repeats whatever his prompters tell him. One might have thought the sense of service had left this veteran long ago. But as we weren't saying our mea culpas fast enough on our own, the exploiters of our defeat pushed him forward and gave him the task of reading the act of contrition and submission they had written out for us beforehand.[27]

Stupidity and hypocrisy reign triumphant—the Moral Order, the virtue of the rich. The bourgeois ladies are rejoicing. In the market, they won't have to compete for chickens with women in house dresses anymore. At last, everyone will be able to eat according to his rank.

The defeat of France is merely one episode in the European civil war. The conflict of nations hides a deeper social conflict. Each nation is so seriously divided within itself that one of the parties which composes it can think it has won when the country has lost. Thus, for one group of Frenchmen, the misfortune of France is the occasion of a victory it hardly dared imagine.[28] The republic lost: so they won.

The days we are living through now reveal what men are like. As we consider the history of the past fifty years—the extraordinary effort of so many Frenchmen to attain some kind of well-being and dignity—we discover, we understand, what suffering the former "notables" must have felt at such an ascension. What pleasure is there in possessing what everybody else possesses? Some people are like that: they feel less happy and less free as soon as others are as happy and free as they are. The happiness of others seems licentious, anarchical, and soon, a menace to them. And hatred for those upstarts, those thieves, is born inside them. That's what we have come to. A hatred which goes back fifty years thinks it is having its revenge today. Our misfortunes probably sadden these "notables," but they have their compensations. They think they will be the only happy, free men again from now on. The idiots! They talk about our unhappy country the way a master speaks of his sick servant: they call it a loafer.

---

[27] Pétain and his ministers blamed the supposedly anti-militarist Republic and its "progressive" morals (rather than military incompetence) for the defeat of France. On June 25, 1940, for example, Pétain said France's "slackness" had led to its defeat, adding: "the lust for pleasure destroyed what the spirit of sacrifice built" (*Discours aux Francais*, op. cit., 66; see the *Translator's Introduction*, p. xvii). France had to repent and change its ways. The press and radio repeated the theme constantly.

[28] A "divine surprise," M. Maurras would say.—J.G.

Charles Maurras used these words to hail the triumph of Pétain and the Vichy government.—D.B.

The little people, always ready to believe, are stunned by their misfortune. Rubbing their eyes, they wonder if they aren't actually even more guilty than unfortunate.

Is it so necessary to condemn those who are suffering? Must they also demean them? Cover them with shame? Is that the way to give them back their courage? Now I know better than I ever did what it means to belong to a people. I feel this more strongly in its distress than I ever felt in its glory. To all the men of my country, I would like to make a sign of fraternity.

We're not "notables." Our country is only an idea. It is a country that cannot be invaded. It is our inaccessible refuge where shame cannot reach us. What connection does this idea have to the shortage of planes or armored plate, to the stupidity of the generals, to the cowardice and schemes of the traitors? They have a habit of demeaning people, of drawing all things into their own little interests. We know that their faults are going to bring great suffering upon us. We will bear that suffering, but we refuse dishonor.

And then, we know very well what history is like, its immorality, its cruelty. It takes its revenge on legends as often as it can. It seems it is jealous of the gods that a people carries within itself. It takes advantage of any inattention, of every minute of sleep during which we lose sight of those gods who lead us. So it makes us limp and fall. But the fall itself wakes us up. We find our profound faith once again.

Must we stop loving France as we do, and love another France in a different way? But it has been here for centuries. One might as well plane down its mountains, stop its rivers, and turn it all into a swamp. One can do no more against an idea than against the sky and the stars.

We won't allow anyone to tell us that the France of the past fifty years was so ugly and so low. The whole world envied it and would testify against these calumnies. If it is true that France was happy, is happiness such an ugly thing? Who are the Pharisees who pretend to scorn it? True, we have made great efforts to attain happiness. But perhaps all men are French in this sense, and envy alone inspired the German critic who accused God of becoming a naturalized French citizen.

God, that eternal spectator, if he exists, if he is neither absurd nor cruel, if he doesn't think men must work just to work, but to make the earth more beautiful, if he likes men to raise their heads sometimes and look at the heavens—yes, when God himself, between two clouds, glanced at France, all things considered, he must have been not too displeased with us.

The domain of the French, the plot that God had reserved for them on earth, was rather well cultivated. The summits of the mountains lay fallow here and there. For they had found the means to fertilize the plain. They had more bread than they could eat, more wine than they could drink. They gave their wheat to the chickens and heated their wine. The villages, which were still a bit dirty, had never been so clean nonetheless. The new slate or tiled roofs were sparkling. Between the church and the town hall, God could perceive a fine house where little children learned to read, write, count, and think. To think—what ambition! Everyone claimed to become a person. What aristocrats, those French democrats! Through the wheat, the vines, the woods, the meadows, from one village to another, from one town to another, the roads went gleaming between the plane trees, a web spread out over the whole domain, a network of sociability. The automobiles—blue Peugeots, black Renaults—ran to meet each other, like friendly thoughts. The cities swelled out, the outskirts grew longer as if they were pulling the countryside to them. And yes, there was much to be said about these new suburbs. The urbanists protested. What disorder, what anarchy! These French would never learn. A race of country-folk, they all want to have the whole horizon to themselves: they set up their city houses like farmhouses, making every effort to turn their backs on their neighbor, to be alone, to be really at home. They would rather have given up the sun than live in straight lines.

From the strange assemblages they made in the cities where they lived together and yet alone, great debates sometimes arose, like rising dust blurring the landscape here and there. Prophets made their heads spin for a moment, but when the dust settled, these inveterate individualists calmly went back home, dreaming of bread and the means to earn it—bread and freedom. For that was their trademark: they never separated those two things, bread and freedom. And they dreamed of them not only for themselves, but for all mankind. They had the mad idea of never dreaming or thinking only about themselves; they were sometimes vain about little things, but generous about big ones. A people who gave good service to the mind, good service to humanity.

In the summertime, in front of tents set up like a caravan, the little children would play at the edge of the sea, at the edge of the world. This horde of little brats knew that France did not end where it seemed to, at that first wave which destroyed their sand castles: rather, it would surge up again beyond the ocean; it was an idea among ideas and thus, like a star, owed its light to the whole world.

But what really gave God tender feelings as he glanced at France between two clouds, I imagine, were the hard-working artists he could see in glass houses, cutting marble, painting canvas, or covering white paper with black lines in front of shelves loaded with books. There were, perhaps, no men in the world better able to love his creation. How attentive and subtle they were, and so clever at detecting connections, mixing tones, encapsulating mystery in a clean line. When things had gone through their skillful hands, it seemed they were clearer and more precious at the same time. Stones, colors, and words all sparkled, brand new. Then God himself would find a new interest in his world. He hadn't realized he was the author of such great wonders and said, gratefully, "All that must not die."

But what's the use of these fables? Prison entertainment.

Montolieu, August 14[29]

I have finally left Clermont, where I spent one of the darkest, stupidest years of my life. These last weeks were especially painful for me, as stupidity was settling into power. Clermont had become, with Vichy, the refuge of journalists, writers, leaders of opinion, the refuge of everyone who's supposed to think. I knew a lot of people. I could see how they were bowing to the new powers that be. It was frightful. How quickly thought and liberty can die! Last vision: the sidewalk café of the Glacier in Clermont; Monday, around 6 p.m. I recognize a few of my former comrades. I can distinguish two types: plump, heavy-lipped faces, swollen with rancid fat, bags under their heavy eyes. And thin faces, gnawed by envy, hatred, and ambition. All of them making a lot of "dough," as they say; they don't give a damn about reasons for living, as long as they're living. Around them, their Muses and their whores, a blonde swarm wreathed in cigarette smoke.

I'm only here for three or four weeks at the most, likely to be called back at any time: for from now on, France is working, and the cabinet ministers are taking in hand those lazy civil servants, of whom I am one. But I feel an inexpressible happiness at being here again, in my village. Oh, nothing like their idiotic "Back to the land."[30] But it's as if there were thick walls of air and the whole sky between that cowardly world and me. I would like to think of a few beautiful things.

August 15

This used to be the village fête, with the girls and boys dancing for three days. Today they are doing penance. Those dissolute ways are over and done with. They celebrated the religious holiday.[31] Around four o'clock, a procession of women led by the priest who thinks he knows all their sins went through the streets of the village singing *Ave*'s to Mary. They were more numerous than they had been these last few years, sent out by their husbands, themselves preoccupied with finding work and customers, and already submitting to the new order.[32] Next year, if this order lasts, they will come themselves and carry the canopy. The wisdom, the terrible wisdom of these villages, so quickly submissive, so obedient. Stuck in the thickness of the earth, solid on its rock, this one like all the others thinks it is alone under heaven, with its cemetery in its back, all those

[29] The village of Montolieu in south-central France near Carcassonne was the native town of Guéhenno's late wife, Jeanne, who had died in 1933; the couple had bought a house there, which Guéhenno still owned. For Clermont, see note 10, p. 1.

[30] One of Pétain's propaganda themes: the French should return to their peasant roots, cultivate the land, reject the "false progress" associated with cities, etc.

[31] Catholics celebrate the Assumption (the bodily ascent to heaven) of the Blessed Virgin Mary on August 15.

[32] For Vichy's "new order," see the *Translator's Introduction*, particularly note 23, p. xvii.

dead so close to it, teaching resignation. What does the village care about the ideas of cities? It swears by Pétain as it used to swear by Blum or Sarraut.* The master is the one who controls the price of wheat or wine. What matters is to be on good terms with him so he gives you the best price. Is this cowardice or wisdom?...This evening, I no longer know. Tired of feeling alone? What happened to the joy I felt yesterday? I thought I had escaped the wretchedness of these times for two weeks. I find it again inside me. These past two days, I have avoided going outside. I was afraid of meeting people, discharged soldiers, of being obliged to speak to them. The French are at the point where they don't dare look one another in the eye. They are ashamed of one another.

But night has descended on the village like a huge white basin turned upside down, with a spot of gold at the very bottom. The black hills all around seem the limits of the world. The village is stretched out on its rock terrace, asleep. What silence! Sometimes a window lights up for a few moments: it is a woman, leaning on her elbows, who wants to look at her man—her male—after love. Everything continues, everything will continue. I listen to the roar of the river, the song of a toad. And I, too, submit. Well, no!

> *Und so lang du das nicht hast,*
> *Dieses: Stirb und werde.*
> *Bist du nur ein trüber Gast*
> *Auf der dunklen Erde.*[33]

August 17

Yesterday I spent the day in Carcassonne. Met Paulhan,* Benda,* and—for the first time—Joë Bousquet,* and it was a great pleasure. We told each other our reasons to have hope.

Benda is a strange little old man. (He's seventy-two.) Unbearable, and yet likeable. I find him living in a furnished room. He took along a few things, a few books; he explains that if he's careful he has enough money to live for six months, but he is just as placid, just as nasty, just as inaccessible as ever. The order of the world has changed? Why should M. Julien Benda change? He is merely the one who explains it. M. Julien Benda speaks for God. Dire poverty, which may be very near, does not frighten him. He is preparing to make progress in the spirit of poverty. It is very necessary to the learned scholar.[34] Besides, there is nothing

---

[33] The last stanza of an 1806 poem by Goethe, generally considered to be Germany's greatest poet. Literally "And as long as you do not have that,/[Then] this: Die and become./You are only a gloomy guest/On the dark earth."

[34] Guéhenno uses the word *clerc*, an ironic allusion to Benda's best known book: *La Trahison des clercs* (translated as *The Treason of the Intellectuals*, 1927); the journal *Gringoire*, mentioned later, alludes to it, too. "Éleuthère" and "Belphégor," further on, come from the titles of two of Benda's other works.

tragic in his situation yet. In Carcassonne he has rich friends who have an excellent grand piano, and Julien Benda—Éleuthère—Belphégor—goes to their home every evening to play the piano. He has even talked them into leaving him all alone and Belphégor gets drunk on harmony. On his table he has meticulously arranged all his papers, his notes for his next books. In the left hand corner, a copy of Aristotle's *Ethics*. He is putting the finishing touches on a book he was writing last April: *The Great Ordeal of the Democracies.* He is delighted with his title. He is also working on a novel where this falsely impassive man will talk about his difficult love life. He talks exclusively about himself, about his last article. He is exultant because this very morning *Gringoire*[35] published a caricature of him with this title: "The bloodthirsty 'learned scholar' who dreamed of sacrificing France to Israel." Pascal's definition of man does not seem quite right to him. Man is not a *roseau pensant*, a "thinking reed";[36] he is merely a *bien pensant*, a "right-thinking" or self-righteous reed. Chance soon gave him a new proof: in the restaurant that noon, a lieutenant-colonel about to sit at the table near ours suddenly recognized him as the bloodthirsty Jew denounced by *Gringoire* that morning; consequently, this noble officer asked the waitress to move his table outside, on the terrace, explaining that he could not possibly have lunch in the same room as that individual dripping with blood. This interested Benda to the highest degree.

I admire Paulhan, the breadth of his mind that makes him a friend of Benda the philosopher as well as of Bousquet or Robin,* those "elf poets," as he calls Robin. Sometimes it seems he has, in order to weigh the nuances of words, those scales made of spider-webs that Voltaire spoke of in reference to Marivaux,* and yet no one is better at recognizing the force of an idea than he is. Precious and solid. What made me like him yesterday was especially that gentle curiosity that he has for all that is rare and secret, his admirable patience to seek out, in so much mumbo-jumbo that young writers send him—among so many obscure, impenetrable signs, so many stammering, aborted poems, so much nonsense, so many dreams—the stanza, the sentence, the word that is the trace of God among men, that immortal breath of inspiration that only rarely even goes beyond poets' lips. And I was grateful to him for having taken me to see Joë Bousquet in the afternoon: I didn't know he lived so near me, near my village. At the door, he said to me: "You know he's in bed... he's been in bed for twenty years... During the other war, a bullet in the spine... He should have died twenty years ago... And his kidneys are turning into stone now... Have you read his poem in the March *NRF*?"[37]

---

[35] A well-known weekly, first pacifist and then pro-Vichy.

[36] The great 17th-century philosopher and mathematician defined man this way in his *Pensées*.

[37] Founded in 1911, the *NRF* (*Nouvelle Revue Française*) was—and still is—one of France's most prestigious literary magazines. Published by Gallimard, which became synonymous with those three letters.

With his stone shoes
In each of his hands
The graveyard guard
Made the path dance.[38]

And we walked into a large bedroom where at first I couldn't see anything. And then, in the middle of the room, between three lit lamps, I made out a man half sitting up in bed and holding his arms out to us. He has been there in that half-darkness for the past twenty years, and he arranged it for his half-life, before the night turns completely black. A beautiful Pascalian face pale from being shut up indoors, racked by suffering and solitude, long hair that framed eyes gleaming with fever, a hooked nose, thin lips, a youthful look, as if being shut in and alone had preserved his twenty-year-old flame, the flame of the day he was struck down like this. He talks with the ardor of the south. He talks, he talks with so much intensity that you can't take your eyes off him. He explains to me that at eighteen he was the best shot in the province. I think of d'Artagnan.[39] I feel him haunted by the sense of honor. Oh, this man has certainly not been vanquished, and hasn't given up hope for France! I surreptitiously look around me: the walls are completely covered with surrealist paintings, with images that are impenetrable for me; I glimpse fetishes, African masks, and flamboyant dragons from China. Joë Bousquet has worked hard to fill his cell with all possible dreams.

August 23

That old cliché according to which the vanquished are supposed to have civilized the victors, the Greeks civilizing the Romans—what a joke. What a decline, from Aristophanes to Plautus, from Homer to Virgil, from Demosthenes to Cicero and from Plato to...nothing. I don't want those consolations for today's France.

August 24

On June 13, the very day of the debacle, I met an old history teacher, and as I was asking him about the causes of such a speedy catastrophe, "Ah!" he said. "We should not look for the causes too close to us, in our most recent history. It's the outcome of a tragedy that has been developing for more than a hundred years. This is where M. Guizot's* advice has got us: 'Get rich!' Don't smile. The spirit of the bourgeoisie has finally killed off democracy. It invaded everything by contagion, transmitted from the bourgeois to the peasants and workers. Republican virtue has been lost. We taught personality: people understood personal interest. Michelet* had foreseen all that. Just recall his great books of

---

[38] *Avec ses souliers de pierre/Qu'il a pris à chaque main/Le portier du cimetière/A fait danser le chemin.*
[39] The bravest of Alexandre Dumas' *Three Musketeers.*

civic education, the cult of effort, that Herculean cult he recommended. Remember his denunciations of mercantilism, industrialism, capitalism, Saint-Simonism,[40] all systems that put administrating things over educating people. There are no more peoples, there are no more men—only the masses. That is why the Republic has lost."

August 25

What a time, when retaining a bit of pride is enough to make you suspect. The villagers are uneasy. We hardly speak to each other. And I felt that they found the red Breton sailor's jacket I wear during these summer days unseemly. If say the old Marshal is senile, the old moles get scared and murmur "Good Lord!" and think to themselves "What a rude man!"

The most servile are naturally the same ones who went swaggering around last August talking war. X..., who admired someone like Daladier* as a father of the people, since he seemed to have saved him some money by reversing social programs, is now in a hurry to have him shot. Oh, what idiocy!

Paris, September 4

We returned home yesterday. Trip without any real problems. I was able to give the exams in Clermont and we went back to Paris Monday morning. I had been eager to go back for weeks, but at the moment of our return, an unidentifiable anxiety took hold of me at going to lock myself into this prison. We crossed the line at Moulins,[41] after waiting our turn for hours at Saint-Pourçain. Nowhere did I see traces of the war on the roads, but everywhere traces of panic—abandoned, looted cars. There never was a war. Fear had made it impossible.

Never had France, "Candide's garden,"[42] seemed as beautiful as yesterday morning. I looked at it with such tenderness! Crossing Nevers was forbidden and the "occupying authorities" forced us to take an impossible road full of potholes near Marseilles-les-Aubigny and Baffes. We couldn't reach the Loire River again until La Charité. But by prolonging our ride, this very detour gave us the opportunity better to understand the reasons for our love. How beautiful that golden countryside was, with canals cutting through it, and foamy rivers, with those great green masses of forests on the horizon. And so obviously impenetrable, inaccessible in its heart. And the "gardeners" just kept at their work. Here and there, at crossroads or on the bridges, a character out of a Guignol puppet show

---

[40] The doctrine of Henri de Rouvroy, Comte de Saint-Simon (1760–1825); it has been called utopian socialism.

[41] The "Line of Demarcation" separated the two main zones of occupied France. In the Armistice agreements, the Germans cut France into the Occupied Zone in the north (Paris, etc.) and the smaller, so-called Free Zone in the south, where Pétain's government had its capital in Vichy.

[42] At the end of Voltaire's satiric tale *Candide* (1759), after many adventures, Candide advises his old mentor to stop philosophizing and "cultivate his garden."

dressed in gray, with a little saber and a small rifle, recalled the historical fable of these years which is claiming to upset an old, old reality. I have hope.

At Saint-Pourçain, among the mass of refugees, a sick woman made ugly by illness is talking to her son while her husband has walked off. Her son suggests she sit down next to his father when they leave; he himself will sit in the back of the car. But she says: "No, I'd rather your father doesn't see me up close for the moment." The father returns. She makes up her face, puts on some rouge and smiles.

September 7

The day before yesterday I ran the errands I had been asked to do. It was long and painful. Nothing but the Metro to go all over Paris. The city seems dead. The street is almost empty. Nothing but German military vehicles. The Frenchman is a pedestrian and a cyclist. The Occupation, after all, is not very dense in Paris. I am pleased with the Parisians. They pass by the Germans the way they pass dogs and cats. It seems they neither see them nor hear them.

I went to see Mosco's uncle as I had promised. A scene out of Dostoevsky. In a rich apartment on Rue de Maubeuge, I found an old Jew. It smelled of moving out, and death. The apartment was still furnished, but all that was left were carcasses of living-room furniture; the cabinets and shelves were empty. In the middle, a table with cards spread out on it: the old man was playing solitaire. What was he betting? His own life? His son's life? (One of his nephews had committed suicide three months ago.) I told him all I knew about his family in the other zone. He was crying. I offered him my services and left. He waited until I walked down one floor. Then I heard him bolting his door. He hasn't dared go out for weeks, he'd explained.

And he probably went back to his solitaire.

Planes have been rumbling in the sky all day long. And at every moment that gives me, once again, a sense of the vastness of this battlefield: it is the world itself. I feel that even the battle of France was merely an episode. The event (the transformation of Europe and the world) will continue to develop for a long time. If only we could look down at it from high in the heavens—like God! In such large spaces, there is still room for hope.

And yet what A…was telling me yesterday hardly held out any hope of an English victory. He explained to me how Germany's air power was still at least twice that of England's, and always would be. English industrial production is, he thinks, having far more difficulties than German industry. And if we take into account the map of the war and the distances the two combatants have to cover, the ratio of transported and transportable tonnage would be one to fifty. The same plane that can carry three tons of bombs for 200 kilometers can carry no more than 500 kilograms for 1,000 kilometers. A German bomber can make five trips when the English bomber only makes one, etc. But I don't trust this kind of purely technical calculation.

September 12

Churchill spoke on the radio yesterday to warn his people. It was admirable, grandiose. He announced that next week would probably be a "very important" one in the history of the English Empire and the world. All the intelligence gathered by the RAF shows that the concentration of German troops and ships is drawing to a close. Now we have been warned, too. A terrible and wonderful era: if there is a new battle of Salamis,[43] the whole world will watch it. Next week we'll follow this battle, crucial to our destiny, hour by hour, as if we were at a play by Aeschylus.

I make an effort to read those new newspapers coming out here under Goebbels'* surveillance: *Le Matin, La France au travail, La Gerbe, Aujourd'hui*.[44] Most of them have editors-in-chief known all too well for their infamy. I hesitate to judge them, however. What holds me back is that life must go on after all, creep in and seek its path. All of them "make good dough," as they say, out of defeat and shame.

I agree that life must go on. All the same, they're in quite a hurry.

This morning in *La Gerbe*, a curious article by Drieu la Rochelle.* He reproaches us for our hesitations, our "shilly-shallying": what are we waiting for, to choose at last? And, of course, choose Europe against England. "For Germany," he writes, "is Europe for us, even if we enter this Europe with a very sad and humiliated countenance." And this nonchalant Gilles with a drawling voice, the laziest man I've ever known, puts France back to work and plays the reformer. He does confess his own laziness—and with a kind of glee. It seems that he is still rolling around in his sheets. But that's all over with now. He's going to work. He is working. As a Frenchman he was lazy, but now he's a good European: under Hitler, he promises to work like mad. A strange reformer. I hesitate for a moment: is this life, seeking its way? But no, all things considered, I'm afraid it's still laziness that's making him so docile, so servile, so submissive. This man "with an empty suitcase" has nothing to save.[45]

---

[43] A naval battle between the Persian Empire and a Greek coalition led by Athens (480 B.C.E.). The Greeks were outnumbered but won. It was a turning point in their struggle against Persia. Eight years later, Aeschylus wrote a tragedy dealing with the event: *The Persians*.

[44] As Hitler's propaganda minister, Goebbels was ultimately in charge of all newspapers. *Le Matin* (*Morning*) was an old far-Right morning paper that naturally turned pro-Nazi and anti-Semitic. The others were founded in 1940: *La France au travail* (*France at Work*) was a daily written by right-wing journalists trying to attract a left-wing readership. *La Gerbe* (*The Sheaf*) was a pro-Nazi literary and political weekly fusing Catholicism and racism. Jean Cocteau, Jean Anouilh, Sasha Guitry, and Colette published in it—one example of "literary collaboration" by prominent non-fascist authors. *Aujourd'hui* (*Today*) was first an independent daily but then became pro-Vichy and anti-Semitic. Some editors of these papers were tried for treason after the liberation of France.

[45] Since Nazi Germany occupied practically all of Europe, "European" had a very special meaning in 1940. "The Empty Suitcase" is the title story of Drieu la Rochelle's 1924 collection *La Valise vide*, well known at the time. In his novel *Gilles* (1939), the hero of that name ends up fighting for the fascists in the Spanish Civil War.

Perhaps it is Hitler's genius to have understood that by playing on people's cowardice between 1930–40 he could do anything: the memory of the Great War and its horrors left room in European consciousness only for fear. He doesn't make war, he organizes panics. Last night all the German radio stations were working at organizing an English panic. Will he succeed?

September 14

I would like to lose myself in some big piece of work. Nothing else is possible. I have two projects. My *Jean-Jacques*, the story of man who does not surrender, the story of a man who remains, despite everything (and perhaps at certain times despite himself), faithful to his origins. And also those narratives, *Changer la vie (Changing Life)*, which would be the story of a more difficult kind of faithfulness—but also, unfortunately, a less exemplary one: the story of another man, myself.

It rains and rains, and people are silently rejoicing at the thought that such bad weather may make all action impossible on the North Sea.

September 16

I could feel something had changed in the house. But I had tried vainly to discover what it was. And then yesterday, while we were taking a walk in the Bois de Boulogne, Émilie told me all the birds were dead. That was it. It seems all the birds died in Paris when the large oil and gas tanks were set on fire as the Germans approached. As the black smoke spread out over the city and the parks, it poisoned everything. What is certain is that nothing is moving or singing in the trees behind the house, and Émilie throws breadcrumbs out the window after dinner and calls in vain. The birds have either left or they're dead, and that adds to our sadness.

Poor Paris. Those lines in front of the stores. And that great silence in the streets. It's Thebes or Memphis,[46] but not Paris. I decide to shut myself in my house and go out as little as possible.

September 19

I am vainly trying very hard to work. All my projects seem silly to me. What's the use? I spend hours with my head in my hands, strangely prostrate, like the country itself perhaps. What? After all they're still the same men in the same skin as a year ago, or two years ago. But no, something has been broken. This people doesn't think, feel, or want anymore. Two weeks were enough to turn it into a herd. Yesterday I waited on line for five full hours to get our food rationing cards.[47] I listened to the people. But their heads are as empty as their bellies. The

---

[46] Guéhenno is referring to the ruins of the ancient Greek and Egyptian cities.

[47] Food rationing was established almost immediately after the fall of France and lasted for over six years after the war had ended.

confusion of their minds is frightful. The crowd has no hope; they are resigned. One would like to hope for the victory of the English. But some of the demobilized soldiers feel this would add to their shame. They have a selfish interest, out of self-esteem, in seeing the English beaten as they themselves were. Nobody talks about the Germans. But it's clear that everyone never stops thinking they're here, and keeps quiet. The main thing is not to starve this winter. And they all wait, like animals, for their turn at the trough—in the office that distributes rationing coupons. Sometimes a well-nourished soldier in a dashing gray-green uniform goes by on the street. He represents order, and he certainly has the means of maintaining it amid all this docility, this wretchedness. What is to be done? This country has lost her soul. What event, what new ordeal could give it back to her? Suffering will not suffice: the country would have to do something, to find herself committed to some action in which she could recover her pride. Nothing can be built on shame.

Today I had to sign a paper through which I "solemnly declare, on my honor," that I have never been a Freemason and have never belonged to any secret society. Oh, what stupidity!

September 20

Met Mauriac,* in despair. "What is to be done? What is to be done?" he asks.

For the anniversary of Valmy[48]:

If France ever died, it would not die from being France but in fact from having failed to be France, from not having been faithful to its essence with enough daring. We were weak because we were not pure enough. We were not deliberately enough of what we were.

I felt the calamity coming. Perhaps we no longer realized how much freedom is worth. We talked about it too much. We thought we enjoyed it already. But for too many people it was a word that no longer had any power. They unconsciously submitted to a thousand constraints, made themselves prisoners of "propaganda," swearing they were free citizens all the while. Enthusiasm for freedom had been deadened by 150 years of bargaining and scheming. As early as the 1850s, Renan was telling the liberals to talk less about liberty and try harder to think freely: liberty would live better from this effort than from all those declamations.

In 1939 there were certainly a few free men. They were a few artists who attentively sought to destroy the force of habit in themselves at every moment and renew the interest of their lives. That freedom was all too often merely the luxury of good fortune, the freedom of rich men trapped in boredom, the whims of sleeping-car dreamers who seek the ardor they no longer find inside them

---

[48] September 20, 1792: the first battle of the new French Republic against the surrounding European monarchies. French troops defeated an Austro-Prussian coalition at Valmy, thus saving the Republic.

everywhere outside themselves. But where was, then, the hard-won, lively freedom of a struggling soul?

The men of 1789 knew what liberty was: for they were emerging from servitude. Perhaps we will know it again soon, if we go back to servitude.

In June 1939, to escape from the lies of the day, from its cowardly confusion, to find joy again, I studied the Revolution. Time had pitilessly brought in its 150th anniversary. The French government was in a difficult situation: it had to celebrate, as the very principle that established it, an act, a principle, that is always a threat to all governments and to itself. The Revolution would have what it deserved: a service and a fine funeral.

The greatest celebration was to be held September 20, 1939! It was proclaimed that on this day, a magnificent "military ceremony" would take place on the battlefield of Valmy, "with markings set up on it beforehand." What bonded surveyors would take over this terrain, guided by what topographer-historians? Would they re-enact the battle? Would they play it as a comedy? Which conscripts of 1939 would put on the Brunswick livery, which the blue and white of the "French guards," and which the blue and red uniform of the national guard? Who would play Kellerman and Dumouriez?[49] Would they also find out where the artillery was placed and even where the cannon-balls fell? The ditches where the conscripts would make believe they died? And that light fog surrounding the French armies and victory all through the morning of the real battle—what smoke-making machine would spread it out over the hills? "On the Valmy battlefield with markings set up on it beforehand..." Was that all that history could do, then? Put the children's footsteps exactly in the steps of their forefathers and point out how far they are free to go, and put markings on the hill and the ditch where all their enthusiasm must end up?

Drunken force was raving all over Europe, and it seemed that we were ashamed to keep our reason in the midst of all those drunkards. The real tragedy of France was not all that threatened it from the outside. Its danger was neither Chancellor Hitler nor M. Mussolini. The danger was within itself: it was the crisis of confidence it was going through, the fear of being itself. When you considered them individually, French boys were as active and intelligent as ever. But they lacked the sort of shared hope and dreams which are the sign of health in a people. The fact that the celebrations for the 150th anniversary of the Revolution were only funeral commemorations revealed that weakness, that lifelessness.

It was so clear that the only right way of celebrating the Revolution would have been to continue it. What makes France France is a certain alacrity. We would have had to believe strongly enough in liberty and justice to present them

---

[49] The Duke of Brunswick was the commander of the Austro-Prussian forces. Marshal Kellerman commanded the French Army of the Republic along with Charles-François Dumouriez.

to Europe as the means to peace. But we lacked faith, and for the last twenty years we have been dawdling on the way.

On September 20, 1939, the day of the anniversary of Valmy, the French armies were beginning to sink into the mud of the Maginot Line.[50]

When the fighting began, all those stories I thought had taught me about how one can live in freedom—under what conditions—took on a different sound in my ears. I found the word death on every page. "Liberty or death." "Equality or death." "The welfare of the people or death." "An absolute republic or death." That grave, heavy sound, like the sound of a bell, was the accompaniment to every word those French of bygone days said or wrote. They did not shout "Long live liberty" off the top of their heads. But that bass, lasting note—that held note, as if underlying all that the mind conceives, meant a commitment of one's whole being, and a commitment one's whole being was making. They never wrote, or said, or ever thought simply "Live free," like avid pleasure-seekers, but they never failed to add "or die." They knew that otherwise it would have been just talk. They knew that it is not so simple to "live free," it is not enough to desire and sing it. They knew that liberty is threatened by death at every moment, and that to conquer death one must be ready to die at any moment. For only death can balance out death, only the readiness to die can defeat death. They knew that liberty is something one seeks inside oneself, that it can become something that can make one burst out beyond human powers, something that must be desired, which desires to be desired; it is not at all something natural. And finally, as non-liberty is the part of God in our lives, liberty is the part of man, his will and his creation.

In the famous Declaration of Rights,[51] they had written: "Men are born and remain free and equal in rights." But they didn't fool themselves. They proclaimed it against destiny, against nature, against all tyrannies. They knew what we were inevitably up against; they knew nature doesn't care a whit about that justice which is only inside us. But if, at every moment, nature undoes what we do—liberty, equality, fraternity—that is all the more reason to redo it through our will, through our laws, and to set up human order against natural disorder. And be ready to pay the price for these pretensions. The precondition for the great life they dreamed of for themselves and all humanity was really—and this is not so easy—to keep themselves ready for life, but also to keep themselves ready for death.

Whatever they may have been—Feuillants, Girondins, or Montagnards[52]—on this point they all were the same men. The idea that they had "virtue" was their honor and their life. If virtue died, they might as well die, too.

---

[50] See the *Translator's Introduction*, p. xvi.

[51] "The Declaration of the Rights of Man," adopted by the National Assembly after the Revolution of 1789, is still part of the preamble to the French Constitution.

[52] In the National Assembly after the Revolution, the Girondins were moderates who opposed the more radical Montagnards. For the Feuillants—and for Saint-Just in the next paragraph—see note 23, p. 7.

"Liberty or death." A target of calumny by those who pretended to believe that this cry was only a threat to others. But the death they named and called on in this way is only their own. "The day," said Saint-Just,* "when I am convinced that it is impossible to give the French people gentle, energetic, sensitive values—but values inexorably set against tyranny and injustice—I will stab myself... It is a small thing to leave an unhappy life in which one must vegetate as the accomplice or impotent witness of crime... I scorn the dust I am made of, and which speaks to you; that dust can be persecuted and killed. But I defy anyone to take from me the independent life I have given myself... through the centuries and in the heavens." Not only was he unable to live without the air of liberty, but he thought he was responsible for it both in the present and before the entire future. He had proclaimed that and promised it: if liberty died, he had to die. The memory of this final sacrifice, at least, would be preserved by the centuries, and liberty would be reborn from that memory.

No matter that this heroic tension in the founders of freedom could never become the tension of a whole people. Nor does it matter that for the past 150 years the history of our liberty was all too often the history of our mystification. The only guilty parties are the mystifiers. It is, perhaps, rather remarkable that it has always been the candidates for tyranny who take such pleasure in denouncing our freedom as being an illusion. So much charity should put us on our guard. Besides, those dialecticians, so expert in explaining the fraud that would victimize us, are confident of their own freedom, which is a will to power and total domination. They would not hatch so many plots to destroy the illusion of freedom if they were not afraid the illusion would end up by creating freedom itself. To believe in freedom is to begin to be free. It is quite possible that a "free country" is merely a country in which people think they are free. But it is surely not the same country in which people know they are not. That difference is enough for us.

We feel, more than we know, what a free world is. Light does not shine only on men who are able to define what light is. A free society is that society in which light reaches the humblest, at least as a reflection, and stirs them to wait for dawn even in the thickest darkness. It is possible that France was still merely waiting. But that wait was its very climate.

If liberty dies, France will be dead, too.

I think of those millions of Frenchmen who are now working to earn bread for their family under the surveillance of the foreign authorities. They serve, but they know they are serving. They are serving temporarily, and with so much disgust that it wouldn't take much to make them lose their taste for bread. But one thing saves them: they have not lost the taste for liberty. If you tell them they are "collaborating," they burst out laughing; inside themselves, they know what the situation is. Their soul isn't in their work. But they are full of scorn: that is the part of liberty. And they grumble at their work, they wait, and they hope.

Leave us to our suffering. To be aware of our servitude is the only honor we have left.

September 24

L'Oeuvre is on the stands again in Paris.[53] Déat,* with all the resources of *Normalien* sophistry, argues that we should accept the facts with good grace and get to work. He is off to conquer the future.

Life is all-powerful. And these extremely fast adaptations are perhaps inevitable. But are Déat and those like him really setting out for conquest or are they drifting along with the flow?

I think I'm watching a dirty river when the ice is breaking up. The river rolls on. The ice floes whirl in the eddies of the river, and the passengers they carry whirl around with them, dismayed, their arms raised to the sky, sometimes turning to the past, sometimes to the impenetrable future. They are shouting— ambitious madmen who believe they command the river that is carrying them away.

But it is no better to remain on the bank watching the dirty river go by, and feel that you are outside of life.

It is painful to think that the same people among us who worked the most consciously toward the creation of Europe yesterday should be the most disoriented today, at the very moment when Europe, they say, is being forged. Europe? No, but a *certain* Europe. Not the just Europe we wanted. What means do we have to promote justice and reason once again? We were "European" against the nationalism of separate nations. What will we be against this false Europe? Are we doomed to be in the opposition forever?

I do not want to drift; and yet I feel that I will not consent to remain calmly on the riverbank for very long, either. Must I wait for the river to be a bit less dirty to throw myself in? One would have to think rather far ahead into the future.

The poster announcing the new publication of *L'Oeuvre* is disarmingly cynical: "Everyone who did not want to die for Danzig,"[54] it says, "will read *L'Oeuvre*." Cowardice masquerading as common sense.

September 25

How can one still write? I can sense the deep connection that links a writer to his era as I had never sensed it before. I suddenly feel eighty years old. All the frameworks of thought in which I thought and lived have, perhaps, been

---

[53] Marcel Déat* wrote over 1,200 front-page editorials for this pro-Nazi daily, which had had been left-wing and pacifist before the Occupation. Like Guéhenno, Déat went to the École Normale Supérieure.

[54] "Must we die for Danzig [Gdansk]?" (*Faut-il mourir pour Dantzig?*) was the title of a well-known Déat editorial in 1939: in other words, if Hitler wants to take Poland, let him!

destroyed. I feel completely insecure when I write. My thoughts seem to me those of a madman. It is the world which is mad around me. But the effect is the same. The connection between it and me has been destroyed.

It was not only pressure from the outside, perhaps, but the ruin inside, too, that reduced German and Italian writers to silence so quickly. It is all abominable.

September 27

"Dream the future? No, make it!" Those are the headlines, one on each side, of *L'Oeuvre*'s front page this morning. Oh, what proud, honest workers! I will not associate myself with those slaves.

I must confess to myself that I no longer know exactly where I'm at. The future? I have proclaimed often enough that I lived at the vanguard of my time and was fearlessly forging ahead to new discoveries. But I felt in perfect intellectual security. I was living with a naïve philosophy, an inordinate faith in man. The revolution I dreamed of hardly meant more than accelerating an evolution that seemed inevitable to me. I did not see it as a break with tradition. The future was to be the fine fruit of the past. I was watching it ripen with my feet in my slippers.

But I am obliged to see that the path is not as straight as I thought, and men do not deserve such confidence. I have just read Rauschning's book *La Révolution du nihilisme*,[55] an admirable explanation of these cursed times; it leaves us with little hope for the immediate future.

I lived and thought inside a civilization (and much more than I thought). I am going to have to live and think among and against the barbarians. But the time has come, perhaps, for real work, for solitude, difficulty, and knowledge.

In my eyes, the problem of problems has remained the same: to ensure the greatness of man, and establish the social system that will enable the greatest number to participate in that greatness. That is my fixed point, my star. But my optimism of the past years is beginning to seem stupid to me.

A rule for my work: useless, now, to think of undertaking some long book. It would be in order to lose myself in the task, and I wouldn't have the heart for it. But I will have to take advantage of the slightest breath I have, work on little things, little essays, without letting myself be put off by their insignificance— work at all costs.

Lunch yesterday at a restaurant. Two little whores were sitting near me. They were talking about their boyfriends: Jean and Maurice. Jean's girlfriend was praising Maurice. "Gee, Maurice is really nice to you." Maurice's girlfriend was praising Jean. They'll steal them from each other soon. And then, at the vain

---

[55] Gallimard, 1939. Herman Rauschning left the Nazi Party in 1935. He saw Nazism as a form of nihilism (*Nihilismus* in the 1938 German title). Oddly enough, it was translated into English as *The Conservative Revolution* (1941).

exclamation of one of them ("Oh, life is so complicated!"), they spoke of André, Georges, Philippe—other lovers who were prisoners of war: "You understand, I do have to write to Georges. It wouldn't be humane." And I have the impression of two little animals, lying, wheedling, so sure of the power hidden there in their center, under their dress; that power sprouting out into a whole body, arms, legs, a pretty face with mysterious eyes, the better to hide.

They are happy. The Germans are now allowing people to come home at midnight. That's one more hour to spend with Jean and Maurice.

October 4

No entries in this diary for days. Silence and misery over the city. When calamity becomes habitual, it, too, can be uneventful.

October 10

I'm back at Henri IV,[56] where I'm going to replace one of my colleagues, a prisoner. The *khâgne* students in whose company I'm going to spend the year have passed through my classroom three or four times, but I don't know them yet. There are about fifty of them. A few intelligent faces. But—am I being too demanding, deep inside myself—I would have wished, for these first meetings, to find them more vibrant, more uneasy. They're "back to school" like each year, and seem to think only about their exam, the École Normale, and their Greek-French and French-Latin translations. In short, they seemed to me somewhat spineless. I told them that this year's work would have a still more serious meaning, that my job was to teach them France and French thought—that is, something which, as skeptical as I may be about history, seems to me as solid as the Alps or the Pyrenees; this solidity would be our guarantee and nothing and nobody could make France something different from what she was, and luckily her history could not be changed; I told them that Montaigne, Pascal, Voltaire, Michelet, Hugo, and Renan were its guardians, and that consequently, according to the law of my profession and out of simple honesty and faithfulness to myself, to Europe, and my country, I would speak to them as I had always spoken. I told them victory would not have changed anything in my way of thinking, so defeat could not change it, either.

October 16

Winter is coming. We are slowly sinking into grayness and cold. "Rationing" is, according to the official announcements (Caziot's speech),[57] "abnormally low." The other day a biologist explained to me that it was barely sufficient to keep people alive provided they remain lying down and don't work. Now there's

---

[56] Lycée Henri IV is probably the most selective secondary school in Paris. For *khâgne* and the École Normale in this entry, see the *Translator's Introduction*, p. xiv.

[57] Pierre Caziot was Vichy's Minister of Agriculture in 1940. He was a big fan of "family farms."

something promising! There are more than 60,000 unemployed in Paris. It seems people are beginning to sell their coupons. The poorest sell the richest their right to live and eat.

The Germans have settled into the school on the other side of the street, all shiny and well-fed; they sing when ordered.

What will become of this country in the depths of such wretchedness?... I dream of a sign by which one might recognize men who still have some pride.

October 18

Saw Paulhan yesterday. He tells me how dismal the streets of Paris are, said he just passed five trucks full of prisoners. I "buy it."

"What, you saw French prisoners?"

"Of course not—Germans."

We go to the *NRF* and walk up to his office. He shows me a drawing posted on the wall over his table: "It's the angel of the *NRF*. It saved the publishing house," he explains to me. "When the Germans saw it they gave up their idea of occupying the house. They were disgusted. They found its profile far too Semitic." I look more attentively at the drawing: the angel does have a rather large, hooked nose and Asiatic hair, like all Jean Cocteau's angels.[58]

But this same Paulhan, so amusing, is rock solid about serious, essential things. He refused to bring out the *NRF* under German control. He's losing his job. He is unemployed.

October 19

The victor is inoculating us with his diseases. This morning the Vichy government published the "Statute Regulating Jews" in France.[59] Now we're anti-Semites and racists. But against what race? Hard to say. I think of my good Jewish friends M...and L..., so generous and intelligent. But that's just it: they're taking revenge on them for their intelligence. I feel full of shame.

Doriot* has launched a new newspaper: *Le Cri du peuple.* The list of contributors is most edifying. An honor roll of renegade drudges. It is consoling, however, to see that they're always the same ones: they simply start over again with new expenses, new salaries. They go indifferently from one paper to another. It's the same public toilet. Everything goes down the same sewer.

---

[58] Jean Cocteau (1889–1963) was an eminent artist, poet, filmmaker, playwright, and novelist.

[59] This *Statut des Juifs* was the first in a series of anti-Semitic measures taken on Vichy's own initiative: Jews were first excluded from professions, the civil service and military, the media, etc., and then from all public places. Mass deportation to concentration camps came later, under German orders. The commemorative plaques seen today on the walls of Paris schools from which Jewish children were deported are precise and accurate: the Nazi deportation of Jews was carried out "with the active complicity of the Vichy government."

October 24

Yesterday evening all the newspapers were shouting out the great news: "M. Pierre Laval has met with the Führer." And since then, the whole country is trembling. What could that horse-trader have done? For what price did he sell us down the river? As early as 9 p.m., the English radio was announcing the conditions of the deal: but what can we really know about it? Did the Marshal reject them? Are we going to be forced to put all our hopes on the resistance of that old man? This tyranny is too absurd, and its absurdity is too obvious to too many people for it to last.

For we have been plunged into vileness, that much is certain, but still more into absurdity. The Vichy government—this is as clear as can be—does not represent France. After France suffered a kind of fainting spell, a few men were able to take power. They are nothing, represent nothing. Everything they may decide has been reduced to nothing beforehand.

October 25

I wrote last July: "Only free men are daring, or can be daring."

The French were asked to participate in a National Revolution and regeneration.[60] But the truth is that the French, each and every one, have been reduced to utter powerlessness. Two complicitous tyrannies are watching us. Everyone must now think only on order; all his good will, and all his will, is lost. The stupidity and muddle of the barracks prevail. A strange regime, in which everyone must hide the best thoughts he has. Who is left to carry out this pseudo-revolution? A clique of failures and cowards, quite ready to think on command if it gives them a position.

We hear there are close to 2 million unemployed. But in fact all the French might as well be unemployed: what I mean is that it's all set up so that no French person has any interest in maintaining his own conscience, his own drive forward, the conscience and life of France, nor does he have the right to do so. Being French by order is not a good way of being French. The only way to give life back to this country is to give it back its freedom. Once freedom is dead, France is dead, too.

So I feel as if I'm unemployed. I read enormously, to kill time. These past weeks I have been passionately re-reading Andler's great book on Nietzsche.[61] It's a bit long, sometimes a bit hazy, but an admirable piece of work nonetheless. Andler wanted to follow Nietzsche day by day, in all his thoughts, in all the adventures and voyages of his mind. He wanted to re-read all the books Nietzsche

[60] For the special meaning of these terms under the Vichy government, see the *Translator's Introduction*, especially pp. xvii–xviii.

[61] Charles Andler, *Nietzsche, sa vie et sa pensée* (*Nietzsche: His Life and Thought*), 1920. The great German philosopher Friedrich Nietzsche (1844–1900) was much admired by Hitler, who misunderstood and distorted his ideas.

himself had read. And in my turn, I am fascinated to rediscover the voyage of one of the greatest humanists through all the systems of philosophers and poets, through so many fables they told themselves about the world. I discover myself, always more ignorant and more eager to learn. I feel sorry that I used my time so badly. I rummage around all those sacred cast-offs, like a woman in a bazaar among the many-colored rags trying to find a dress. Among so many fables, ah, what if at last I found the one that would give me the meaning of the universe, and of myself?

How I regret that I had such bad guidance when I was twenty. I had to find my way alone, and I went where circumstances and my passions of the moment drove me. If I could begin my life again it is this world of myths, of sacred legends, of demons and gods that I would like to explore. I like to linger in this smoke and these flames. Or perhaps I would be a musician? Dreams don't cost a thing.

In the Metro this morning in the middle of the crush, right next to me, a dark, handsome young man, Adam, squeezing against a young red-headed woman, Eve. He covers her lips, her curls, her ears with little kisses, in other words continues to prolong his pleasure, as if they were still in the earthly Paradise, or in their bed. I hear him whispering in her ear: "You're not too chatty now?" He triumphs like a rooster—afterward—and a sudden flash in their tired eyes recalls all the joys, all the transports of the night.

October 26

Jealous of the horse-trader, the Marshal wanted to meet Hitler, too, and it appears we are moving into Collaboration without any further ado. In its turn "France is aligning itself with the Axis,"[62] as they say. What will be the conditions of this "alignment"?

These days are still heavier than the days of June. I listen to conversations in the street, in the Metro. People are stupefied by what is being done in their name. "The only thing left for some Frenchmen to do now," writes *L'Oeuvre*, "is to understand." But all of France does not understand.

Perhaps one should try to understand. That's what my friend A… is doing, I'm sure. But I'm afraid I'm a desperate case. I'm just too proud and stupid: I think I have already understood. And I think of myself as an old, untuned guitar.

October 29

If I had time and were not so overwhelmed by my job, I would write a book on the French moralists, like a protest and a testament, an appeal from France to men of the future. "The French Art of Living" would be its title.

Nietzsche himself praised the French for being the people most attentive to "cleansing the mind."

---

[62] The Axis: Nazi Germany, fascist Italy, and Japan.

Today Europe is full of dirty minds. That filth is causing all its misfortunes. I call a mind dirty, a people dirty, a mind or people drunk on music, which gleefully submits to magic and enchantment—a mind or people that sings on order, in a rush to let itself be seduced by every fine, false story that a master sorcerer tells it about its genius and its destiny; eager to get rid of itself, eager to obey.

These past days I had to re-read some great passages in Montaigne for my students. Now there's a clean mind. In fact that cleanliness is the whole principle of his strength, and will always make his thought effective and active. I note that he distrusted music as well as vague ideas. He was horrified by all pretense, the "ceremony" which not only forbids us to show ourselves what we are, but even prevents us from knowing what we are by filling us with reverence for false ideas about ourselves. He wants us to know ourselves. No one had wanted this with such energy since Socrates. He dares to look at everything that's happening inside him. He looks without horror and without pride. He neither prizes nor despises himself. He dares to say all he sees. "I find myself here [writing his *Essais*] hobbled by the laws of ceremony, for ceremony does not allow us either to speak well of ourselves, or badly. So we will just leave it alone." And thus begins through him, in his *Essais*, the exploration of man which had been forbidden for so long by all-powerful "ceremony," by religions, governments, customs, and myths. And ever since, the men of Europe have never stopped dreaming that a true human order can only be an order founded on that exploration, beyond ceremonies.

Rabelais, Montaigne, La Rochefoucauld,* Fontenelle, Voltaire, Chamfort,* Stendhal, France, Gide* ... so many writers who exposed "ceremony."[63]

There is a certain pathos in the *Essais*. I can feel it everywhere in the variants— those additions, those corrections that let us watch the story of a mind, its very attentive searching, its ripening, but also its aging (and the aging of the body with which it wants to be in tune). A "for some time" Montaigne adds to his text of 1580 suddenly warns us that he "eludes himself every day." His voice cracks at this "for some time."[64]

I know only one other book that ripened in this way, and grew old at the same time as its author. It is Whitman's *Leaves of Grass*.[65] And it is no accident that each of them could say in almost the same words: "Whoever holds my book in his hands holds a man." Four centuries apart, they were moved by the same individualistic ardor, drier and more intellectual in Montaigne, more generous in

[63] Guéhenno is linking five centuries of French literature: Rabelais and Montaigne lived in the 16th century; La Rochefoucauld's* "Maxims" appeared in the 17th, and Fontenelle wrote in the 17th and 18th centuries; Chamfort, the late 18th; Stendhal's great novels appeared in the 1830's; Anatole France worked in the late 19th and early 20th century. André Gide was twenty years older than Guéhenno.

[64] Likely referring to "the beauty of his soul, as that of his body has been withered for some time" (*la beauté de son âme, celle de son corps estant pieça fanée*)—"On Friendship," Book I, Chapter 18.

[65] Walt Whitman published the first edition of his collected poems himself in 1855; he revised and added to each successive edition until his death in 1892.

Whitman, as if in proportion to a new freedom, a new world in which an individual no longer has to develop *against* others, but *with* others, and realizes that he enriches himself by becoming more fraternal.

November 3

Montaigne again. He writes: "I have a soul all my own accustomed to behave in its own fashion." This in a flat tone, as if it were the simplest, most natural, most ordinary thing in the world. And again: "Extremely idle, extremely free, by both nature and art, I would lend my blood as easily as my care." Notice: not "as uneasily," but, in a firm tone, without raising his voice, just "as easily." A stoic or a blusterer would cry out: "Go ahead and kill me, I will remain what I am." As for Montaigne, his self-assurance is enough for him. He knows he will not flinch. He is unable to be different from what he is, that's all. In fact, through a kind of elegance, he presents this firm tranquility as the result of his "thinking, lazy and sluggardly" disposition[66]—the fruit of his good fortune, too, his luck that had him come into the world without ever having to exert himself unduly nor submit to someone else in order to live. But who could be fooled by this and not recognize his exemplary virtue, the ever-active principle of his thought and work—to whatever he may owe it—in that "ability to sort out what is true, that humor free to easily submit to its beliefs"? "To have a soul all one's own."

November 6

I am re-reading Valéry's* "Sketch of a Serpent," very skillful but very precious; and that other admirable sketch of the same "reptile" in *The Genius of Christianity* (I, III, Ch. II)[67]:

"Our century has haughtily rejected anything miraculous; but the serpent has often been the object of our observations, and, if only we dared to say so, we thought we saw in it that wicked spirit and that cunning which the Scriptures attribute to it. Everything is mysterious, hidden, and astonishing in this incomprehensible reptile. Its movements differ from those of other animals; it is impossible to say where the principle of its motion lies, for it has neither fins, nor feet, nor wings and yet it flees like a shadow, it vanishes magically, it reappears, and then disappears like a wisp of blue smoke and the flashes of a sword in the darkness. Sometimes it draws itself into a circle and thrusts out a tongue of flame; sometimes, standing on the tip of its tail, it walks in a perpendicular position as if by enchantment. It throws itself into an orb, rises and lowers itself in a spiral, rolls its rings like a wave, circulates among the branches of trees, slides on the grass of the meadows or the surface of the waters. Its colors are as

---

[66] "thinking": *pensant* in the original; "thoughtful" would be more natural, but the French is not "natural."

[67] This work in poetic prose (1802) by François-René de Chateaubriand* prefigured the Romantic Movement.

indeterminate as its walk: they change according to various aspects of light, and like its movements, they have the false brilliance and deceptive variety of seduction."

And that is why Eve's tempter, quite logically, could only be a serpent!

A large number of cultivated Catholics now seek and find their strongest reasons to believe in Baudelaire, Rimbaud, Mauriac, and Claudel.*[68] A whole new exegesis leaves behind the Saints and Martyrs as being decidedly ancient and out of fashion, and seeks evidence in the life and work of the greatest sinners. That certainly makes for a more exciting theology. Who will write the new "Genius" of this new Christianity?

November 9

Air-raid alert last night over Paris from 9:30 to 10:30. But not a single bomb bursting, not the noise of one plane. It was only a prank of the "occupying authorities."

A little story...Paulhan tells it. "You know the Führer convoked the Grand Rabbi to make peace between the Jews and him. On one condition: the Grand Rabbi has to reveal Moses' secret to him—how he crossed the Red Sea."[69]

November 10

Another heated exchange with X...last evening. I hadn't seen him since June. Vainly did I try to make the conversation drift over indifferent subjects. I felt he could not contain himself. He spoke of the coming peace and its conditions, as an "unexpected good fortune." The "statute on Jews" does not bother this self-hating Jew. Two of his grandparents were Aryans.[70] Rather, the statute reassures him: it is a text which establishes his Aryanism from now on. I had to tell him that for my part, I was remaining faithful to my errors. Then, with his beard trembling and his round eyes flashing like an old bird, he said: "Well then, you will be dismissed." "No, no, not yet," I answered. "I didn't realize that what I'd been teaching for the past twenty years was scandalous. Now I can no longer close my eyes to it. But that's just too bad! The texts, the facts, and what I think France is have not changed. So I will continue to be scandalous...And then, perhaps we'll become more intelligent, and perhaps, if we have to, more cunning." He was red with rage.

---

[68] Finding Christian faith in Baudelaire and Rimbaud, those great poetic rebels of the 19th century, is quite a feat. François Mauriac and Paul Claudel, however, were both committed Catholics.

[69] We recall that the one challenge to Hitler's control of Europe was then right across the Channel.

[70] The notion of the superior "Aryan race" opposing "the Jewish race" and other "decadent races" was a basic tenet of Hitler's racist fantasies. For Vichy, Jews (and Masons) were not *really* French, and thus should be excluded from the life of the nation; extermination was a Nazi invention that Vichy, however, facilitated.

Men of this sort have a terrible fear that their "victory" will elude them. We are in a civil war. I could not resign myself to believe that there really was treason last June. But why are they so attached to France's defeat and enslavement? Why does any surviving resistance or pride seem a danger and an offense to them? I cannot describe how ugly it was to see this man's hatred. The idea that workers in Belleville are reacting and still have hope,[71] that the University— professors and teachers—is not yet on its knees made him literally tremble. From now on I will avoid this kind of spectacle.

November 15

Around 5:30 on Armistice Day, November 11, I went to the Champs-Élysées. I saw French policemen following German orders and taking away the flowers that passersby had thrown at the foot of the statue of Clémenceau.* I saw German soldiers charge young people from the schools on the sidewalks of the avenue with their bayonets, and officers throw them to the ground. Three times I heard machine guns firing... Today the Sorbonne is closed: the students have been sent back to their provinces. Students from Paris are required to show up at their local police stations every day. I feel such disgust that I cannot even write what I saw in any detail. Submerged by idiocy. At a moment like this I don't know what I think anymore. I no longer have any desire to think anything. I need to start over from this zero and rebuild a soul and a mind once again.

Drieu is continuing his sermons in *La Gerbe*. A strange priest. He thinks his advice is "urgent." He is urging us not to wait anymore, to enroll in German Europe. Let us wait.

Monod and Rivet*[72] warn me that we may be "purged" soon. We'll see.

These notebooks might help me more to find an order, a discipline.

November 16

I'm working on a big essay: *Changing Life*. But I can't seem to get out of the preambles. I am continually re-drawing the portrait of the painter. It is high time I began to paint for real. What stops me is that I no longer have much belief in myself. I no longer feel I have a sufficiently intense connection to the world, a grip on life. I don't have the heart for it, or to be exact, my heart no longer finds any use for itself. They have plunged us into too much despair. The same flame is still burning within me. But I can no longer ignore the fact that it is burning for nothing and warms no one at all. I should have the strength to settle into this despair and build on these ruins.

---

[71] Belleville has traditionally been a working-class, left-wing part of Paris.

[72] Undoubtedly Jacques Monod, who joined the Resistance in 1940 (and won the Nobel Prize for Medicine in 1965), and Paul Rivet.

And yet I could work in a marvelously disinterested way, since the odds are that everything I write from now on will never be published. I could slowly, patiently, try to construct a great image of human effort as I have been privileged to witness it during these fifty years of life. For my own improvement alone, and to see more clearly. But all my thoughts are vague and tenuous and dissolve at the same time they are formed. Communication with the public creates a most useful constraint. It is not enough to say that thought is action. Every thought that is not action is vain. The cloud gets lost and diluted if it does not crash into the mountain, where it could become a storm.

November 20

I have received a letter from Montolieu. My dear "grandpa,"[73] who is sick, informs me that he'll send me a card every Monday. And I am to understand that when the card does not come, he will be dead. I can't even send him a telegram.[74] I could only send him one of those cards with a printed form authorized by the Germans. It will get there in a week. If he dies...I won't even be able to go to the funeral. This prisoner's life is crushing me. A world of savages.

I am reading my students' papers and suddenly I understand better than I ever have, perhaps, what culture and civilization mean. There are some original temperaments among them, magnificent young barbarians, and I think of the triumph of Apollo, whose chariot is drawn by all the beasts of creation, finally tamed. There are, naturally, young eagles in this class. But there are also young lions, young tigers, as well as a few less dangerous animals. Not for anything in the world would I want to destroy these temperaments. I know all the harm I could do. I am afraid to put out the eagles' eyes and pull out the lions' teeth. And yet I do have to discipline all these young animals...Yes, I feel more strongly than ever that a cultivated man is a temperament tamed, but also a temperament that endures and resists. In Europe today I can see a few wild temperaments, and a mass of slaves. So we live in barbarity. Nothing is finer than a temperament that has been tamed, regulated. And I enjoy taming these sincere young animals. I respect their sincerity, I am careful not to kill it, but I gently get them to recognize the world, the others around them, and to match their inside with the outside, their violent sincerity with the truth.

I am thinking of old Langevin* in his prison. He's in with the common criminals, no fire, no light. Night now is thirteen hours long. He is seventy-two; he made some of the finest discoveries of modern science. He was the story-book picture of a real scientist, one who believes in the people, who sees in it the reservoir of all spiritual energy and thinks that their science must make the world happy. These are all his crimes.

---

[73] Guéhenno writes *Bon-papa* for his late wife's father—an obsolete, childish word for grandfather.

[74] Montolieu was in the Free Zone. Communication between the two zones was strictly limited.

November 21

The newspapers are announcing this morning that Langevin and Rivet "have been relieved of their functions" by the Vichy government. I call Rivet. He had heard it last night on the radio. Langevin will learn the news in the prison he was thrown into by the Germans.

The "settling of scores" that X… had promised me in June appears to be in full swing.

November 24

A… was telling to me yesterday how the new conditions of the war are creating a singular state of mind in German or English aviators. Everything is in their hands. They are the only ones fighting and they know they are destined for death—given to death. Champions of their people, of their race. The rest of the army hardly does more than watch them. A… also pointed out to me that air combat is always a voluntary combat: the planes have to seek each other out and their pilots, as they seek, are seeking death. No struggle demands more ferocious determination. No wonder these men become frightfully hard-hearted. Since they must die, it might at least be for something, they think. And thus, it seems, there are no greater, more demanding Teutonophiles in the German camp than the men in Goering's air force. And it is the same, no doubt, in the English camp.

November 26

I know this with ever-increasing clarity and certainty: all dignity consists in seeking one's order inside oneself and in trying to sort out what is true, as old Montaigne said. And once we think we have found it, in holding on to it without any consideration for the passing follies that triumph around us. All that necessarily gives rise to melancholy, and in the storm that is carrying away our lives there may be some vanity in not limiting oneself simply to *be*, instead of presuming to explain and understand oneself. In this forced retreat where I find myself, I occasionally think of myself as an old abandoned guitar: it no longer sings, but if you strike one of its strings in passing, a pure sound arises, showing that all music is not lost, evoking an eternal order.

November 29

The newspapers are lamentably empty. This morning, however, I find the speech that Alfred Rosenberg, the high priest of Nazism, delivered yesterday from the podium of our Chamber of Deputies.[75] For it is from there that Nazism is to hold sway over France. That is what they have decided, out of a sadistic taste for giving offence.

[75] The most influential proponent of the Nazis' racist, anti-Semitic theories, Rosenberg was executed for war crimes at the Nuremberg Trials in 1946. The Chamber of Deputies, of course, is the main legislative body in the French government, although it lost its power under Pétain.

It's not a speech, it is the prophecy of Joad: "Heavens, hear my voice! Earth, lend me your ear."[76]

The history of the 19th century, he claims, is nothing but one great fable: the struggle of blood against gold. "But today, blood is victorious at last...which means the racist, creative strength of central Europe." I am recopying it exactly. "Out of chaos, misery, and shame the racist ideal has arisen, in opposition to the international ideal. The victory of this ideal in all areas of life is the true world revolution of the 20th century."

Must one be an anti-Semite to speak like a Jewish prophet? I will not decide whether the prestige of gold in the 19th century was mythic in character. As far as I'm concerned, I haven't the faintest idea. It is possible, but I can't believe it; nor that there is any value other than work. And gold can only be worth something as the sign of accumulated social work...But must one substitute one myth for another? Race? Claiming to rebuild Europe on a fable like that— how absurd!

When Rosenberg writes about the French Revolution, one might possibly agree to discuss this: "Its slogans led men to fanciful conceptions, foreign to real life. They separated the individual from his old native soil, they overestimated the constructions of the intellect..." These criticisms are not very new...But why must he go on to say "By that development, foreign to life, they led the people to abandon its blood by accepting a parasitic people in their midst— Palestine." This unexpected intervention of the unfortunate Ahasuerus reveals your own mythomania all too well, O Rosenberg![77] Occasionally a madman will speak reasonably for some length of time and we begin to regain hope for his mind, but suddenly a word he says will plunge us back into despair. Once he's under way, M. Rosenberg doesn't stop. All is purple and gold in his hallucinations. He bathes in regenerating Aryan blood with sheer delight. He swims in it. He dives into it. Then, surging out of the mystic blood, he shakes his ears and prophesies like a new Parsifal.[78] If we are to believe him, the great French books of the 19th century are the books by Gobineau and Lapouge (naturally), but also *The Jews, Kings of the Era* by someone named Toussenel, *The Jewish Danger* by someone named Mousseaux, and *Jewish France* by Drumont.[79] Well! We shall have to read these new classics.

---

[76] In Jean Racine's classic tragedy *Athalie* (1691): "*Cieux, écoutez ma voix. Terre, prête l'oreille.*"

[77] Ahasuerus: husband of the Biblical heroine Esther and a character in another tragedy by Racine, *Esther* (1689).

[78] Hero of Germanic myths and of operas by Richard Wagner.

[79] Drumont's *Jewish France* (*La France juive*, 1886) was an extremely influential anti-Semitic book. Mousseaux and Toussenel are utterly obscure. Arthur de Gobineau's *On the Inequality of the Races* (*De l'inégalité des races*, 1884) is notorious, but Lapouge is almost unknown today. Guéhenno is, of course, being sarcastic when he calls all these books "classics."

November 30

The *NRF* publishing house is locked and sealed (the Germans are asking it to fuse with a German house), but the journal *NRF* is going to reappear all the same, with Drieu la Rochelle as editor-in-chief. In the December issue: Gide, Giono,* Jouhandeau... In January: Valéry, Montherlant*...[80]

The man-of-letters species is not one of the greatest species in the human race. The man of letters is unable to live out of public view for any length of time; he would sell his soul to see his name "appear." A few months of silence, of disappearance, have pushed him to the limit. He can't stand it anymore. All he quibbles about now is the size or font of the characters that will print his name, or his place in the table of contents. Of course he's chockfull of edifying reasons: "French literature must go on," he says. He thinks he *is* French literature and French thought, and they would die without him.

Why keep on writing? It is hardly possible to doubt the absurdity of exercising a profession of such a personal nature any longer. These times call us back to modesty. Men seek the new conditions of life for their species. Poor species. Flabbergasted by its discoveries, lost on earth because it has transformed the planet, a dupe of its own creations. We are still one of those pleasure-loving, greedy apes who, when they were surprised by the ice age which threatened to kill them, survived through strenuous efforts and became men. What will we become this time? No doubt what is happening does not concern the individual conscience very much, and only makes the human pipe dream seem more fantastic—that pretension each of us has of existing by himself and being the magical, predestined mirror in which the vague universe finds its order and beauty.

All France, all Europe is in prison. All over the countryside, at the doors to schools and town halls, on bridges over rivers, at crossroads, the green men stand on guard with their legs spread and their eyes in a vacant stare. Sometimes there is a sharp clack: one boot is striking another; one of them, like a clockwork puppet, has activated his joints, clicked his heels, presented arms, and now there he is, looking stupid and miraculously still more motionless than he was before. He has saluted the new order, a general with a high cap going by in an automobile. This farcical scene is played a thousand times a day here and there throughout Western Europe, and we're supposed to look at it with reverence. It would be truly scandalous if the landscape itself did not snap to attention when the general goes by. But the gentle wind keeps on blowing through the eternal countryside; the birds keep singing, the leaves trembling. We, too, will escape this mechanical phantasmagoria. We will not snap to attention.

[80] All well-known literary figures, then and now. See note 37, p. 15, for the *NRF*, which had the dubious privilege of being the only literary magazine the Nazis allowed to be published—with a fascist as editor. It disappeared in 1943 but appeared again with a very different cast after the war, regaining its position as a distinguished literary journal.

We need to paint the walls of our prison. I don't know what I'll paint on the walls of mine, but I am sure that all my old dreams and all the images of my faith will be on them. This is not the time to change my faith. On the contrary, it's the time to be dangerously faithful to it. In my heaven the spirit of liberty will still be flying. The prison term may well be long. I will work deliberately. Now the time has come to write for nothing, for pleasure. Here we are, reduced to silence, to solitude, but perhaps to seriousness, as well. And after all, whether our cell is full of light or not depends on us alone.

We are being flattered. By attributing so much importance to our thoughts, a tyrannical power is forcing us to recognize how singular and scandalous they are. It is giving us back to ourselves. We did not dare think we were so interesting. We were growing old, our best thoughts were becoming too habitual to us, and freedom was making them too facile. They are going to begin to cost us something once again. Good. The odds are that these writings will never be published. All connections with living people have been cut off. Gone is the hope of reaching them immediately, and that vain pretension of changing them which obliges us to force our voice and turns the most sincere among us into liars. To write like a dead man and expect only Judgment Day—all things considered, these aren't such bad conditions in which to work. I am as free on my paper as I am inside my head. Nothing can keep me from the truth except myself. And that can be the most difficult and cunning obstacle, I know…Still, what an opportunity to attain an intimacy and depth that one has never reached! Let us work.

Literature. Nothing is nobler than its play when it is the flower of freedom, but nothing is baser than when it is the means of doing without freedom, of avoiding the risks of freedom—when it is entertainment and a cover for the servitude one has accepted. What are we to think of French writers who, in order to be sure not to displease the Occupation authorities, decide to write about everything except the only thing all French people are thinking about? And better still, who, through their cowardice, are furthering the project of those authorities: that everything in France should appear to go on as it did before? I will say nothing of those who are used to taking things from any hand and deliberately turn themselves into servants of the victor and preach to us about the delights of servitude.

But French thought will indeed continue. Against them, despite them.

But the republic of letters is holding up pretty well, when all is said and done. The "collaborators" are rare: a few old, unfulfilled artists, always aching for fame or money, all the greedier for the sound of their name being whispered about once more as they can feel above them, closer than ever, the shovelful of earth that will definitively stop up their ears; a few young failures from the latest broods eager to make themselves, in the disaster and silence of France, the reputation they accuse her of having denied them when she was happy and could speak; and finally a few pitiful braggarts who were born unable to keep quiet.

Voltaire invented the expression "man of letters" to designate a new responsibility and a new honor. As there had been "men-at-arms," and "men of the robe" to conduct the social ceremony in other centuries, from then on there would be men of letters, free men, makers of free men, and freedom would be their arm and their honor.

We are free or slaves in proportion to our souls. A true man of letters is not a purveyor of small pleasures. His freedom is not the freedom to be lazy or to dream. The vain contemplation of himself cannot be enough for him, nor the subtle games of his mind. For every man with a heart, freedom is, even more than his own liberty, the freedom of others. He cannot feel free when 2 million of his fellow citizens are so many hostages in a victor's prisons, when 40 million men around him can save what dignity is left them only through silence and cunning.

December 8

The Greeks are handing the Italians a serious defeat. So in the corridors of the Metro you can read this warning to the Germans, scribbled by some cocky Parisian kid: "Watch out, it's the Greeks!"[81]

We're living in myths, fables. We need to get out of this phantasmagoria. Why should I be taken in by all these lies? Neither Germany's cause, nor England's cause, nor Russia's cause is deeply mine. Not to let myself be destroyed by propaganda, invaded by "society." Return to simple ideas, to the one, the only problem: how a man becomes a man, becomes more of a man.

December 12

The *NRF* has indeed come out again. I'm reading the December issue. It is appalling, even from a purely literary point of view. Intelligence is taking its revenge. It seems that most of these gentlemen have lost almost all their talent. My friend Duval* tells me it's a Turkish ceremony.[82] But the ceremony lacks gaiety. The *mamamushis* are ill at ease in the brown shirts of their new role.

So many contortions. There is every conceivable way to dissimulate. How to be a traitor without being a traitor? How to celebrate France without offending the new master? Drieu la Rochelle wiggles out of it by using amplification. "France, the country of gentle hills." What non-entity invented that howler? France is not a country of gentle hills, France is a country of mountains...He writes an essay on this theme worthy of a high school literary prize.

---

[81] *"Vingt-deux v'la les Grecs!"* (commonly *"...les flics!"*): literally "Twenty-two, it's the Greeks!" This is a slang expression meaning "Watch out, it's the cops!"

[82] The "Turkish" allusions, including *mamamushis* further on, are references to a farcical scene in Molière's 1670 *Le Bourgeois gentilhomme* (*The Bourgeois Gentleman*).

M. Jacques Chardonne,[83] more abject and less skilful, celebrates the cognacs of Charente. He reports the dialog of a man from that region—a veteran of Verdun—and a German colonel:

THE CHARENTESE: I can only praise your soldiers, and I think everyone who lives around here has the same view. Moreover, the soldiers don't seem to complain about the welcome they have received.

THE COLONEL: The soldiers are happy.

THE CHARENTESE: The Charentese willingly offer whatever they have.

And he offers the colonel a glass of cognac, authentic 1820 vintage.

THE COLONEL, TASTING THE COGNAC: *Sehr gut…sehr gut…* It must distress you to see us here.

THE CHARENTESE: I would rather have invited you. But I cannot change the way things are. I hope you appreciate my cognac. I am glad to offer it to you.

In his last page, M. Jacques Chardonne outdoes himself, according to all the rules of rhetoric: his fawning reaches the sublime.

He quotes—makes up—this letter from another Charentese to a German captain who is occupying his house:

I am sorry I arrived after your departure and could not thank you in person for the way your soldiers behaved during the occupation of my house. The propriety of conduct they displayed is one of the best pieces of propaganda for mutual understanding between our two countries.

One could not be nicer. "That's France for you," as M. Jacques Chardonne goes on to say.

M. Fabre-Luce,[84] when it is his turn to sing, has some delightful songs about Paris and Parisian women. He informs his American friends that Paris has never been purer and more majestic, the *Parisienne* more elegant; that "the elegance of Paris can be seen much better in these Spartan times;" and finally that "the divided skirt, an effect of the shortages of gas and coal, has gained prestige."

Since André Gide has the most talent of them all, it is quite just that he should outshine them all in the art of dissimulating as well. This sincere man is a master of dissimulation. A true monomaniac—in his pages, he continues to hold forth with gentle obstinacy about his little "difference," and as he says next to nothing

---

[83] Pen name of Jacques Boutelleau (1884–1968), a pro-Collaboration novelist and essayist, imprisoned at the liberation of France. Verdun refers to the bloodiest battle of World War I, where Pétain commanded the French forces, finally victorious despite heavy casualties.

[84] Despite his pro-Nazi, Collaborationist writings, Alfred Fabre-Luce (1899–1983) had a long career as a journalist.

about the war, about whatever is tormenting our "multitude," he gives us this edifying excuse: "Out of modesty, in this notebook I shall only deal with things not connected to the war; and that is why I have written nothing in it for so many days. Those are the days when I could not get rid of my anguish and could think of nothing but that."

"Ah! The poor man!" as Orgon says.[85] That bleeding heart, that indescribable anguish, that distress which no words can express, that moving silence...Now there's something our little Tartuffes couldn't have come up with. It takes the genius that makes great stars. But why doesn't he simply keep quiet?

December 13

Chancellor Hitler's speech to the workers of the Reich. I have just read the text in German. As far as I can tell, his language is horribly impure, vile, but there is a movement in it that gives it eloquence and guarantees that it will take. The thought is confused but brutal, astonishingly well adapted to his public. It might as well be a speech by Thaelmann or Thorez.[86] Every clear idea gets lost in this mess of words. Communism and National-Socialism come together through what is lowest in each of them. How can the wretched crowd find its way in all this? It follows along, it can only follow. And all that is absolutely sickening.

December 15

Someone who analyzed the Vichy and Paris press this morning (and the news flashes on the radio, too) would surely find plenty of fine examples of the malpractice, distortions, omissions, and lies that constitute what is called news reporting in the European prison.

Last night around 9:00 I got Vichy on the radio just at the moment when Marshal Pétain was ending his reading of a new address to the French people. I was enraged. I did hear enough to understand that M. Flandin was replacing M. Laval as Minister of Foreign Affairs, and that M. Laval was no longer "heir apparent."[87] Besides, the Marshal was assuring France—and M. Hitler—that he was obliged to part with M. Laval solely for reasons of "domestic politics," and that France's foreign policy would in no way be modified because of it.

So, the conflict finally exploded. Pétain has dropped Laval. Had he promised the Germans too much, and Pétain resisted and found himself "painted into a corner"? Or was the affair really only "domestic"? I went to bed, impatient for more news.

[85] In Molière's comedy *Tartuffe*, Orgon applies these words, quite mistakenly, to the main character: Tartuffe is the archetype of a religious hypocrite.

[86] German and French Communist leaders, respectively.

[87] Pierre-Étienne Flandin (1889-1958) was Foreign Minister when Hitler invaded the Rhineland in 1936; France did not budge (nor did England). He would be Pétain's Vice Prime Minister for only two months.

This morning I rushed down to the newsstand. The papers have not arrived. Writing them under German control last night must have been quite laborious. Finally they do arrive, a good two hours late. Not a word about Laval, no trace of the Marshal's speech. But a great piece of news, an incredible piece of news that must make the heart of every Frenchman leap for joy: the ashes of the Duke of Reichstadt have been taken from Schönbrunn back to Paris. December 15, 1840–December 15, 1940. A hundred years later, the son will be reunited with his father under the dome of the Invalides.[88] Such is the magnanimous decision of the Führer. "Collaboration." Hilarious!

The ceremony took place during the night, lit by torches. (Why? That, too, would deserve analysis.)

In his speech, Ambassador Otto Abetz* was careful to declare: "It is M. Laval who created the atmosphere of collaboration, and for us, he is its sole guarantor." Words charged with lightning.

At 1:30 I am hoping Vichy radio will at least give us a follow-up to last night's news. No, nothing. It doesn't say a word about it. It is clear that after making a fuss about Laval, the Marshal had a bit of a fright. He is speaking again. But it is merely to address a message only to Parisians, about the Duke of Reichstadt . . . and to thank M. Hitler once again.

Let us wait.

December 16

I'm thinking about this "magnanimous" gesture of the Führer. I learn that the great celebration of "collaboration" would supposedly have taken place yesterday in broad daylight if the Laval-Pétain affair hadn't intervened. Goebbels had the idea of adding this scene to Rostand's play *L'Aiglon*: Germans and French, reconciled, carried the ashes of the Duke of Reichstadt to Les Invalides . . . But instead of that, nothing but a discreet ceremony at night. A night of dupes,[89] and M. Hitler got nothing for his "magnanimity."

Is M. Hitler really so uncultured himself, or so convinced of human stupidity, that he thought the return of the Duke of Reichstadt's ashes weighed as heavily as the return of Napoleon's ashes in French public opinion? That Rostand's eaglet had as much worth for propaganda as Victor Hugo's eagle? . . . But perhaps, deep inside, he was pleased to renovate that sanctuary of a people— that tomb of a genius, Les Invalides (where he jealously came to meditate last

---

[88] Les Invalides is the monumental building in Paris housing the tomb of Napoleon. His son, the Duke of Reichstadt, reigned briefly as Napoleon II; his ashes were taken to Les Invalides on December 15, 1840, and later sent back to Austria. Edmond Rostand (1868–1918), author of *Cyrano de Bergerac*, wrote a play about him: *L'Aiglon* (*The Eaglet*). Victor Hugo admired Napoleon I but not Napoleon II or III: see next entry.

[89] *Zilda, ou la nuit des dupes* (*The Night of the Dupes*) is an 1866 German comic opera and a 1934 French film. It became a common expression.

August). He turned it into a family tomb, the edifying tomb of an unfortunate family, something like Juliet's in Verona. From history, we fall into fiction. M. Hitler is probably thinking of his own future tomb and he's getting rid of the competition.

December 20

Still in the dark. It is clear that serious things have happened in Vichy: but what? The newspapers are mysterious. We're like prisoners whose cells have been changed. We grope around in the darkness to recognize the walls of our new dungeon. We have not yet seen the face of our new guard.

In the lycée, my students offer me their season's greetings. Using a phrase of Alain's,[90] they wish me: "think spring."

December 23

Cold and hunger for many people. Dire poverty. And this frightful silence. But on the other side of the street, in that school they've transformed into a barracks, our guests are setting up a Christmas tree and the poor people of the neighborhood watch the trucks full of provisions for the festive evening going into the courtyard.

How to keep a diary of emptiness?

For all Europe is a prisoner, but the prison regulations are nowhere more perfect than here in France, the country of Montaigne, Voltaire, and Renan. We speak, read, and write only on command. If we do not speak, write, and read following orders, we don't even have the right to breathe. The best part of ourselves is the most suspect, the most forbidden—and especially that urge we may have sometimes to say a sensible word or two, just a word, pointing to those silly things that are happening on earth, sea, and sky. It would even seem we have lost the knowledge of good and evil, and even the ability to tell one from the other...Renan smiles, Voltaire snickers, Montaigne wonders.

Wait. Nothing to do but wait. But wait for what? Oh, how tempting it would be to decide that the follies of this phantasmagoric world do not concern us...but it is harder and harder to fulfill our material needs; potatoes are becoming rare.

In the depths of this distress, it seems to me I've wasted my life in a kind of "idea-fight." As early as eight years ago, I decided to believe only in creatures, in individuals, in goodness—more precisely in a certain kindness which is, as it were, the flower of goodness. I believe in it, I want to believe in it, all the more, perhaps, as I have been less and less able to do so. But it is all I desire. It lights up the human face with a smile; it lightens our lives. So here I am, a great philosopher. And must one have lived fifty years to feel such naïve things with some

---

[90] Pen name of Émile-Auguste Chartier (1868–1951), a moral philosopher who was influential at the time and profoundly democratic and liberal.

depth? The desire to please, without trying, or study. To please. And thus to reconcile the people one meets with things, with life, with themselves, with oneself.
To soften their severity for a moment. To end their distrust and fear so they are
obliged to smile in their turn, and, for the first time, it seems to them that heaven
and earth are welcoming them graciously.

But at twenty we think we have the task of changing the world, and when we
discover how very imperfect it is, we think we've fallen into an ambush... Thus I
remember being deeply shocked by the inadequacy of creation and vowing to
correct it. I toiled for thirty years. I was hard, and full of anger. I looked at my
contemporaries as so many enemies every time I found them inclined to accept
a world in which all I could see was poverty and injustice. I brandished like a
sword a few little ideas that I of course thought had come from the depths of my
being, whereas they may merely have been prompted by the furies of the day. I
strove to frighten people, as if that were a good way of persuading them. I fought
with all my strength and condemned as cowards those who did not commit
themselves to the battle with the same heart. I wore out the best of myself in
those battles. It was not enough; I almost forgot to live. (For life cannot merely
be that vain brawl.) Perhaps pride as well as suffering persuaded me that I had a
mission, that my life would only be justified by this battle, "my battle," *Mein
Kampf*, as the fellow said—that king of madmen, that man typical of all today's
arrogant stupidity.[91] I used up the years that were given me to love a few human
beings kindly and modestly in fighting for the love of humanity. I lived badly,
loved badly. I didn't take the time for it.

From March on, the flowers of the almond trees have warned me about this
dozens of times. I did not heed their warning. What kind of coward could look at
the earth blossoming again? I was angrily scribbling out my battle orders. The
letters on my blank sheet of paper intersected, crossed like rapiers in a fencing
bout. And now the fine weather has gone, and the creatures—those I should
have loved—are all dead, or almost all of them. And I still have kept my love for
humanity, with no use for it, no object to satisfy it except my fight to the death,
as soon as I can begin that once again.

I should make better use of this time of silence and prison. Sometimes I think
I've fallen into the depths of despair. In the last analysis, what I have seen the
past thirty years is a real enigma to me. How did the milk of human kindness
turn into the blood of battles? How, out of love, have we ended up killing each
other so conscientiously?

December 24

The "dupes," the other night, were not exactly the ones I thought. Today's
L'Oeuvre hypocritically analyzes the event by evoking this "historical precedent":

---

[91] The title of Hitler's infamous book *Mein Kampf* means "my battle," or "my struggle."

the "day of dupes" (1630).[92] The paper is triumphant. "They wanted," it says, "to get rid of a great minister and he's still there; they wanted a change in policy and it has been reinforced; they hatched a plot, and they were its victims." Unfortunately all that is quite likely, and we must conclude what no newspaper dares say clearly (though after a week went by, we were beginning to suspect it): at Hitler's wish, M. Laval has remained our master.

December 25

It's Christmas. We're stifling. All this freezing, empty day I have been desperately repeating Audiberti's poem for prisoners like us to myself:

A blow for a, two blows for b

. . .

Nothing will be of that which was.[93]

December 26

I'm re-reading Léon Blum's book *Stendhal and Beylism*[94] in the hope of finding a few revelations about himself in it. But the revelation, if it is one, is only in the choice of subject. It is no doubt rather remarkable that before he became the leader of the Reds, Léon Blum should have been a Beylist, an admirer of Julien Sorel, a "Reddist" as they used to say around 1885, and that his career should culminate, in 1914, precisely in this little book. No doubt he saw himself in that Stendhal whose genius, he writes, is to "combine the coldest clear-sightedness with the most ardent sensitivity, to adapt his rigid method to an infinite faculty for suffering, to an almost lyrical taste for passion." At least he dreamed of such combinations, too.

I think of him in his prison. I can see him as he was when he used to greet us at the Hôtel Matignon,[95] when he was surrounded by the love of a whole people. He fairly quivered with sensitivity; he was so "nice," and yet so oddly distant. I remember our last meeting in Clermont last July in the offices of the regional paper, *La Montagne*. After re-reading this book, I feel I have a better understanding of that ironic, far-off air he had as he told me about

---

[92] The name given to the events of November 10–11, 1630: Louis XIII unexpectedly renewed his confidence in his minister Richelieu and got rid of his political opponents. For *L'Oeuvre*, see note 53, p. 25.

[93] "Prison," by Jacques Audiberti (1899–1965), a poet, playwright, and novelist. Guéhenno is quoting the first and last lines: *Un coup pour a, deux coups pour b. Rien ne sera de ce qui fut.* The poem ends with the prisoner arising.

[94] Henri Beyle was Stendhal's real name; further on, Julien Sorel is the hero of his masterpiece, *Le Rouge et le noir* (*The Red and the Black*, 1830).

[95] The Prime Minister's official residence. Blum had been arrested in September—by the French, not the Germans.

the days in Bordeaux.[96] I can see his fine hands trembling over the table as he analyzed the event with assiduous coolness. From that moment on, he probably knew he was beaten, and was no longer able to feel anything but disgust.

Since on the eve of the war, in 1914, he was well aware that his master's doctrine "tends toward an idea of happiness in which there is no room for action," how is it that just after the war, in 1920, he threw himself into action? How could he not have thought more carefully about Stendhal's declaration: "I had and I still have the most aristocratic tastes; I would do anything for the people's well-being, but I would prefer, I think, to spend two weeks out of every month in jail than to live with shopkeepers"? How can one imagine Stendhal as the head of a party, head of a government? And if the intimate contradiction at the heart of Stendhal's genius led him to write the most beautiful love stories but to have rather pitiful love affairs, where, then, would the same contradiction very probably lead in the realm of political action? "Sublime," Stendhal used to say about himself, "In your extraordinary castles in the air, not good in this world at all..."

But it is a rather noble thing to have been politically committed, compromised, and lost through what is best in oneself.

December 29

I ought to have the patience to listen somewhat diligently to Vichy radio and especially to the lectures, news stories for the young and for the family. Hypocritical voices, the same who read the impious declarations of the Popular Front two years ago, take pains to read out, unctuously, sermons on work, family, country, and religion.[97] It seems it's always the same Tartuffe who's talking. The same soppy nonsense on the family, the crafts, folklore (there is an overdose of folklore in Vichy), flowing interminably on like a dribble of dirty water. It seems that for the past 150 years we had been living in the darkness of sin. This dirty water, like a new baptism, is supposed to regenerate us. The night before yesterday, live commentary on the radio from La Grande Chartreuse![98] We know the Carthusian monks returned to France on the heels of Hitler's armies. Ah, how edifying it was! The prior general, full of scruples in front of the microphone—

---

[96] Fleeing the German advance, the government moved to Bordeaux on June 10, 1940. Exactly one month later, the Chamber of Deputies voted to give "full powers" to Marshal Pétain, thus ending the Republic.

[97] The Popular Front: the Socialist-centrist-Communist coalition that governed France in 1936–1937 and introduced social security and paid vacations for workers. "Work, Family, and Country": Vichy changed the national motto from "Liberty, Equality, and Fraternity" to this slogan of the French State.

[98] La Grande Chartreuse, a massive monastery in the Alps, is the mother-house of the Carthusian order, which was expelled from France at the Revolution and again in 1903.

that diabolical machine which chases away silence everywhere—resigned himself to telling the world what the vocation of his monks was: "Contemplation in solitude." At which, with no transition, in a voice mellowed by grace, the reporter related how the secret of the Chartreuse (the liqueur) had been providentially transmitted from prior to prior for ten centuries. So much vulgarity is offensive, but what is truly exasperating is that this edifying radio is, in the last analysis, well adapted to the facile religion of so many excellent parishioners: every Sunday, they go to eleven o'clock mass, take communion, "eat the body of Christ," then lunch copiously; and since digesting so many good things is rather difficult, they turn to the Chartreuse of the good fathers as a *digestif* around two o'clock.

Vichy propaganda is evident in an appointment-book, *Agenda de La France Nouvelle 1941* (Calendar of the New France 1941). Along with pages for appointments, the booklet has illustrations and short articles: justifications of Pétain's policies, attacks on freemasonry, and advice for coping with food and energy shortages. Propaganda was not limited to the radio, the press, and posters. It was everywhere, even in calendars and appointment books. *Courtesy of Jean-Kely Paulhan.*

On the front cover, the French banner (blue, red, and white in the original) winds around the happy family of a worker; a factory is in the background. The back cover (not shown) depicts a happy peasant family: workers and peasants were supposedly the pillars of the Vichy regime. The illustrations on pages 49 and 50 were in this appointment book.

La rafale.

"The Gust of Wind" of New France (Vichy) sweeps away symbols of the old Republic: the Chamber of Deputies, the Senate, "Marianne," and the top hat and briefcase of "plutocrats" who supposedly ran the old regime. *Courtesy of Jean-Kely Paulhan.*

La terre ne ment pas.

"The land does not lie." The value of "roots" in pure French soil rather than the "decadence" of the city was one of Vichy's themes, as this illustration from inside the appointment book shows. In actual fact the Germans were requisitioning masses of farm produce for their armies. *Courtesy of Jean-Kely Paulhan.*

Philippe Pétain, Marshal of France,
Head of the French State. Library of
Congress *LC-USZ62-77383*.

December 30

Something new to offend us every day. Last night they announced that Place
Jean Jaurès* in Toulouse will be called Place Philippe Pétain from now on. This
morning Tours, Algiers, etc. have already applied the same decree. The new prefects certify and guarantee the spontaneity of the decisions. All this is more
stupid than tragic.

Just before the news announcing this revolution in street names, the Marshal
delivered his pitiful homily to the youth of France. Anger and disgust made
me run to my library. I got out Jaurès' "Address to the Young" and read it to
Louisette.[99] Where can one learn to love this country any better than there?
We regained hope. Through those ample sentences catching their breath and
breathing after each ending, I could hear the great wind coming down from the
Montagne Noire, the bracing Cers wind that awakens and revives the gentle
plain around Toulouse. Harmonious, rhythmic speech has the effect of commu-
nicating the fervor of the man who said it, the movement of his heart. I have
never felt, for anybody, the sense of what a great man was so much as for
Jaurès—a force so ample that it cannot find all its use in the man who has it; it
grows and nourishes the other people around it, awakening a life inside them
that they had not even been able to conceive of by themselves.

[99] Guéhenno's daughter Louise was then eighteen. Jaurès gave the speech in *1903* at the Lycée of
Albi (in the south, near the Montagne Noire), where he had been first a pupil and then a teacher of
philosophy.

1941

1941. It is snowing. The silence of Paris is merely a little deeper. Misfortune has made people modest: they timidly wish each other a "better" year.

The newspapers—*L'Oeuvre*—are beginning to imply that December 13 was a bad day for Collaboration.

The great hypocrisy of Déat* is to present himself as a pacifist, as if he had no idea that Collaboration with Germany, which is fighting a war, necessitates France's growing participation in that war.

The way events are developing makes the position of the Empire stronger every day.

Life in Paris is growing very difficult. We have ration tickets, but we can't buy anything with them anymore. The shops are empty. At home, we've lived exclusively on parcels sent by friends and cousins in Brittany for the past two weeks.

"There's a new moon," writes Déat. "Before it is full, many things will be put in order." Now there's something promising.

I don't know if I've already noted my deepest reason for hope. It's just that all this is too absurd. Something as absurd as this cannot possibly last. It seems to me I can read their embarrassment on the faces of the occupying forces. Every day, they are increasingly obliged to feel like foreigners. They don't know what to do on the streets of Paris or whom to look at. They are sad and exiled. The jailor has become the prisoner. If he were sincere and could speak, he would apologize for being here. No doubt that pitiful revolver he carries at his side reduces us to silence. And so? For how long will he be carrying it, will he have to carry it? For, without a revolver...Will he be condemned to wear it forever and live in this exile, without any other justification, any other joy than that little revolver? The occupier hasn't thought enough about this remark of his fellow countryman Hegel: "All that is real is rational. All that is rational is real." There is not enough reason in his victory for it to be real. That's what I was thinking to myself a little while ago as I was going to a Feldwebel to ask him very respectfully for the authorization to send a bit of money to an old relative who lives in the other zone.[100] The Feldwebel will give me his answer in two weeks.

What are the names of those two lovely stars that we see in their zenith around eleven o'clock? The other night they were flying through the sky and I thought at first they were two planes coming into Le Bourget.[101] But half an hour later they were still there, and only then did I realize that they were really two stars behind the clouds quickly going by in front of them. They seem very close and shine with extraordinary brilliance. I'll have to find out.

January 8

I'm re-reading *War and Peace*.

January 10

A new issue of the *NRF*. Valéry* has his *Cantate de Narcisse* in it.[102] I can't help being sorry to see him go along with the ploy of our occupiers, who want everyone to think that everything in France is continuing just as it did before. Besides, the poem is charming, but no more than that. We prefer La Fontaine's *Adonis* and *Psyché*,[103] which he sometimes copies rather brazenly; this work of his is far from a masterpiece. Now, only perfection could justify a publication like this. So the occupier would be fooled by his own trick. Why do you not show the world, Valéry, what kind of victories we can still win? But if all you can do is amuse us, keep quiet.

The whole issue is very weak. A few strange pages by Montherlant.* As naïvely vain as ever, this time he plays at being a "knight," evokes his 13th-century ancestors, gets all worked up about the Teutonic Knights (a courteous bow to the German censor), the Templars (another bow to the pederasts), the Orders of Castile, takes pains to be a Montherlant as one might be a Bourbon or Condé or Bragance, and as the last shoot of a noble family tree, appears to wash his hands of the defeats and misfortunes of a beggarly, plebeian France. Saint-Simon was less proud of being a Duke and Peer of France than he is of being a knight.[104] A "Knight of Literature," one might perhaps say, but real knighthood is never an affectation.

---

[100] Feldwebel: sergeant. Guéhenno uses the German word, as he does for others in use during the Occupation.

[101] Le Bourget was then the main airport of Paris.

[102] Valéry wrote his "Narcissus Cantata" for the composer Germaine Taillefer in 1938.

[103] Light erotic works by Jean de La Fontaine (1621–1695), whose rhymed *Fables* are classics.

[104] The *Memoirs* of Louis de Rouvroy, Duc de Saint-Simon (1675–1755)—not to be confused with the utopian socialist of the same name—are still read today. Proust loved them. The Bourbon dynasty ruled France for almost three centuries; Condé and Bragance were great noble houses.

And yet, all through these pretentious pages, these theatrical rants, a noble manner, like someone who cannot be soiled by the dirtiness of the day, an individual propped up and protected by the old dream of his lineage.

January 12

A visit from N... He is a young Indochinese man, astute, elegant, and sensitive. He was my student two years ago. He wrote French with a kind of love, the same meticulous care he probably exercises when he paints his Chinese characters. Yesterday I could feel that he was disturbed, and surely had come for help. He no longer knows where he stands. He told me what France meant for his friends and for him in the Saigon lycée four years ago, how they loved her with a romantic love, so strong and at the same time so vague and so endangered. So far away, and what a paradise she was, according to the dreams they had as they read beautiful books and flawless poems together. He talks of this slowly, taking the time to reflect between every sentence. He loves France still, he wants to love her. But am I aware of the wretchedness of his fellow countrymen now in France? How they have been abandoned, living only on the aid of the Red Cross and the Salvation Army? And over there, in Indochina, am I aware that any willingness to do something is suspect and watched over suspiciously, and how they treat young, cultivated Indochinese, what care they take to maintain them in inferior positions...? And suddenly his face lights up, his eyes shine, his cheeks grow pink, and it is only now that I feel he is absolutely sincere: "You have to be young to understand this," he tells me. "You can't understand what Japan means to us."[105] That's what had been so hard for him to tell me: what he had just told me—this new love, no less romantic than his love for France had been. He explains to me that Japan isn't what it is thought to be in Europe. There is the shining, hard Japan of the Samurai, but there is another Japan, one which has not forgotten the tender, humane lessons of the Buddha... And I listen to N..., somewhat embarrassed and ashamed. I am obliged to feel that we have not done our whole duty, and that since France had not believed strongly enough in herself—in her essence—she missed her chance for greatness; and disappointed, I fear, the love of so many young people whom she should have turned into free men, our equals and our brothers. We're paying for this lack of faith, we're expiating this sin. How can we expect these young Indochinese men to defend the Empire against Siam and Japan? They would be generous indeed if they didn't take some pleasure in seeing us humiliated by an occupier as they were by us.

---

[105] Vichy allowed Japan to use the French colony of Indochina (Viet Nam, Laos and Cambodia) for the transport of military supplies in September 1940; a full-scale Japanese invasion and occupation followed.

January 13

Certain *pensées*—"thoughts"—of Pascal allow us to see his meditation at a particular moment in his passionate reading.

I think I can see him reading Psalm 136[106]:

Super flumina Babylonis, illic sedimus et flevimus, cum recordaremur Sion...

What does he care about the strict meaning of the text, its historical meaning? Only its mystical sense captures his attention. *Sensus sublimior*, as the theologians would say. All he is looking for is a rule for his life.

Zion is the celestial Jerusalem, the paradise that original sin made us lose: we are nostalgic for it and we will find it again in death. Babylon is the world, the earth; its rivers are lusts, their flow, the flow of life, the vanity and sin of our desires.

Flumina Babylonis... His eyes stopped on these words. His passion goes beyond the text. No, it is not enough for the rivers to flow. "The rivers of Babylon flow and fall and drag us along. O holy Zion, where all is stable and nothing falls." "Flow and fall and drag," are these three verbs, at least, enough to express his own horror of the earth and life? And that invocation, that geometrical antithesis, that "reciprocal" formula: "O holy Zion, where all is stable and nothing falls" enough to proclaim the certainty of his hope?

Again he looks at the text: *Super flumina Babylonis, illic sedimus...* That *Super* is strange. Literally *On* the rivers of Babylon, where we sat... Why *On*? Why not near, or at the edge of the rivers of Babylon? Scoffers might wonder if that *Super* is not a bad translation of the Hebrew text, a mistake.

But he has no doubt and sticks to the letter of the text. The sacred psalm says *Super*, On. So it is "On" that we must understand. The *sensus sublimior*, the spirit of God is in all the words, and in that *Super* itself. And Pascal is dazzled, and comments:

> One must sit on the rivers of Babylon, not under or in, but over; and not standing, but sitting: being seated, to be humble; being over, to be safe. But we will stand in the entrance to Hierusalem.

He insists on nothing so much as this *Super*. Isn't it the means to his most moving antitheses? "Under or in," rolled and swallowed by the rivers of desire, fought and beaten down by pride, such is man. But "over"—such is the Christian, and such is Pascal himself.

But as he trembles at having conceived of a rather proud joy—for the Demon is subtle, and knows all the pathways—he catches himself up immediately: "And

---

[106] Guéhenno writes 136; it is Psalm 137 in the King James Version: "By the rivers of Babylon, there we sat down, yea, we wept as we remembered Zion." Pascal would have read it in Latin.

not standing, but sitting"...The *sedimus* of the inspired book returns him to humility: "being seated, to be humble; being over, to be safe." Thus must one live, in a faith that is never a rest, but somewhere between fear and hope, the continual torment of purity and greatness.

Pascal pursues his meditation. Sometimes rigor and fervor, which are usually mutually exclusive, lead his thought. He watches the rivers of shameful, vain desires flowing around him. The rivers of Babylon are flowing. That is the theorem. Then suddenly a corollary appears to him and this corollary will be a rule for his life: "Let us see if this pleasure is stable or flowing: if it passes, it is a river of Babylon."

What? The pleasure one has at seeing a smile on a face is "a river of Babylon"? What—all poor human pleasures as guilty as the orgies of Sardanapalus? What eloquence! But what geometry! And what is the use of such strong thinking if it is used only to destroy life?

January 17

Never have so many people in Europe known how to read and yet never have there been so many herd animals, so many sheep. In times gone by, a man who didn't know how to read would save himself through his distrust. He knew he was ignorant, as Descartes did, and he was wary of anyone who spoke too well. He thought by himself—the only way to think. A man today who has learned to read, write, and count is utterly unprotected from his vanity. A degree certifies his knowledge. He believes in it, he's proud of it. He reads the paper and listens to the radio like everyone else, with everyone else. He is abandoned to the tender mercies of advertising and propaganda. Something is true as soon as he has read it. The truth is in books, isn't it? He doesn't realize that the lie is in them, too.

I can see this confirmed more every day. Our teaching is far too much about teaching results. All too often, it fosters only the gift for pedantry and a docile memory. A hundred young people I talk to are far more knowledgeable in geometry than Euclid, but few of them are able to reflect that Euclid was a great geometer and that they are nothing. More than the results of the sciences, we should teach their history, reveal to young minds the nature of a moving, active intelligence and communicate the deep meaning of science: get them to understand that a scientist is not a man who knows but a man who seeks, crushed and exalted at the same time by the idea of all that he does not know. Thus we could produce independent, strong men and not vain, servile animals.

January 23

Too many of the days when I record nothing in this notebook are days of despair. I know—one mustn't let oneself go. And besides, we keep on living. We live out of habit, if that is living. We hold on, we last. But submerged by solitude and sorrow, overwhelmed by the very awareness of our own impotence. We have no temptations, no desires. Very rarely, a thought dares to spread its wings. It sinks as soon as it rises. What's the use? The snow has melted in Paris; there's a thaw. We merely think we're going to be a little less cold.

My recourse, my refuge, is my profession. I work hard at it, I wear myself out at it, I lose myself in it. I give to it all the taste for perfection of which I am capable. I only find a bit of freshness in front of those fifty young men, my students. At the door of the lycée, before going in, I stand up straight, out of consideration for the judgment of others. My students are waiting for me in the classroom. I walk in, and immediately I am sure that all the misfortunes of this country are temporary. The hope that is merely an act of the will for me is organic, as it were, in these young men. When they offered me their season's greetings three weeks ago, they wished me: "Think spring." But as for them, they live spring. Nothing will prevent spring from blossoming again. So I try to describe Racine's reverie or Pascal's torment to them. We forget together, and for a few moments it really seems that modern idiocy has been utterly abolished.

Paulhan* has a kind of logical imagination, the funniest in the world. Yesterday he was telling us: "Do you know what Hitler told Pétain at Montoire?[107] He has him in his pocket: he threatened to withdraw his troops from the Occupied Zone." Everyone laughed. But it is quite true that no measure would be riskier for the Vichy government and would embarrass it more.

January 24

Drieu* has collected his latest articles and sends them to me with this dedication: "To J.G. who will give me an article on Voltaire one day." We have no means of telling these gentlemen what we think of their activity. At least they might leave us in peace. To crown it all, they try to present our silence and our decision not to publish anything as cowardice. "Fortunately," one of them writes in the last issue of the *NRF*, "Neither Voltaire nor Diderot reasoned like that."[108] Those men, holding out their hands to be chained and passing themselves off as Voltaires…All one can do is gnash one's teeth. Impossible to reply without offering to enter the prisons of our occupiers.

January 29

Around 10:30 in the evening I often get Budapest radio. They play gypsy folk music. It is a long growl, ceaselessly recommencing, like a man brooding endlessly over his unhappiness yet never resigning himself to it. Always the plaint

---

[107] A smiling Pétain shook hands with Hitler when they met at Montoire on October 24, 1940.

[108] As Guéhenno well knew, Voltaire often had to publish anonymously, and in Holland rather than France; at Diderot's death in 1784, he had left his most subversive writings unpublished. Both spent time in prison for their free spirit when they were young.

starts up again, like a new protest, a new entreaty to gods who shut their ears to it. That music makes a rather appropriate accompaniment to our thoughts. This is how we groan and growl in our prison, in the night.

January 30

Yesterday afternoon, a new speech by Hitler at the Sportpalast for the eighth anniversary of his accession to power. Never has he been more frenzied. Never a better demagogue. I noted some signs of fatigue, however. Three times he seemed to get lost in a word. He stammered: Uh...Uh...He was no longer in command of his tongue, or of his head. An *Etwas*...held him back like glue. *Etwas...Etwas...Something*...But he eventually started up again. And what thunder. He brandished all his anathemas. Then he affected tranquility. Jealous, perhaps, of Churchill's humor, never has he been wittier. I heard the loud laughter of the crowd and I could imagine the shaking paunches. The finest moment was when he related that a certain English "mister," thanks to a certain method, had calculated that he, Hitler, had made seven mistakes in the course of the year 1940. "Seven mistakes," he went on. "That man made a mistake. I checked. I did not make seven mistakes. I made seven hundred and twenty-four of them." The crowd could not contain its joy. He let the paunches regain their composure and then began again: "But I went over the count again and I counted that my enemies had made four million three hundred and eighty-five thousand mistakes..." Then the crowd went mad. But who was speaking? Hitler, or the clowns Footit and Chocolate?

This morning I re-read the speech in the *Pariser Zeitung*.[109] In vain did I look for a political sentence that was somewhat thought out and could give rise to discussion in one way or another. No, he simply wanted to "pump up" his people. How to think of the coming weeks without horror. The other day Bouché* was telling me about airplane crews—what courage, what technical knowledge they have. And three or four thousand of those crews may fall— ten thousand of the most intelligent, determined, and courageous men in Europe.

Ever since yesterday, the Paris papers have been full of threats. They give us a choice: either servitude or Collaboration. This morning *L'Oeuvre* gave us to understand that we would have no more than twenty-four hours to decide.

It seems that the Italian defeat in Libya has renewed Vichy's courage to some extent. And Pétain probably doesn't want to leave Weygand* the advantages of his position and the virtues of resistance.[110]

---

[109] "Paris Newspaper": the official daily German newspaper of the Occupation, with some articles in French.

[110] Maxime Weygand was then Vichy's Delegate-General for France's North African colonies. British forces destroyed the Italian Tenth Army in Libya in December 1940–January 1941.

February 5

The argument between Berlin and Vichy continues. Berlin makes threats, but apparently hasn't dared take any decisive action, fearing dissidence in North Africa. Vichy tries to gain one day after another and tries cunning, crawls, gets up for a moment and goes back to crawling. What this argument is, exactly, we don't know, we can't learn a thing about it. We can sense shameful blackmail. And this unfortunate country postures and wriggles like a slave under the lash, just to hold on to a bit of life and honor.

Paris has been under the snow again for the past three days.

February 9

"It takes twenty years to bring man from his vegetable state inside the womb to the purely animal state, which is the lot of his early childhood, to the stage where he begins to grow into maturity. It took thirty centuries to learn something about his structure. It would take an eternity to learn something about his soul. It takes only an instant to kill him." (Voltaire, *Philosophical Dictionary* ["Man"].)

February 10

What genius future historians will need to recognize the real causes and real motives for the events in those texts, those communiqués, in which not one word is honest or accurate. And how can a whole people be expected to understand? But it is saved by its genius. From so much hemming and hawing it can only conclude with total certainty that Laval* is Hitler's man, and *collaboration* is merely a fine word for servitude.

Churchill spoke on the radio last night. What a contrast to Hitler's shouting. The throaty, heavy voice of an old man, but sensitive in every phrase—*the unconquerable will* that Milton spoke of. There is where our hope lies. He concluded by these words, addressed to the Americans. Their very simplicity made them deeply moving: *Give us the tools. We will finish the job.*

Symbolic: every evening at the Opera, I am told, German officers are extremely numerous. At the intermissions, following the custom of their country, they walk around the lobby in ranks of three or four, all in the same direction. Despite themselves, the French join the procession and march in step, unconsciously. The boots impose their rhythm.

February 14

My profession as a teacher is the main part of my life and I blame myself for noting nothing or almost nothing about it here. It's the time of year when I begin to talk about the 18th century, for my work is regulated in such a way that every year I must go through the same cycle, following France in its revolution like a heavenly body. It is a great privilege. Ten centuries are condensed into ten months. Three hundred days. Toward the month of February we enter—France enters—the sign of liberty at the same time as the sun is entering the sign of Aquarius. It's the finest moment there is. It is springtime for France. The "nation" begins to know itself and stir. Eyes open and light up. Hope trembles like the first shoots of wheat. Writers are going to celebrate that moment. From now on they belong to "the nation," and not to the king or a grandee. They are men of letters in the same sense as there had been men-at-arms. Liberty is a new honor for them.

Yesterday, for the first time, we heard the laugh of Voltaire. We were discussing a fragment of his *Letters Concerning the English Nation* and we were watching freedom being born from the alacrity of a mind and a feeling for the public good. Around four o'clock, I suddenly realized that the classroom was filled with an astonishingly serious silence. All the students were pale with attention. None of them were even thinking of taking notes anymore. To give the text its full meaning, I was reading fragments of letters, of poems—the poem on liberty, from 1734:

Liberty in man is the health of the soul,

and the poem on the death of Mlle Lecouvreur![111]

What! Can it only be in England
That mortal man dares to think?

They were listening, they were completely bound up in listening. Was it the circumstances? Were we all watching the birth of something which is perhaps dying at the present time? The texts spoke for themselves. We felt inside ourselves the spirit that made France. I left at five with my heart full of joy and yet on the verge of tears.

As I came out of Henri IV I met Monod,[112] who told me the Occupation authorities had just arrested a teacher of German in Lycée Janson de Sailly; he had been denounced by a student. It seems the Occupation authorities pay a hundred francs for such denunciations....What, one wonders, have I deserved, for reading those fragments of Voltaire? How will I teach, in the coming months? The star of France is going to continue its revolution. There is really nothing I can do to stop it: Voltaire, Rousseau, Diderot, Danton,* Robespierre,* Chénier,* Hugo, Michelet*..., I have nothing to discuss but suspects.

Never have I eaten with more pleasure and gluttony. It's because when we eat, from now on it always seems to us like a godsend.

---

[111] Adrienne Lecouvreur (1692–1730), probably the greatest actress of her time, played in Voltaire's tragedies. To his indignation, the Church refused her a Christian burial—unthinkable in England. Voltaire's *Lettres anglaises* (1734) wittily contrast the free spirit and tolerance of England with the hidebound intolerance of France under the ancien regime.

[112] See note 72, p. 34.

February 17

So Admiral Darlan* is becoming the heir apparent. In order to remain in control, the Marshal has only to brandish his last will and testament. A dark comedy. A collaboration between Tacitus and Regnard.[113]

February 21

It's snowing again. But the few nice days we've just had were frightening. The planes were beginning to make their rounds again. This bad weather gives us some respite, but anxiety never leaves me. The green men whom I pass on the street seem pitiful to me. They have the silly, vapid look of soldiers in every country on earth, dragging their boots around uselessly while they wait to give blood in accordance with the rules of their job.

One feels rather ashamed to eat. The poor people in the neighborhood have no more bread. As of now, they have used up all their February ration tickets. If we're still eating in our house, it's because we're members of the bourgeoisie and can send for packages from Brittany at great expense.

What can one say about those prescribed postcards which are the only authorized correspondence between the two zones? What a testimony to the degradation we are enduring. The text is printed in advance and we only have the right to leave it or cross it out according to the circumstance: it anticipates that a man can be "in good health," or "tired" or "slightly or seriously ill" or "wounded" or "killed" or "prisoner." So much for the state of the animal. As for his needs, it allows us to "need provisions or money." Finally, as the average Frenchman sometimes goes wild about exams, as we know, it is indicated that he may "have gotten into school" or he has "passed the examination." That's all. After which, "Affectionately. Love." We can neither love more nor less.

In addition, one card out of two is rejected. Louisette's card to her grandfather came back this morning. It did say that I was "tired" and that is permitted. But she had added "like last year" and that is forbidden. A stroke of a blue pencil showed her mistake.

Yesterday I received an authorization from the Feldwebel to send some money to the other zone. I had waited two months for his answer.

Rivet succeeded in getting through to the other side. It was high time. He left Monday morning. In the evening, the Gestapo searched the Musée de l'Homme[114] and arrested fourteen people. Julien Cain, the former administrator of the National Library and a Jew, has been arrested. The grounds: he was too visible.

---

[113] Publius Cornelius Tacitus (56–117 C.E.) was the very serious historian of corrupt, tyrannical Roman emperors, while Jean-François Regnard (1655–1709) wrote comedies and satires.

[114] "The Museum of Man." A group of anthropologists who worked there founded one of the first Resistance networks in France and an underground newspaper. Jean Duval,* one of Guéhenno's close friends, was in the network, as was his friend Jean Blanzat.*

February 22

Dr. Mondor has just published the first volume of his life of the admirable Mallarmé, and it was a pleasure to follow the poet in his chimerical adventures for a moment.[115]

In the depths of the abyss, in the depths of this prison we are in, what a temptation it is to flee, or to imagine one has fled, to turn one's back on "the dazed herd of humans," at least in dreams. But after all, we know how such flights end up. Poor Mallarmé was all too aware of it himself:

> Those heroes enraged by trivial ills
> Hang themselves from lampposts, ridiculously.

Still, for that one must be a hero, a real poet—Gérard de Nerval.* But what about us? Always after those flights we find ourselves back among the herd, only a bit more dazed by the race and the dream.

Those poets mislead us. One does not change life by oneself and to be free in dreams means nothing. The problem of freedom concerns the whole flock. The whole flock will be free or not one beast will be. As for me, I deeply feel, I will never have enough courage, I will never rise to such a height where I could judge human ills as "trivial." I am of that "dazed herd" and I always will be. There are first impressions from which one does not recover, from which I cannot recover. I lived in a stable for too long in my youth. I cannot forget it and I'm making a virtue out of necessity. I can feel as well as anyone all that is noble, delicate, and heroic in the intellectual adventure of someone like Mallarmé. He was tempted by perfection, as Pascal had been in another realm. But when I am confronted with attempts of this kind, however attracted I may be to them, I feel that I am an incorrigible barbarian. I will never be capable of being an angel. Resigned to being a beast among the beasts, I think only of saving the herd.

February 24

The herd, however, is not pleasant to contemplate when it is gathered together. I saw it yesterday. The political party that Déat is trying to organize to "take power," the Rassemblement National Populaire, was holding its first rally.[116] But I would like to think that the only part of the herd which was there were representatives of a particularly low order.

[115] Henri Mondor (1885–1962) was an eminent surgeon—two hospitals bear his name today—with a passion for the great Symbolist poet Stéphane Mallarmé (1842–1898). In addition to his substantial medical writings, Mondor published many volumes of literary history, including a critical edition of Mallarmé's complete works for Gallimard's *Pléiade* series. The quotation in the next sentence (*le bétail ahuri des humains* in the original) is from Mallarmé's poem "*Le guignon*" ("Hard Luck"), as are the next lines quoted.

[116] The RNP (literally "the National Popular Gathering") urged closer collaboration with Nazi Germany and a fascist regime in France. Like Hitler's Nazi party, it claimed to be "socialist," but "European"—in Hitler's Europe.

They had taken great precautions in preparing the meeting. People could only get in by showing their Party card and the invitation. One of my friends had received a card for two people. I decided to go and see.

There were five or six thousand people in Salle Wagram.[117] Not one worker. The great majority was composed of shopkeepers, clerks, office-workers, and pseudo-intellectuals—the same people who made up the troops of the CSAR, the PSF, and the Cagoule three years ago. When their former leaders appeared on the platform, they applauded. The movement is neither national, nor "popular" (of the people); one can be sure of that right away. The common species of frenzied petty bourgeois in shiny cotton oversleeves was the only species represented.

The meeting was supposed to be informational, but naturally we were informed of nothing. When Blanzat and I walked in, Jean Goy* was ending his speech. Then a certain X… took the mike. He declared himself a Breton and gave me many new reasons to be modest about my own origins by claiming that all Bretons were like him. "People of Paris," he shouted, "I swear before you…" It was too stupid for words. This all too sincere paranoid was followed by a kind of huckster. His voice, his gestures, his acting—everything gave him away: the most sincere crook in the world. The far-Right herd immediately recognized its shepherd. I felt a strong urge to flee, but, just as he was working up to his climax, the poster of the RNP collapsed next to him from the breath of his voice. That restored my serenity.

At last, Déat spoke. It is obvious that he has a different dynamism than his teammates. He still has the same Auvergne accent that he had twenty years ago at the École Normale, a kind of rustic force disciplined by the rhetoric one learns at the École. I dare not judge his faith, his sincerity. No doubt he has the sincerity common to his profession: he has been aspiring to power for twenty years, and he continues to do so. A politician must want to exercise power, he says to justify himself. He wants to be a leader and he'll be one in German if he can't be one in French; he'll be a führer, if that's the language of the new Europe. What does the herd matter to him, as long as he's the shepherd. One real passion inspired him yesterday: hatred of the Vichy government, which did not make him a minister.

In the mess we're in, what are the odds that this prodigious stupidity, exploited, disciplined, and organized by this peasant out of the École Normale, will succeed? I don't think they are very great. Stupidity of this sort does not have deep enough roots in the country. But, Lord, is that herd ugly!

Let's have some fun. In Digoin, in a train station on the Line of Demarcation, some workers from the south of France are unloading requisitioned material.

---

[117] Salle Wagram: near the Arch of Triumph, one of the oldest concert halls in Paris, it is also used for sports events and other shows. In the next sentence, the CSAR (Comité Secret d'Action Révolutionnaire), the PSF (Parti Social Français), and the Cagoule (literally "the Balaclava") were far-Right organizations active in the 1930s.

They have finished their job, but the Feldwebel neglects to check the delivery. So one of them says, with that strong Provençal accent:

"Hey, conqueror! Come over here, there's some work for you."

"All right. But I already told you not to call me 'conqueror.' I'm telling you, it's silly."

In a train station in Savoy, some young people are chatting near two immaculately dressed Italian officers.

"You know that uniform?"

"It's the Romanians, I'm tellin' you."

"Nah, they're Hungarians."

"Not at all, I'm tellin' you, they're Serbs."

One of the officers says pompously:

"Gentlemen, you have obliged us to hear your conversation. You are wondering to what army we belong. You really should recognize the uniform of the victorious army."

And one of the young people says: "I told you they were Greeks, didn't I?"[118]

February 25

New speech by Hitler. As far as I can tell, he is putting on a more serene air to reassure his people as the decisive test approaches. One word, however, betrayed his uneasiness. "I have a fanatical confidence in the future!" Why fanatical?

He is a marvelous actor. For a long time, in the first part of his speech, he did imitations of his former adversaries. The crowd was delirious with joy. A shout occasionally revealed the frightful hardness of this leader. He answered those who threatened him with Revolution in a whistling voice: *Wer die Revolution machen soll, das weiss ich nicht. Nur eines weiss ich, dass es in Deutschland nur ein paar Narren geben kann, die an Revolution denken, die aber hinter Schloss und Riegel sitzen.*[119] To conclude, he flexed his muscles, recalling all the former contests from which he emerged victorious and rejoicing at the coming spring which would allow him to measure his strength once again. And then, the grace of God is with him. And with that, music.

February 28

Bouché and I were invited by X...to come see him around three. He had "things that may be important" to tell us. Bouché and I were somewhat surprised to find ourselves at his place. He had told neither one of us that he was calling us both. Why?

---

[118] Italian troops invaded Greece on October 28 and were routed by the Greek army. (Germany came to their rescue by invading Greece later in the year, as Guéhenno will report.)

[119] "Who might make a revolution, I do not know. I know only this: in Germany there are just a couple of fools who can dream of revolution, and they are behind bars."

X...is convinced that Germany "has won." He knows all the miseries that "Vichy repression" has inflicted among civil servants. He suffers at the thought. He can't wait to swing into action. Thus he agreed to meet with representatives of the Occupation authorities; together, they thought of founding a new republican newspaper: secular, socialist, and European. And yesterday X...actually asked us to be the editors of this paper, along with him.

Bouché and I—each in our own way—wasted no time explaining to X...that for eight months now we had accepted being victims, but not slaves.

But what clearly comes out in those conversations with the Occupation authorities (and this is, after all, rather comforting) is that they have not succeeded in making contact with the real France. X..., who does have a certain taste for mischief, seems to have given them a real surprise by defining what a newspaper capable of bringing together the honest masses of the country should be. They had a very hard time understanding what "a serious man" is in the eyes of the little people of France: neither Deloncle nor Fontenoy nor Déat will ever appear serious to them.[120]

Bouché talked—admirably—of our helplessness. Despite all our good will, we cannot be useful. There simply are no conditions that make good, honest action possible: on the other hand, if we are not careful, we are sure to be used. War means the helplessness of men. It occurs precisely when the good will and rationality of men can no longer do anything to govern the relationships between them. Then men are merely used by forces foreign to themselves. The development of technologies has changed the face of the earth. It must digest these techniques. But that digestion may take a long time. And men may be victims for a long time. In order not to be slaves in this chaos, all one can do is to remain faithful—every man in the depths of his being—to a certain idea of man, and keep that idea alive for the day when the earth's digestion will end and Man will begin again.

There are moments when all our liberty is reduced to the awareness of our servitude; it is like a great memory that continues to guide us, and we never cease to know from what direction the day will break.

March 1

Yesterday in the Metro, a German soldier was looking through his guide to Paris. He finally asks an old worker. He's looking for the Bréguet-Sabin station. The old worker informs him, but does not succeed in making himself understood. Then, overflowing with sincere pity: "Poor guy. Man, are you dumb. What the hell you doing here? It's too complicated for you."

---

[120] Eugène Deloncle (1890–1944) was one of the founders of the far-Right Cagoule (see note 117, p. 62). Jean Fontenoy (1899–1945) was an ardent collaborator who committed suicide in Berlin when Germany lost the war.

March 3

I'm finishing Mondor's book on Mallarmé and I just took down some interesting excerpts from the new book that Halévy* has written on Péguy.* Biographies of exemplary men make us confront our own contradictions. One does not change life by oneself, I wrote the other day, from an old distrust of those too singular adventures, those flights of scornful archangels. I do suspect those who claim to live above "the dazed herd of humans" of excessive pride; I want my cause to be the common cause.

But if one only thinks alone, and if all salvation lies in thought, one can only save oneself alone. When all is said and done, nothing is as valuable as a certain instinct for perfection, and that instinct, variously employed, is the same in a man like Péguy or Mallarmé. The common cause may merely consist in awakening or liberating that instinct in everybody.

These past few days I learned Socrates' beautiful prayer by heart again—the one Jeanne had taught me long ago.[121] Socrates addresses Pan and all the gods who make the day so bright and the water so transparent in the country around Athens. "...O dear Pan, grant me, too, inner beauty." That is enough, no doubt, enough for everything.

Yesterday, as we were explicating Book VI of the *Aeneid*, we came across these words of Aeneas when he has decided to return to combat: *Arma, viri, ferte arma*...The student who was translating naturally took care to mistranslate: "To arms, citizens!"[122] he cried, and we laughed, seriously. After which, he very judiciously pointed to the eloquent conclusion of the second hemistich: *Vocat lux ultima victos.*

This morning, as I came into the classroom, I find this inscription on the blackboard:

Una salus victis nullam sperare salutem.

That teacher at Lycée Janson who was arrested the other day after he was denounced by a student—he had given his class a text of Schiller's on freedom to translate—was finally released. But the student who denounced him doesn't dare return to the lycée. He's afraid his classmates will beat him up.

---

[121] Guéhenno's wife Jeanne Maurel, a historian and the mother of Louise Guéhenno, died in 1933. Jeanne had translated the letters of Sacco and Vanzetti, anarchist Italian immigrants to America executed for murder in 1927 after a trial that became internationally famous as a scandalous miscarriage of justice.

[122] Virgil's *Arma, viri*...means: "Weapons, men, bring weapons." The student has changed this into a rousing line from the chorus of the *Marseillaise*: *Aux armes, citoyens!* The next quotation means "The last light (death) summons the vanquished." The final one is from Book II of the *Aeneid*: "The one safe hope of the conquered is [to have] no hope."

March 5

For the past eight months, people in the Vichy government have been abusing a word in a very strange way. To hear them talk, France was rotten, the workers were rotten, the civil servants were rotten, the parliament was rotten. The university, elementary school—rotten. The Republic was merely a great enterprise of rottenness.

No doubt there were, in the Republic, corrupt, rotten people—if one must give in to fashion and find a use for the word. They were not so numerous and they were both rotten and failures. But the defeat, the "divine surprise" as M. Maurras* says, finally gave them a chance and opened careers for them; what is remarkable is that these are the men who are now throwing around this slogan about the rottenness of France.

No, history will say that there was, at the western headland of Europe, an old people which had, from its very age, a more advanced political conscience than any other, a people that believed in reason and happiness, wanted peace and rejected war with all its heart. Their only folly was to believe that their neighbors were as wise as they were, their only fault to be too wise too early. But their time will come.

March 7

Persian Letters. "How can one be a Persian?"[123] ask the Frenchwomen and Frenchmen as they turn curiously around Uzbek, so strange with his long, silk puffed-out pants, his long frock coat that goes all the way down to his feet, his high belt, his daggers, and his turban. But how can one be a Frenchman? That is the question this mischievous book is asking, for the very first time, and that astonishment heralded many storms to come. The wise Montesquieu himself could not have predicted where that passion for questioning would lead us. How can one be a monarchist and a Christian? Believe in the Holy Ampulla and the Trinity, etc.?[124] And finally, as Paul Valéry wonders, "How can one be what one is?" Whoever asks this question has already given up being just that. "Nobody," says Uzbek under the eyes of so many curious people, "nobody was so much in the public eye as I was." The French, around 1720, saw themselves so much they no longer could see themselves. They were what they were out of habit. But when they began to look at themselves again and everyone felt the eyes of all the others upon him, they had to change, like a woman at the Opera who feels all eyes upon her and arranges a lock of hair, smoothes her eyebrows, moistens her lips, and lights up her eyes—the Revolution.

---

[123] *Comment peut-on être Persan?* is a famous question Parisians ask Uzbek, the Persian, in Montesquieu's epistolary novel *Lettres persanes* (1721).

[124] "The Holy Ampulla" was a glass vial filled with holy oil supposedly used to baptize Clovis, King of the Franks, in 481 and subsequently used in the coronation ceremony of French kings.

At the École Normale Technique, we were studying Michelet's admirable text about Hercules in *The Bible of Humanity*.[125]

> What does it matter to you, young man? Rather, come with me. Let us sit at the feet of those heroes of bronze blazing with the rising sun of Delphi. All the mountains are crowned with a pure, living light. Their finely indented peaks, like clear steel against the azure, pierce the sky. One peak, calm and strong, looking from on high at all its neighbors in Thessaly, triumphs in his glory. It is Mount Oeta, the funeral pyre of Hercules.
>
> May the heroic legend struggle against Bacchus. May the good, great Hercules strengthen and support the wavering young man and hold him firm and high in the holy party of the lyre.

And old Michelet, I am sure, would have been happy. His words were giving back their pride to these young men, vanquished only yesterday. As moved as they were, I explained to them what history meant for Michelet: not dissecting a corpse, but putting the past itself to work for the present and the future; and a call, always a call to the lifeblood of the nation. A call specially addressed to them. I did what I could to pick up their step. For, according to that grand idea, they, who are lucky enough to be twenty years old, were now fighting on the front of history, marching in the first rank, in the first battalion of an immense army that came from the depths of Europe and the centuries. Countless dead are pushing us along, and we cannot betray their hopes; they are forcing us to go where they wanted to go, toward the light, toward freedom. The frightful reality around us filled Michelet's phrases—perhaps they are a bit too eloquent—with new life.

March 9

When Péguy was killed in 1914, the Church was about put him in its Index of forbidden books. All "right-thinking" people today speak of him as a kind of saint. The Church is wonderfully skillful in taking advantage of the temporal glory of its sons. It condemned Pascal, but once Pascal had decidedly succeeded in this world, his success had to resound to the greater glory of God. From then on, no one has spoken of Pascal more tenderly than the Jesuits.[126] They canonize the same dead men they persecuted when they were alive.

---

[125] The École Normale Supérieure de l'Enseignement Technique (ENSET), "Higher School for Technical Education." The ENSET, like the École Normale Supérieure (ENS), was an institution of higher education but trained engineers and technicians. Guéhenno taught in the "General Culture" program (since abolished); he was a strong believer in the value of general culture for technicians. Michelet's *Bible of Humanity* (1864) is an outline of the history of religions. He views Hercules as a great *worker*, transforming the earth.

[126] The Jesuits were responsible for the Church's official condemnation of one of Pascal's major works in 1656.

Halévy tells the story of Péguy's life and has written a fine book. But out of conformism, he, too, gave in to hagiography. Péguy was far from being a storybook hero. There was nothing namby-pamby about him. He was a rough, sly peasant, a man who stood alone, a heretic in every way, a man who supported the Republic and refused to vote, a Catholic who refused to take communion. He had a faith—his faith—but he could not have a political or religious party. Halévy quotes this phrase of Barrès*, to contradict it: "Your Péguy is really a Baillard"— Baillard, the heretical visionary of *The Sacred Hill*.[127] Barrès is right. Péguy himself was one of those wanderers in history whom he loved. Perhaps all heroes are wanderers. Ordinary history is flat and orthodox.

Whether he was a socialist, as in 1900, or a Catholic, as in 1910, his religion was the same: he had hope, he needed to hope. For him, the cardinal virtue was hope. He was a Christian the way an old supporter of the Republic could be Christian, a Christianity which damned no one, for true justice was compassion and love. He was a Christian the way Michelet and Proudhon* were Christians. "No more damned," he cried. "No more saved," Michelet had cried before him. It is the same cry. All things considered (for objections could be made, and this peasant was absolutely not a saint), that purity we admire in him, that stubborn purity with which he pursued his work—Halévy, you'll just have to accept it— that purity was still the purity of a stubborn "old republican" who knows what a man owes to himself and what he owes to his country.

March 11

M. Darlan is proclaiming "Germany's generosity." It is the height of absurdity: these vanquished generals have become our masters, and because of their very defeat, they must fear England's victory and the restoration of France above all. They know they would be swept away by this victory, and more: they would then have to account for their actions. So France must remain vanquished at all costs so that they may keep their power and their honors and no tribunal can interrogate them about their honor.

March 16

Yesterday morning a certain Mme X... (D as in Denise, E as in Ernest, G as in Gustave..., she told me on the phone) asks to make an appointment with me. I don't know her, but she knows me. She is a Belgian. She gave the name of poor Jacques Mesnil* as a reference, as well as P..., H..., and... She would like to talk to me about Mesnil's manuscripts, and... great interests that we have in common. She's at the Hôtel Wagram, 208 Rue de Rivoli, Metro station: Tuileries.

I answer rather coolly and make an appointment for 4:30. I did not know Jacques Mesnil very well and there is no particular reason to see me about him.

---

[127] Baillard is a character in *La Colline inspirée* (*The Sacred Hill*, 1913), a novel by Maurice Barrès.

I ask P... for information: "Mme X...," he answers over the phone, "is a big, likeable vixen. You must see her."

At 4:30, I'm standing in front of the Hôtel Wagram. As I expected, it has been requisitioned by the Occupation authorities, one of the hotels of the Gestapo. Should I go in? I thought about it under the big red flags with their black crosses. And if I go in, will I get out? I go in. Mme X... is waiting for me in the hall. She tells me a few things about Jacques Mesnil, about his death in an asylum in Limoges in June '40, about the debacle, about the publication of his manuscripts (if they are found). Would I not be ready to help her? "Of course, that's my job." But she wants to talk to me about more serious things.

"May I offer you a cup of tea? It's still quite good in this place." I'm sure it is. To the waiter: "Two teas." "Just plain tea?" asks the waiter. "Yes, just tea." I don't deserve bread and jam. Mme X... reassures me. She is in this hotel because one of her daughters married an important German before the war and she was able to get the necessary *Ausweis* to give her access. She had been a regular here, hadn't she? So... She has an apartment on Quai Voltaire, too. But she hasn't been able to open it yet. She has important things to tell me. Ah! The atmosphere of Paris is unbreathable. Things have to change. It absolutely cannot go on like this. She has turned to me as she has to other friends—to D... (for her, D... is old D..., so old is the esteem she has for him) and to P...—because she has read all my books so many times, because she knows how humane I am...

I give up trying to record the whole scene. Mme X... acted brilliantly. One can swindle someone through his humanity as well as through vanity. Exactly what did she want from me? Was she supposed to transmit a report on me? Or was she merely to inform her agency about the opinion of French intellectuals? I was on my guard and still I acted badly. I'm not used to this kind of game and, incorrigible as I am, I told her only what I thought. The big men with shaved necks crossing the lobby at every moment should nonetheless have reminded me to be prudent.

Her problem, explains Mme X..., is to open her house on Quai Voltaire. She will no doubt succeed, by moving heaven and earth. She will be authorized to leave Antwerp for Paris. The best Germans and the best Frenchmen must get together. Would I not agree to... There are left-wing men in Germany, Communists. P... was just telling her that the police were everywhere, but she can't believe it. She asks questions, gets the lay of the land, jumps from one topic to another, from one name to another: Déat, Laval, Abetz,* the RNP. One must save the human element. Ah! the human element! What do I think of de Gaulle? Of V...? Of S...? Ah! If only all honest men... And above all, I mustn't begin to think that she wanted to see me for any other reason than to... My books are what decided her to call me. The human element. Nothing but the human element.

I was patient for a long time and then I exploded. I answered that I did have many misgivings about doing nothing, but it seemed to me the conditions for any common action with the Germans did not exist; I, too, was from a "race," after all, since she was talking about race—my name made that clear enough—and I was prepared to be subjected to foreign rule, but I would keep my freedom. I knew Germany was unable to make contact with the French people, it was doomed not to make contact with them in the future and we were all slipping together toward something frightful; but events would develop and then we might see that there was reason to act, perhaps—and even with certain Germans; German military victory was perhaps an established fact, but the victory of Nazism had never been further removed; the triumph of Germany had merely consisted in spreading its own misfortune over all of Europe—a misfortune that excused its rage to conquer, perhaps, but a misfortune which, after all, we had the right to refuse.

This outburst had calmed me down. I was master of myself once again. I got up and told her as nicely as you please that if she opened her house again I begged her to inform me; I couldn't promise her anything but then I would certainly tell her yes or no after thinking it over very seriously.

"If I find Mesnil's manuscripts, I'll be counting on you," she said at the door.

I went out. I walked up the Avenue de l'Opéra in the sunlight, slowly, full of disgust, as if I had just been chatting happily away with a crook. As a result of dragging myself through that filth, it seemed to me I was lifting fifty kilos at every step.

I phoned D . . . right away. He did not dare answer me. I could feel he was afraid of a wiretap. He kept repeating to me that he was telling me nothing, he was telling me nothing, he had told me nothing.

This is the kind of air we are living in. While I am taking these notes, Mme X . . . must be writing up her report. We'll see . . . And these first days of spring, so beautiful nonetheless.

The Vichy government is handing over to Hitler the two leaders of the German Social Democratic Party, Breitscheid* and Hilferding,* refugees in France. It is an abominable disgrace.

I'm reading Kierkegaard's "Concluding Unscientific Postscript." According to K, Christian truth cannot be the object of "consideration." "For," he says, "it has two eyes to see with and it is even all eyes. Now, it would be quite unpleasant—impossible, in fact—to examine a painting or a textile if, when we wished to make this examination, we found that these things were actually looking at us. This is exactly the case for Christian truth . . ." And K's translator adds this note: "Just as a poet wrote that there is, between the sun and the moon, this difference: the sun looks at us, whereas we look at the moon. We might perhaps see in this what essentially distinguishes the God of philosophers from the God of Christians."

What strange apologetics! What preciosity! What gongorism! I think of that curious phrase of Balzac's comparing a beautiful sunless day to that beautiful blind woman that Philippe II was in love with . . . [128] Those fine images pleasantly occupy the mind for a moment or two.

March 21

The planes rumbled by constantly all night. Decidedly, it's spring.

March 24

Three days ago, English radio had asked us to write the first letter of the word Victory on the walls and the pavement as a sign of hope. Since yesterday the V's have blossomed everywhere. A kid traced a monumental one on the door of our house.

But the other day I saw a more curious inscription. In a *pissoir* between the Pantheon and Lycée Henri IV one could read *Heimat, süsse Heimat* in fine Gothic letters.[129] Is it the sad confession of one of the countless green "tourists" who come to visit the Pantheon? Or some perceptive high school kid who made the effort of writing these words, so likely to awaken *Sehnsucht* in the heart of these exiled visitors?

Yesterday, Sunday, we went to Versailles. They are everywhere. There were three of them in the restaurant, big, pot-bellied, unbuttoned, slumped in their chairs, nostalgic, in the hands of three horrible whores billing and cooing, caressing them, pampering them. All of them were stretching and grunting together with pleasure. O German virtue! O Siegfried! It's true that the whore and the soldier are international types. But ordinarily they hide their amorous frolics. A conquering soldier openly flaunts all his rights.

March 28

In this great silence that covers Europe, something extraordinary happened last night. A cry of hope rang out in the prison and was instantly smothered, but everyone heard it. People on the street hardly dared look at each other for fear their joy could be seen. But everyone was whispering to those he could count on and friends were calling each other across Paris: "Did you hear the news?"

The news is that two days after Yugoslavia signed the Tripartite Pact, a people's revolution banished the leaders who signed it, drove out the regent, and

---

[128] Not the great 19th-century novelist Honoré de Balzac, to whom Guéhenno will refer a number of times in later entries, but the 17th-century Jean-Louis Guez de Balzac (1597–1654), best known for his *Lettres*. Guéhenno quotes the whole sentence from this Letter in his entry for October 11, 1943. The Danish Christian philosopher Søren Kierkegaard (1813–1855) is thought to be a precursor of existentialism.

[129] "Home, sweet home" in German; Gothic is the old Germanic script written on the urinal (*pissoir*) wall. *Sehnsucht*: nostalgia, longing for home.

proclaimed a new government.[130] And one must probably wait to judge exactly what this event means. But rightly or wrongly, all the prisoners of Europe had hope last night. It seemed that a young king of seventeen, pushed forward by a whole people, had broken the circle of fear. Could this be the beginning?

I picked up Serbian radio at seven. It was broadcasting a demonstration in Belgrade. How sorry I was not to understand it. But I was listening to history in the making. There was a kind of delirium, chants mixed with shouts: *Pe-tar-Dru-gy*...I could make out a few words more: Hitler, Albania, and sometimes, during the calm spells, the ridiculous sound of car horns honking in the jammed streets. It lasted for two hours.

This morning the papers are as empty as usual, and we begin to wait once again.

March 31

Blanzat has told me that we should never forget. Our feeling about the disaster should not abandon us for one single moment. Only on that condition can we prevent France from completing its destruction. He is right. And yet, yesterday we occasionally forgot. He himself suggested we spend the morning in the Jardin des Plantes. It is one of the most charming spots in Paris; there you can breathe the light, intelligent air of the 18th century. The shades of Jussieu, Daubenton, and Buffon, those curious men, wander through the groves.[131] We stayed in the vivarium for a long time, watching the ground beetles fighting with each other and the bats sleeping; we held toads and grass snakes in our hands as a favor from the director who was giving us a guided tour. And then we went to see the big cats and the monkeys. An orangutan truly humiliated us. So like us, he was walking like a broken old man, with his arms in front of him like two sticks. Except that he had the privilege of being able to carry a slice of bread between the thumb and fingers of his left hand behind him; so as not to walk on it, he took care to hold it in the air. And suddenly straightening up, as if he were tired of walking so naïvely, he climbed up to the top of his cage and walked around the ceiling, hanging by one hand, then by the other, still holding his bread between his toes. His wife, squatting in a corner, was suckling their baby. A mysterious family.

One of my students from last year, Drouet, came to tell me that he's entering the seminary in Issy next October. Already, three years ago, he had spent a year there and then had given it up. But now he is sure he has a calling. I can understand

---

[130] When Yugoslavia allied itself with the three nations in the Axis (Germany, Italy, and Japan), a revolt of labor unions, peasants, church, and army overthrew the government on March 26, 1941, and put the king's young son Peter on the throne. Further on, *Petar, drugy*: "Peter, comrade!"

[131] Founded in the 17th century, the Jardin des Plantes is a park and botanical garden housing the Museum of Natural History and a zoo. Jussieu, Daubenton, and Buffon were great 18th-century scientists.

those strange outbursts in his papers—which incidentally weren't very good—that lovely look he had when he was listening, that profound goodness.

April 7

The newspapers are out, in special editions. The government of the Reich is announcing that it is going to re-establish "calm and security" in Yugoslavia. "I have decided," the Führer is proclaiming, "to entrust the representation of German interests to force; only force, as we see once again, is able to protect right and reason."

Stalin is continuing his game. He is signing, in his turn, a friendship pact with Yugoslavia. Will Pan-Slavism be the first means of maneuver of the Communist Revolution?

A flabby, quavering speech by the Marshal. He denounces the dissidents, doesn't dare name de Gaulle, but declares "Admiral Darlan has my complete confidence." We thought so.

April 9

We are living through the darkest days. I can write nothing in this note-book. The German offensive unleashed against Greece and Yugoslavia seems to be succeeding. It is hard to have hope. Nothing to do but wait behind our barbed wire. It is terribly sad to see other people fighting vainly and dying for our deliverance.

Young R...came to see me. A Parisian woman, a schoolteacher intern in the Yonne region. She's here for the holidays. Her mother, a member of the Communist Party, was arrested and sentenced to a year in jail.[132] The police came in one morning when she was still in bed, searched her place, and found nothing. But while the policemen were doing their job, a friend of Mme R...knocked on the door. The police opened it. She was carrying a packet of leaflets. So they arrested the two women. Young R...does not cry as she tells me her troubles. But I can see her lips trembling from pain and rage. The three women lived together, her mother, her aunt, and her. The policemen are boasting of shutting all three of them down.

Good Friday, April 11

Nothing but bad news. London seems uncertain, worried. Churchill's speech yesterday reminded me unpleasantly of Reynaud's* speech last June. The same appeal to America, and almost as desperate. For the first time, I said to myself that our defeat may be definitive and I wonder what our lives will be like in this prison. Prison for life, at least for people of my age. We were not sufficiently

---

[132] The Communist Party had been decreed illegal since August 1939, under Prime Minister Daladier.

aware of how lucky we were to be born in a noble country whose words—all of them—echoed around the world. How will we live in this impoverished, debased, dishonored country? The most urgent task will be to give it back its honor. There will be a lot of work to do. I was old, I was approaching that age which d'Aubigné* called "the season of use and no longer of labor." Let labor continue. I am ready to work still, with all my heart. But will we even have the right to work? The best of us will no doubt continue to be forbidden to do so and forced labor will be the only kind authorized. Leave? In the midst of this great misery, that would mean desertion. Remain? But then we would run the risk, as Blanzat pointed out, of "retail desertion"—giving in, adapting, and putting up with it. Use cunning? But I am so bad at being cunning. At any price, work and give free rein again to honor and to freedom.

In the past, we would have been in Montolieu at this time of year. We would be moved by the first lilacs, the first irises blooming in the garden. I think of the last sight of that world which impressed me. Of that beautiful tree with shining yellow buds against the blue of the sky bursting out this week like so many little flames. The whole week was nothing but one long rustic ceremony, alternating between joy and gravity. The altar boys would run and get eggs from the farms, shaking their little bells in the streets of the village to remind people of the services. Thursday evening was Stabat Mater.[133] The bells were going to Rome. Then came two dark days of wind and rain, and on Sundays, the earth would resuscitate, at the same time as God. At least I can't reproach myself for having gone through the week too lightly, without the necessary attention. But this year, these days of Easter seem heavier to me, and emptier.

April 12

André Gide's *Journal* is, it seems, the biggest hit in Gallimard's *Pléiade* series. What modesty, to take his place, during his lifetime and alone among living authors, with Montaigne, Plato, Shakespeare, and Cervantes. What assurance of his immortality, down to his slightest words.

Gide himself explains somewhere that one of the qualities of all great works is to be particularly *well-timed*. This quality, at least, is not lacking in his *Journal*. Its success is symbolic, in a way. The French bourgeoisie of 1920–40 and all those in it who had cultural pretensions are present in this journal of Narcissus. That limp elegance, that preciosity in one's pleasures seem to them the height of distinction. André Gide is all that a cultivated bourgeois can be or want to be. His travels, his leisure, his wanderings, his errors, his vices—these are the only

---

[133] The *Stabat Mater Dolorosa* ("the Sorrowful Mother stood...") is a medieval Latin hymn set to music by many composers and sung at this time. In the next sentence, according to an old French Catholic tradition, church bells fly to Rome at Easter to visit the Pope—or at least that's what children were told to explain their silence on the days before, during, and just after Good Friday.

means by which the bourgeois "with no profession" can imagine "assuming the most humanity possible."[134]

I picked up the journal again last night. Is it the circumstances? Never have I been so irritated by that air Gide has, on almost every page, of sucking on a piece of candy. I think I can hear him catching his saliva the better to savor his pleasure. So many delights, so much enchantment—I find it depressing. That "exquisite" world in which he moves is not a real world. He is awfully serious about his pleasure, and no one has ever worked harder at cultivating his sloth. The desire for personal enrichment, to perfect himself, which is perhaps admirable, is his constant guide. But I can only feel a sense of distance from that irresponsible life, his rejection of all commitment. For him, everything is no more than literature, an occasion for pleasure. The greatest books, the most tragic—he devalues them, he debases everything. He thinks he's a Montaigne, but tastes everything and risks nothing. He thinks he's a Goethe. But Goethe trembled, and he merely quivers just a bit, likes to quiver, and the reader sinks with him from *Schaudern* into simple tickling. His reading is enormous, but we don't feel that any book has ever changed him. Why should he have changed? All he has to do is let himself live. Jesus, Montaigne, Pascal, Dostoevsky, and Nietzsche are no more than masks that Corydon[135] wears one after the other to give himself a feeling of greatness—successive invitations to take pleasure in himself in a different way. Always pleasure. He is a man who has time, too much time.

April 14

Belgrade was occupied yesterday.

I think that for these past few days I've been taking out my rage on that poor Gide. "Justness of judgment is useful in all things," says Voltaire. For the sake of justness and justice, I am recopying here a few notes I took at a first reading of this same journal. I had given them the title "André Gide or the Tragedy of Total Liberty."

> p. 20.—He is twenty. And he writes this principle in his journal and underscores it: "*Dare to be oneself.* I must underscore it in my mind, too." What a decision! And he'll hold to it all his life. The admirable lesson that he gives us is summed up in those few words.
>
> p. 45.—What amazing happiness! And at the same time, what a disaster! No outside limits to his experience. If he is not in quest of

---

[134] Guéhenno is quoting from Gide's long prose poem *The Fruits of the Earth* (1897). Further on, with *Schaudern*, he refers both to a line in Goethe's *Faust*—"*Schaudern* (trembling in awe) is the best part of man"—and to Gide, who speaks of *Schaudern* in Goethe.

[135] The name of the Gide's spokesman in his Socratic dialogue of that name (privately printed in 1920, published in 1924) defending homosexuality against accusations that it is "unnatural," immoral, etc.

God, he must be in quest of himself. Now ascetic, now sybaritic. Between him and God, nothing, neither a human being nor a thing to which he feels obliged, by which he feels constrained. He plays the angel or the beast at will.[136] All those intermediary questions, the in-between state that Pascal speaks of, where a real man shows his measure, are settled for him. We don't know if he is more to be envied or pitied for having been able to write as early as his twentieth year: "All I had to do to be happy, perhaps, was to let myself live." True, there is that "perhaps." But all that "perhaps" will do is to sanction the leaps of the angel, the moving voyages, always recommenced, between himself and God, then from God to himself.

p. 46.—I simply turn the page and I find these reflections on "dependency": "You must understand," he says to man, "That independence means poverty. Many things lay claim on you, and many claim to represent you."

That's really him. Where is he? What is he? What does he esteem more, the precise servitudes of the earth or angelic voyages?

But he recovers his liberty immediately when he was tempted to lose it, through this new rule: "Every act must find its reason for being in itself, and not be self-interested." We already see the "gratuitous act" of Lafcadio.[137] Now our man is delivered and decidedly an angel. Because chance chose for him. He was born free, he had the good luck to be born free. He can imagine the servitudes of the earth and get carried away as he speaks of them; he will never know them. Servitude that is truly felt excludes the gratuitousness of the act.

How close he is to Barrès at this moment of his life. They are both the same kind of anarchist. At bottom, the journal is merely a manual of exaltation. But what a magnificent adolescent he is! How he feels things in all their greatness. And he owes this, precisely, to his total freedom. The enthusiasm of the young is almost always constrained by social circumstances. Whereas he was constrained by nothing.

"Things," he writes, "are the interpreters of God." That is the way he feels them, and the way he teaches us to feel them. No matter that he owes the power to give us this lesson to pure luck: the lesson is a good one.

p. 47.—The tragicomedy of the impossibility of choice. It is merely the predicament of a young man from a good family who has nothing to

---

[136] Guéhenno is referring to Pascal: "Man is neither angel nor beast, and he who plays the angel may end up playing the beast" (*Pensées*, 1669, published posthumously).

[137] Lafcadio is the hero of Gide's 1914 novel *Les Caves du Vatican* (translated as *Lafcadio's Adventures*, 1928). At one point, he throws an old man out of a train for no discernible reason—an *acte gratuit*.

do. And that complete freedom is going to set him off in pursuit of all pleasures. The fruits of the earth. Dilettantism.

p. 48.—But now greatness again: the will, which intervenes so early and so firmly, to lead a great life, the jealousy of great men. That is the way the little young man rises up. He decides to use his liberty, all his life, to become great and singular, and few lives show such perseverance in carrying out a design conceived in the exaltation and purity of youth. There is a prodigious stubbornness in him. I find on p. 48 the outline of a whole discourse on the method of becoming a great writer. Few oeuvres will have been so conscious and so deliberate.

I know two Gides. One of them is seated, sprawling back in an armchair with his arms extended, his chest wide, his mouth wide open, and that strange light at the outside corner of his eyes, laughing, shining, beaming, surely a rather good companion. The other is standing, wrapped in his cape with his hat over his eyes and the gaze of a cat, his thin lips curled up to smile—a miserly, tight look to him with his head bent to one side self-consciously, his chest narrow, all buttoned up from top to bottom, surely a rather ugly character.

Photo on the cover.—A bust of meditation. That brow, those lowered eyes, that hand under his chin. What a pose! How many shots before the photographer got the right angle!

p. 215.—Notes on happiness. But I worry about what he is not noting. Is this journal of happiness his whole diary?

p. 219.—"I'm going back home to work . . . " What uneasiness as soon as he can't work.

p. 222.—"Distress . . . bewilderment." Something is hidden from us that he should finally dare to say. But this sincere man is silent about many things.

p. 228.—Apathetic about everything except his work. On every page: "Studied my piano." At the end, it's irritating. And the visits to art shows, to museums. All those occupations of an idle man.

p. 250.—"I am only a little boy having fun, coupled with a bored, puritanical pastor."

Play-acting religion. Sometimes he mimics Pascal. Struck by the greatness given to his *Pensées* by their very incompleteness, he sometimes manufactures notes and brings them to a suitably unfinished point. Everything here is premeditated. The *Numquid et tu*[138] is designed to play the role, in his oeuvre, of the "Mystery of Jesus" in Pascal's *Pensées*.

---

[138] The Latin title of Gide's account of his religious struggles (1922) comes from John 7:52, in Latin; in English: "Are you, too, of Galilee?"

   p. 437—A letter to Beaunier, extremely important for the criticism
of his work...

What would I add to these notes today? I admire unreservedly the astonishing strength of will that André Gide has employed to make a career as a man
of letters, but a marvelously successful man of letters may still not quite be a
man. Perhaps that is what distorts everything in his case. He is an author who
plays at being a man. He has, and he uses (even if he denies it) all the pretensions
of a spiritual adviser. The prestige of his talent has led many of us astray. Myself
among them—and often, perhaps. Every time we have been weak and grew
weary of going in search of the world and its problems, every time we've been
tempted to avoid all commitment and its attendant risks, every time we wanted
to "let ourselves live," his work was able to provide us with excellent reasons, and
even with a method. It shows all too well that one can, after all, spend one's life
rather nobly by thinking only of oneself.

April 19

A visit from my former student R..., who's just out of prison. He's coming
out of it more of a Communist than he came in. I did not listen to him well
enough. There were four of them in the same cell sleeping on the same straw
mattress. His companions were two thieves, a murderer—"such good guys," he
explained. He does not know if he can keep on at the university. His "comrades"
are helping him. This solidarity is the true greatness of that political party. The
other day Olga R... told me what kindness and devotion the "comrades" showed
her mother, too. Every week a comrade goes to the prison to pick up her laundry,
washes it, and mends whatever needs mending.

At the Rue Brasserie near the Gare Saint-Lazare, the "cigarette boy" is a little
old man of seventy, wearing navy blue, a frock coat, a cap with gold braid, all of
it a bit worn, but you could take him for an admiral. Five medals rattling about
on his chest complete the resemblance. All he needs is the big cross and the
decoration. Some jealous politician refused to give him one, no doubt. His whole
being exudes dignity and fame. He walks with a deeply felt step from one table
to another, procures cigarettes, matches, women, and morphine and cocaine, for
all I know. An astonishing caricature of the social order? No, B... tells me, rather
an act of defiance.

It's all over in Serbia. Now to Greece. And the campaign in Cyrenaica[139] is an
even greater concern. How hard it is to hope.

---

[139] The Roman name for eastern Libya, where the German army was then triumphing over British
forces.

My students' papers are sometimes remarkable pieces of testimony. The last ones I have just read show the extent to which the youth of this country lacked masters who showed some manliness. I thought I would provoke them by giving them a text by Boylesve* on naturalism, Balzac, Flaubert, and Zola. A vain provocation. The best students are still following Gide or Proust who, each in his own way, teaches them to delight only in themselves. Most of them had no problem whatsoever agreeing with M. Boylesve that science is "stupid," could not possibly transform the novel, and the "ignorant young man who describes his heartache creates a novel that lasts forever." They don't dare to defend Boylesve's novels *The Child on the Balcony* and *The Scent of the Borromean Islands*, but they think they can recognize Proust or Gide, their favorites of the day, in that "ignorant young man." They would willingly trade Balzac's "Human Comedy" or Zola's "Rougon-Macquart" for Gide's *School for Wives* or Proust's *In a Budding Grove*. I can assess all the harm these masters have wrought, focused as they are only on themselves, so weak, so feminine, so vain. After the audacious, virile investigations of naturalism, what a drop in energy. A few others of these young people follow Valéry into another impasse: preciosity and abstraction. All of them—Gidians, Proustians, Valéryans—are paralyzed by the fear of looking foolish. Just one forcefully denounced M. Boylesve's bourgeois vanity and explained that all of nature cannot be contained in the *Map of Tendre*.[140] How can one restore their taste for risk and give them some energy?

Goethe said: "We are and must be dark to ourselves, open to the outside, and working on the world around us."

April 21

Hitler is fifty-three.

April 23

The situation is getting worse and worse in Greece and Egypt. The occupying authorities have grown bolder because of it. They have resumed their propaganda. The worst of it is that it seems to be acting secretly. The corridors of the Metro are covered with little stickers with this slogan: "To save France, put Laval in power." How nice of them not to use posters. They know we don't read their posters, whereas we run to see all the little stickers. But as usual they've gone too far.

---

[140] Or "of Tender": *La Carte du Tendre* was an allegorical map showing the roads to Love; it was associated with the *Précieuses*, a loosely defined group of ultra-refined women in the 17th century. Balzac's *La Comédie humaine* and Zola's "Rougon-Macquart" are the titles these great 19th-century realists (or "naturalists," for Zola) gave to their series of novels.

What ghost-writer is now manufacturing the Marshal's speeches? Bergery,* who wrote the first ones, was skillful. He had really put himself in his boss' shoes and composed edifying homilies, slightly out of breath, an old man's speech. Since then, two or three other ghost-writers have succeeded him. But the speeches have gotten worse and worse. For verisimilitude, no doubt: the boss is growing old.

April 24

I wrote some notes on the 18th century for a new review which is to appear in the other zone. I was as crafty as I could be, and thought I had succeeded. But Vaillant,* to whom I read these notes last night, guaranteed that they could have no other effect than to get me dismissed by Vichy and then imprisoned by our guests. Besides, the censors would naturally block their publication. So I don't know what to do...Since the 18th century, the means of subjugating people have made the same progress as the means of killing them.

April 26

"If I knew something useful to my country which was ruinous to another, I would not propose it to my prince, because I am human before being French (or rather, because I am necessarily human and only French through chance)." (Montesquieu, *Notebooks.*)

April 28

The Germans entered Athens yesterday. Last night at nine, Churchill spoke on the radio. A somber speech which leads us to fear new disasters in Africa and Asia. At every sentence I could hear him catching his breath deep inside himself. He courageously spoke of all the perils confronting the Empire. The transmission was increasingly scrambled and I was unable to hear the end. On Saturday I had to stand on line at city hall to change my food ration card. (Only gym teachers have the right to a T card: 350 grams of bread. Those who, like me, merely lift words, only have the right to an A card: 200 grams of bread.) For three hours I listened to the conversations. They were stunningly stupid. The majority ask for it all to be over with, to end at any price. They imagine that then everything will begin again as it was before. An infinitely small number of people have some idea of what is happening, and what is ahead of us. Few men deserve freedom. Perhaps that is why it is dying.

May 2

Yesterday the first of May and Saint Philip's Day. That is our Marshal's first name. As early as eighty-five years ago Providence, without any doubt, had thus manifested the particular plans he had for this child. It was written that he was the man through whom class hatreds would be appeased, through whom the red day of the Communards[141] would become the white and blue day of social peace. A decree turns the first of May into the Marshal's Day and Labor Day. But Providence showed its intentions no less precisely by arranging things so that this little child, from string-pulling to string-pulled, to star in the heavens, went all the way to marshaldom. The domain of the military and the domain of the worker coalesce in his person: the marshal of troops and the shoer of horses.[142] These are the Jesuitical idiocies Vichy propaganda was developing all day long yesterday. This is the stupidity into which we have fallen in eight short months. All the walls are plastered with posters. One can make out, delicately set across a blacksmith's anvil, the blue baton with the seven stars of the Head of State. An edifying image!

To celebrate Saint Philip's Day, we went to look at the fish in the Colonial Museum. My friend Paulhan's idea. We spent the whole morning there, alone, in halls lit only by the lights in the aquariums, among landscapes of waving grasses never seen before. We walked forward in this green light, stepping as lightly as possible so as not to disturb the astonishing silence of those depths. We lost our weight, became as fluid as water, algae, eels. We walked along the bottom of seas or streams, in the waves of the Amazon, among the man-eating fish, off the Madagascar coast, among the tortoises and caimans. We set foot on dry land again only at the Porte Dorée Metro station. There, schoolchildren were selling insignias with the emblem of the New Order: the anvil and the marshal's baton.

May 4

A blue and yellow May Sunday. We wanted to go outside and we were wrong. Poor Paris: it might as well have been paralyzed. We walked around the Bois de Boulogne, the Champs-Élysées, on the sidewalks, between the zebra crossings, among the obedient cattle. The street is empty. Just a Mercedes goes by from time to time, with brilliant glass and a few shaved necks. On the lake of the Bois, we passed by veritable squadrons of Germans. We waited on line at the boat rental office. But as the occupying authorities exercise their right of priority for pleasures, too, hardly two or three couples of French lovers were finally rewarded for their patience. The occupying authorities thought they were on the Spree.[143] They had taken off their jackets and were dozing, stretched out in all the boats, with one boot hanging over each side. Phonographs were tinnily playing *O Tannenbaum*... From the occupied shore, the occupied sadly and resignedly contemplated that magnificent repose. A little girl standing near me asked her

[141] The members of the revolutionary Paris Commune of 1871. See also the entry for August 21, 1941.

[142] An untranslatable pun: *Le maréchal d'armée et le maréchal ferrant*. Further on, a marshal's cap has seven stars.

[143] The river that goes through Berlin.

father if she could "get into a boat, too." "Yes," he answered, "when those customers aren't here anymore."

May 6

O my France, O my France,
Do you hear? Do you hear?
Will you be sold out, Will you be sold out
By Darlan? By Darlan?
(To the tune of "Frère Jacques," on British radio.)

May 9

I often feel as if I miss everything: after my love, my country. Perhaps through weariness, through being less in myself, I will finally be able to have some objectivity. I am tired of my own problems. What a pleasure it would be to lose oneself in someone else. I am tempted once again to write a novel or a play. But I would need more time, the necessary leisure for continuous dreaming. I'll try this summer.

My friend Bouché was telling me roughly this, last night: "This war is still more awful than anything we may have thought. The military war is no big affair; the terrifying superiority of one of the combatants reduces losses. Economic warfare is the main thing and it can last a long time. It is a war without visible dead. German bombing of England killed 30,000 people last year. But over a million Englishmen die a natural death per year. So those 30,000 dead cannot be a determining factor. An insurance company would insure that new risk at one percent. The loss of combatants isn't very heavy, either. But there is a kind of tuberculosis sapping Europe. Everything is dying without our seeing it, and without provoking reactions of horror and defense that bloody death would. We rush to the aid of a man we see losing his blood, but we walk by indifferently when someone is dying of cancer or tuberculosis. The carnage is invisible. We'll see its effects when the cemetery is full."

After which we spoke of the increasing difficulties in our life, the famines we should expect. But we agreed in thinking that nothing would stop the catastrophe from developing, that America would soon enter the game, etc.

The new great men of these new times—Hitler, Stalin—are great *mass men*. Back when I studied Lenin, I was struck by that character. A great man in civilized times was great precisely because of what set him apart from the mass: intelligence, willpower and culture, the delicacy of his mind or heart. These new great men are great because of what makes them similar to the mass—a kind of crude common sense, brutality, and lack of culture. The handling of affairs may make them admirably cunning and remarkably good at the practice of politics. But to maintain their prestige and power, they must also maintain their lack of culture and brutality. They must remain primitives.

Hitler's last speech, about his victory in the Balkans, was quite remarkable in this regard. It was an unbelievable historical novel about the last four years; only an extremely clever novelist could have written it. But it is also an excellent serial, and to write it he needed that faculty for forgetfulness, that instinctive violence, and that horror of any critical sense which characterize the masses. Hitler truly has every right to enjoy the confidence of his people.

May 15

Yesterday, in the name of the laws of France, 5,000 Jews were taken away to concentration camps. Poor Jews from Poland, Austria, and Czechoslovakia, humble people with modest trades who were greatly endangering the state. They call this "purification." On Rue Compans several men were taken away. Their wives and children begged the police, shouted, wept... The working people of Paris who saw these heartrending scenes were full of indignation and shame.

Collaboration: French and German authorities in Paris work together arresting Jews to be deported to the concentration camps in August 1941. *Bundesarchiv, Bild 183-B10816/CC-BY-SA.*

Pierre Laval, head of the Vichy government, with Carl Oberg (smiling), "Führer" of the SS and German police in France, in May 1943. Oberg was in charge of deporting Jews and members of the Resistance to the concentration camps. *Bundesarchiv, Bild 183-G25719.*

German soldiers relax in a sidewalk café in the Latin Quarter. *Bundesarchiv, Bild 101I-247-0775-09/Langhaus/CC-BY-SA.*

"The Jew and France." Poster for a "scientific" exposition organized by the "Institute for the Study of Jewish Questions," part of a propaganda campaign to justify anti-Semitic measures under the Occupation. The show ran from September 1941 to January 1942 and was visited by close to 200,000 people. *Bundesarchiv, Bild 146-1975-041-07.*

May 16

As I was writing down these horrors yesterday afternoon, A... suddenly comes in to warn me that the Germans are searching B...'s apartment. I call. Mme B... tells me the Germans just left and took our friend away.

I do not feel free to write everything down here.

May 20

Everything had conspired together for the misery of this country. For over eighty years, Providence had taken care of an old soldier sufficiently avid for honors to make himself Head of State thanks to the disaster, and sufficiently vain and stupid for the sound of the people's protests and supplications to reach him only as a concert of praise and adoration.

May 21

B...was released yesterday afternoon. No doubt in the end the embassy convinced the Gestapo that there was more to gain from releasing him than from keeping him.[144]

A retail business: You had the right to two lines of correspondence. You will have the right to seven. But you will give us your ships...In a few weeks Hitler will have bought everything and Darlan sold everything. The common people look on, impotent and full of shame, as their honor is sold off retail. Will little profits end up making them accomplices? Finally we tell ourselves that our shame is an established fact, we can't do anything about it. And so? We might as well take advantage of small blessings. We're trading our shame, not our honor. That has been lost for a long time. A prostitute takes pleasure in sprawling out on her bed and contemplating the presents from her lovers.

May 21

Yesterday in the Metro, I was coming back from the school library and leafing through Mornet's book *Les Origines intellectuelles de la Révolution française* on my lap when I heard someone say to me: "What you are reading there, Monsieur, is extremely anachronistic..." I looked up. The man sitting in front of me speaking in such educated, precise language was a worker of about fifty, probably a mechanic, judging by the dirty, greasy blue overalls he was wearing. He had read the title of my book upside down and thought about it. I was stunned. As I explained that I was indeed reading a book like this as a defense against the despicable time we live in, he went on: "I was saying to myself, Monsieur, that you were an odd fellow, but I can understand you." And together, each helping the other, we ended up by agreeing that Voltaire, Montesquieu, and Rousseau above all (he's the one who named them) had touched such depths in man, and some of their words had been so strong and just, that they could never die within us. He was the one who ended our discussion by declaring that everything happening around us today was only an accident...He was the one who was the odd fellow. I asked him, pointing to my book: "Did things like that always interest you a great deal?"

"Oh, no!" he said to me, "I simply educated myself. You have to try to understand things."

We were coming into the station at Place des Fêtes. We shook hands. I was filled with happiness.

Drieu has compiled some old essays and poems under the title *Écrits de jeunesse* ("Youthful Writings"). He sends me the new book with this dedication:

---

[144] B...in this incident stands for Jean Paulhan. He owed his freedom to the intervention of Drieu la Rochelle, as we learn from the published Paulhan-Guéhenno correspondence and other sources.

"To J.G., in sign of perfect disagreement." That is rather nice, after all, total as our "disagreement" really is. He has often revised his old texts considerably. He gives different reasons for this—the unequal nature of his talent and the right one has to "extract the best from the worst," and then this: "You correct your work before publishing it; why shouldn't you correct it afterward?" But the last reason is the best of all: "I had to try and save these writings at any price because I am, above all, a prophetic writer. And my only way to defend my work is to clearly display this unusual characteristic," he writes. Humor or naïveté? So he corrects and clarifies his "prophecies" of the fifteen years that have gone by since he pronounced them. It's a job he can tackle again once or twice before he dies. At least, that is my wish for him. But one is sure to lose the last game of this match.

If I had the time, I would try to analyze the reasons for our "disagreement." It could be a rather good way of exploring the history of certain ideas in the course of the past twenty years, and taking the measure of recent developments in France.

The self that one relates in a diary is most often only a loose, anecdotal, and chancy self. The only self worth anything is one that is constructed and desired. An elevated style, which Stendhal mocked, has its value. Its tension can be the tension of the man himself, not of the author. There is an elevated style in Stendhal himself; it is the style of his novels, which is quite different from the style of his diary or of *Henri Brulard*. Stendhal wants himself in his novels; he tolerates himself in his diaries. As for me, I prefer the author of *The Red*.[145]

May 23

For years now, all propaganda has been trying to make freedom suspect. It had become somewhat silly to value freedom. It was as if valuing freedom meant wanting to be a dupe. I myself have overused Diderot's admirable sentence: "To have slaves is nothing; the most frightful thing is to have slaves and call them citizens." This propaganda suggested that we were still nothing but slaves. A language that is fine to use with men who are awakening, not with men who are falling asleep. Like so many others, I would recite the famous Marxist theory of alienation, so well suited to destroy the illusions citizens have about their freedom, but so well suited to destroy the conditions necessary for freedom as well. I should have explained, instead, that we were only beginning to become free men. It is not good to tell men that they are slaves too often. They end up believing it, and grow accustomed to submission or expect others to free them; and when freedom actually is dying out, they have neither the strength nor the faith necessary to save it.

---

[145] *Le Rouge et le noir* (*The Red and the Black*, 1830; Guéhenno writes: "L'auteur du *Rouge*"). *The Life of Henri Brulard* (1835–1836, published posthumously) is one of Stendhal's autobiographical writings.

May 25

My "disagreement" with Drieu. In 1919 we had roughly the same judgment about the adventure we had just experienced. But already, he respected what I scorned—the Leader, or rather the man who wants to be or thinks he is a leader. Nothing has changed since M. de Bonald* and his stick. "In a line of blind men who are all holding each other by the hand, one only needs a stick for the first." Drieu thought all we had to do was follow the stick, with the understanding, of course, that it was only men of his kind who were to hold it.

In 1917, Drieu was a boy hesitating between Action Française[146] and some International, he wasn't sure which. Captivated by Nietzsche, too. A distinguished young bourgeois, he was used to distinguishing himself, whether inside the French community or on the international stage; he had no doubt that he was a leader. "It is because of books," he shouted to the men of the people, "that you go to war. But men like me gave you civilization. And *I* have renewed the gift by being born with a brain." This young brain thought it was the cat's meow, so to speak. "There is," he wrote, "a pact of which no one speaks, between all leaders: to maintain life against the people, who would like to reduce it to nothingness." Vanity was the downfall of these young bourgeois men. Even in M. de Bonald's day those prophecies were nothing but drivel.

I recopied these sentences of Drieu's from the 1917 edition. The new 1941 text is infinitely more cunning. The "prophecy" has been brought up to date. What childishness!

One thing has deeply perverted French political life these past twenty years. It is precisely that ideology of the Leader which had always been, throughout our history, a conservative and reactionary ideology; it became revolutionary through the use that totalitarian parties made of it, whether fascist or Communist. Democracy then became demagogy. The people became the crowd. The general will was no longer the sum of individual wills. The unity and fairness of the Republic were lost.

May 26

I am reading the admirable essay on the spirit of conquest by Benjamin Constant*:

> The vocabulary of hypocrisy and injustice is inexhaustible.
>
> When some governments send their legions from one pole to the other, they still speak of the defense of their homes; one would think they call their homes all the places they have set on fire.
>
> The conqueror will see that he overestimated the degradation of the world. He will learn that calculations founded on immorality and

[146] See note 19, p. 6.

baseness—those calculations he boasted of not so long ago as a sublime discovery—are as uncertain as they are narrow, as deceptive as they are vile.

To know men, it is not enough to despise them.

Ten years ago, in an article in *Europe*, I commented on these pages as a warning
to corrupt, brutal governments. May they help me to have hope today.

May 23. "The *Hood* went down with all hands on board." Half the world
rejoices.

May 25. "The *Bismarck* sank and not one sailor survived." The other half of the
world jumps up and down for joy.

Bang!... Boom!... That's the point we've reached today. These are our fits of
complicity. I had my part in the common rejoicing.

May 28

Little hope of going to the other zone, to Montolieu, for the holidays. According
to the latest regulations, a son may go to see his mother, or vice versa. But collat-
eral relationships must have something Jewish about them. There is no provision
for them. "Every goat tethered to its stake" is a good maxim of government.

Last night at 4:30 I got up to listen to Roosevelt on the radio. I did not want to
sleep if he was announcing our deliverance. But the fading and scrambling were so
strong that I could understand nothing. Toward five o'clock, in the tranquil dawn,
the planes were speeding back from their carnage as if surprised by daylight.

June 3

A curious visit this morning. X..., one of my former students, calls me. He
would like to see me, to "talk to me about something that might interest me."
An hour later, in comes a heavy boy, rather ill at ease. He's coming from Radio
Paris where he has a little job. He keeps the daybooks. Through his embarrassed words, I can make out what had happened. While chatting at the job, he
mentioned that he was a former student of mine. And then, right away, the
occupying authorities ordered him to go see what I was up to. Would I not
agree to give a few lectures full of European propaganda? I set the poor boy
straight without any further ado. I have a strong urge to throw him out. He
tells me he knew what I would answer already, stammers, but runs his errand
nonetheless. He explains that they're looking for names, they pay very well,
etc. I draw him out. The occupying authorities are, it seems, cordial but distrustful. They are very much afraid that their employees might slip in a word
here or there which would make them look silly. They examine all the scripts,
record them, and before every broadcast, they make sure the record is the same
as the pre-censored text. Finally, they are extremely well informed. The other
day, weren't they thinking of asking one Julien Benda* to give a lecture against
the Jews?

Before he leaves, X...asks me exactly what he should tell them. "Because you have to watch out," he says. "With them, it's either honors (!) or prison." We agree on a vague reply which will, I hope, earn me neither one nor the other.

June 6

Vichy is leading us into a war with England. It is turning our airfields in Syria over to Germany. The Muse of History is mocking us. Oh, so you didn't want any more wars. You didn't want to fight. Well, you'll learn how to fight again by fighting against each other, Pétainists vs. Gaullists. There is no war finer than that, or more atrocious.

I am no longer recording the triumphs of the Wehrmacht in this diary. There are too many of them, and they solve nothing. The Wehrmacht, the "defense force" of Germany, was defending it on the Island of Crete last week, 2,000 kilometers away from Berlin. The "defense force" occupied it to be on the safe side.

Men of honor. Brasillach,* an officer prisoner, freed by the occupying authorities to head one of their newspapers in Paris. He's exhibiting the price of his freedom at the Rive Gauche bookstore ("*Rive Gauche du Rhin*," say the students, the "Left Bank of the Rhine"): it's a book, *Our Pre-War*, in which this Frenchman courageously denounces the weaknesses of France for Hitler's benefit.

Another collaborator: X...Famous for his "alternations," but also for his consistent fatuity and cynicism. A young imbecilic creature, more horse than man. He has to champ at the bit, to prance about. Even if it's in mud and dung. It splashes onto others, but it gives him a halo. An accomplished man of letters, as empty as he is brilliant. A star. A spoiled child of fifty who would deserve a spanking; but he would take too much pleasure in it as long as there was an audience.

I meet him the other day at the door of the *NRF*. He is surprised that I have not been dismissed yet. "So you have come to Paris," I say to him, "and you intend to stay here?" "Yes," he answers, "for a few months, until it starts getting cold." The calendar of this bloated tenor has only an eternal summer on it. He is careful about his throat and his voice. The slightest draft drives him from Paris to Marseille, to Algiers, to Biskra. But wherever he may be, he continues his vain little business. He took advantage of the fine weather to come to Paris and sign a few new contracts with the new impresarios. Is it his fault if today these impresarios represent Hitler or Goebbels*?

This same X..., as I was complaining that it's hard to breathe on this side and the air is full of poisons: "Oh," he said, "I prefer *feldgrau*[147] poison to Church poison." This, to charm the anticlerical person he thinks I am. A sort of pederast Don Juan, he claims to be a rationalist. He likes people to think that he saw the

---

[147] "Field gray," the green-gray color of German Army uniforms. Further on, the Commendatore: father of Dona Anna in Mozart's *Don Giovanni*; his statue comes to life to drag the Don down to hell in the last scene.

ghost of the Commendatore on his last night, and of course, did not tremble. It would not displease him if people think he has accumulated sins. He is careful about his biography, and if he thinks of the last scene, he wants a stunning death: a sinner struck down by lightning—dying as a repented sinner. The main thing is that his death be talked about. Literature.

June 9

Still in the same darkness. A piece of news sometimes drops on us and only increases our anxiety. Yesterday we learned that the English and de Gaulle's Free French had entered Syria, where Vichy has military forces. Is this the beginning of a civil war?

I am re-reading Renan*, thinking of an essay I promised Gallimard. Will he teach me to live in this time of idiots? "That love of the universe which makes one have eyes only for it," he wrote—that love distracted him for a long time from the little adventures of his contemporaries. I will never consent to be that wise, or that well-behaved. Was he so wise himself when the ordeal began? What Frenchman today will write the equivalent of his letters to Strauss*?

Noon. The news is little better, confused, but it does seem that Syria is not resisting.[148] We hardly dare think of what might result from a straightforward adhesion of Syrian forces to Free France. The event might serve as an example. A bit of courage, and France could begin to exist again.

June 10

Two years ago I had promised myself to attend only to the "works of God." How badly I am fulfilling my promise. Never have I been more mired in the works of this world.

June 13

Anxiety. The radios are contradicting each other. If we are to believe Vichy, there are terrible combats in Syria. If we believe London, the resistance is not serious.

Be that as it may, the occasion seems lost. If Syria had enthusiastically gone over to Free France, it could have given the impulsion for a great movement. We continue to wallow in shame and treason. The Marshal's proclamations are flabby and Jesuitical as usual. "You are not fighting in vain," he says to his Syrian troops. That is, telling them without telling them: "Fight."

June 14

It is relatively easy for me to shout at the top of my voice that nothing can vanquish me. One needs more humility truly to enter into the miseries of those

---

[148] Here and further on, Guéhenno is referring to French colonial forces in Syria controlled by Vichy, not to Syria itself.

one loves. My inner certainty that I will never yield will remain useless as long as it merely reveals my pride.

Tonight the announcer on Free France will exclaim "Today is the three hundred and sixty-fifth day of the French people's resistance to oppression; German troops entered Paris one year ago." That is the language of our common misery. I have thought too much in my own way. I lacked fellow-feeling. It is not only the framework of my own little ideas that collapsed. A year ago, black smoke was falling over Paris; the trees and the sidewalks were covered with soot. The rare passersby would stop and touch that falling soot and ask each other about it, wondering what it could be. People said the enemy armies were advancing, hidden in a cloud. Paris was almost empty. The whole city was on the roads, toward the Loire, toward Brittany. After the flight and panic of the last days, a prodigious silence reigned over the city. Toward eleven o'clock, we heard music. They were arriving. They marched by all day. The concierge, an old woman who had seen them in 1870, shut herself in her little apartment,[149] the better to cry all by herself. Martel* committed suicide. And seventeen other Parisians. For a year now, they have been here; they don't really know why. Robots serving the machine to enslave others, slaves themselves. They complain that we have glass eyes and we refuse to see them. They are uneasy, they seem lost. For we need the gaze of other people; it is that gaze which guides us and humanizes the light. Today the glass-eyed Parisians, through a secret agreement, are all wearing a black tie: Resistance to oppression! In school this morning, a little girl guilty of wearing a black ribbon in her hair was called in by the principal. "So, what are you mourning for?" "For Paris," she replied quickly, just as she felt it, without taking care not to be insolent. They suspended her for a week, on the pretext that she had no "respect for society." Today "respect for society" is respect for dishonor.

The misery of Europe is composed of these trivial and profound things, and it is infinite. What has been conquered is much more than ten countries, ten states, much more than France. It is that humble honor which, as much as a certain tension of our being, made us stand up and raise our eyes. We no longer dare to look at each other. The eyes of others would only teach us our shame.

But why, why am I ashamed, and of what? I've thought about that and here is what I've found. The deepest thing a man can lay claim to, precisely the one that makes him human, is that of having his own destiny, his and his alone. There was no one, no matter how deprived, who did not think that at the bottom of his bag he had something that could make his life a most interesting adventure. The simplest people were the most honest: when they went to a fortune-teller, they were confessing their conviction that their particular destiny was written on their hands, on cards or stars. The cleverest disdained those superstitions, but

---

[149] Concierges (janitors, but with more duties) lived in a small apartment next to the building entrance—the *loge*—often with their family. In 1870, Paris was besieged and partly occupied by the Prussians during the Franco-Prussian War.

believed no less in their own destiny; they were merely more proud of it being impenetrable. Now, that great idea which gave us courage, that claim which made us always ready to give the great wheel of life another turn with a thoughtful finger, like a player in a carnival game—what a hard time we have holding on to that idea, to that claim! That is why we are ashamed and sad. We are ashamed not to believe in ourselves anymore. We can do so no longer. No one has a life of his own anymore. No point going to the fortune-teller and holding out our hands. No line means anything anymore: neither luck, nor life, nor willpower. The hand of a European is the hand of a slave. No one has the right to his own life anymore. No one can hope to have it anymore. It is the most forbidden thing in the world. "Every destiny is special." That proud certainty of the humblest, rendered ever more certain by an eternity of meditation and effort, the example of wise men, the patience of saints—now that certainty is wavering within us. We live and die en masse. We work and we're out of work en masse. We kill and we are killed en masse. Without vices and without virtues. Never responsible...

The only way we can manage to live and think for ourselves is by being crafty, by cheating. An effort like that is against the law, against order. I will be crafty, I will cheat...

Well, no. My sadness is silly and cowardly. My dreams do not belong to me alone. They are so important only because they concern everyone else and because they are everyone else's dreams, too. And that in itself is the guarantee that they won't be defeated. No doubt I'm still not humble enough. A bit more humility and my disappointments will seem unimportant to me. *Man* is not disappointed and will not be disappointed. My dream and mankind's dream will win out. How can one be sad, working for an inevitable victory?

The conscience of our old Europe protests against all that we are being subjected to. I can go along with it if I say: there is no greater suffering than seeing a man fall away from that humble honor which should make him himself before God and man. I cannot stand to see men degraded. A man can only construct himself on his courage and through his courage. True order between men can only come from the influence of their dignity. I want to be able to look at all men as my brothers. But the man whose first look at me is to discover, cruelly, the weakness, need, or unhappiness which would guarantee my submission is no brother of mine. I can only love those who hope for my courage and my pride.

June 16

M. Xavier Vallat himself has commented on the new decree he just issued against Jews; it institutes the severest measures against them.[150] His commentary

---

[150] One of a series of statutes excluding Jews from French life (see note 59, p. 28). A well-known anti-Semitic politician, Xavier Vallat (1891–1972) had headed Vichy's High Commission on Jewish Questions since March. Further on, the tenor Tino Rossi (1907–1983) was a popular romantic crooner and actor.

is a triumph of Jesuitical style. "As for those," he writes, after enumerating the means of terror, "who find these measures insufficiently drastic, we answer that for us it is sufficient that the measures be effective, and the effects of justice are more durable than those of persecution. On the other hand, to those whose liberalism is alarmed by what it considers a manifestation of sectarianism, we answer that anti-Semitism has never been aroused by anything but the Jews' unsociability and their intrinsically inassimilable nature." How well said that is. The quota reduces the number of Jewish students admitted to the universities to three percent. No doubt they will take care to keep only the most stupid. It is in the logic of the law and the only way definitively to preserve the nation from the malice and intelligence of that race.

They're fighting in Syria. We must resign ourselves to believing it.

I've timed it. I can't stand Vichy Radio for more than three minutes. Oh, never has a state been more faithfully represented! Stupidity, sermonizing, and growling in a vulgar accent all day long. Nothing can give an idea of the voice of those announcers. All have the same unctuous, sing-song voice, prolonging the a's, rounding the o's, simpering on the I's, wetting the l's and r's until you feel nauseous. It's Tino Rossi from morning till night. The radio vocalizes on Work, Family, Country, and Collaboration. It says "the Marshal" as it would say "my love." The miseries of France are bits of sherbet that melt in its mouth.

June 18

The Republic of Letters is decidedly not too rich in people with character. X...is preparing his conversion. Naturally he avoids peremptory declarations as he usually does, but if you ask him about Germany, he explains that it has made immense progress over the past twenty years, that it has become more...democratic. About America? It, too, has changed a great deal. It is no longer the still young, colonial America of 1909, but a cowardly country from which one may expect nothing...He leaves it to you to draw the resigned conclusions that his words suggest. He himself is resigned to seeing his plays put on in Paris as soon as possible.

Duhamel* and Mauriac* save our honor. Yesterday a certain X...gave a lecture on "François Mauriac: Agent of French Disintegration" in the Ambassadeurs music hall. We went there to boo him. A Dominican, Father Maydieu, led the noise and at first it went rather well. But the lecturer was really too stupid and we soon grew discouraged. From *Young Man in Chains* to *A Woman of the Pharisees*, he enumerated all the illnesses that the heroes of Mauriac's novels suffered from, without forgetting measles. France, according to him, supposedly died from repeated bouts of whooping cough. We left.

A sociological problem: Why so many pederasts among the collaborators? C..., F..., M..., D...(who, it is said, goes both ways). Do they expect the new order to legitimize their loves?

Mauriac, who sees all the exploits of the collaborators from close up, gives this explanation: "You don't understand this because you're not a Catholic. Believe me, on the day of the Last Judgment, men will continue to climb ladders, feverishly. It will always be a simple matter of standing one rung higher than the others..."

Hervé,* one of my former students, a teacher of philosophy arrested last week on the pretext that he was spreading Communist propaganda, was judged yesterday by one of the "special tribunals" and acquitted. "No matter," said the police. "You have been acquitted because we couldn't prove our case, but we are absolutely certain that you are guilty." And they put him in a concentration camp.

St. John's Day, June 23

I have written nothing in this notebook for the past few days. The enormity of events makes this diary seem silly. The French experienced great happiness on Sunday morning. During the night, the Reich had declared war against the Soviets. As the enemies of our enemies are our friends, from now on we have 180 million more friends. And then, all Frenchmen could say to themselves that at least this time Hitler would be busy for a while. However quickly his machine may advance, this time it has a long way to go. Some people, especially the Communists, had other reasons to rejoice: in their minds, order was restored. They began to be sure again that the argument of our time is between fascism and communism.

I was elated, like everybody else. And yet I confess I do not understand all these turnarounds very well. For the first time Hitlerian fanaticism is going to come up against another fanaticism. If communism succeeds in resisting Hitler, it has a good chance of gaining all of Europe. We'll be Communists out of gratitude.

June 27

Depressed again by feeling how foolish I am. For days now, I've been afraid of meeting people. It seems to me that my stupidity is visible, and I am ashamed. That drives me back inside myself and I would so like to get out. But it is possible, too, that this humility may put me back on the true path. Then I return to the problems of Caliban. I hardly dare raise my eyes. I begin to explore my canton of the world again, what is within my field of vision, without any vain pretension. All I need to do is to do this well. The action of real artists is out of bounds for me. The worst that could happen to me would be to become one of those hybrids that Michelet denounces in *The People*.[151] If I meet Blanzat, Paulhan, Mauriac, and all the others, I feel frightfully heavy inside myself. After five minutes I don't

---

[151] In Chapter III of this 1846 work, Michelet talks about the suffering and difficulties of educated workers who can't really take advantage of their education. Michelet does not "denounce" them, however: he feels for them.

dare say anything. I'm afraid of boring them. I would like to leave. If I stay, it's out of idiotic politeness. I can feel myself growing more and more stupid. But once I return to my solitude, I find it desolate and I can't stand it. The world of Caliban was not solitary: it was the world of the heart. I am no longer simple enough to be happy in it and I was born too stupid ever to be at ease among brilliant minds. Have the strength to remain alone.

June 30

The Germans are advancing in Russia, marching on Leningrad and Moscow. I always felt rather removed from Communist tactics: that mix of cunning and violence. But if Soviet Russia, if communism, is annihilated, I will feel that defeat as a great intellectual and moral downfall—which it will be, in fact. All the peoples of the world will be in mourning for their greatest effort and their greatest hope. For it doesn't matter how people lived in Moscow in actual fact. Nowhere did men ever have so much hope.

> For weeks now,
>> On the walls and street you see
>> Sprouting everywhere, the V.

London has relaunched its inventive propaganda campaign. It noticed that the signal for V in Morse code was three dots and a dash, which is also the rhythm of Beethoven's Eroica Symphony.[152]

From now on those four notes, those four beats, will be the rallying sign of hope in the prison of Europe. Is it our fault if we are reduced to such childishness? We have to live like children. Our servitude is absolute...A rhythm is contagious in a way that an inscription is not. If that heroic call rang out everywhere, it would, perhaps, give people more courage.

"It was a time full of agony, of heavy hearts, wrinkled brows, tense minds, mute in themselves or devastated by the news, the waiting, the disappointments, the senseless hypotheses. In those formidable circumstances, what could one do, when all one could do was bear it, and people were deprived of any action that might respond to the extraordinary excitement of a furious era of the world?"

I came across these lines last night. They were not at all written to characterize the world we are in, however it might seem. They are in Paul Valéry's latest work, *Mélanges,* and define the four years he spent, he explains, "trying every day to solve extremely severe problems of versification." Doubtless the four years of the other war, 1914–18. He does not explicitly say so. One does not name what one despises.

---

[152] A slip, of course: it's the beginning of Beethoven's Fifth.

He continues:

> Perhaps nothing less was needed, but the vainest and subtlest quest: that which applies to delicate combinations of the multiple values of language simultaneously composed to arouse all one's will—for they require it—and all the obstinacy in that will, which could maintain one part of the mind sheltered from the terrible effects of anxious expectation: resonances, sounds, imaginations and contagions of the absurd.
>
> I made myself a poetry deprived of all hope, which had no other end and almost no other law than to institute a way of living with myself during one part of my days. I did not envision an ending, and I put up a sufficient number of conditions to find in it the matter of a limitless task.

What wisdom! What mighty scorn! And no doubt it is admirable to resist the absurd so victoriously. But when the absurd is life itself... Poetry cannot be that escape from our confused suffering. No book of Valéry's had given us the opportunity, as these *Mélanges* do, to hear his conversation with himself, to listen to "his inner voice." And it is most often admirable.

That a great intelligence cannot find something to which it can devote itself, nor its object, is always tragic. I know an exceptionally intelligent old man in a village who has never really done a thing in his life. But it is hard to conceive how inventive his idleness can be. In quarreling and making peace with his fellow villagers he employed as much genius as Talleyrand* did in making and unmaking Europe. His schemes and tricks are superior to those of Machiavelli's *Prince*. They invent and create their object.

In our villages, any mind that does not devote itself to daily tasks turns to cunning and deceit. It nurtures malicious gossip, which is the literature of villages.

July 1

When I wrote to Valéry, I did not dare call him *Cher maître*, "Dear Master." I am not sufficiently sure of having even opened the door to the studio where he works.

Leconte de Lisle's* *Solvet Saeclum*[153] makes one think of a gob of spit. What an idea, to end a book with a gob of spit.

July 4

Dubreuil,* in *The French Knights of Labor*, recalls an old custom of the workers. If they had a demand to make, when it came to signing the document "they

---

[153] The title of Leconte de Lisle's last poem in his *Poèmes barbares*, it comes from "Dies Irae," a medieval Latin hymn: *Dies iræ, Dies illa/Solvet sæclum in favilla* ("Day of wrath, that day/Will dissolve the world in ashes"). That event is celebrated in the poem.

would write their names one after the other in a closed circle that they had first penciled in, whose diameter was exactly calculated so that the series of signatures left no intervening space." This, so the boss could not discover the leader. Dubreuil states that during a strike in 1908 in Paris, the workers suggested resorting to this expedient. Caught between courage and fear, no one dared to be the first to speak to the master.

July 5

In the depths of despair and self-disgust, what a need to pray. But ready-made prayers can no longer suffice. No sect, no philosopher, no priest spoke for me. Each person must invent his prayer. I remember those nights when I begged the beauty of the world to preserve what I loved, to grant it a few more years, while what I loved was suffering and dying at my side. Beauty of the world, I would say, save what is beautiful. Sweetness of the world, save what is sweet. But we are the ones who create helpful powers. They do not exist before our prayers. And what is beautiful dies, because we have not prayed enough in time.

Some mornings when I feel all my shortcomings more strongly, I dream of magic words that would open up the world to me, make me at ease among men and things, make of me a true living being, grateful and kind at last. But I still don't know *my* prayer, and I'm afraid I will spend my life looking for it.

July 9

Old Groethuysen* and his girlfriend are sad and uneasy. They are Communists, but were never happy about the Russo-German war. They lament that the first socialist state should be, like capitalist states, forced to make war and for a time must put their fate into the hands of their armies. As if a test of strength could ever be a test of justice. The anguish of these two people, so pure, teaches me more about the spirit of communism than many books. They make one feel to what an extent it is a spirit of peace and work. The parallel between the methods and tactics of Stalinism and Hitlerism sometimes led me to confuse them. But a political regime is defined, after all, by the kind of man it tends to produce. Now, the man that communism claims to make is a happy worker. The man Hitlerism produces is only a soldier. Somewhat too many engineers in both, perhaps, but one is an engineer of peace, the other an engineer of war. One would like to manufacture life serially, on the assembly line (and the series, the line are uncalled-for), but the other manufactures death.

Caliban and Prospero have remained more or less out of harmony inside me. And that adds some confusion to almost everything I say or write. As long as I have not succeeded in bringing them into agreement, it would doubtless be better for me to try to speak and write like Caliban or like Prospero, letting each have his voice and his accent. The hybrid, the intermediary—Trinculo, Bevilacqua[154]—has nothing worth saying.

Prayers. Believe in words.

July 11

The other Sunday, we went to the Vallée-aux-Loups with P...and M..., and for a few hours we forgot everything while we walked around the park, accompanied by that old lady who knows about Vicomte François-Marie-René de Chateaubriand* everything there is to know, everything including the names of all the exotic trees he was proud of having planted, everything, up to the last centimeter. I asked her point-blank: "Was the Viscount tall, Mademoiselle?" "1 meter 63, my dear Sir. That's neither tall nor short." How far away the war was. But I learn today that in the depths of this very peaceful park, the Germans shoot people who have been sentenced by their courts martial—most recently a young Frenchman accused of Gaullism and a young German aviator who had lingered three days too long with his mistress. Dr. le Savoureux had charitably hidden all that from us.[155]

So many things that I don't understand. Yesterday, a show of André Lhote's* work. An antiques store specializing in late 19th-century objets d'art. Under glass globes, fruits, artificial flowers, hair frames—all the horrors of a monstrous fashion. Among this bric-a-brac, Lhote is showing his watercolors, which seem to me to reveal a different perversion of the spirit, and not a lesser one. The drawings and colors are equally thought out. But are the effects he has obtained worth so much work? A few images seemed agreeable to me and not without charm. But charm is assuredly the last thing this painter who dreams of "humanized geometry" wants. And so? It is all too clear that I do not understand. I cannot believe that reducing objects to skillful diagrams is a means of giving them eternal life. A painted apple is an apple that does not rot, but it must remain an apple, an apple one might wish to bite for all eternity. It is not just a circle with a vermilion spot.

The other evening, Caillard* was talking about Van Gogh, his master, and he was marvelously attached to *things*. I could feel that the world, and the world in its slightest object, had a reality for him that I will never know, perhaps; but it is precisely that reality which is all I want to know and all that is worth knowing, a reality that seems eternal, and for that very reason, scandalous. It is the body of things that is, for painters, eternal. All their work is a struggle against the inevitable

[154] Trinculo is the drunken butler in Shakespeare's *The Tempest*; Bevilacqua is a minor character, skeptical, lucid, conservative, and moderate, in Renan's *Caliban: Suite de la Tempête* (1878); see the *Translator's Introduction*, pp. xxv–xxvi.

[155] Henri le Savoureux, a psychiatrist with literary interests, bought the property where his favorite writer had lived, then turned it into a mental hospital and, later, a literary *salon* and a refuge for some writers who were in the Resistance. It is now the Chateaubriand museum.

rotting, the continual deterioration of created things. "The way of all flesh": that terrible Christian saying cannot seem true to them. *Fiat Lux*[156] is their saying, and fruits and flowers and Adam and Eve are born from their fingertips, never to die.

Well no, it's more complicated than that. The painter paints an eternal instant. And it must be only an instant, but the instant must triumph over death. Death must always be there, hidden in the light itself. Decidedly I understand nothing about it. I do think, however, of a portrait I saw three or four years ago in the Tuileries. In the foreground there was a young woman in her beauty of one evening, living forever in her dress, her jewels, the bracelets and rings of the 1890s. Oh, how I envied the painter for having so clearly saved what he loved from death!

July 12

Because I ran into Mauriac a few times recently, I read his new novel, *A Woman of the Pharisees*, with more care than any other book he wrote. What cruelty in that nice man! He gives you the idea that purity is always silly, and intelligence is above all the sense of evil. I don't know if the novel is good. A few pages seem somewhat botched to me. He doesn't rise sufficiently above the anecdotal. Still, it must be rather good, for one retains the impression of a vile little world, terribly alive. What a nasty swamp! So much the worse for silliness! Long live purity—progressive purity, obligatory and secular! Let us not fear mockery. If the Christian fable can produce monsters like these, if it changes the world into that stinking swamp, if it commands us to look at the world with such cruel, dirty eyes, we should destroy it. What an upbringing! It makes us either too humble or too proud. Excessive humility or excessive pride both dispense us from effort. A saint's humility, beaten in advance. A Pharisee's pride, triumphing in advance. Man's real stake lies between these extremes. The sin of all sins, self-esteem, is the one principle of his self-perfection.

Who made you so cruel yourself, dear François Mauriac? The priests who taught you, who revealed evil to you above all and put you on guard against yourself and other people? "Evil" became your obsession. You had no trouble discerning it in those mistrustful bourgeois among whom you were born. Did they not have the same upbringing as yours? Soon you saw it everywhere. You were unlucky. No one and nothing to give you the idea of what a man can do for himself. And as you were a poet, the Christian fable, as you came to understand it better, did not fail to seem more and more true to you, since its fictions proved you right about that fallen creation, that disaster you had learned to despise as a very young man.

But I think of you in friendship. For your cruelty doesn't spare you, either. As for your faith, do you really know where you're at? What terrible irony in a sentence like this one: "That familiarity with which I lived with God, the belief that

[156] "Let there be light."

nothing happened to me in which the uncreated Being was not involved, and that nobody entered my life who was not in a sense a delegate to me from the infinite..." It's the narrator of *A Woman of the Pharisees* who is speaking, and I am well aware that you have warned us the narrator is not you, but "a very particular character who paints people's portraits in a cruel light, a character who seems to be slaking some obscure thirst for vengeance..." But what if you yourself were taking your revenge?

The Christ of the Gospels claims to give a meaning to pain. But the Christ of a distrustful and pettily happy bourgeoisie gives a meaning only to evil. And for them, evil is hardly more than anything that threatens to disturb the tranquility of their families, the solidity of their inheritance—that taste for life which spurs "the prodigal son," "the young man of means" into a life of adventure. What a degradation of the Faith!

July 17

Noted nothing these past days. Fatigue and boredom.

On the afternoon of July 14, we walked out on the boulevards. The unfortunate Parisians really did all they could to make their resistance known. What ingenuity to bring the three forbidden colors together, one way or another. It was easier for the women. A few of them seemed rolled up in flags. Louisette in her red-and-white checkered dress and her blue scarf came down from Belleville like a Republic. Men had fewer means of doing it. They let one of those match boxes decorated with a blue-white-and-red emblem stick out of their jacket pockets. Never had people looked at each other more carefully. Each one worked at recognizing the others' intentions. The blue shoes, white stockings, and red dress of one woman. The red jacket, blue purse, and white gloves of another. What pathetic efforts. But not wasted, after all. That mutual attention ended up by creating the joy of a communion.

On Boulevard des Italiens, the crowd had gathered in front of the recruiting office of the Anti-Communist Legion[157]—magnificently empty—when someone shouted "Get on line. Get on line. Line up!" There was a great burst of laughter.

Nothing else to note down but prison stories.

Someone came to see me the other day about Hervé. He escaped from jail with twenty comrades. Their basement received its light from a small barred window that gave onto Place Dauphine. For a few nights, people on Place Dauphine could hear them sing. Never had anyone seen such joyful prisoners. One of the prisoners was sawing away at the bars while the twenty others were singing.

[157] Guéhenno writes *anticommuniste*: actually the *Légion antibolchévique*, recently formed by pro-Nazi French leaders outside the Vichy government. It was later recognized by Vichy and renamed the *Légion des volontaires français*. Its members wore swastika-like emblems and black uniforms and berets; some fought alongside Hitler's armies.

Roulier was arrested last week at Saint-Lazare station. He was having fun shouting *Heil Stalin* and raising his fist under the nose of every German officer he met. He's not a Communist at all, just a pig-headed Frenchman. He explained that he simply couldn't stand them anymore. He would raise his fist and shout *Heil Stalin* to make fun of them, absolutely delighted when one of those oafs, completely dumbfounded, would sometimes answer *Heil* and raise his arm out of habit.

A...and Bernard...were arrested as Communist militants. Now, in 1938–40 both of them never ceased to denounce the Soviets. Since the Armistice, only fear of other people's judgment stopped them from "collaborating." It is incomprehensible. Yet it is clear that the occupying authorities are misfiring.

One cannot even be afraid of going to jail anymore. That seems the best way of fulfilling one's destiny. The whole political order today tends toward prison. That is where it finds its perfection. Especially for free men.

Yesterday I gave my last class at the lycée; rarely have I spoken so badly. I can't stand it anymore. I am thinking of ways to organize my time and work over this vacation so as not to fall into neurasthenia.

July 25

There is a real battle of the V's. To respond to English propaganda, the Germans have decreed that V is supposed to be the sign of German Victory. Everywhere they have raised big white flags decorated with a monumental V, and pasted red posters with a black V over the swastika. V is supposed to mean Victoria, and Victoria is supposed to be an old German word. But people wonder what brand of cherry brandy that might be, or think of the Queen of England, and they keep on cutting out V's for *Victoire*, H's for *Honneur*, or the cross of Lorraine in their Metro tickets.[158] They're blooming all over the sidewalks.

Taking advantage of France's powerlessness, Japan has occupied Indochina. In fine Vichy style, this becomes: Japan and France have agreed to confront English threats to Indochina.

And every day in Paris, recently, you could meet French sailors who were prisoners in Germany and were now being sent to Marseilles or Toulon so that they could ship out for "a repeat performance"—but against the English. Poor men. Poor country.

July 26

I can only write if I can imagine with some precision who will read me, just as I need to see the eyes of the person I'm talking to when I speak. Otherwise my thought wanders without an object.

---

[158] The double-barred cross of Lorraine was the symbol of the Free French Forces headed by de Gaulle.

Paulhan, Blanzat, and I spent the morning at the Musée de l'Homme. I was filled with wonder in that Museum of Man. Around the world in two and a half hours. It is hard to know which is more striking: the Unity of Creation or the variety of human crazes. But finally I was, as we left, rather appalled at everything I am or could be.

We see our own faults more easily in others than in ourselves. It costs us less. Yesterday, as I read the book by my friend Jean Grenier* called *Inspirations méditerranéennes*, a beautiful book in which one can feel a marvelous nostalgia for greatness at every instant, I found myself full of severity for something "Barrèsian" in his language, for the false decorations, the all-too-carefully shaded inflections of the phrase, the feigned swoons, the cleverly drawn-out little speeches, the *bel canto*...but those are vices I know well: I know them from the inside.

"How strange it is," Grenier writes, at once Pascalian and Barrèsian, "to bear within oneself a lasting being, and to be interested only in what happens to him through chance encounters." Well, no: what lasts is the world we encounter; our being passes, and if it is interested in what it encounters, it is to flee itself, to flee the death that is in it. The encounter we have with the world is the occasion we have to grasp the eternal. If we had not put our eyes to a telescope one day, we would only have had a rather paltry idea of infinity.

July 31

Louisette will leave alone for Montolieu tomorrow. I finally obtained the necessary authorization for her. It's the first time she's leaving me, the first time she will be the only one responsible for herself. She's leaving for two months. How long these two months are going to seem to me. I'm still trying a last trick to be able to leave, but I have hardly any hope. We are in a prison. That's what we really have to understand. I cannot get used to it.

I think of the little cemetery, the terrace over the torrent, the fountain between the cypresses, the wind over the garrigue, the fine August nights in the valley, and the shooting stars.

Conversation with Blanzat. He talks magnificently to me about what our writings should now be, when we write about France: a great simple, natural cry, without dialectic, without "literature." Write and speak like a man, like anybody at all, forget you're an intellectual. But apparently ever since Gide, no French writer has been able to forget it.

August 1

Culture is a tradition and a hope. We will remain faithful to both. Western man is that conscience, that individual whose moral value was defined by Socrates, for whom Jesus died, to whom Descartes taught the means of his power, the individual the Revolution of the 18th century established in his duties and his rights. Three thousand years of reason and courage definitively guided the *way of man.* Totalitarian propaganda and squawking, the noise of tanks and planes, the *zusammen marschieren*[159] of armies, constraints, and miseries will not change it. German Nazism betrays humanity. It betrayed Germany itself, as it only managed to set up its reign against the thought of the greatest sons of Germany: Luther, Kant, Goethe, Nietzsche, those theoreticians of the individual.

Jean Wahl is in prison. In prison, that little philosopher so sensitive to the cold, who unraveled the concepts of Kierkegaard and was afraid of drafts. But he has committed a great crime: he is Jewish.

August 2

Vichy now seems to have perfected its methods. A year has been enough for those Jesuits to assimilate all the knowledge of their Nazi masters. A quick news bulletin informs us that a "device" exploded in Montélimar in the hotel room where Marx Dormoy had been under house arrest for a few weeks. Killed on the spot. Good work. Marx Dormoy, Minister of the Interior in the Blum government, no doubt knew too much about the killers of the Cagoule, the assassins of the Rosselli brothers, who have become, thanks to the Marshal, top officers in the police.[160]

The fighting in Russia is terribly bloody. B…heard that when the Russians pick up fine young German corpses that show little damage—corpses with a bullet in the heart, for example, plunged into sleep—they tie them two by two, hang them from a parachute and throw them into the German countryside, where some harvester can find them with this inscription on their chests: "What Hitler has done to German youth." B…has not succeeded in verifying the authenticity of the story. But whoever thought it up, what a horrible idea. It would make Goebbels jealous.

August 5

Under the title *Vent de Mars,*[161] H. Pourrat* has published notes he has taken for the last three years about the life of the peasants among whom he lives—"the green life," as he says—and it is the book of a nice man; but it seems to me there is a great element of illusion in this evocation of a Christian peasant order.

Throughout this narrative, the war rumbles like a storm. The horizons are blurred for a moment. But that passes, Pourrat leads us to think, and the green life continues, the eternal countryside…

[159] Literally "marching together," in German.

[160] See note 117, p. 62, for the Cagoule. The Rosselli brothers were anti-fascist Italian intellectuals. One man widely suspected of being an accomplice in their murder was appointed to an important position in Vichy's High Commission on Jewish Questions. Many streets and a few schools in France bear the name of Marx Dormoy today—in Paris, two schools, a street, and a Metro station.

[161] "March Wind." It was awarded France's most important literary prize, the Prix Goncourt, in 1941. Whatever the value of the book itself, it fit Vichy's cultural program perfectly: the "eternal peasant" and the moral value of rustic life compared to the cosmopolitan "decadence" of the Republic were themes of Vichy propaganda.

It is true that already the thunder of the war is no longer heard in the countryside and has not even made a dent in the mountains. Things, animals, and men (not all of them) are in their accustomed places. But, my dear Pourrat, I assure you, the thunder continues to be heard in London, in Berlin, even in Paris, all over the earth; cities are collapsing, countless men are dying and all humane relations have been destroyed. You yourself, open your ears! Can't you hear? The fact is, from now on the green life is far from being the whole life of men. What a many-colored life we have. Return to the soil, sings the chorus of Vichy angels. But the very ones who have not left it are demanding phosphates and sulfates from Vichy along with a thousand products of the devil and the city. Finally, o abomination! When the ancient man with the hoe himself is set before a tractor, he stands there overwhelmed with admiration.

August 7

Solution to a sociological problem: Why do pederasts collaborate?

Their joy is the joy of the boarders in the brothel of a small town when a regiment goes by.

Idiocy abounds. For the fourth time I had to swear on my honor that I am neither a Jew nor a Freemason.

August 9

Rabindranath Tagore* has died. I remember that day during the other war, around 1916, when, by chance, I discovered the messages of this poet unknown to me in a Far Eastern newspaper. From the bottom of the world, with an immemorial wisdom, he denounced all the causes of our miseries: the will to power of the West, its frenzy for machines; the cruel, abstract logic of nationalism, the dehumanizing effect it is threatening to have on the whole world. And his laments and accusations came together with the thoughts I had in the trenches. Then, I felt one of the deepest joys of my life. Those messages in my hand from the other end of the world, when everything seemed to be tottering, assured me that man's faith was safe and sound. When the war would end, I wanted to get to know the poet's work, and the first essay I ever published was merely a commentary on it.

Yesterday they burned his body at Santiniketan. Smoke disappeared into the sky.

I leafed through the collections of his poems. He said:

I was not aware of the moment when I first crossed the threshold of this life.

What was the power that made me open out into this vast mystery like a bud in the forest at midnight?

When in the morning I looked upon the light I felt in a moment that I was no stranger in this world, that the inscrutable without name and form had taken me in its arms in the form of my own mother.

Even so, in death the same unknown will appear as ever known to me. And because I love this life, I know I shall love death as well.

The child cries out when from the right breast the mother takes it away to find in the very next moment its consolation in the left one.

And also:

When I go from hence let this be my parting word, that what I have seen is unsurpassable.

I have tasted of the hidden honey of this lotus that expands on the ocean of light, and thus am I blessed—let this be my parting word.

In this playhouse of infinite forms I have had my play and here have I caught sight of him that is formless.

My whole body and my limbs have thrilled with his touch who is beyond touch; and if the end comes here, let it come—let this be my parting word. (*Gitanjali*, 96)[162]

August 11

This morning I tried once again to obtain the *Ausweis* necessary to go into the other zone. Useless. As early as 5:30 a.m., in the dark, I was on the first Metro with the fishermen. They were getting on at every station, with their fishing-rods, their landing nets, boxes of worms, folding chairs, and so many hopes. They were all rushing to take their places on the banks of the Seine and got off at Châtelet. Toward 6 a.m. I was at Rue du Colisée, where the occupying authorities have their headquarters. It was much too late. But how could I get there earlier, unless I walked there during the night? It is forbidden to go out before 5 a.m. Three hundred people were already there; they lived in the neighborhood or had slept in the hallways nearby. As the authorities only examine about 50 cases a day, at least 200 of them were there for the third or fourth time. People were bickering with each other. It was all rather frightful, a scene out of Maupassant. Each one wanted to have the most dangerous illness in his own family. Peritonitis was at a premium. The luckiest had a corpse, and, to get in with the first in line, brandished their telegram.

What's more, I was told they were examining only "urgent" cases and mine did not even deserve examination. After two hours of waiting on line, abandoning all hope, I left.

---

[162] *Gitanjali*, or "song offerings," was first published in 1913.

I walked along the Champs-Élysées, completely empty. Only a few *"feldgrau"* and a few *"gretchen"* were making their way to their offices, clicking their heels on the asphalt and giving the Hitler salute. Then I got the idea of going all the way up to the Arch of Triumph, to go for a moment near the Other One, up there under his slab of stone.[163] I stood there for a long time. The policeman on duty was bored. The pathetic little flame danced in the wind. Do I know what I was thinking? I was looking. There he was, that man, killed twenty years ago...a corpse has no age. Are you less dead after twenty years than after a thousand? But all around me there was Paris—admirable—and France, like a ruin, in that astonishing silence, and also those *"feldgrau"* and those "gretchen." That dead man, alone among all the dead, decidedly did have an age, an age given to him by the history of his country. For how long will that flame keep burning? Why, then, was it lit? It all felt to me like an insult. Unknown comrade, whom they let neither live nor die, offended in your life which was stolen from you, offended now even in death, you poor man loaded with glory and shame that you did not desire, o you, truly my brother...

August 12

Blanzat explains to me that the devil would have to be invented if he did not exist. He hates people who, when they are in accord with their own mind, think they are also in accord with everyone. Nothing is so annoying as the pride, the assurance, and the ignorance of the pure. They find nothing inside them that is real life, which is a swamp. All this about a Protestant girl we meet and whom I praise lavishly. It seems to him that life must die at the feet of a girl of such obvious virtue. He is mistaken. Purity has its own disquiet, its own violence. And in fact I know few girls more alive than that one, who often has a cold expression on her face. It's true, even her smiles are voluntary, but that itself makes them more moving. They seem to engage her completely, and they are so honest they are disconcerting.

August 13

The Marshal has spoken. A vulgar, convoluted, threatening speech. He does have to recognize that France is not behind him. He claims he will put it there by force and promises to persecute us. We shall see.

The logic of treason is obliging the government to be increasingly treacherous. But the logic of suffering will increase the nation's resistance to treason every day.

At the beginning of his speech, the Marshal announces that he has serious things to tell us. But it is quite remarkable that the "serious things" he says are not the ones we're thinking of. Everybody was expecting a speech on foreign

---

[163] The Tomb of the Unknown Soldier, killed in World War I.

policy and waiting for him to talk about Germany and peace; he talked about Freemasons and the obstacles they were putting in the way of the National Revolution.

To sum up: he's going to double the powers of the police the better to defend the French against themselves.

August 17

Vainly has German propaganda tried to appropriate the V's. The battle continues and no confusion is possible. The German V's are not very numerous but colossal; they are spread out over public monuments, on flags, on posters. The V's of the Resistance are tiny, but innumerable: Metro tickets folded into a V, matches broken into a V . . .

Wednesday, Friday, there were fights around Saint-Lazare, at the Porte Saint-Denis. It seems some Frenchmen and a German were killed. Impossible to know anything precise, however. Only "notices" posted everywhere warning us that whoever encourages Communist propaganda will receive the death sentence.

Roulier is in prison for three months. I wrote him yesterday. He is in Fresnes. Cell 236. A strange address for this lively man, so nice, so generous. He had his clientele in grand hotels and his wife brought him a package of extraordinary victuals in this time of famine: a lobster, a ham, and packs of cigarettes that his "customers" sent him. I can imagine the faces of the prison guards when they "visited" the package, and the joy today of Roulier and his four pals in cell 236; you take whatever revenge you can get.

This story is making the rounds: toward 4:30 this morning, a man was walking in the night. He was going to Rue Galilée to stand on line for an inter-zone pass. He meets a patrol. Panicked, he starts running. The patrol opens fire and he is killed.

August 19

Yesterday, by means of its little posters, the occupying authorities were offering a million to anyone who discovered the authors of various "attacks against trains and rolling stock." Early this morning, other little posters were promising a thousand francs to anyone who ripped a star off Darlan's epaulettes, two thousand to anyone who ripped off two of them, and three thousand francs to whoever killed him.

August 21

The air is getting heavier and heavier, unbreathable. In some neighborhoods the police are closing off the streets. A whole arrondissement (the 11th) has been searched. Jews have been arrested, Communists shot. Every morning, new posters invite us to become informers and threaten us with death. The worried "occupier" is organizing a reign of terror. In this "communard" neighborhood where

I live, between Rue Haxo and Rue des Rosiers, the poor working people, who have been resigned for a long time, are falling into despair. There is nothing to eat. For the past two weeks, all meat has been confiscated. The news from Russia is bad. The workers feel that their dream is collapsing. They walk around with closed faces. The moment is approaching when no one will have anything left to care about and the flame of revolution will flare up. We can feel ourselves slipping into something unknown and frightful. We are stifling. From the bottom of my heart, I wish the poor people in whose midst I live courage and patience. There is nothing we can do now, and there will be nothing we can do for a long time to come.

Forget about "I think, therefore I am": people conclude "I am, therefore I think." What pretension!

I returned to the Vallée-aux-Loups, for I wanted to see. We follow a path along the vegetable garden, jump over a little wall, and cross a path. It is there. The occupying authority "used the terrain," a rather deep hollow in a sparsely wooded area. Bullets have slashed into the slope. People who have no doubt come from town are turning around a bunch of skinny tree stumps like the ones I saw twenty years ago in the Ardennes. We draw near. It is really there. The tree has been sawed off, ripped apart by bullets at the level of a man's heart. It was used all last winter, four or five times every week. The earth is all trampled down at the foot of the tree. It has lost its bark. It is black from the blood that drenched it. It can no longer be used now. It was shot too many times. It ended up collapsing, too. The people from a nearby farm carried off the top of the trunk and the branches. I am absorbed in looking at it. In the thickness of the trunk, a V—yes, a V—has been carved out with a knife. By whom? By the Germans, to sign their crime? Rather, no doubt, by a French boy, as a tender greeting of friendship and hope to the men who came to die there, and a promise to avenge them.

A few meters away, here's the tree that's in use today. It's a beech tree. It is hardly wounded yet. Its bark has burst, however, and we can already see its white flesh with blood stains still at the same height, the height of a man's heart. No trace of a bullet underneath. The firing squad has good aim.

I am full of suffering, disgust, and horror.

August 25

I am finishing my reading of *Germany's Third Empire* (*The Third Reich*), that prophetic book by Moeller van den Bruck, a young Nazi philosopher who signed it with his death. It is quite full of somber enthusiasm and helps one to understand the frenzy of those young Germans who have been seeking victory or death for the past two years all over Europe. As hate-filled as the book may be, it does not arouse our hatred, but rather our pity.

In it, one can clearly see that Germany's sickness is that very youth. It is suffering from jealousy and envy, from its having fallen behind Europe by two or three centuries, badly constituted as a nation, without any political consciousness yet and simply instinctive, when England, France, and other nations had already become empires and laid down the foundations of civilization and law throughout the world.

But the worst of it all is that these young philosophers claim they will cure the illness through the illness, youth through youth. They proclaim "the right of young peoples" as if it were quite obviously superior to the right of more ancient peoples. It seems to them that the last-born child is always the most intelligent. We have never yet been a nation, they say. We shall thus be the Nation itself. We have never yet thought politically, our politics will thus be Politics itself. The romantic myth of youth also distorts all their reasoning. Adolescents intoxicated with themselves, with their unhappiness and their hunger, according to whom the ideal is not to become a man, but perpetually to remain a young man. They want— these are Moeller van den Bruck's very words—"to create a politics out of the immense danger which emanates from them." A big thank-you from humanity.

Europe's first duty will be to help Germany grow older. Nonetheless, this "young man," precisely because he looks at us with hatred, is excellent at seeing and discovering all the gaps, all the weaknesses and hypocrisies of our faith. Things are said in his book, as his master Nietzsche recommends, "in the most corporal and bloody manner." I note a few maxims on which it would no doubt be rather profitable for us to reflect:

1. "Ideas that have been put into practice are dull images."
2. "Who knows what good is blown by an ill wind?"—Hindenburg.
3. "The whole mistake of socialism resides in one sentence of K. Marx: 'Humanity only poses those problems which it can solve.' No. Humanity only poses problems it cannot solve, and therein lies its greatness. That is the genius which leads it."
4. "Conservatives are those who think of legalities that are always re-established, while progressives are those who cultivate hopes that never come true."
5. "It is not economics but politics which determines history."
6. "Liberalism is the freedom to have no definite opinion while affirming that that absence of opinion is itself an opinion."
7. "Liberalism is the party of upstarts ... It is based on the desire felt by all men to have a personality, even if they have none."
8. "Democracy can mean: stoicism, republicanism, toughness, severity. But it can also mean: liberalism, parliamentary chatter, frivolity."
9. "Whoever wishes to be a proletarian is a proletarian."
10. "Only the examples of republicans who become the symbols of their conviction, only acts that demand respect and give us liberty can maintain the Republic."

August 26

As the Russians withdraw, they leave behind them nothing but desert and ruins. L…observed that the law of communism favors the strict implementation of Stalin's orders here. In France, a small landowner in June 1940 could not make up his mind to burn down his house or his barn. A worker on a kolkhoz, does not have the same scruples, since the farm is collectively owned.

We are sinking deeper into horror. The day before yesterday in Versailles, they were presenting its flag to the Anti-Bolshevik Legion recently formed by Deloncle, Déat, and Constantini, when shots rang out. From the very ranks of the Legion a man shot at the officials present at the ceremony. Laval and Déat, the colonel commanding the Legion, were wounded, along with a Legionnaire.

Yesterday morning, the whole people of Paris had difficulty concealing its joy when it read the news. The joy of a terrifying hatred. The people thinks only of taking revenge on its masters, the masters of taking revenge on the people, and the same impatience reigns on both sides. Big headlines in the newspapers are announcing that only yesterday, by order of a court martial, three Communists were executed.

Déat is wearing a brown shirt and a beret in the photos, and looks so very proud of his uniform. Already, twenty years ago at the École, after the war, he couldn't get over having been a captain. He has never been cured of his desire to command. That is the story of his life.

But who is this Paul Collette who is going so deliberately to his death?[164]

August 30

This morning two new notices were posted: Five workers from Paris or the outskirts were shot for having "taken part in a demonstration against the German army," two other Frenchmen and a Dutchman for espionage. The tree in the Vallée-aux-Loups will soon be cut down. At the doors of the newspaper vendors, in the cafés, and in the Metro, no one dares to talk anymore.

September 3

A young writer (in the *NRF*), the same who called for war in 1938–39 and displayed such great haste to have a bloodbath, now finds in defeat an occasion to put on the same show. He must pose as a hero at all costs. He took his bloodbath. He was wounded last year, and he shouts it from the rooftops; he is not far from believing that he was the only one to fight, and the lost war seems to him a swindle of which he was the sole victim. Now he is concerned that they don't swindle him out of the Revolution, *his* Revolution. For the Revolution belongs to

---

[164] The Nazi-controlled Paris press claimed the assassin (Collette) was a Communist; the French police investigation concluded the young man had no connection to any left-wing party. Surprisingly, Pétain commuted his death sentence to life. Collette was eventually deported, survived, and was awarded the Legion of Honor in 1985.

him, too. So he sets up as the leader of his generation. (You say to yourself: now there's French pride!) Incidentally, this boy maneuvered so well that he became secretary to a minister in that same ministry he suspects of sabotaging the Revolution, and this article is an occasion for him to court the occupying authorities—people in a hurry do have to reckon with them today—by proposing "the admirable German irregular forces of 1919" as an example to the French youth of 1941. He says to himself, "France needs a Goebbels: why not me?"

But the Revolution, the real one, belongs to no one. Above all it does not consist in replacing the sly ambition of the old with the frantic, ruthless ambition of the young. It is a very old cause and it was not born with you or with us; one needs a certain humility to serve it.

The utilization of youth as a separate force is one of the new, singular traits of contemporary politics. Youth is rather proud of that separation. Today's politicians would have youth believe that it is leading the world, when in reality they are merely exploiting its frenetic energy and its thoughtlessness. Totalitarian ideology is completely instinctive and naturally must make use of the fervor of youth. And there is something in it for a few young sharks, but the mass of young people have never been more skillfully deceived. They give themselves up completely for a black, brown, or blue shirt, and use their energy to make a world in which, when they grow older, they are ashamed to live. For youth does not last. It is for men that the city must be constructed, not for young men. The goal is not to put a club into the hands of young people who take an idiotic pleasure in brandishing it, but to put tools that will make their lives safe into the hands of men.

September 17

I went on a trip to Brittany for a change of air and to try to get food supplies, for life here has become increasingly wretched. I saw some good friends. I saw the sea. I spent a few afternoons on the water, and I was singing with joy, but by the third day I was eager to come back here. I went to Camaret, to Brest, Saint-Brieuc, Fougères, and Saint-Germain-en-Coglès, in the very village where I was brought up. Everywhere I found the same absurdity. I recalled the songs we sang as draftees:

Never will the Prussians come
And eat up our soup in Brittany.

The song lied. On the sea, on the moors, in the forest, on the paths of Saint-Germain, just when I was going to forget about him, suddenly the gray soldier was there in front of me, with his rifle and his face of an all-powerful, barbaric moron. But it is impossible that he himself cannot feel how vain is the terror he is wielding. The sailors of Camaret make fun of him openly. The peasants of the interior remain impenetrable. He will go away as he came; he will have gone on a long, absurd trip.

The first piece of news I learn upon my arrival in Paris is the execution of ten hostages (ten Communists and five Jews), shot yesterday "as a repressive measure."

Old Saint-Pol-Roux, the poet, was finishing out his life in Camaret, in the "manor" with his daughter, Divine, a woman servant, and his dog. The manor is solitary, far from the village, on the edge of the heath in front of the sea, on a cliff. One evening a year ago, around ten o'clock, a German suddenly walked into the house on the pretext that Englishmen were hidden there. Nobody. They walked back to the living room. Then the soldier sent away the dog. Then, in front of the poet, his daughter, and the servant, all terrified, he laid two revolvers and a dagger on the table, saying he was expecting his buddies. An hour went by in terrible silence. Toward eleven o'clock, the old poet asked the soldier to leave. Then the soldier, with a revolver in each hand, demanded that everybody go down to the cellar. They went down. The soldier shot and Saint Pol was wounded; the servant who wanted to protect Divine was killed. As Divine was running away, the soldier shot again and she collapsed, with a broken leg. Then he dragged her into the living room and raped her. The dog, who came in through a window of the living room, chased him away. Divine wandered over the heath, where she was found in the morning, unconscious.

Since then, old Saint Pol has died of sorrow. Poor Divine was taken in by the dead servant's sister. She would like not to remember. She walks on crutches. She can't do anything, not even read.

To be fair, let us note that the soldier was executed. Divine recognized him in the midst of a line-up they made for her. He confessed right away. He had seen Divine swimming at the bottom of the cliff. So . . . The occupying authorities, decidedly considerate, gave Divine and the old poet the privilege of watching the execution. After which she occupied the "manor."

September 18

As the tree in the Vallée-aux-Loups had become a shrine, the occupying authorities blew it up with dynamite. The firing squads have worked elsewhere ever since.

September 20

Two more Communists were executed yesterday.

From the 20th to the 23rd, curfew has been brought back to nine o'clock. For three days, we must go to bed as soon as the sun sets. They punish us like children, "for our own good," declares General von Stülpnagel.* We are guilty of not denouncing the authors of attacks on German soldiers. The occupying authorities have not been able to arrest a single one of them. Why are we not child informers?

The feeling of oppression hardly ever leaves us here. In Fougères, and especially in the village, in Saint-Germain, how far away the war was, despite everything; joys and sorrows continued to be natural joys and sorrows, as they always had been. I helped to thresh the buckwheat, and it was still a fête. As for sorrows, I encountered one in the image of that old peasant whose wife, "*La Fine*," died three months ago. At the end of a path lined with chestnut trees, I found him in his gray house, his "shack"; he works hard to keep it all shiny and bright in honor of *La Fine*. "I'm getting used to it," he told me. "But it's real hard, every time I get back. No fire, no flame, no woman, no nothin'." And then he showed me, leaning against the bed pillow, a big photo of *La Fine* and him, "only five years ago." *La Fine* had a big smile.

September 22

Yesterday evening, in a few unbelievably trite words, Pétain denounced the criminal attacks against soldiers of the occupation army (which is his job), but he also asked us to seek out the guilty parties and give him, to this end, our "complete co-operation" (which is a misuse of authority). Of the 30 men shot last week, he did not breathe a word.

Clémenceau* was "old man victory." De Gaulle has just christened Pétain "old man defeat." The quip has a future.

Twelve hostages were shot the day before yesterday as reprisals for an attack on an officer in the German army. And Stülpnagel is warning us he'll do much better next time.

At the other end of Europe, Leningrad, Kiev, and Odessa are under siege, and every day thousands of men are dying. This thought hardly ever leaves me.

September 23

Another nickname for the Marshal is being whispered about: Pétoche.[165]

September 24

The mother of that young man of nineteen who was shot as a hostage the other day is supposed to have killed a German in the street and supposedly gave herself up. The wife of another executed prisoner supposedly did the same. A myth, no doubt, but laden with meaning.

Last night the birds were shouting in the trees of the garden. Paris is so dark and quiet that screech owls will soon come and perch here as if in the middle of the countryside. We'll hear the cuckoo, as in Montolieu.

Met X...the day before yesterday. To avoid me, he dives toward a shop window covered with wire mesh where there was nothing to see, but I am going to ask him what he's doing. "You know my opinions," he says to me. "And you know mine," I reply. Then, whether as a provocation or an interrogation, he talks about leaflets

---

[165] [*Avoir*] *la pétoche* (slang): "scared stiff."

I'm as familiar with as he is, he says, that are supposedly inspired by my thought, or commenting on sentences from my books or taking them as an epigraph. I assure him that I have not seen them and have just learned of their existence from him. I ask him to send them to me. It is clear that he did not believe me.

A collaborationist writer is speaking of a fellow writer whom he did not succeed in converting: "His position is childish," he tells me. "He thinks he's a world writer and doesn't want to do anything that might take away his worldwide public. But if one thinks a bit, one can quickly see that for him, the world is America, where he is very concerned that his books continue to be published and sold. So he will publish his next book in Switzerland, so that the Americans can't suspect him of having been subjected to censorship."

The dollar he did not mention illuminated his words like a sun.

September 26

I admire the gift Jean Paulhan has of lightening up life all around him. What a delightful friend and how he will have helped me to live in this prison! He walks along like a tightrope-walker, standing on tiptoe at every step, and if you're walking next to him, almost immediately you find that you're walking more lightly. When things threaten to get heavy, he takes off. A way of conquering heaviness, of thumbing his nose at it. He is rigorous and subtle. He likes all games. But especially those which consist of inventions, transformations, ruses, metamorphoses. Games seem to him the best school for life, as if to live well, basically all you have to do is to look at things from the right angle, and the way we look depends on us. The other day at the flea market, which he likes for the strange discoveries you can make there, he stopped in front of a cigar box, struck with admiration. It was one of those octagonal boxes where if you press a button, all the panels pop open, forming different geometrical figures. He worked it several times. He wanted to buy it at all costs. I think he was contemplating it both as the product and the symbol of the most marvelous human power that he knows, that of seeing and showing things precisely as we wish. You push a button, and with astonishing precision and a sharp click, that closed, graceless box opens on all sides, through all its walls, onto so many little scenes where you expect tiny stars to appear. It is full and it is empty, one and multiple. It is day and night. The curtain opens and shuts, as you wish. Life is a theater in which you yourself put the enchantment of your choice on stage. For Jean Paulhan has no doubt about it, we want to be, we can be "the poets of our lives."

I am recopying here Nietzsche's admirable aphorism about "What one should learn from artists." It is a good rule.

> What means do we have for making things beautiful, attractive, and desirable, when they are not...? And it seems to me they never are, in themselves! Here we have something to learn from physicians, when, for example, they dilute what is bitter, or put wine and sugar into their

mixing bowl; but we have still more to learn from artists, who in fact, are continually concerned with devising such inventions and artifices. To withdraw from things until one no longer sees much of them, until one even has to see things into them in order to see them at all or to view them from the side, and as in a frame or to place them so that they partly disguise themselves and only enable perspective views or to look at them through colored glasses, or in the light of the sunset or to furnish them with a surface or skin which is not fully transparent: we should learn all this from artists, and moreover be wiser than they. For this fine power of theirs usually ceases with them where art ceases and life begins; we, however, want to be the poets of our lives, and first of all in the smallest everyday matters. (*The Gay Science*, 299)

September 29

By 10:00 yesterday morning I was at Sainte-Périne hospital and all day I was almost constantly under the influence of what I saw. During the night, a telegram had warned me that our old friend had died there. They led me to the funeral parlor of the hospital. It's at the end of the grounds, a little house like a gardener's house, and I remembered that they never wanted us to take the path that led there when we walked around with her. A room hung with black drapes. The last dormitory. There are five or six places, five or six beds always made. Just one was occupied yesterday—by our old friend. Between the dark drapes, daylight was falling on her through a window at the head of the bed. I could see her against the light. She was covered up to her chin by a white sheet; the hard, motionless shadows of her eyes, nose, and mouth dug into her waxy, pitted face. The left eye, half open, was full of fear. That witness-face pursued me all day. Because of it I forgot the war, our miseries, our artificial prison, and the fighting in Russia. I have seen only a few dead people in my lifetime. But I remember those motionless faces like military markers that trace the way.

I thought again of those Mexican mummies a year ago in the Musée de l'Homme, mummies of women: when they die they are piled on each other in a bag to take up less space. They are squatting there behind the display windows, terrifying and yet so natural, as if they were still busy poking the fire. Louisette was with me and I was sorry for that. "Not at all," she said to me. "It's quite useful. You have to familiarize yourself with what you are."

October 3

I had an unpleasant conversation yesterday morning with an administrator. At first I attached too much importance to it, but at least it forced me to become aware of the unbelievable luck I've had for twenty years: I have earned my living as a teacher without thinking about it, without even noticing it, without being subjected to any constraint. It is not only that I loved my profession. I was always able to exercise it in complete freedom, in the spirit and with the methods of my choice, and, it seemed, for no other reason than pleasure. As I worked, I don't think it even occurred to me once to calculate the profits I would get from my work. I just about never had the feeling of working for money. What extraordinary happiness, after those years of my youth where I worked ten hours a day only for the pay, twenty-five francs per month, then thirty, and then up to forty-five francs.[166]

But yesterday morning, I was asked—nicely, I must say—to give my teaching a more technical and practical turn. A sign of the times! They are now suspicious of a certain influence I have in the École and the very education that ten years ago they had asked me to give.

The history of ideas is suspect from now on. Why didn't I speak, instead, of the rules for the agreement of participles? I immediately had the idea of resigning. I was held back by the thought of the 10,000 francs I earn in this school, and my need for them. But I am going to look for ways to earn them elsewhere, and in the meantime, I will take these administrative recommendations into account only as much as I like. The idea that I would go there just to earn a few hundred francs more every week is unbearable. One cannot do this job for money. One can only do it well for pleasure, outside of worldly interests. The administrator went into Latin, and said to me: *Cedere tempori, id est necessitati parere, hoc est sapientia.*[167] Such wisdom is not mine. I do not have to be prudent; I only have to be truthful.

I feel that for years I have known a marvelous freedom. A school of the Republic could be a fine thing. With a hundred or so young people, I was seeking truth, with nothing but truth at stake and in all serenity. We had no other passion but truth. Must I bring into the classroom the preoccupations of the times, politics . . . I think of the words of Scripture: "The Lord was not in the wind."

October 5

I've given up keeping a record of the stupidity and vileness of the times in this "diary." The day before yesterday bombs exploded in all the synagogues of Paris . . . They're announcing a few new executions by firing squad . . . All civil servants (and I am one) will have to swear an oath to the Marshal, etc. Let us wait, with resignation.

Luckily tomorrow I'll see my students once again.

October 10

The terrible battle continues in Russia. Perhaps our fate is being decided over there. But we hardly think about it. We are enjoying the sun, which stayed away

---

[166] Although prices were very different then and it's hard to calculate, we can say that the top salary young Guéhenno earned in the factory was extremely low: somewhere around nine dollars a month in pre–World War I dollars. In the following paragraph, École refers to the École Normale Supérieure Technique (see note 125, p. 67).

[167] "Yielding to the times, giving in to necessity; that is wisdom" (Cicero, *Ad Familiares* [*Letters to Friends*], IV, 9).

from us all summer, and these fine days of autumn, like a truce before the hard winter to come.

It is clear that official pedagogy does not wish to think that certain writers of the past thought very much. As I was explicating Rabelais these past few days, I was struck by the effort that some commentators—university professors— make to reduce their ideas to naught. M. Plattard quotes Victor Hugo's lines only to make fun of them:

> Rabelais whom no one understood.
> He cradles Adam so he should sleep
> And his enormous burst of laughter
> Is, for the mind, a bottomless deep.[168]

If we are to believe him, Hugo and all the Romantics were fooled. There is supposedly no reason to seek out the "substantific marrow" in his work. It is not there. He himself has flatly said so. And Professor Plattard takes him at his word. If it is there, it is, in any case absolutely not anti-religious. Wasn't Rabelais a cleric? So Professor Plattard leaves us a choice: either Rabelais was a Catholic, or he was a hypocrite. As one cannot suspect him of hypocrisy, he must therefore be a Catholic. Don't say that at a time when a Borgia was pope, a Rabelais might well be a monk... Besides, concludes Professor Plattard, "his serious ideas [so he had some!] are merely of historical interest..."

And that is how, from sophism to sophism, a magnificent old wine can be changed into a cheap, flat red. For above all one must shun all debate, arrange everything, and to do so, neutralize everything—everything. What fear of ideas! But they are tough and resist these little tricks. Those industrious pedagogues will not reconcile the Joy of Rabelais and the satisfied misery of the Catholic ideal. We will continue to turn to Rabelais in quest of courage and energy, despite their glosses.

One of the ideas that believers find most disagreeable is that the Faith, too, has a history, and the faith of Guibert de Nogent is not quite the faith of Joan of Arc, the faith of Joan of Arc that of Pascal, the faith of Pascal that of Chateaubriand, the faith of Chateaubriand that of M. Maritain.[169] The flame wavers, dwindles, and rises in the wind of the centuries. It seems that when you

---

[168] *Rabelais que nul ne comprit./Il berce Adam pour qu'il s'endorme/Et son éclat de rire énorme/Est un des gouffres de l'esprit.* In the next sentence: Rabelais' Prologue to *Gargantua* famously invites his readers to "break the bone and suck out the substantific marrow" of his work (*rompre l'os et sucer la substantifique moelle*)—in other words, to seek out its deeper meaning. In a comic turnaround, Rabelais then says there is none.

[169] Guibert de Nogent was an 11th-century Benedictine abbot; Jacques Maritain (1882–1973) was a contemporary Catholic philosopher, an eminent specialist in the thought of St. Thomas Aquinas.

point that out you're playing a dirty trick on them. They look at you with resentment. What if the flame were to go out as it lit up...

Montherlant has come out with *The Childhoods of Montherlant,*[170] letters and drawings from his tenth year of life. Why not? We do say "the childhoods of Bayard." Now, this man of letters upholds the same relationship with his era as the Chevalier de Bayard with his. His whole life supposedly helps him to compose a "mirror of the perfect charlatan."

To redirect the hatred of the French people, Vichy has published the names of the Freemasons. But this publication did not have its intended effect. It would be hard to do a better job of destroying the legend of the power of Freemasonry. This list clearly shows that being a Mason could easily lead to being a schoolteacher or even a tax inspector, but almost none of the great names of the Third Republic are on it. So Vichy, feeling silly and wanting to make up for it, has explained today that we should not be fooled: "Masonry is a doubly secret society; it hides its activities not only from the public but from part of its membership," etc.

I find it prudent to put these "notebooks" in a safe place. From now on I will keep this diary on separate sheets of paper.

The news from Russia is bad. Once the Germans take Moscow, will the same political decomposition that occurred last year in France take place in Russia? If the Soviets survive, if they don't sign an armistice, if the war continues in one way or another (a war analogous to the one the Chinese have been waging for seven years), perhaps nothing is lost.

The new prefect of police—an admiral, of course—boasts of having arrested 1,100 Communists or Anglophiles.

Langevin,* who was under house arrest, has been jailed again. Borel (sixty-six years old) has also been arrested.[171] The Gestapo has declared all of academia under suspicion.

The Germans' repressive methods are such that there is not one Frenchman who will not feel his debt to the Jews and the Communists, jailed and shot for us. They are the veritable sacrificial victims of the people.

The occupying authorities are offering writers and journalists a free trip to Germany. The small fry will surely make a three-day trip. But the most distinguished and devoted writers will spend a whole month visiting the marvels of

---

[170] *Les enfances de Montherlant.* The next allusion is to the Chevalier de Bayard (1473–1524), who became legendary as "The Knight Without Fear and Without Reproach."

[171] Émile Borel (1871–1956) was a world-famous mathematician and an active left-wing militant.

the Third Reich. Among them are several knights of the green carnation[172]: J...,
P..., F...

October 19

For ten days now German propaganda has been announcing that "the Eastern
campaign is virtually over." But the terrible battle continues.

I have no taste for noting down the little horrors we suffer here. What's the
point: we're in a state of numbness. Every morning the paper gives us the name
of another man who has been shot. We grit our teeth as we read. People are
hungry. Little Jojo in the house next door found a job and is quite proud of earning 8 francs 24 an hour; but his eyes are all sunken; they put him at a lathe and
he eats too little to sustain himself. The Marshal has spoken: in the name of loyalty, he is inviting all French children to become informers. The urge to throw up
scarcely ever leaves us.

The Marshal was a handsome man, they say. He's proud of it. Over 300 painters
or engravers made his portrait in the past few months. Only one was awarded a
prize by the ministry: it received a gold medal. So the others complained and the
Marshal ordered them to bring 300 portraits to Vichy. He had them hung on the
walls of the Hôtel du Parc[173] and inspected them. After this, he dictated and signed
a letter of thanks to his 300 portraitists. One would like to see the letter.

October 20

Yesterday I read Blanzat's new manuscript; this morning, old letters from
J...And now I am overwhelmed by the feeling of my heaviness. I have lived so
grossly, paying so little attention to other people's souls. It seems to me that I
can see what determines the principle of my grossness...I had no modesty in
myself and had a hard time imagining it in others. I always revealed everything
I was, fairly ready to make a rule of that indecent, naïve frankness. I did not sufficiently reflect on the fact that there are more discreet souls, wrapped in modesty as in a veil, and sometimes I must have been insufficiently careful not to
offend them. I thought other people were only as I saw them. Idiot! Will I still
have the time to live with a little delicacy?

I admire how nice Blanzat is. His little boy has returned to Paris, and Blanzat
is full of fear at the idea of so many offenses which may hurt him. His tone of
voice when he says: "My son!"

October 21

Discussion with J.P. about language.

---

[172] Ever since Oscar Wilde's habit of wearing a green carnation in his lapel, it had become a sign
of gay underground culture.

[173] This hotel was the headquarters of Pétain's government in Vichy.

What is the essential quality of language? Is it not to express one's thought as closely as possible? And thus to write well is to think well, and to think well is to write well. It's always a question of the same difficult probity. I think of that Christian idea according to which the word of Christ, the Gospel, is another body of Christ. I would be ready to secularize that idea. The language of men is another body of men. And as our body bears our spirit, our language must bear it, too, and bear it completely. And as the defects of our mind end up by affecting our body, they sometimes affect our language. Too many contemporary writers are vain and irresponsible: they use language in a flabby, cowardly way. As they are not men of their word, they never keep the promise of their language. And that is how one becomes a "man of letters"—a charlatan, a bad actor. Language deserves more reverence...

October 22

Anniversary of the meeting of Pétain and Hitler at Montoire: the "Collaboration" inaugurated by that meeting is chugging along nicely. Have we reached the depths of horror? This morning the papers are publishing the following notice:

NOTICE

Cowardly criminals paid by England and Moscow shot the Feldcommandant in Nantes (Loire-Inférieure) in the back and killed him on the morning of October 20, 1941. Up to now the assassins have not been arrested.

In expiation of this crime, I have ordered, as a preliminary measure, the execution of 50 hostages before a firing squad.

Given the gravity of the crime, 50 other hostages will be shot if the guilty parties have not been arrested between now and midnight October 23, 1941.

I am offering a reward totaling 15 million francs to the inhabitants of the country who contribute to the discovery of the guilty parties.

Useful information may be left at any department of the German or French police. This information will be used confidentially upon request.

Paris, October 21, 1941.

Der Militärbefehlshaber in Frankreich

Von Stülpnagel

General in the Infantry.

The newspapers, docile as they are, have printed the figure of 15 million francs in large capitals; it seems it's a new prize in the National Lottery.

But fifty citizens of Nantes faced the firing squad this morning. What Frenchman did not hear the salvos? What silence and what anxiety, a while ago in the Metro.

At two o'clock, the Marshal spoke to us once more. He denounced foreign plots, hatched in England, and invited us to become informers.[174] "Do not let them," he said to us, "hurt France in this way." And just in case we hadn't noticed, he took care to point out that his voice was breaking.

October 23

The list of the forty-eight who were shot (they spared us two) has been published in the papers. True, they did push it back to the third page, out of fear or shame. Naturally the forty-eight have been declared "Communists." In Belgrade, in Sofia and Brussels, the same mass executions. This is the new order. We can think of nothing else. The boys in the École Technique this morning were appalled.

October 24

News from the French writers in Germany. One of them writes that they are being waited on hand and foot. Every morning, for their small expenses (cigarettes, etc.), they are given pocket money.

October 25

A German major was killed the day before yesterday in Bordeaux and von Stülpnagel decided to execute a hundred new hostages. But, on the other hand, "days of grace, 72 hours, have been accorded for the complementary groups of hostages in Nantes and Bordeaux." Are we to understand that fifty hostages were shot in Bordeaux yesterday morning? And that fifty others will be shot in Nantes on the 27th and fifty more in Bordeaux on the 29th, if the occupying authorities have not discovered the "assassins" by then? We are lost in horror.

October 26

Met M... yesterday. He tells us that V... saw Pétain, and we're being too hard on him. Pétain himself says he is an anchor preventing France from going adrift. And he resists as much as he can. And he is maintaining Weygand in Algeria against Darlan, against the occupying authorities.[175] Maybe...

The other day, B... was defending the same point of view and reminded me of Montesquieu's quip: "It's not the ministers who are small, but the problems that are great." True, but must we have so much indulgence for men who cheated their way into power and claimed to play the great ministers, only to reveal their smallness for the world to see?

---

[174] An accurate summary of Pétain's *Appel du 22 octobre 1941* (*Discours aux Français*, op. cit. pp. 203–204).

[175] Darlan was thought to be more pro-Hitler than Weygand.

The hostages in past wars were noble or bourgeois, "notables." This time it's usually just unimportant people who run the risk of being shot. But they're shot by the dozen, so that the quantity should make up for the "notability," no doubt. Thus the war has kept its character: mass warfare.

If the authors of the recent attacks really are Communists, they are not giving themselves up, knowing that their comrades are the ones who'll take their place among the dead. And I hear people proclaiming that it shows they're all the more cowardly for that. But this doesn't take into account the pact which unites the comrades, the solemn commitments they made together, the orders they gave each other, mutually, at great risk, and dying for each other: the assassin may be in the hostage's place, the hostage in the assassin's place, as luck may have it. Each one holds to that pact with all his will, and does what he must do in his place. And that is frightful, but it has its grandeur, too.

The "15 million" tempt nobody, so the authorities are trying another way: it is announcing that it will free the prisoners of war belonging to the informers' families.

October 28

Monsieur J.C. has published a new book: perseverance. He chose a strange title: *Seeing the Face*.[176] Because he had a vision: he saw the face of the new Europe. Thus current events have no mystery for him. He understands everything and explains to us that if we don't understand anything, it's because we haven't been lucky enough to "see," like him, "the face." As for him, gratified by his vision, he prophesizes. He even understands what will be.

But through the book, I can glimpse only his own face. Even so, it is a bit blurred; a few grimaces, however, a few wrinkles, reveal old passions: a love, as if from the family, for cognacs from Charente and porcelains from Limoges, a totally bourgeois vanity, and a solid scorn for the people. These are the virtues that make Monsieur C...a "good socialist" and a "good European," according to the new definitions Germany has given to these words. He is truly exasperated by our stupidity. What, they're giving us a chance and we're not jumping at it?

In vain do I seek the enthusiasm of someone with his heart in the right place in this pretentious drivel. Monsieur C..., we haven't waited for you to see the face of the new Europe. But now there is all this blood around us. This blood *they* are draining from France every morning. As for me, I have only that blood before my eyes.

October 30

From America, Jules Supervielle* has sent this poem:

---

[176] *Voir la figure*, by the novelist Jacques Chardonne (1884–1968). After the Liberation of France, he was imprisoned for collaborating with the enemy.

At night, when I would like to change my active brain
Into a sleep that wants no part of me, but leaves me
As I am, my weary body unable to complain
And I cannot put it out, that brain,
The dead man I shall be stirs inside with ease
And says: "Time is beginning to drag for me,
What can still keep you here on this earth
After our defeat and France in misery?"
Unwilling to answer him who follows me everywhere
I look ahead for a world in which to disappear,
Smother the saddest part of my being inside
And feel myself become the humble son of night.[177]

October 31

Following what Jean Pommier has pointed out, I re-read the story of Nehemiah in Renan's history of Israel. Renan tells how Nehemiah reconstructed the walls of Jerusalem; he endows his story with symbolic grandeur.[178] The jealous neighboring tribes tried in every way they could to distract Nehemiah from his task. "On four different occasions," Renan writes, "Sanballat and Geshen invited Nehemiah to a conference in one of the villages of the plain of Oho, near Lydda. Nehemiah gave an answer that those who have a duty to fulfill in life should always have in their minds: "I am doing a great work, so that I cannot come down: *Magnum opus facio et non possum descendere.*"

And Renan himself, according to Pommier's testimony, had inscribed this admirable line on the cover of his Bible so that he would always have it before his eyes. I have re-read the greater part of his work these past three months. What exemplary application to that work which Bossuet* called the works of God. (It does not matter that their God was not the same one. The feeling they had about his works was the same.) His life ended when the work he had assigned to himself in his youth was over. Once he had written the last line of the history of Israel, he prepared to die "in the communion of humanity, the religion of the future."

Yesterday evening, with my brain somewhat heated up through thinking about him, the idea came to me for that work that I thought so often of composing and that I would call: *The Spirit of the French 19th Century* or else: *History of the Revolution in France in the 19th Century.* The idea kept me awake for a long time.

[177] *La nuit, quand je voudrais changer dans un sommeil/Qui ne veut pas de moi, me laissant tout pareil,/ Avec mon grand corps las et sans voix pour se plaindre/Ma cervelle allumée, et je ne puis l'éteindre,/Le mort que je serai bouge en moi sans façons/Et me dit: « Je commence à trouver le temps long,/Qu'est-ce qui peut encor te retenir sur terre,/Après notre défaite et la France en misère. »/Ne voulant pas répondre à qui partout me suit/Et cherchant plus avant un monde où disparaître,/J'étouffe enfin en moi le plus triste de l'être/ Et me sens devenir l'humble fils de la nuit.*

[178] Jean Pommier (1893–1973) was a Sorbonne professor whose scholarly work spanned the whole range of French literature. He particularly admired Renan and devoted a number of studies to him.

But, this morning, the fire is almost out, and I no longer dare to make the commitment to myself that I was so ready to make around midnight. On what could I better spend the years I have left? I am almost sure I can see the subject in all its greatness. And it could be the occasion for a last, great surge of energy. But again I feel the obstructions of my life, the weight of my job, and all my limitations.

The prestige of the writer was a peculiarly French phenomenon, I think. In no other country of the world was the writer surrounded with so much reverence by his people. Every French bourgeois might well fear that his son might become an artist, but the whole French bourgeoisie agreed on the almost sacred preeminence of the artist and the writer. It is only in France that the writer could consider himself a kind of magus.

Men of letters today still enjoy this traditional respect. But how clear it is that they no longer deserve it! All too many of them are merely merchants. But as the respect they were given by other people finally made them excessively vain, they think they are above the miseries and servitude of their country, and beyond responsibility, like gods. Thus one can see them continuing to go about their business—under Goebbels' surveillance. Their little business, their sacred work. Nothing can interrupt it. Is it their fault if their merchandise must bear a little Hitlerian flag in order to be sold? You have to live, say some, the most honest. Others will explain to you with some embarrassment that their masterpieces will be the first revenge of France. Still others, the most cynical, paint their very works with the new colors.

In times gone by everybody in France believed in ideas, both writers and readers. That faith made France France. For some time it has seemed that nobody believes in it anymore. I dare not conclude...

The occupying authorities are, for the time being, giving up the idea of shooting the "complementary hostages" so as to leave time for the French to do their duty and denounce the guilty parties.

November 1

A new weekly has appeared: *Le Rouge et le Bleu*.[179] With the white of the paper, here's the whole flag recomposed. It presents itself as the "journal of socialist thought." What audacity. I find in it the names of Socialist politicians who delivered France to Pierre Laval in June '40,[180] of a few failed or corrupt journalists. In the first issue of the weekly, not one word about the only fact that has filled the minds of the French people this week: the execution of a hundred hostages. O freedom!

I wander through the house, not knowing where to take refuge for my work. It is very cold, and we have to keep the coal for December and January... I used

---

[179] *The Red and the Blue*, punning on Stendhal's *The Red and the Black*.

[180] Of the 150 Socialist deputies in the National Assembly and 17 senators, only 36 voted against giving "full powers" to Pétain (actually in July), a measure pushed through by Pierre Laval. Soon afterward, Pétain appointed him second in command (Vice-Président du Conseil) and Foreign Secretary in the new French State.

to lose myself in work. What will become of me if even that is no longer possible? But there are greater misfortunes.

November 2

The *NRF* has published a few pages, often very fine, by Montherlant: *June Solstice*. It is rhetoric of the very best, the lyric song of a Chateaubriand gone vulgar. A few great poetic connections, associating earth and sky, the cycle of the seasons, after Spring Equinox the June solstice, solar and pagan signs and the swastika triumphing over the Christian cross, the victory of Hitler; and this declamation takes on a profound air: "Thou hast *been* conquered, Galilean!"[181] On June 24, 1940, Montherlant, sitting at a sidewalk café in Marseilles, thought he heard this cry over the same sea which had heard another prophecy 2,000 years ago: *Great Pan is dead*, meaning: "Thou hast *conquered*, Galilean." And there we are! Fate has been reversed. A whole philosophy of history seems to go into this change of one syllable: German victory is the victory of paganism over Christianity. Not to mention the fact that the declaimer maintains his reputation as a demon at the same time. How very serious all this is! (When, oh when, will I resign myself to the idea that a very great artist may not have a very great character?)

"In truth," writes Montherlant, "Current events have never been important to me. I only liked them for the rays they produced inside me as they passed through." Now there, at least, is a sincere statement. A German debacle would have made other rays inside him, that's all, and inspired another song no less lovely, no doubt.

But perhaps at the next solstice . . . Perhaps Montherlant has already gathered his plays, his images, his words to celebrate the next victory of the Galilean: a changeover. This "knight" always rallies around the strongest side. A matter of taste, he would say. We know he has a taste for force. So fine a rhetorician would surely have no lack of good motives to explain his "betrayals."[182]

But his real fault is no doubt not to be able to keep quiet, ever. Perhaps he is merely a silly man.

One must look at men as they are if one wants to get the most pleasure possible from them. And above all not expect something that can merely amuse you, to "save" or elevate you. And it is also silly constantly to claim one is "saving" others or "being saved." At the end, vain people are less bothersome than proud people.

So let's have some fun: Montherlant doesn't know Latin very well, but he's one of those people who are quite proud of knowing it, and then, a Latin quotation always sounds good in a declamation. When he evokes the Emperor Constantine, he could not fail to play on the well-known words: *In hoc signo vinces.* He cries his scorn for the Galilean: *In hoc signo fuges.* That's really opening

---

[181] The last words of Julian the Apostate (Emperor of Rome, 361–363) were supposedly "Thou hast conquered, Galilean," recognizing the triumph of Christ. This, of course, is the opposite.

[182] "Betrayal" in his language is merely a synonym for "changeover" or "alternation." True, he puts it in quotation marks. But how he would regret missing one: "Will we be there to betray once more." *Solstice de Juin* ("June Solstice"), p. 15.—J.G.

one's mouth too wide and letting out a false note. The Galilean, who decidedly is God, has already taken his revenge by feeding him this barbarism.[183]

November 9

It is my profession to produce *Normaliens*. This is a species I know pretty well. I don't think there is, anywhere in France, a gathering of young people more devoted to beauty, to truth, to all the ideal values, than in the École Normale or in a class preparing for the École Normale, a *khâgne*. But then, too, no doubt, nowhere can one see what an evil power culture can have, what a vile instrument the *Logos* can be.[184] A rather large number of these *khâgneux* and *Normaliens* go on to have brilliant careers in French society. And some of them without ever betraying their first vocation. But a few others are among the most notorious adventurers in business, politics, or journalism.

There is in every good *khâgneux*, at the same time as a mind able to devote itself to noble, disinterested research, a dangerous dialectical skill from which he is always tempted to profit. The practice of the *Logos* makes him capable of doing anything at all, to serve a lie as well as the truth. Among these marvelous young men I deal with every year, I have hardly any difficulty in discerning, unfortunately, those who a certain lack of character, too much greed, too much haste, or their very excess of cleverness will turn into the new sophists, serving institutionalized power—vile servants of the strongest, whoever the strongest may be. They are "maids of all work." Thus each class of *Normaliens* has its lot of *Graeculi esurientes*.[185]

One of the latest products of that ambiguous discipline seems to be this Pucheu,* from the class of 1919. In a hurry to make his way, he immediately gave up on the *Agrégation*,[186] left the University for business—from history to the steel industry—and, from boardroom to boardroom, from committee to committee, rose to be Minister of the Interior today, in an administration where, under the guise of maintaining order and virtue, he devotes himself to safeguarding the interests of the Trusts that gave him his position. It is said that he boasts of "holding France in place for at least fifteen years." Through his *Logos* and his police, no doubt. But his classmates say he was wrong not to prepare for the *Agrégation* in History: he would be less sure of it.

Other masterpieces of the École and *Logos*: Déat, Brasillach, etc. . . .

---

[183] Montherlant is using the wrong form of the verb *fugere* ("to flee")—no small matter in Latin. *In hoc signo vinces* means "in this sign, you will conquer" and supposedly appeared to the Roman Emperor Constantine in a dream. Christ ("the Galilean") told him he should use the sign of the cross against his enemies.

[184] Guéhenno is using this theological term in the general, secular sense of language, mind, reason.

[185] "Hungry little Greeks." An expression used by the Romans to mock the conquered Greeks, some of whom were their teachers.

[186] A long competitive examination—in the humanities, five days of written tests, followed by an oral—that can lead to a university career. The next entry is November 11: the day of the Armistice that ended World War I.

November 11

All demonstrations are forbidden today. Students will be kept in school until seven in the evening...A good way, after all, to make them think together of what each one might perhaps have forgotten if he were left to himself.

November 12

Hitler spoke about November 9.[187] A rather embarrassed speech, all in all, in which he explains that if he hasn't already occupied Leningrad and Moscow, it is because he doesn't do anything by the clock, he doesn't particularly care about that. And he warns America that Berlin does not claim to be the capital of the world, but that Washington will never be the capital, either. (So would that be London or Paris?) But it will be a long time before there is a capital of the world.

Some Catholics reproach me for considering Pascal with my whole mind. That would supposedly be a way to understand nothing. One must be irrational oneself, they explain, to understand the irrational: in other words give up trying to understand. Must one also be mad to understand madmen?

As for me, I dislike the idea of finding a kind of pleasure in not understanding. I can't stand those who think there is never enough mystery, people who add to it as much as possible. One must try to live with clarity.

Most contemporary Catholics expect us to speak of Pascal as a saint, in an edifying way. But if we denounce his paralogisms, it becomes obvious that the *Pensées* are decidedly insufficient to establish Catholic truth, so they suddenly turn around and treat him as a heretic. They expect him to be useful to them. If not...

Nothing is more intolerable than a mind which always postulates that all education can only have the goal of justifying its own prejudices. And what an insult to Pascal, using him only to justify one's own conformism, one's habits, one's flabby, earthly religion. They cut everything down to their size. And perhaps in the end what they hate the most, in my way of talking about it, is the care I take to show what his faith really was: terribly hard and demanding. They shrink before those conclusions—conclusions they are quite decided not to draw. They "love" Pascal, like music or tennis, but having read him would not change their lives in the slightest, of course, as they are all too sure they are Catholics from the start. Come to think of it, do they read him?

November 17

"What I wanted to do in criticism," writes Sainte-Beuve,* "was to introduce a sort of *charm* into it, and at the same time more *reality* than what was there before—in a word, poetry and at the same time a bit of *physiology*. Physiology has gained its place through the years." (*Nos poisons* ["Our Poisons"], p. 120.)

---

[187] The anniversary of the 1923 "Beer Hall putsch" in Munich, a failed Nazi coup attempt which sent Hitler to prison. November 9, 1941 was also the day the British destroyed an Italian-German convoy on its way to Libya.

I came upon these lines yesterday and they seemed to me a new warning. As I get older, "a sort of charm" is what I increasingly hope to be able to put into my writings and into my life itself. I have worked too much all my life. But perhaps "charm" cannot be learned or acquired. At least, if I thought of it all the time, I might manage a bit of relaxation. There is something "brusque" in me that disgusts me. ("To be nice, calm, and strong," J...used to say. Are these not, precisely, the instruments of charm?)

Live as an artist, not as an ideologue.

November 21

All the display windows of Rive Gauche, the German bookstore on Boulevard Saint-Michel, were shattered last night. It's the second time. The occupying authorities demanded that everything be repaired by the end of the day. But all day long, students walked by the piles of broken glass with their mouths shut, but laughing and talking to each other with their eyes. One of the windows was filled with photographs of Montherlant at every age (two years old with his maid, ten years old with his mother), of his first letters to friends, his first literary essays. The *Childhoods of Montherlant*. All that was smashed to pieces by the explosion of the grenades. What an irreparable loss!

"General Weygand is retiring." We gather the occupying authorities demanded his recall and Vichy obeyed. To crown it all, while relieving him of his duties, the Marshal is awarding him the Order of the Nation.[188] That makes a lot of lies.

They are quietly leading us into a war with England.

English offensive in Libya. But the news from Russia is not good.

November 25

It is no doubt rather remarkable that attacks on individualism are almost always the work of pretentious egoists who long for tyranny. They have doubts only about other people's ego, not their own. They preach so well and advise us so eloquently to lose ourselves in the state or the Party only in order to make sure they have an easier reign.

On Sunday, Paulhan (it could only be him) dragged me off to the Society for Psychic Studies. A gentleman in striped pants and a black jacket gave us a lecture on astrology. He produced great proofs of the influence of the stars on the condition of men, not to mention on gravitation, on tides, the regularity of the seasons, and then on our loves and the menstruation of women. How could we not have noticed that the angle the Champs-Élysées makes with the meridian line—that avenue which goes from the Arch of the Carrousel to the Arch of Triumph—is precisely the angle of the ecliptic; that the sun sets twice a year in the very axis of this avenue under the Arch of Triumph on the day Napoleon

---

[188] A distinction officially given for "services or acts of exceptional devotion performed for France at the risk of one's life."

was born and 18 Brumaire;[189] that the lid of the Emperor's tomb in the Invalides has precisely the form of the zodiacal sign of the Dragon, only reversed and flattened, etc. After that, how can one doubt that Paris had been promised to Bonaparte by the stars themselves?

But we had come especially to hear the news from "clairvoyants." They only showed us two. The first was a dyed blonde with a strange, rather handsome face, tense and serious. She read, in coffee grounds, the fate of three or four old ladies who had come to the meeting as we did; their age did not seem to have made them less curious about the future. She promised them lots of good things, advising them only to watch out for their legs. An accident can happen so quickly. The second clairvoyant, a brusque, curt, vulgar brunette, had other methods and a very different power. All she needed, to see into the depths of the future, was her glove and her hat. But what trembling did she subject them to, rubbing them, stretching them, beating them hard enough to burst their stitches. But the fluid went through. A very round man with the face of a born cuckold wanted to know what heaven had in store for him. He had a fine black hat. Here is what the clairvoyant pulled out of the hat after a few skillful questions:

"I see, I see..." (silence) "Your wife is not in the room?"

The patient: "No."

"Yes, but she's inside more often than out, right?"

"That is correct."

"Give me your hand. Ah! You do have a lot of fluid!"

"Correct."

"Yeah, well, I'm telling you, things aren't going good at home. Right?"

Then the poor man had to hear that he needed to be careful about his reflexes, he was kind of violent, his wife was playing fast and loose with him, he had a linoleum floor in the hall, he had two fellow workers in the shop, a tall one and a short one.

The patient: "That's correct."

"Yes, and the tall one uses the file and the short one turns the screws."

"That's correct."

The poor man was just reciting to her, out of control. She was reading him like a book.

"Well, remember what I'm gonna tell you: You're gonna leave her pretty soon, your wife, and watch out! The sooner the better."

"Correct, correct," the man answered, in a daze.

Nobody laughed; we were a bit ashamed of being there.

I haven't yet read in the papers that the patient killed his wife in the past three days. Let us wait, and if he fails to do so, it won't be the clairvoyant's fault.

[189] The day of Napoleon's coup d'état, November 19, 1799—that is, "18 Brumaire," Year VIII of the new Revolutionary Calendar. For more on that calendar, see note 225, p. 159.

As we went out, we found ourselves next to the two prophetesses. The brunette was complaining to the blonde about her fatigue.

"What a bad house!" she was saying.

"Why is that?" we asked.

"It's hard to say. There are days like that, when there are too many radiations..." and she stretched her body, which was pierced by rays of another light.

Charlatan or sibyl? Who will ever know?

November 28

The other evening Drieu reported the rumor from the German embassy that the Marshal was resigning. I'm inclined to think he is threatening to resign: it could be a fairly good way of resisting their new demands. According to another rumor, Italy is making a separate peace treaty with England. Living like this without knowing anything is one of our miseries. Nothing we can count on to construct the slightest reasoning, the slightest hope, in a sort of mental cloud made of vague rumors, false news, self-serving lies, and idiotic illusions. In this blurry world, courage is as vain as fear. Another habit we must get used to: being cold, after being hungry. We huddle up more and more. The worst is that all this suffering may well be just silly. For the struggle is not about the fate of France, it is about the fate of Europe, of two or three empires, and there is something silly about judging all that from the point of view of France. But we cannot do otherwise. For a sick man who is afraid of death, the edge of his bed is the limit of the world.

Drieu has published a new essay: *Notes to Understand the Century*. A hundred and eighty pages, a few texts sophistically employed, and sheer nerve are all he needs to throw together a philosophy of history. The book does not lack a certain movement, but it is terribly unreliable. The Middle Ages were the real Renaissance, according to him. The Renaissance and the last three centuries were merely the decadence of the Middle Ages. Luckily we are entering the new Middle Ages at last, under the sign of the swastika. What verbalism!

I can accept the idea that history is only what the living agree that it is, and I know that the past is merely the reading we make of it according to our hearts, and that at each Revolution we give it a new reading. But, Drieu, we need another force, a force from further away than the one that drives you. In the name of what, of whom, do you speak? Who do you represent? What new man driven by what old forces as yet unrevealed, and thus able to re-read the past as well as to command in the future?

December 3

The 18th arrondissement (Montmartre) is being punished. Curfew at 5:30 p.m., etc. For once, I was able to get some reasonably precise information. In a bordello at 41 Rue Championnet the other evening, German officers were enjoying themselves with the ladies. The idea comes to them to turn on the record player.

A time bomb was hidden in the record player. The bomb exploded. Three of those ladies and two of those gentlemen were killed. *Heldentod*,[190] my friend added amusingly when he told me the news; and he spoke of the noble letters which would tell their families and all Germany of the death of those heroes.

Nothing is more dismal than the posturing of servitude. That is what I call the poor efforts of those men of letters who can't keep quiet because of their habit of showing off. They would like to show a bit of courage in their writings occasionally; but at the first courageous word they may have ventured, terror returns immediately to make them feed some compliment to the authorities watching over them. Every criticism turns into a bow that degrades them still more.

I read this in a recent book: "The German knows the truth. The truth is this: the Germans may have conquered France, but that will not give them French painters and they know it as well as I do." What daring! But the author adds, in the same breath: "And they certainly hope not." And that little phrase is the posturing of servitude to get the rest through... So why don't you just keep quiet? Who is forcing you to posture?

Michelet speaks of the contortions and posturing of the slaves whose life had been spared by the emperor; he would give them freedom if, in the midst of the lions and tigers, they succeeded in going through the circus carrying an egg rolling on a plate. But that was a question of life and liberty. *Our* posturers are merely afraid of being forgotten.

But perhaps this is not so serious. I'm still making my old mistake. The history of these last two centuries led us to give the man of letters credit that he does not deserve. He is, most often, an entertainer among other entertainers. And to assure his welcome, like any other salaried employee, he sometimes postures before the boss.

A new armed attack on Boulevard Magenta. A German officer killed. Now it's the turn of the 10th arrondissement to be punished. And all Paris is threatened with the most vigorous reprisals if we do not denounce the guilty parties before December 10.

God owes his existence to the confusion of the human mind. This morning, that struck me as glaringly obvious as I listened to young people talking about their faith. They were celebrating or denying God with the same frenzy. But aside from the fact that each of them would have been quite hard put to define him if asked, you couldn't have found two of them with the same definition. God is the noblest of our vague ideas. The only way of believing in him seems to be not to wonder too much about what he is. He may be everything we lack but we lack so many things... Rarely have I better understood the revolutionary character of clear, distinct ideas than when I was listening to them ramble on.

I did not dare take the discussion very far and show them what "monsters" they are without knowing it, what paralogisms they were contenting themselves with, believing something quite different from what they think they believe, and

---

[190] "A heroic death." The German word has an old military history but was particularly favored by the Nazis.

what contradictions they are living with. All the same, I lit a fire in front of the hive and that was enough to stir up a fine buzz. I could no longer leave. At noon, all of them were still around me, killing me with questions, each wrestling with himself and with that God who exists or does not exist. Nothing excites us more than what we lack, and vague ideas enjoy a great deal of prestige.

There are as many Descartes as there are Descartes commentators. Each one turns the text to suit himself: Delbos, Chevalier, Gilson, Gouhier...But there is only one Cartesianism. If I were in those gentlemen's shoes, I'd be careful. There is, no doubt, a good chance that the real Descartes is the one recognized by universal consent: the founder of Cartesianism.

D...has become a seminarian and writes that he prays for me often. I ask you, he adds, not to take offense at what you may consider silly naïveté or the maneuver of a "converter." No, no, D..., I even believe in the efficacy of your prayers. I don't at all think it useless that men should think about each other a great deal and I thank you for it.

December 5

New armed attacks by the Resistance. We're sick of this atmosphere of murder.

L...has a strange profession.[191] As he can understand a large number of languages, the Ministry of Information gave him the task of listening to various radios; he spends his nights listening to the world, and every morning he writes up a report. There are, no doubt, few men better informed than he is. He knows everything anyone can know, allowing for censorship, about the propaganda spewing out all over.

The news he's bringing back these days is comforting, after all. Japan is hesitating, out of breath: it absolutely needs Indochina and Thailand in order to eat this winter, but America knows what urgent needs are pushing it. The Russian-German war is increasingly taking on the character of the Sino-Japanese war. The German army only holds the big centers in Russia. It is at a standstill before Moscow. Behind it Russian bands are organizing and every day the guerrillas are growing in strength and number. Let us be patient.

Last night around 5:00 a.m., I wake up with a start as the phone is ringing. I run to pick up the phone. And I wait.

"Here are three messages. First message, 22.30.15.20, etc."

I shout that I don't understand, while the enumeration of numbers continues.

"You don't understand...(A short silence.) Guéhenno?"

"Yes."

"This is Touchard. You didn't get a letter from Commune this morning?"

"No, I don't understand."

"Well, you'll get it. Just take these messages. First message 22.30.15..."

---

[191] Undoubtedly Guéhenno's former student and friend, Armand Robin.* Oddly enough, we know from Jean Paulhan's correspondence that he is also "X...", the poet Guéhenno threw out of his house on August 4, 1940.

"I don't get it. Go to hell."

I hang up violently.

A bad practical joke, a test by the police, entrapment by a snitch? I lose myself in conjectures. What a weird life!

December 8

From now on until further notice, we can no longer go out between 5 p.m. and 5 a.m., the Metro will stop running at 5:30, the restaurants will close, etc.

It is 6:30, I watch night fall. Not a sound, not a whisper. This is Paris!

Behind the window panes ("For the duration of the curfew, windows must be closed," the authorities have ordered), the people in the house facing mine are looking, as I am, at the empty street. We wave to each other. Prison solidarity. But suddenly, in an inner courtyard toward the end of the street, the sound of a loud bugle call: a cocky Parisian kid is thumbing his nose at our servitude.

December 10

Sunday morning Japanese planes bombed the Hawaiian Islands, the Philippines, Hong Kong, and Singapore. The war has now spread all over the world. News has come in every hour since then, proclaiming American and English catastrophes. Vichy-Footit[192] trumpets them out as if they were its own victories.

I am too full of emotion to note anything here. The world is undergoing a revolution, and all France is doing is watching, like a coward: the mistake committed in June '40 appears more enormous every day. Whatever may happen, France can no longer be anything but what the victor will allow it to be.

Again this evening, all Paris will be in bed by 10:00 like a punished child.

December 12

(Sick for a few days, I was unable to go to work on Thursday morning.)

The firing squads are in action again. Eleven people in Brest the day before yesterday, five Parisians yesterday. The "crowning achievement of the campaign:" the police have announced the arrest of 1,200 Communists in the Free Zone, "which brings the number of Communists arrested since November 1 to 13,000." Now there's a victory for you!

A year ago, public opinion was limp and cowardly, ready for anything. Vichy and Berlin have worked so well together that now the whole country feels its servitude. It feels enslaved, not governed. It is bubbling with hatred and does not yet know what it wants, but at least it knows very well what it does not want: precisely everything it's being subjected to. I hear eminent members of the bourgeoisie say that "the Republic was not so bad." So why did they betray it and hand it over? But we haven't reached the depths of horror yet. Vengeance will

---

[192] Footit: the circus name of an English clown who had a career in Paris. Lautrec drew his portrait in a lithograph.

call for vengeance, for a long time. What man, or what event, could give this country back the sense of its own dignity? It is living in such conditions that for a long time it will only be able to act in reaction to outside events: Germany's defeat? The triumph of communism in Germany? The events themselves find it divided. France has lost the initiative of its thoughts and its actions.

But in fact perhaps there are no more nations. It is important how, and under what conditions, the world will change. How, under what conditions, will work and bread be distributed to each person? They've already settled the score of the German Caliban. The American and Soviet Calibans are still to come. Each of them has his own idea of the world and the best way of distributing the soup. O, the time when Caliban's mother heated the pot in the cave for her little family! But now we are all like the crowd of soldiers waiting for soup around a rolling kitchen. And the pot has been overturned, out of fear that there wasn't enough to go around!

Few Catholics have a sense of the paradoxical nature of their faith. They don't even like to see it emphasized. *Credo quia absurdum* is absolutely no longer their motto.[193] Their religion is hardly more than an indulgent set of regulations for life which they like to think is reasonable. What disarray and what surprise, the other day, when I was explicating to my class the conclusion of the funeral oration for Henrietta of England, those pages where the paradoxical faith of Bossuet bursts out so splendidly. The death of Henrietta of England at twenty-six, in all the splendor of her beauty and fortune, becomes a "miracle of grace." "God acted in haste," and that haste itself is a sign of his goodness. Bossuet drives the argument home with implacable rigor and force, and, to hear him talk, we can only rejoice that the blood of Jesus, with which Madame, thanks to her piety, was already "quite penetrated, quite colored," had passed all the way into the veins of this young, mortal woman to wake her into eternal life. This mystical realism, too, was so foreign to these young Catholics! It was extremely hard for me to communicate my own emotion to them. The ancients did say: "Those who die young are beloved of the Gods." But what a platitude, compared to what the Christian myth enables one to say about it. Bossuet actually found the way to the sublime in Christian paradox.

My friend Vaillant, to whom I was relating these things, remarked that calling religion "the opium of the people" no longer has any validity whatsoever. The people don't care a hoot about it. Now it is merely "the opium of the bourgeoisie." In other times, and not so long ago, the bourgeoisie was itself irreligious and counted on religion to lull the people into inaction, but at present they are overwhelmed and, not knowing where to turn, try to find tranquility and sleep in gibberish and a religion of pure habit: if they must die, let it be in their sleep.

December 16

(Still sick. Dizzy. Sweats. Extreme weakness. Nervous impatience.)

---

[193] *Credo quia absurdum*: "I believe because it is absurd." The Latin phrase is famous in theological discourse, supposedly invented by one of the Fathers of the Church.

The curfew has been brought back to midnight, but General von Stülpnagel is announcing new reprisals: "A fine of a billion francs on the Jews. Deportation of Jews and Communists to Germany, execution of a hundred Jews, Communists, and anarchists." Neither Jews nor Communists, he explains, are French, and X...comments in *Aujourd'hui*: "However severe the news may be, it was welcomed with relief by public opinion because it allows for innocence." Now there's something we should remember.

How long will this last? A year, two years, ten years perhaps. We'll have to find a way to live through this horror, to settle into it, to wait. But how? We're in blood up to our bellies and all around us. How can we not see it?

December 19

New attacks by the Resistance all over Paris and the outskirts of the city. But impossible to learn anything precise.

Is Vichy changing its policies? On Sunday, its radio protested (oh! timidly!) against the new German reprisals. And yesterday it dared to declare that "the *Saint-Denis* was not sunk by an English submarine." That is an accusation against Germany and Italy. Cordell Hull[194] told the American press: "The French will be able to stand up to Germany. France will be completely independent in the near future."

Many mysteries here.

The German armies are retreating in Russia. "An alignment of the fronts," according to Goebbels' propaganda. A total debacle, according to Stalin's propaganda. Wait and see. Yesterday I leafed through Tarlé's book *La Campagne de Russie 1812*, and I am ashamed of the wicked joy I felt for a moment. If Hitler's armies suffer what Napoleon's armies suffered, "Now that's a bit of all right!" as Fabrice's camp cook says.[195] The parallelism of the facts is unbelievable. Of the horrors, too, no doubt. Tarlé's book came out last March. The Occupation authorities would not let it appear today: too many French readers are going to rejoice as they read it and find comfort and hope in the narrative of so many horrors. Such are the finer feelings servitude is cultivating in us.

December 25

It's Christmas.

Yesterday my friend Bouché was trying to re-awaken the sense of joy in us. He had received a turkey and invited us. What a fête, when it was brought to the table, well browned and so fat, so fat. We had not eaten so much in 18 months.

Last night on the radio, I listened to Germany sing. The program was composed of folk songs from the all the provinces. It was often admirable. What

---

[194] Secretary of State during the Roosevelt administration (1933–1944).

[195] Fabrice (in some translations, Fabrizio) is the hero of Stendhal's *La Chartreuse de Parme* (*The Charterhouse of Parma*, 1839).

enthusiasm and what life. But an uncontrolled life, which always runs after triumph or disaster. Hitler announced three days ago that he was firing Marshal von Brauchitsch and was taking over the command of his armies, trusting only to his intuition from now on. Will it make the snow melt in Russia? Will it unfreeze his planes and tanks? Will it give clothes to his soldiers?

B . . . and I agreed yesterday that the French are no more conquered today than they were conquerors in 1919. Their mistake is to believe in their defeat. One mistake leads to the other. They will have to be made aware of both.

December 26

"We have been defeated. Do you want us to be despised into the bargain, and rightly so? That is what depends on us alone, and always will. The armed struggle is over, but as soon as we wish, the new struggle, the struggle of principles, character and mores will begin. Let us give our guests the spectacle of a faithful attachment to the country and to our friends, of incorruptible honesty and an incorruptible sense of duty, of all civic and domestic virtues; let us offer our present guests this friendly gift so that they may take it back home with them the day of their departure, which will come sooner or later. Let us take care not to incite them to despise us. The surest means of getting them to do so would obviously be to fear them inordinately or to try to give up our way of life to adopt theirs, and try to resemble them. Far from us, certainly, the senseless idea of urging individual provocations. But the safest attitude is to follow our own path everywhere as if we were absolutely among ourselves alone and to have with them only the relations that the circumstances impose . . . No doubt we will sink lower and lower, depending on the circumstances of chance and in part, too, depending on the intelligence and good will of those who have subjugated us. But to rise again—that depends on us alone. And assuredly, we will never recover any sort of prosperity if we do not know how to get it for ourselves, and more particularly if each of us does not act in his own domain as if the salvation of future generations rested with him alone."

That is Fichte,[196] speaking in 1807 to the students of Berlin, which was occupied by French troops.

The Dean of the Faculty of Medicine of Bordeaux probably thought it was clever to quote this text in a speech he has just given to his students. Such mischievousness seemed to him the height of daring and he is quite proud of it. But why did he follow this quotation with a commentary that was just so much posturing, the posturing of a slave? The Dean, above all concerned with "not making waves," found the way of presenting this text as something like an appeal for "Collaboration": the submission of the conquered people of times gone by supposedly authorized the submission of the conquered of today.

[196] Johann Gottlieb Fichte (*1762–1814*), a German philosopher.

Jean Guéhenno in 1942 in the courtyard of Lycée Louis-le-Grand, one of the schools where he taught. *Photo courtesy of Jean-Marie Guéhenno.*

1942

The year will surely be better; we are nearer to the end.

Hitler spoke to his people. What happened to the big fighter who was flexing his muscles a few months ago? No more cries of victory. Nothing but a prayer to God (on whom he had never relied so heavily) to save Germany. "Germany must listen to me if I say that I would have preferred peace to war." The author of *Mein Kampf* presents himself as someone who has worked for peace, distracted from his job, despite himself, by "bunglers." The Jew Ahasuerus is solely responsible. On further whole his appeal has a violently socialist tone, and this is no doubt significant. Is he afraid of a communist movement? "Comrades in the Party," he says, "I fought Marxism for years not because it was socialist, but because a socialism financed by the *Frankfurter Zeitung*[197] and the Jewish or non-Jewish aristocracy of money could only be a lie..." It seems this man does not quite know where, in his people, his real support may be.

Pétain spoke on the radio last night too, and was no less curious. The difficulties his master is struggling with are giving Vichy an unheard-of audacity. In a tone still modest, but insinuating, the Marshal explained that France was still something—an empire—that the occupying authorities would be well advised to understand... He complained of living in semi-exile, of only being semi-free, and if he did not denounce Germany by name as the author of all his misfortunes, he said enough about it for us to think only of Germany. Here and there, too, some curious words, against the press, the radio, and "the deserters" in London and... Paris. Strange!

There was a painful moment when he read a whole paragraph of his speech twice without realizing it. How could one not feel an immense surge of pity? That old man whose attention wavers at every moment—how could he represent France? Naturally, the Paris newspapers aren't breathing a word about his speech this morning.

One of the cleverest tricks of Action Française was to create a kind of snobbery of the intelligence. Since Maurras* presented himself as its unique defender,

---

[197] A daily newspaper that still exists today.

each of his supporters had every reason to think he was the keenest and subtlest of men after him. Unfortunately, their faces gave these young snobs away. They glowed with stupidity and pretentiousness, and it was painful to see the mind celebrated by such obvious idiots.

January 3

The Paris papers still haven't published Pétain's last radio address. But Déat* and all the other "deserters" are seething.

Moreover, Vichy is clearly frightened again and is back to flinging mud at England and Churchill; if they comment on the Marshal's speech, they pretend to consider it a speech about domestic politics. The fact is—and I did not sufficiently notice it the day before yesterday—the speech was also a strange admission of helplessness and a quasi-desperate plea to the French people.

January 7

One by one, the statues of Paris are disappearing, the balloon on Place des Ternes—Fargue amusingly said it looked like a vaporizer—Chappe and his telegraph, and the two pharmacists at the end of Boulevard Saint-Michel.[198] The other day, on the Place du Panthéon, I saw them taking down Rousseau. Poor "Citizen," you're going to become the soul of a gun.

All that remains is bare pedestals in the middle of the public squares. Do they want us to think harder about the great absentees? It seems now that all those pedestals used to support the same statue, the statue of liberty.

January 11

Chateaubriand,* in *Mélanges littéraires* (p. 508), after recalling Lucan's vile verses in praise of Nero, seeks an excuse for that degradation and writes, in his magnificent manner:

> Show me, in the revolutions of empires, in those unhappy times when
> a whole people, like a corpse, no longer gives any sign of life—show me,
> I say, a class of men ever faithful to their honor and who never yielded
> to the power of events, nor to weariness from suffering: show me that,
> and I will immediately condemn men of letters. But if you cannot find

---

[198] The Germans were melting statues down for their metal, in short supply as the war went on. The statue on the Place des Ternes, designed by Bartholdi (1834–1904, the sculptor of the Statue of Liberty in New York), was erected in honor of men who used hot-air balloons to communicate with the army when Paris was under Prussian siege in 1870. Léon-Paul Fargue (1876–1947) was a poet who also chronicled Parisian life in prose. Claude Chappe set up the first telegraph in 1792 on the highest point in Paris, and a bronze statue on Boulevard Saint-Michel honored Pierre Joseph Pelletier and Joseph Bienaimé Caventou, who isolated quinine in 1820.

that order of generous citizens, single out the favorites of the muses for accusation no longer, but groan over all of humanity.

No doubt, but men usually hide their treason; "the favorites of the muses," if they are traitors, actually insist on proclaiming it from the rooftops. It's a question of habit: doesn't everything that comes from them deserve to be known? I even know some who have become traitors merely in order to be talked about. They are afraid of being forgotten and rekindle Reputation any way they can.

January 21

We are so cold we can hardly think of anything else.

January 24

For the last few weeks I've had the greatest difficulty in going on with this diary. It is because events, I feel, are now evolving in a predicted and in a sense inevitable way. What's the point of keeping the diary of stupidity and fatality? The defeat of Germany is absolutely certain from now on: the Germans themselves are beginning to realize it. But I don't even feel any joy in writing it down here. All we can do now is wait. The stupid things countries do are like the illnesses that strike individuals. They must go on to their end. Cancer cannot be stopped. From now on, we (and Hitler himself, perhaps) can see how all this will end. But the illness must continue to eat away at Europe and a few million young Europeans must die, pointlessly.

But perhaps it is necessary to be outside of the fight, as we are, to see how useless and stupid it really is.

Toward ten o'clock on the night before last, bombs fell close enough to the house to make the window-panes and lamps shake. Around Le Bourget, it seemed to me. I couldn't get any specific information. Apparently the snow makes it easier for them to spot their targets. It has been a long time since the English came…

January 25

How could I have written what I wrote yesterday? How ridiculous all that is. Do I know if Germany will be defeated or not? Rather, I'm afraid today of what will happen this spring. The Russians may be worn out by April. And then… How can I come up with one clear idea? Not to think at all would be my wish. Just one thing remains certain: the base stupidity of these times.

January 26

Old Madame Étienne, the concierge of number 7, has died. She will have worked the bell-pull until her very last hour.[199] She was already very weak yesterday

---

[199] Guéhenno lived at 9 Rue des Lilas in the 19th arrondissement; after hours, tenants had to ring the bell of the concierge's *loge* to enter (see note 149, p. 92), and she had to pull on a rope to let them in.

evening. But she opened the door for the tenants until late into the night. She was found lying on the floor this morning around nine o'clock, numb with cold, in her unheated little apartment. She died a few moments later. She said to us a few days ago: "It really bothers me to go like this, without seeing my prisoner again, and leaving France in such deep misery." In her was all the delicacy and kindness of Paris.

We have no master but ourselves, and that master must be tough…

January 27

I have ample proof, unfortunately, that the teaching of literature in the Sorbonne and the Universities has become pathetic. The abuse of history, of the footnotes of history, has destroyed all critical sense and taste. I know a professor who spent a whole year giving a commentary on Lamartine's* "*Le Lac.*" He traced the history of a little pink or blue notebook in which Lamartine had scrawled a few stanzas of his poem. He related what hands it passed through, he counted the pages, analyzed them…That required several lectures. When the last one came around, neither he nor his students had read the poem yet. To these so-called historians, it seems that all the artists of the past suffered, wrote, and lived only to provide matter for a few bibliographical index cards. They have confused research with education. We must have researchers. But "researchers" are not professors. Let the researchers do research and the professors teach. They are two distinct functions. No one has more admiration for scholars than I do. And yet I would wish them never to lack a sense of quality, a more global approach, and never forget that there is a hierarchy of values, ideas, and facts. But it's up to the École des Hautes Études and the scientific institutes to train them.[200] It's not up to the Sorbonne or the Universities. They have to train teachers who will then make men. They should awaken a great sense of curiosity in students, a sense of what is universal and human, so that later, when those students will themselves have become teachers, the fever of knowledge and a kind of human fervor become the driving force even in the smallest schools of the nation. But in the best of cases we train bookworms; from the age of twenty on, we accustom them to remain inside one drawer of index cards, we train them to compile notes and work their way through it. We cultivate petty vanity in them. For them, knowledge will always consist in adding a card to their file, like a gram to a kilo. Knowledge will distract them from their life, which it should rather enrich and govern. Their curiosity about small things will dispense them from being curious about great ones. Without critical sense, without taste, without

---

[200] The École Pratique des Hautes Études is one of the great research and educational institutions of France. Its goal is "practical" in that the research and methodology of its scholars in the social and hard sciences are designed to be taught in seminars and laboratories rather than simply published in scholarly or scientific journals.

ardor, mediocre researchers and worse teachers, they can only maintain our society of quantity in its vain illusion of being a civilization.

I always return to Barrès,* "my old enemy," with the same pleasure. Yesterday I re-read "An Empress of Solitude" in *Amori et dolori sacrum*.[201] After all, it doesn't matter what he thought, or thought he thought, or his biases and prejudices. He had an instinct for grandeur, the very shape of his sentence, the sort of emotional pull it produces, that uneasiness in his own skin, that tension at the end of its tether, those discouraged downturns, that effort eternally recommenced—it all moved me too much when I was twenty, and I have learned too much from him not to recognize my debt. And now that everything has been destroyed, now that all ideas are flattened, more than ever those all too vague words "To have some soul"—words that stirred us into fervor when we were twenty—seem to me to define the only possible revenge. To have some soul, at least to suffer well, if we can do nothing else. To have some soul, to say no.

Let me note here the joys that my profession sometimes affords me. There is no greater pleasure than to give a mind some confidence in itself. You have before you a boy who is all tied up in knots, distrustful, despairing; and a question you ask him, and you help and oblige him to answer, or a word from him that gives you something to latch on to—a few confused sentences he wrote that you bring into clarity—suddenly reveal his mind to himself and give him the thread out of the labyrinth in which he thought he was lost forever. And in fact, from test to test, now he is finding his own order, his light. Oh, one does not often have that opportunity! But then we feel paid a thousandfold for the countless hours of work and boredom. Such moments give us the idea of completely pure tenderness, completely intellectual, from mind to mind.

January 31

"Love thy neighbor as thyself," says Christianity; but that's not saying a lot, if it first advises each of us not to love ourselves. Christianity finds the creature suspect.

The Führer spoke last night. I listened to him scolding and howling without saying anything for two whole hours. But he has an admirable sense of oratorical action. The crowd around him was delirious with enthusiasm. Re-reading the text of his speech this morning in the *Pariser Zeitung*, I find nothing in it that has the slightest interest. It is all in the manner of conducting the paragraph, of varying the tones, scolding, acting modest, seeming to reflect, to offer himself as a sacrifice, to shout insults, to command. At the end it is not a prayer he is addressing to God, but a demand. Eloquence for the masses never had so great a master. No doubt at all that he writes his own speeches, as Napoleon drew up his battle plans himself. These are his battles. How not to think of those pathetic ministers we have known and know in France, who leave it to ministerial attachés to write

---

[201] *Dedicated to Love and Sorrow* (1903).

their speeches, either because they accord little importance to them, or because they are incapable of writing them. Has a great political leader ever acted that way? Can you imagine Mirabeau*, Danton*, or Robespierre* reading their secretaries' speeches? The movement of the speech must be the movement of the man himself. There is nothing more carnal than true eloquence. It is violent and dominates the crowd like a woman. But that takes real men. It is understandable that eunuchs simply give up. At least Hitler does not leave his work or his pleasure to others. One fine moment came when he shouted "If I am alive, there will not be another 1918!" But what did he mean? Has he sometimes envisaged the defeat of his country? And if that happened, has he decided to die?

I am reading M. Leroy's book on *Sainte-Beuve's* *Politics*. S.-B. would like his politics merely to be an "enlightened empiricism," a prudent administration of the circumstances and facts. And perhaps it would indeed be the wiser course while we wait for it to be the exact science desired by Saint-Simon and Comte.*[202] But I am afraid politics of that kind can only be the politics of those who watch, and watch for a long time. S.-B., like Renan,* hardly did anything but watch the show. Like Renan, he found his pleasure in SEEING. Renan himself writes this word in capital letters in "*The Future of Science*." But the actors in the show cannot be so prudent. Still less the politicians: they know they have to manage passions. And in a time like ours, what passions! The monstrous passions of the masses. I doubt that the most reasonable, most enlightened empiricism would suffice. Some passion is essential. Great politicians necessarily have great biases. Each one tries to remake the world according to his point of view. That is assuredly not prudent and turns history into one long brawl. But can it be otherwise? Order can only be found gradually, by struggling, and in the struggle. Those who are in it are hardly going listen to somebody who is looking at them and can only look at them.

And then, I distrust formulas that seem so prudent and so moderate. M. Maurras also speaks of "an organizing empiricism." And yet we know in the service of what frenzy, of what prejudice he puts that "empiricism," *Petano regnante*.[203]

My barber was a little Jewish workingman. But he no longer has the right to cut hair. He is the plague: he is forbidden to ply a trade that puts him in contact with the public. In order to live, he goes out after nightfall to cut the hair of his co-religionists in the neighborhood.

February 14

Nothing can express the monotony and the resigned stupidity of life in Paris. It is very cold. Everyone is huddled in his house without a fire. The only ones who

---

[202] For Saint-Simon, see note 40, p. 17. Auguste Comte (1798–1857) was the founder of positivism; he wished to apply scientific method and data-gathering to the social sciences. He invented the term *sociologie*.

[203] Latin for "under the reign of Pétain."

can eat are those who are lucky enough to have relatives in the provinces to send them provisions. It is scientifically designed scarcity. And during this time the old world is collapsing. The English were announcing the fall of Singapore as early as the day before yesterday. It seems that this country is dying, as if thrown on the scrap heap of the world. And its death is only the smallest little human interest story, cut off from great events. If I have written nothing in these notebooks, it's because it is not very useful, no doubt, to note that it is snowing, that we are hungry, that we are cold, that the executions are continuing, two or three every day (they no longer even have the honor of being on the front page of the papers), that people no longer think about it, except perhaps Marcel Déat, who adds a stanza to his cantata for the new order every morning.

I try to lose myself in work. I have begun a book that would oblige me to read an infinite number of books. It would be called *Jean-Jacques: In the Margin of the Confessions.*

February 16

Last night English radio suddenly announced that M. Churchill would speak an hour later, at 10:15. The old man wanted to announce the terrible news himself, to the Empire, to "his friends." His voice was grave and worried. He first evoked all the perils the Empire has already surmounted these past two years. He spoke about the difficulties of a struggle which obliges England to be present everywhere and divide its forces, but also about the reasons to continue to have hope, the example of tenacity and resolution that Soviet Russia had given last fall when the German troops were only a few kilometers away from Leningrad and Moscow, the fidelity of the Russians to their government at the height of the danger. He clearly asked if his old, free country would not have, in that ordeal, the same sangfroid and the same invincible confidence. And then in a dull voice, muffled by emotion, he said approximately this: "*I speak to you at home, to you all, my friends* . . . (and he enumerated all the lands in the Empire), *I speak to you in the shadow of a great defeat: Singapore has fallen.*"[204] It had incomparable grandeur. Everyone the world over who is attached to the great humanistic, industrious tradition of Europe through love and hope felt himself behind this old man in his London room. What a strange life we have, where the greatest events lose all their mystery and we hear the walls of Jericho falling and empires collapsing. But let us avoid words of ill omen!

February 20

The cold has settled in, and it gets on people's nerves and drives them mad. German requisitions have never been so heavy. I have this from a good source.

[204] In English in the diary. Guéhenno first translates it into French, unlike his Latin and German quotations. Churchill's exact words were "I speak under the shadow of a heavy and far-reaching . . . defeat."

Fifty-two thousand horses and a few hundred locomotives these last months. Naturally Vichy says nothing about it, and that is enough to judge this regime. For after all, no clause in the Armistice forbids it to make these requisitions public, every month, every week, and every day. It would be fairly clear what effect this publicity would have. But Vichy, like most governments, puts its faith in trickery alone, when it comes to governing. Only lies and illusions seem effective to them. All politicians think they must be Machiavellians. They don't realize that when everybody lies, being truthful can be a clever move. Among gamblers who made cheating the rule, the one who didn't cheat would beat everyone else. The worst of it is that Vichy is playing the enemy's game. It dissimulates those requisitions, after which the nation quite naturally blames the government alone for its pain and suffering. Will there never be a politician who believes in the force of truth and bases his action and power on it? I see no other means of taking this country out of the confusion and weakness in which it is losing itself, and awakening its conscience. And as for those requisitions, isn't it clear that making them public is the only means we have to rein in the voraciousness of the enemy?

"Community": it's a fashionable word now, the new hypocrisy. The fear of communism has invented this play on words. In reality, under the pretext of a war on individualism, all they want to do is maintain and conserve the community the way it is, each one remaining strictly in the place he occupies, rich or poor, privileged people or scapegoats. The poor would be quite ungrateful if they didn't understand that the privileged are more deserving than they are, by using their privileges only to serve the community, while they offer only their suffering; ungrateful if they were not won over and emulate that sacrifice. Vichy is quite content if the community dominates persons, as long as it doesn't dominate property. The privileged will find themselves quite at home.

February 24

Yesterday began the vile farce in Riom.[205] It is monstrous that the old man who exercised the greatest military authority during these last twenty years in the army itself, in the high Council of War, should be the one accusing others of being responsible for the defeat. It is true that he has no doubts about anything anymore. Yesterday, for the first time, when the prefects were being sworn in, he was greeted like Napoleon himself, as the band played the consul's march. What a farce!

"It's over," my friend Paulhan* told me on the phone, "For our friends."

"What?"

"Yes, it's over. Since yesterday afternoon."

---

[205] The town where the Vichy government tried Léon Blum* and other important figures in the Third Republic for their role in the fall of France.

So the plea for clemency sent to Berlin last week was useless, and they were shot yesterday afternoon. Seven men and three women, almost all of them from academia. We knew them a little because of that. For one of them, I can imagine what his last look was like, in front of the firing squad...[206]

February 26

I have some more information. The women were pardoned, no doubt. They shot the seven men Monday afternoon, one after the other, every five minutes...No notice appeared in the newspapers. Thus, when they tell us almost every morning that one or two men have been shot, it's only to keep us in suspense. The reality is still more horrible than anything we can know.

Hunger, cold, misery, terror. The country is in a sort of prostration. Nowhere can I feel life. Truth, the daily publication of the truth about all its suffering, could alone revive the country: first make it aware of its existence once again, then of its duty, and then of its faith. But the little world of intriguers in Vichy only thinks of saving itself, even if it is against France. It is enough for it to get by from day to day, in silence or through lies and intrigue.

Now the collaborationist writers are actually denouncing each other to the occupying authorities. *La Gerbe* and the *NRF* are accusing *Comœdia* of being soft.[207] It's not enough to betray your country. You have to betray it right, with all your heart. As the vanity of men of letters is involved, the farce is sometimes rather amusing. The author of *The Paths of Writing*[208] rages against the wishy-washiness of *Comœdia* more than anyone. That's because *Comœdia* didn't talk about his book.

I am trying to work on my Rousseau. Perhaps I will manage to stick to it. The subject itself is a great help to me. Experiencing as I do the life of my hero day after day, I am sometimes as curious about the next day as he might have been himself. We have just left Geneva, yesterday we saw Mme de Warens for the first time, last night we dreamt of her lovely eyes, and in a few days we'll be baptized in Torino—an apostate.[209] That makes many adventures, and soon we'll be sixteen.

I'm sure I could not find a better way of escaping from myself.

---

[206] "Our friends" here are the founders of the Resistance group in the Musée de l'Homme (see note 114, p. 60). Its leader was Boris Vildé, a linguist and ethnologist. The men were shot at Mont Valérien, the usual place of execution. The sentences of three women were commuted; they were deported and survived German concentration camps.

[207] *La Gerbe* was a pro-Nazi weekly (see note 44, p. 19). *Comœdia* was a Paris daily that covered theater, film, and literature; it became a collaborationist weekly during the Occupation, yet eminent non-fascist writers like Paul Claudel* and Jean Anouilh, actor-director Jean-Louis Barrault, and filmmaker Marcel Carné contributed to it.

[208] *Les Chemins de l'Écriture* by Bernard Grasset, founder of a publishing house that bears his name and is still alive and well in Paris.

[209] All events in Part I of Rousseau's *Confessions* (1765–1767). Madame de Warens was his (much older) aristocratic lover; he was born a Protestant, so his Catholic baptism made him an apostate.

March 3

The first thing Monday morning they told them they were going to be shot that day. Vildé saw his wife that morning and had the strength to tell her nothing. In the afternoon, they drove them from the prison in Fresnes to Mont Valérien. They went through all of Paris piled in a truck with their guards. They were singing. Each of them had a white paper square pinned over his heart and they were killed at nearly point-blank range. Vildé, as he had asked, was executed last.

March 4

Last night, in the moonlight, the English bombed the Renault factories in Boulogne-Billancourt. A massive, continuous bombing, really the first we have undergone. To see better, I walked up to Place des Fêtes with Vaillant,* but even from there you couldn't see very much. Nothing but rockets, the glow of fires from the other side of Paris, and twice, above the square, two planes like shadows in the clouds. We talked with the people. Nobody was indignant.[210] Most of them could hardly hide their jubilation. The occupying authorities had not even sounded the alarm. There were 500 dead and more than 500 wounded. At two o'clock this afternoon, all the sirens wailed—for nothing, of course. The occupying authorities were having fun.

Tomorrow morning, the execution of twenty hostages.

I'm working on Rousseau. There is surely no other writer in our literature into whose life I can enter so easily. From fourteen to twenty, I had the same experiences, the same adventures, the same temptations, and the same humiliations. But *he* was carried along by his genius, he touched the extremes. An idiotic sense of moderation has maintained me in the in-between. I worked, I put things together in a petty way, so that at twenty-one it was over, I was a student in the École Normale and a civil servant for life, sitting in an armchair. My mediocrity had saved me...or rather, damned me. Adventures, the real trials, were over. You only have the ones you deserve. And yet all I have to do truly to understand this, it seems to me, is to remember.

March 6

For the past three days, Vichy-Tartuffe has been chopping the dead to pieces to add to the horror. There are 500 dead, Vichy would like 2,000. To listen to its radio, it's Paris that the RAF bombed, and there never was a certain Renault factory in Boulogne-Billancourt.

Looking for distraction, I turned to the radio. A sermon. Reverend Panici is preaching for Lent at Notre-Dame. It is not just mediocre. If I were a real Catholic

---

[210] The next morning the collaborationist press was full of indignation at this bombing just outside Paris. Pictures of flattened buildings were featured on the front page along with the number of people killed.

I would blush for shame. The Reverend Father is speaking about order, which he defines as "what is suitable." "Suitable," "unsuitable," "fitting" are words that came back a hundred times in his sermon. Never has a more vile conformism been presented as the teaching of Jesus Christ.

March 16

A nation of men is already ridiculously vain, what can you expect from a nation of supermen!

These past few days, the papers have been publishing an incredible protest of "French intellectuals" against English "crimes":

> Great Britain, which has always displayed the deepest contempt for the colonial populations it had conquered, remains faithful to its conception that the Blacks begin in Calais. The country of millionaires and unemployed does not shrink from distributing, by means of its bombs, corpses, and unemployed. The country that tried to steal his brilliant invention from our great Branly,[211] which really never learned anything and never forgot anything either, has taken the liberty of a criminal impertinence (*sic*).

This idiotic text, full of irrelevancies, clearly translated from the German, is signed Abel Bonnard* of the Académie Française,[212] Ramon Fernandez, Jean Ajalbert, Denys Amiel, Brasillach,* Céline,* Maurice Donnay, de Chateaubriant, Drieu la Rochelle,* Abel Hermant, Luchaire, La Varende...

March 21

But the sweet light has returned. And that is stronger than everything. This morning, toward 11, I took the longest way to walk back home, along the quays. The air was silvery over the Seine, the palaces, the city, so peaceful. The sun was inflaming the poplar trees and the windows of the Louvre. The streets were just about empty. What silence! Never, for centuries, had spring set up its quarters

---

[211] Édouard Branly (1844–1940) invented one of the first great steps in radio communication, which then was further developed by the British physicist Oliver Lodge—and then developed still further by the Italian Guglielmo Marconi.

[212] Founded by Cardinal Richelieu in 1635, the forty members of this venerable institution are supposed to watch over the French language; new members are elected only when old ones die. Aside from those in the *Biographical Dictionary*, the most important names in this list of Collaborators are Jean Luchaire (b. 1901), a prominent journalist who urged support for Nazi Germany, fled there just before the Liberation of Paris, and was executed for treason in 1946, and Ramon Fernandez (1894–1944), a respected literary critic who wrote for the pro-Nazi press and served as a censor during the Occupation.

so tranquilly in Paris. The river was bubbling. The nymphs of the Seine had come into the city... Should I have turned my back on this felicity?

On the quays I bought *The New Voyage to the American Islands*, by the Reverend Father Labat. Something to make a fine trip next week: to go to the West Indies around 1700.[213]

March 25

The Triumph of Life. There is a good deal of lying in this new essay by Giono.* It displays the cunning of a peasant and the vanity of a man of letters. As usual he puts on his genius act. At the beginning of the book, a portrait—his portrait. He has composed a head for himself, with hair flying in the wind of disaster and eyes staring into the unfathomable. What an actor! I read him with embarrassment. Because I know him too well, I know too much, I have had too many occasions to see how he lies, even in October '39, and I can see through his tricks. I did read the first fifty pages nonetheless, but I doubt I can go any further. The sentences, the paragraphs move forward on rope-soled sandals. The walk of a thief. He has stolen from everybody. Sometimes he has the cynicism of Montherlant,* but reduced to a cheeky, slovenly vulgarity. He fishes around all over. Sometimes the false good humor of Péguy*: his repetitions and parentheses, but without his ardor, his deep breath. Sometimes the broad beat of Walt Whitman, and for a moment the sentence fills up like a sail. Naturally, a few Bergsonian themes: memory, being...[214] But nothing is really his except a kind of low trickiness. The defeat of France is a triumph for him, Jean Giono. There is no question of Pétain's stealing it from him. I told you so! he sums up. "The Return to the Soil" and "Youth" and "Handicrafts."[215] Who but I had foretold all that—I did, me, Jean Giono! And complaining, without complaining, while complaining that the ungrateful Pétain had not yet made him his first agent, if not his minister of propaganda. And it is true that no one could praise the stupidity, cowardice, and lies of these times better than he would.

And yet, he was a real poet and a great one. I remember that admirable night when we read the manuscript of *Hill of Destiny*,[216] and how in the morning I ran to Halévy* at Grasset's publishing house to tell him of our discovery. Two days later, the contract was signed. I have not had more happiness in my whole life as a reader... And we remained friends, as long as he was only a poet. But he was increasingly taken over by the prophet, the demagogue, and the liar, and we went our separate ways.

---

[213] Jean-Baptiste Labat published *Le Nouveau voyage aux isles de l'Amérique* in 1722. The quays of the Seine are lined with the stalls of booksellers, some specializing in rare books.

[214] Themes of the philosopher Henri Bergson (1859–1941).

[215] All themes of Vichy propaganda. See the *Translator's Introduction*, p. xviii, and the entry for December 29, 1940.

[216] *Colline* (1929), Giono's first novel.

March 27

I am making myself read Giono's book; I was unfair, the day before yesterday. The lie ends around the fiftieth page, or rather Giono finally imposes it on us, and—why beat around the bush—that really is his kind of genius. He forces us to live with him, in his world. The lie consists in this: living outside our time (and aware of that), he still claims to be a guide and a prophet. He burrows into his own world, and thus makes it easy for himself. It is not enough to say, like Guilloux,[217] that he can't think straight. He can't stand truths that might disturb him. He is voluntarily blind to them. And he rambles on as far as the eye can see. His book is so bad—sometimes unreadable—only because of his confidence in himself. But somehow in this vainglorious jumble, what an admirable taste for things can appear, what pleasure in naming them: just by naming them it seems that he is feeling them, caressing them with his thick god-like fingers, and creating them with letters. A poet! What a marvelous sense of life. Life is not truth. And if he lies, it is perhaps because life lies, too.

April 1

The other day, the students in the École de l'Enseignement Technique[218] put on a review and I could see myself on stage. They caught and portrayed details of my character rather well: gestures, my way of reading, and certain shouts. My mustache, in this clean-shaven world, was enough to make me recognizable. The satire was not nasty. On the contrary. But I always find it disagreeable to see myself. I hardly need someone else to be disgusted with myself . . . And then, it is rather painful to discover that even the best part of oneself may still be merely silly. I try to arouse the sense of what is rare and perfect in the souls of these technicians, who are almost solely interested in what is useful; so they see in me a master of abstruseness, a Valéry* maniac; my *khâgne* students, on the other hand, always tempted by the rare and the difficult, would instead discover in me, I am sure, my taste for common values, a Hugo maniac. Am I wrong to teach them each above all what they are not? But this spectacle of myself was not useless to me. I will try to reform. Perhaps I should be more cunning? I have too strong a taste for frankness, not enough for secrecy. Since then I have seen my technicians again. I reminded them of the last line of Spinoza's *Ethics*: "But all things excellent are as difficult as they are rare."

I have said "no" too much all my life. So much time lost in recriminations, in purely critical and negative tasks. We must say "yes," however little the times may help us, seek for what we can say "yes" to, and say it. It is the only way to heighten life.

---

[217] Louis Guilloux (1899–1980). A well-known novelist (the subject of Alice Kaplan's 2005 book *The Interpreter*) who had much in common with his friend Jean Guéhenno: the son of a Breton shoemaker, he, too, became an active left-wing intellectual. Their correspondence is voluminous.

[218] For this school, see note 125, p. 67.

April 9

For two weeks now, we have had some new entertainment. The English have come almost every night. The sirens howl. But people are fatalistic; they don't go down into the shelters anymore. They open the curtains of their windows to watch the fireworks from their beds. Unfortunately, our house is too low. I can only see the reflection of the bomb flashes in the sky. I can hear a plane rumbling by and I can guess its path. I follow its trace from those stars and exploding shells that pursue it. Sometimes the whole room is filled with light, and that lasts a few minutes. It's a rocket the English have fired to see better, and carried by the wind, it swings above the houses. The shadows of the trees turn around the bedroom, on the furniture, in the mirrors. The whole sky thunders. It comes and goes like a storm, but commanded by men. The sirens bellow again to signal the end of the show.

April 11

In Vichy, Laval* is having mysterious conversations with the Marshal. No doubt we have some more progress to make in shame and degradation.

April 13

It seems to me that I am escaping myself, little by little. I would also like to escape from these times; otherwise, how could one live? But here I am, more curious than I have ever been, more preoccupied with all those lives that I have not lived. I am going to make every effort to dream and keep the notebook of my dreams.

April 20

It's done. Hitler wanted Laval to be the head of the French government and he is. The old man is giving him his full power and has now become a ghost even before he has died. He spoke last night without much energy. We can guess that he yielded to an ultimatum. Two weeks of intrigues ended in a strange combination. There are, when all is said and done, two governments: military power in the hands of Darlan,* and civil power in the hands of Laval. Does the old man hope to save a bit of independence by playing one against the other? What is certain is that France, the 40 million French citizens, want neither one nor the other. The Pétain government had a few cowards behind it. The Laval-Darlan government has no one. Even the cowards are ashamed.

All along the Seine, between the Porte du Carrousel and Place de la Concorde, all the plane trees are displaying a big V around a cross of Lorraine carved deep into their bark. I admire the daring of a piece of work like that. No doubt it took a whole team. The occupying authorities had the inscriptions tarred over, but that makes them still more visible. The black stains attract the eye. And the inscriptions are going to grow for years, with the trees.

April 21

The clumsiness of our guests is truly admirable. They are taking care to do everything necessary to eliminate the possibility that any Frenchman would even be tempted to believe M. Laval. In their newspapers, Déat and the others may well celebrate the "new climate." But the "commander of Greater Paris" keeps publishing his "notices" as a commentary on their articles. These "notices" have been announcing "new measures" since this morning: fifty-five Communists and Jews will be shot in the next ten days as "jointly responsible," and fifty-five others will be deported.

These past days a poster could be seen on the corner of the street showing a muzhik, a Russian peasant (Stalin), opening the door of a France who is shouting to him "Get out!" But the night before last, people in the neighborhood pasted Laval's picture over the muzhik's face.

April 24

I am reading *Mein Kampf.* It is high time. A friend lent me a copy of this edition, the only complete one, which two brave translators tried to put out in 1934; it was immediately withdrawn from sale after the intervention of Hitler himself and the German Embassy. The French government gave in. Already! The very fact that Hitler wanted it banned should have opened their eyes. Why did I not read that profession of faith as soon as it was published? Perhaps I would have understood sooner! The translators were right. This book had become a bible of the German people and all French citizens should have been familiar with it: "When someone has thrown such precise threats in the face of a people (France)," say the translators in their preface, "normally, one no longer has the right to prevent it from knowing what those threats are."

April 27

Yesterday Hitler suddenly called in his deputies to ask them for new powers. What powers did he not already have! He gave an incredible lecture on the violent changes of empires. He went all the way back to the Flood, as usual, and then launched into his ordinary commonplaces: Jews! *Juden! Juden!* A good moment came when, with admirable sarcastic force, he enumerated all the reasons for the confidence (*Ermutigung*) of Churchill and those around him. But that positive part of the speech seems to be the last. He threatens civil servants and judges, and asks that his deputies grant him the right to dismiss anyone, civil servant or judge, who does not seem to him fully to be doing his duty: "*Ich erwarte dazu allerdings einiges: dass mir die Nation das Recht gibt, überall dort, wo nicht bedingungslos im Dienste der grösseren Aufgabe, bei der es um Sein oder Nichtsein geht, gehorcht und gehandelt wird, sofort einzugreifen und Heimat, Transportwesen, Verwaltung und Justiz* (what a list!) *haben nur einem einzigen Gedanken zu gehorchen, nämlich dem der Erringung des Sieges.*" What is happening? Can things be stirring in

Germany? Could people be organizing resistance here and there? Or did he simply have a fit? Are these new demands merely the sign of his frenzy? Now he is the supreme judge, for naturally, on Goering's order, all the deputies instantly rose to grant him what he was asking. Unfortunately I only heard the end of Goering's speech on the radio. "My deputies" then sang, according to the ritual, the *Deutschland über alles*.[219] But am I mistaken? It seems to me they didn't put their usual enthusiasm into it. Were they themselves dumbfounded by this tense, menacing speech?

But we can be sure that terror everywhere, *überall*, will make new progress.

April 28

"The Spanish tragedy is a mass grave. All the mistakes Europe is now dying from and trying to disgorge in frightful convulsions have come here to rot together...A cesspool like this, the image of what the world will be tomorrow..." (Bernanos* in 1938: *A Diary of My Times.*)[220]

May 4

I have lost myself in the life and work of Rousseau; now I fear it will be a grave and its silence, all too perfect. I have been reliving his life day after day but forgetting to live my own. I was hoping to work on something else at the same time. I am utterly unable to do so. I have even neglected this diary for a few weeks.

We are in that cesspool Bernanos was talking about. The worst is that we manage to live in it. Toward the end of a meager meal, we turn the dial on the radio. We calmly listen to them say that fifty-five hostages were shot in Lille, two divisions were exterminated in Russia, Malta has just undergone its 2,000th bombing, etc.... Then we savor that drop of wine we had been saving for the end of the dinner, we keep it in our mouths for a long time, dreaming of wine-cellars and barrels; finally we make up our minds to swallow it. And then we talk of the war that's coming, inevitably—civil war—and of this one and that one, too, who will have to be killed so they won't kill us. We walk over to the window. The first iris has opened in the garden...

I am ashamed of this monstrous apathy. Have I forgotten? I *know*, however. I saw men die. Could I no longer feel anything of that immense pity I was filled with at the age of twenty-five? Have these past twenty-five years worn away all our humanity?

---

[219] The German national anthem: "Germany above everything." The stanza with these words is no longer sung.

[220] *Les Grands Cimetières sous la lune* (literally "The Great Cemeteries under the Moon") p. 153: a passionate condemnation of Franco's side during the Spanish Civil War by the Catholic novelist Georges Bernanos. He had first supported Franco's revolt against the left-wing Republic but was horrified by the actions of Franco's fascists. Among other atrocities, they used Hitler's air force to devastate Spanish cities. France and the other democracies remained neutral.

May 7

The English have occupied Madagascar[221] the master Tartuffes of Vichy ful-
minate against it or say their prayers, each according to his genius. As events
evolve, the tremendous mistake of signing the Armistice appears ever more
clearly. The mistake was not to think of France as an empire, and to think all was
lost because metropolitan France was lost. Not one French politician took the
true measure of the war and saw that for the first time it concerned the whole
earth. It was ridiculous to think they could safeguard the Empire through a
European armistice. We would remain in the war, whether we liked it or not,
because of all the territories we possessed in the world: they would be so many
possible strategic bases in this planetary war. Simply crying "Uncle!" like children could not possibly be enough to keep them, and those who kept on fighting
would be sure to get the most they could out of it. Japan pulled Indochina into
its game; the Anglo-Saxons took Syria, the Pacific Islands, and Madagascar.
When will it be the turn of Senegal and North Africa? Everything will go!

The Anglo-Saxons are proclaiming that the French Empire will be restored
through victory, despite the Armistice; and no doubt they are sincere. But the
war may end in confusion and every one of those pieces of empire that we have
defended may become the object of bargaining. If that happens, the Armistice
will have been a sort of official abandonment and everything may be lost.

May 10

Sunday. Saint Joan of Arc's Day. Anniversary of the German offensive. The
radio is bellowing all over Europe: "We Germans are born to win," *Wir Deutschen
zu siegen*...The trombones are playing themselves hoarse. The triangles are
clinking. I think of those Tyroleans who used to lead bears through the streets of
Fougères in my youth. They had little bells on their hats and carried a whole
orchestra on their persons.

But this stupid, euphoric bear dance is going to last all day...I take refuge in
Rousseau.

May 11

Churchill, that old bulldog, spoke last night on the radio. His assurance con-
trasted with Hitler's anxious frenzy the other day. But it is clear that the game is still
only beginning. Answering Hitler's threats, he regretted that his burst of pity for
harmless civilians should have come to him so late, after the bombing of Warsaw,
Rotterdam, Belgrade, and countless French and English cities; and he solemnly
asked the German population to evacuate the industrial cities and ports and take
refuge in the countryside, from which they can contemplate at will the miseries to

---

[221] Madagascar was then a French colony, as were the other places listed at the end of the paragraph; Syria was a French mandate.

which they have subjected others for the past two years. The wheel has turned. It is their turn. The bombing will last all summer, then the fall, then the spring, then the summer, then the fall, then the spring again, etc.... Until the end.

May 16

Vichy is a kind of African kingdom or satrapy. There, defeat and servitude are celebrated with fanfare. A hundred generals watch the Company of the Guards parade by. After that, the court writers recite their new panegyric. I note, among other admirable strokes, that the Marshal called Pierre Laval to power for the same reasons that Jesus decided to build his church on Peter, that the Marshal is a new Joan of Arc, except for the difference in age...Never has this regime been so stupid.

The French West Indies after Madagascar. The Americans are settling in on Martinique. Déat rages: "France has resigned"; "No more Empire, no more France!" Indeed. But conversely, as long as the Empire was not conquered, France was not conquered. Your mistake is not to have seen that. And the whole Empire will come back into the war but despite you and against you, not under your orders. And North Africa could well be the decisive battle, one day.

The new school of history in France with its claims of "impartiality and objectivity" has a kind of horror for the philosophy of history. I see in it a great sign of our moral decline. Germany gave us this illness when it was already over it. That so-called impartiality was only impotence, cowardice, and dilettantism. Great peoples are peoples who dream. The philosophy of history of a people is its collective consciousness. Bossuet's* 1682 *Discourse on Universal History* was a hymn of confidence in the Catholic monarchy. Michelet's* *Introduction to Universal History* in 1831 displayed the new faith of France in its power to liberate and conquer. In those times, the French were striding ahead: they thought they would take possession of the future. They even subdued the past. It had to serve them. History was not the disenchanted exploration of necropolises. They went to the sources of life, of their life. Every great era naturally, spontaneously reads the whole past in a new way, and that is its philosophy of history. It is a strange mistake deliberately not to allow oneself to have a philosophy—the sign of a strange weakness of character. It means not allowing oneself—at the same time as judgment—choice and action, preferring all the dead to the living. They take pleasure in a life already lived in order to save themselves from living today. Impartiality? But truth is not neutral, history is a movement, life has a bias, it is a plus, not a zero. We must serve life and have a bias for it, go along with that plus, go forward and continue history. And what an odd way of respecting the dead themselves, to treat them as so many definitively abolished beings; choice and love are excluded. The empire of death is not that dust, nor that confusion. It is the deep humus which nourishes the forest. Peoples who are truly alive seek it out and find in it the principles of their hope and strength.

It is spring. In Germany, they have restarted the mechanism of enthusiasm. The days of great bloodletting have returned. I am sorry for the German people, who have been subjected to this moronic scientific mechanization through all the principles of mass psychology. Today, around 12:30, all the radio stations announced that they would soon transmit a special communiqué from the Führer's headquarters. And the show began: for more than half an hour the circus bands worked at creating an atmosphere of alarm and joy. The music was sometimes interrupted, the time for the speaker to announce: "You are going to hear a special communiqué from the Führer," and the impatience of the listening crowds kept growing. Finally toward 2:30, the music became graver, more solemn. A few great Wagnerian chords could be recognized. From the depths of the forest God himself was going to speak. A great silence, and the voice of Wotan pronounced: "The Führer's headquarters is announcing: Kerch has been taken.[222] The city and port are in our hands." Then a rumble of thunder and music, for the whole earth, played *Hosannas!*

Wotan has a patent from the Institute of *Massenpsychologie*.

But won't this propaganda, this mechanism, end up by defeating itself? Don't German women shudder every time they hear that frenetic music once again? Wotan is calling: "I need all your sons! Give them to me. What's that one doing, huddled in your skirts, woman of Germany? Come on, hurry up! Kerch has been taken, but I have a spot for him near Moscow. And that one? And that one? I want all of them! Russia is vast. There is room for many, many dead."

May 27

We are undoubtedly entering into the decisive months. Anxiety hardly ever leaves us. We can guess that the fate of the world is being played out—and what a game—at this moment near Kharkov. Perhaps in a few days we will know how much time our misfortune will still take. One or three or four years. The Russians are pushing forward near Krasnograd, the Germans near Izium. Each is trying to encircle the other... They are fighting day and night and men are dying by the tens of thousands. France watches in a sort of lethargy, and listens, still completely dazed. It has emerged from its surprise only to find its shame. Slowly it realizes that it would only succeed in living again, would only awake if it got into the action once again. But there is no way of doing that.

May 28

I am reading *Mein Kampf*. I'm forcing myself to read it, for although that frenzy is surprising at first, it soon grows tiresome. Four years ago at *Vendredi*,[223]

---

[222] One of the oldest cities in Ukraine, on the Sea of Azov. Wotan (Odin in Norse mythology) was the supreme god in the old Germanic religion and in Wagner's *Ring* operas.

[223] "Friday": Guéhenno ran this left-wing pacifist weekly from 1935 to 1938 with two other well-known intellectuals after resigning as editor-in-chief of *Europe* when the Communist Party took it over (see the *Translator's Introduction*, p. xiv).

someone I didn't know wrote me roughly every two weeks to give me his advice. He would write in small letters or capitals and underlined his sentences in blue or red pencil according to the importance he gave to his opinions. It's a mania well known to psychiatrists. I thought of him as I read Hitler.

Like him, Hitler uses italics or roman letters, lower case or upper. He surely regretted not being able to print his book like a poster. *His* truth must be strikingly obvious to you, dazzle you. Don't talk to him about that humble truth that some seek patiently and spell out prudently in plain language, so modest that it leaves the reader free to seek further. Hitler *knows*. He has always known. He has a marvelously simple mind with a marvelous gift for simplification. "Fortunately," he writes in the first line of his book, "I was predestined to be born in Braunau am Inn, a small town situated precisely at the border of Germany and Austria." And that is in fact the principle of his passion. It is there in Austria, but at the German border and born German, that he could feel it most strongly: the humiliation of belonging to a decadent empire devoured by Czechs, Hungarians, Slovaks, and Serbs, and the ambition of going back to the great Reich of Frederick and Bismarck. It was there that he could feel most strongly what it is to be part of a race, "and that the same blood must belong to the same empire." What was true in Braunau is a universal truth. Hitler's racism was at first merely anti-Czechism, anti-Slavism. In Vienna, Munich, and Berlin it became anti-Semitism and pan-Germanism. Then Hitler had no more doubts that there was a master race—his; and that he himself was the Master of masters. I am absolutely not drawing a caricature here. Hitler is deeply convinced that force and energy have an eternal privilege. That's what he calls "the aristocratic principle given by nature." Now, the superiority of the German people over all other peoples is obvious, and Hitler finds in himself the assurance of his own superiority over his fellow citizens. Many centuries ago Callicles already had the same certainties, and he never heard the small objections Socrates was making to him. Since then, the argument has never ceased.

May 29

The Marshal is still a firm believer the spirit of penitence and defines the duties of the army in this way: "We don't have to become aggressive..." Could he sense some impatience in the army of the Armistice itself, among the generals who were prisoners yesterday and who paid for their freedom with the oath not to fight anymore? "You must read my messages in your families... The country must know that we have been beaten. I spent three months after the Armistice saying it all around me, and for two years I have been repeating it to myself every morning. This must dispel any pretensions we may have."

But he will not persuade France of this, which sees more clearly every day that it was surprised and betrayed, not vanquished, and that nothing is over.

June 6

"We ordinarily think that the world of society is the theater of great passions; I think, on the contrary, that it is only the theater of little tastes, and one does not have to be very experienced to convince oneself that the great strokes of passion in all the genres were all produced by lonely, melancholy hearts." (Rousseau, *Memoir for the Education of M. de Sainte Marie*.)

June 8

London has begun re-transmitting American news reports twice a day. They are as ingenuously vain as can be, but also bold and confident. The theme music is in the jive genre, a kind of wild Negro dance. Then comes the news, as fast as possible: German cities collapsing, Japanese ships sinking; American planes, tanks, and ships filling the air, land, and sea. It seems that even the rhythm of the war has changed: it comforts you for a moment and then you're overwhelmed by the feeling of the foolishness in which we live.

June 9

Whitman, p. 7. His thought that his real life must remain unknown.

Laval knows better than anybody that politics is the art of the possible. But what is possible is based in reality. Now, reality is the NO of all France to what is, and what it is undergoing. It is only on this NO that it can be rebuilt. No one is more impossible than Laval himself.

June 11

"Bordeaux, June 10.—After a speedy, energetic investigation by the sub-prefect of Saintes, the mayor of Tounay-Bretonne has been suspended by a decree of the Prefect of Charente-Maritime."

This mayor was tolerating a Marianne[224] in his town hall, painted red (!), while the Marshal was only represented by a small photo.

The people of a nation has the songs it deserves. *La Marseillaise* for the soldiers of Year II, and for those of today, "Marshal, Here We Are."[225] Never have French songs been so vulgar and so inane. There is a whole song cycle about the Marshal. B...brought me a "Complaint for the Present Times" in thirteen stanzas. It reeks of stupidity, forgery, lying, and sycophancy. Here's the first stanza:

---

[224] This female statue representing the French Republic had been traditional in town halls and other public spaces. It still is. See note 15, p. 4.

[225] Written in 1941, *Maréchal, nous voilà* unofficially replaced the *Marseillaise*—banned in the Occupied Zone—as the national anthem, since Pétain had replaced the *République Française* by the *État Français* (the "French State"). Year II (*l'An II*) is 1793 in the new Republican calendar established by the Revolutionary Convention: since the monarchy was abolished in 1792, that year became "Year I."

A gleam in the night, a presage of dawn,
What will day bring? Misfortune's spawn?
Pétain watches alone, from the top of the tower,
A motionless figure, his eyes going round,
What thoughts does he have in that sentry box,
What times will come out of his constant thoughts,
Like a statue standing high on the ground,
With motionless brow, but eyes going round?
A gleam in the night, a presage of dawn,
Will the night we are in be finally gone?

It is all just as strong as that. "Olde France" fabricated by swine!

This diary is not at all what I would like it to be. It is too external. I don't use it enough for inner prayer, to construct myself.

Life is escaping me. I do a hundred things, but not, perhaps, the one necessary thing. I still lack consistency of thought. My life is only the continuity of my habits, of my regular tasks. All the rest is chance. My memory is bad and I feel that the will, too, is a kind of memory.

All I have to do would be to better define to myself the relationship I have with this world. To succeed would be to make myself master of that relation and truly live.

I keep on with the Rousseau, but I'm afraid of losing myself in it. It's good to relive Rousseau's life and to watch *his suns* rise with him every morning. But I should also watch my own suns rising. I have grown older. The new day no longer surprises me.

I would like to find simplicity again. Twenty or thirty years ago, I thought I knew who I was and what I had to do in this world. Now I have trouble finding my way. How hard it is to grow old well. I cried out the revolt and hope of Caliban, and that came from the deepest part of my self, from my childhood. (Although books had already perverted me and taught me to put too much order in my cries.) Now Caliban needs to talk like a new man, the new lawgiver. A great simple heart could do so. But I lost myself in books. I was thick as thieves with them: I read, read endlessly, and now feel only despair at my ignorance. Sometimes the hunger for reading takes hold of me. Last night it was for the sequences and prose of the liturgy... But I am well aware that I will die starving. The only book one must discover and read is that one, unique book Mallarmé dreamed of, which will never be written. My soul, like my house, is littered with papers and knick-knacks. Perhaps I should burn all that.

June 16

"The man who, in a turbulent era, is turbulent himself, aggravates the harm and spreads it more and more, *but the man who persists in his thought forms the world around him.*" (Goethe, *Hermann and Dorothea*, quoted by Barrès, *Cahiers* ["Notebooks"] VI, p. 78.)

We do not have, cannot have, such high ambitions, but we know that our fidelity is not useless. Through this fidelity, thanks to it, France survives in this disaster, in this shame, in this chaos. And if we are faithful enough, perhaps in a year, in two years... Europe, exhausted by its very disorder, might form itself around France, around a certain high, pure idea of man that a few men will not have compromised for a moment.

For a week now, Jews have been forced to wear the yellow star and call public scorn upon themselves. Never have people been so nice to them. It's because there is no doubt nothing more vile than forcing a man to be ashamed of himself at every moment and the good people of Paris know it. As Nietzsche knew it. "Spare every man," he said, "from being ashamed."

Just by seeing the Jews of this neighborhood, we can verify how fully they represent "international capitalism": most are obviously wretchedly poor and all the working people are indignant that the authorities should try to dishonor poverty in this way.

June 19

The church of the 17th century condemned Pascal, but the church of the 20th century speaks of him as a sort of saint. The church of the 18th century condemned Rousseau, but the church of the 20th century speaks of him as the upholder of religion. If we are to believe M. Guillemin, the quarrel between Rousseau and the Encyclopedists is nothing less than the battle of good and evil, and the struggle of a saint against the enemy. His book, *Cette affaire infernale,*[226] quite clever besides, is a veritable brief for the canonization of that poor Jean-Jacques.

I can't abide those paralogisms: what probity is there in dragooning into the service of the Church writers whose books were burned by the same church in another era. Barrès and Péguy gave us the example of that horror of truth.

June 20

At Mauriac's* yesterday. He had wanted me to meet Guillemin, and "organize a corrida," he said. The corrida wasn't very lively, but it was not useless. I felt more keenly than ever what I should never do: this morning, I even doubt whether I should continue to write that long life of Rousseau. I'm afraid in the end it will seem no more than a work of scholarship. They'll think I merely wanted to put anecdotes in order, classify events and documents. Simple notes

---

[226] *That Infernal Affair.* Shortly after its publication, Henri Guillemin, a left-wing Catholic historian, was denounced by Brasillach's fascistic weekly *Je Suis Partout* (*I Am Everywhere*) and prudently fled France for Switzerland, Rousseau's native land.

on Rousseau would perhaps be better, notes where one could feel that I am in quest of a soul. All I want to do, if I can, is to recognize a man in all his truth—a man to whom I feel infinitely close, whom I neither love nor hate, but admire; and for whom I feel sorry.

Guillemin did not justify his sophisms or his annexations very well. But Mauriac intervened for a moment. "We don't want to annex anything, really," he said to me in an emotional voice. "But we would like to find Christ everywhere. We think he is everywhere. It is such a great thing, the Incarnation! But how hard it is to see its effect, in the world, in the whole world." And he closed his hands as if to hold a very tiny thing. "So we seek. Yes, we would like to find Christ everywhere." And this cry moved me far more than Guillemin's ratiocinations.

June 26

Laval is closing factories in France and then compelling the unemployed to leave for Germany.[227] And I do not know if there is anyone more representative of our miseries and degradation than those workers: to live and feed their families, they must, against their conscience, go manufacture weapons to destroy the very country in which they have put all their hope for twenty years—the Soviet Republic. But what world does Vichy think it's building in doing such violence to the soul of the masses? The masses will get their revenge.

No doubt we are going through the darkest weeks. Germany is going to win more battles, in Egypt, in Russia, and perhaps conquer the entire Mideast. We will need solid nerves. But those victories don't settle anything. Germany can build nothing on that immense hatred it has awakened everywhere. Hitler does not even garner, like Napoleon, the admiration of those he has subjugated. Europe is not even surprised. It watches the growing power of an infernal machine, but knows it will be broken.

Our memory retains everything. That's what makes the tragic element in history. The legend of Hitler might do the same harm in the 20th century that the legend of Napoleon did in the 19th. The legend left by such men is even more harmful than their actions. It insures that the cult of force will continue and makes newcomers have doubts about reason and justice.

The news more somber every morning, the fatigue of the year, hundreds of student papers to read, and now this foolishness: hay fever. I can't take any more.

And then the last days of the school year are all too moving: students come to see me at home. They talk more freely to me, and sometimes I discover that they are rather different from what I thought they were like. All year, I try to treat them only as minds. It is actually that which makes the greatness and purity of a class. There is nothing purer in the world. I don't want to know where they

---

[227] For the Compulsory Work Service, see note 7, p. xxxii.

come from, what their parents do, rich or poor... Their greater or lesser appetite for truth, their passion, their skill in seeking it out, makes all the difference between them in my eyes. But these conversations at the end of the year reveal them to me the way they are among their classmates, in their family, in the nation—already bound by all kinds of interests, "on board." I have pleasant surprises, but also disappointments.

All in all, what a mystery they are, these young men! Especially at this end of the year; I look at them with so much concern, at the idea that their whole future is postponed. How I would like to have given them a taste for lucidity and courage! But I'm beginning to know them well. I have seen a lot of them. How these young monsters know how to protect themselves. Don't trust them. They neither lend themselves nor give themselves.[228] Sometimes they make believe. Their fresh, shining skin is impenetrable, and the brightness of their eyes serves only to dazzle you and prevent you from seeing through to the bottom. They are nice, and inaccessible. They are getting ready to take hold of life, at any cost. That's the bottom line, and it is just; it's their turn. And we must repeat that to ourselves constantly in order to understand and sometimes excuse what they will become.

We are told that Pascal's fright before the infinite spaces and their silence[229] is a feeling shared by all men. But the longer I live, the more I am persuaded that it is not the irrational that frightens most men, but the rational. The great mass of minds only finds ease and pleasure in the irrational, in prejudices, superstitions, songs, music... It swims in that dark sea. It only fears understanding. And the greatest courage is needed to accept living only in clear ideas. Only lucidity is frightening. And Pascal himself would not have been so frightened before the depths of the skies if he had not been such a fine geometer.

I have just read more than 300 essays for the entry examination to a great scientific school, and it is hardly reassuring as far as the breadth of the human mind is concerned. You have to have such experiences truly to know what low habits still generally make up the life of the mind—and these are minds that have been subjected to strict discipline for ten or twelve years. No, common sense is not the most common thing in the world. But still we must continue to act as if it were. It will be. There is no other hope.

July 10

For some time now our guests have been committing their crimes in silence. They have been executing people every day in the prisons, but no notice was

---

[228] Guéhenno is thinking of a maxim in Montaigne's *Essays*: "one must lend oneself to others and only give oneself to oneself" (*il faut se prêter à autrui et ne se donner qu'à soi-même, Essais*, III, 10).

[229] "The eternal silence of those infinite spaces fills me with fear" is a famous line from Pascal's *Pensées: Le silence éternel de ces espaces infinis m'effraient.*

published. Just today they were tempted by publicity once again, as if not having the glory of all their crimes was finally beginning to weigh on them. At five o'clock in the corridors of the République Metro station, I saw a crowd gathering around a yellow poster (already ripped up). People said nothing, but horror was written on every face. It was so badly torn it was hard to read. But fifty yards away, another gathering. And this time the poster was intact. It's an announcement by the head of the SS in France,[230] who, moreover, does not give his name. He first addresses his revolting compliments to the great mass of the population for its discipline at work and its good conduct, but, he explains, the sabotage committed by a few is obliging him to take new measures: since the saboteurs run away and hide, he has therefore decided:

1. All male relatives of the runaways over eighteen (cousins and brothers-in-law included) will be shot;
2. The women will be sentenced to hard labor;
3. Children under eighteen will be sent to reform school.

July 11

Yesterday's notice has disappeared. It is not published in the papers this morning. M. Laval must have warned our guests that really, it was better to act without talking about it.

July 13

The notice is in all the papers today.

Yesterday, the distribution of prizes at school. By chance, I found myself seated near the house snitch. He alone among the lycée personnel was wearing the Vichy insignia. At least we've been forewarned.

This morning I learn that all the Jews in central Europe are going to be deported to Russia and their children put into camps.

Montolieu, July 17

Finally allowed to come back here, after two years, as the "accompanier" of a university train. I was the "head of the car," in charge of twenty little children, boys and girls, a veritable kindergarten. At the Line of Demarcation, slight incidents. Each child or each student should have been at the numbered seat of a chart of the train drawn up by the French and German authorities. But all kinds of mistakes had been made on both sides and it was a complete mess. Forty-odd children had to remain on the train platform in Paris; we can imagine their despair. At Vierzon, the occupying authorities naturally did not forget to inter-

---

[230] The SS was the "elite" Nazi organization most heavily responsible for committing crimes against humanity.

rogate a dozen little girls whom they treated like spies. At Châteauroux, we were in the "Free Zone," a strange country, a sort of principality where everyone, from children of six enrolled in "youth organizations" to "veterans" wearing *francisques* or Legion insignias, seemed to be in uniform.[231] Where is France?

I went to a little cemetery scorched by the sun. For a long time, L...and I sat there in the shade of a cypress, without talking. Nothing but a big slab of granite burning in my mouth, with lizards running on it and the light dancing, and all around the same eternal countryside, the great country sparkling and silent, and so absolutely identical to what it was two years ago when we left it and nine years ago when J...left it,[232] when we closed her under that stone. What difference between her and us? We returned—why shouldn't she? What does it mean to be dead? To be absent from certain things, but present for others, perhaps, as we ourselves had been for two years. Where is she?

July 18

Careful! "Past the age of forty, a man is responsible for his face" (da Vinci).

The village gravedigger, a foul-mouthed idiot who gets a bonus for every ditch he digs, meets old M..., who was sick all winter.

"You've really lost," he tells him (it's a way of saying: you've gotten thinner).

"What d'you mean?" answers old M..., who doesn't understand at first.

"You've really lost," the gravedigger says again and shows M...that his clothes are floating on him.

"Well you," old M...says, "you lost more than I did."

"How's that?"

"You didn't bury me."

The gravedigger rubs his nose, which is enormous.

July 19

I've gotten into *Dichtung und Wahrheit*[233]; I want to read it carefully during these two months. Right away, what self-assuredness! What stature! And at the same time, what humility! When most people tell their own story, they are only preoccupied by isolating what makes them different from others. They passionately seek their little difference and feel great pleasure in showing it—a wart, a desire, a spot on their muzzle that distinguishes them from the species, something they think they alone possess and which is enough, in their eyes, to

---

[231] The Legion was a French pro-Nazi paramilitary organization; the *francisque* was the emblem of Vichy (see note 6, p. xxxii).

[232] Guéhenno's deceased wife Jeanne (see the *Translator's Introduction*, p. xv); L...is, of course, their daughter Louisette.

[233] *Poetry and Truth*: Goethe's autobiography (Parts I–III, 1811–1813; Part IV published posthumously in 1835).

make them admirable. Goethe, on the contrary, is a man who knows everything that links him to the world:

> It seems that the main task of biography is to represent man in his temporal relationships, to show how much the world resists him, how much it favors him, how he forms from it a conception of the universe and of man; and, if he is an artist, a poet or a writer, how he reflects them outward. But for that, one condition is necessary which is, so to say, out of our grasp: that the individual know both himself and his century. Himself, to the extent that he has remained the same in all circumstances; the century, to the extent that it sweeps along with it those who want it and those who do not, and determines and shapes them, so that one can say that a man, if he were born only ten years earlier or later, would have been quite different, both as far as his own culture is concerned and the action he exerts outside of it. (pp. 12–13)

And that same preface gives us a glimpse of a remarkably noble sense of the function of the writer. No desire to show off, no ostentation, no vanity. He only tells his life to help those who trusted him to better understand his work, to "contribute in this way to the education of those who were educated with him in the past, and according to him." He knows he is responsible. He was a man whom others took for a model. It's the least he can do to let them know him exactly, to follow him still, or to stop doing so if they think it right. He has no need to interest them in him as if he were a magnificent monster. He will not cater to their vain, low curiosity. He is not expecting them to worship him. He is not preparing a chapel for himself: his memoirs, like his other books, have no other object than to offer his readers, once more, the opportunity of taking the measure of a man, and their own measure. That example will be himself—a man, it is true, in a rather large format. But he does not seem to think about that largeness, that greatness, as if the stars and fate alone had determined that.

And I note this epigraph:

Ὁ μὴ δαρεὶς ἄνθρωπος οὐ παιδεύεται

Man, if he is not beaten (skinned alive), does not grow.

July 25

The men of Vichy are greatly concerned to keep people in their zone ignorant of what's going on in the other one. To feel more at ease as they betray their country, they need to maintain public opinion in a degraded, lifeless state. Above all, nobody must know what the requisitions have been like, or that thousands of Frenchmen have been shot … In saying this as I say it, and putting in front of people's eyes the issue of *L'Oeuvre* announcing the new measures taken by the head of the SS, not only am I making myself suspicious and provoking the village stool-pigeons, but I can feel I'm making everybody uncomfortable. They don't want to believe me. As those figures became enormous, did they also become unbelievable? They would rather not know. They've gotten used to it. The men of Vichy have made two countries out of France, and they degrade one so that the Germans can cut the other's throat in tranquility.

One might have thought—such had been the enthusiasm of the last demonstrations before the elections—that France counted 38 million republicans in 1936.[234] What happened to them? The whole German people have gone Nazi; 7 million German Communists have become Nazis, but we are no better than they are.

July 27

"Nothing is more real than poetry; it is what is completely true only in another world." (Baudelaire, quoted by Crépet, *Mesures*, July 15, 1938.)

July 28

Night is falling, so gentle, so beautiful. The stars are rising, millions of worlds between which we are lost like a speck of dust in the folds of a coat. I listen to the gurgling of the fountain. It is gurgling about eternity. How can one imagine that tide of fire washing over the other end of Europe near Rostov at this very moment, and the frightful slaughter? How can we think that we are personally concerned by it? That people are dying for us at this very moment?

August 2

The graves of rich people, so dignified, so serious, between the tall cypresses— the last lie! False witnesses, sumptuous monuments of an eternal love that the members of one family supposedly have for each other, in death as in life. They want to be together, with the family, *in saecula saeculorum*.[235] Under those edifying stones, in those tombs, in the secret darkness, what storms there would be if their inhabitants were in death what they were in life, if they still had some memory, if they continued the "scenes" they made when they were alive! And since they're waiting for the Last Judgment, among all those people who know all about them, what opportunities for denunciation and vengeance! How could they not have taken better advantage of death, which could have returned them to solitude? The poor are more fortunate. Each alone in his hole in the ground with only his remorse and his memories. A score to settle between him and him. Nothing but him. He has as much peace as one can have.

---

[234] "Republicans" in the French sense, of course: those who support the Republic.

[235] Literally "for ages and ages": forever. The end of a line in the Latin hymn *Gloria Patri* ("Glory to the Father").

August 4

Yesterday, a "poetic" day, of the kind I would like to have more often. Perhaps I owe it to Thomas Mann. I had re-read *Death in Venice*, and it had taken me out of myself, out of my anxiety and my discipline, and inclined me to some kind of license. Daydreamed more than I worked. A delightful indolence: a state where the miracle of spontaneity happens at every moment, where it seems that all things touch you directly and you are naked, like a leaf whipped around by the wind.

The morning was spent in quest of memories for the portrait of my father I would like to write. Brittany. My part of the country. The beautiful chestnut trees. The little town. The "reds." The sordid war of the rich against the poor, my great hope, my life changed, my faith. And then I went to the grocer's funeral. The old church. Imagined thousands of bodies stretched out at this same spot where *she* was laid out in her turn, where, nine years ago...where in a few years...And all those chants, all that incense, those scents, all those promises, for her, the fat woman from whom I used to buy pepper and sugar. And crossing through the village, the last path, the last car. And the tomb opened and inside, M..., the mason, as comfortable as he would have been on a roof, working fast, putting that new coffin in its place, as close as possible to the others, allowing for the future.

On the way back, a friend and I had stopped a moment to chat with Pierre M...Pretty Mme K...walked by, followed by her little dog, and the little dog came over to be petted by Pierre M...and then ran to catch up with his mistress. She was going to buy bread. We were still there when she came by again, and once again the little dog left her to get petted by Pierre M...As for me, I hadn't noticed anything, but my friend has remarkable eyes. When we were alone:

"What traitors these dogs are," he said. "They give away all our secrets."

And as I did not understand, he said sententiously:

"The little dog dearly loves his mistress' lover."

It would have been good to work during the afternoon, but I was unable to do so. Thomas Mann, but also the book by Cumont about Eastern religions,[236] were going through my mind. My head was full of gods: Cybele, the Great Mother, the "mistress of wild beasts," and Attis and Isis, and Serapis, and Adonis, and Hormuz and Ahriman. All those gods that at least made death in the ancient world greater. We die more dully. Swastika, fasces, *francisque*. Emblems of modern stupidity. If we must have processions of morons, I prefer the adepts of Mithra. We no longer know how to be madmen, just cruel and stupid.

Toward evening, I went to "the end of the plain." The shadows were already long: I sat down at some distance from that fine line of trees along the river to

---

[236] The Belgian historian, philologist, and archeologist Franz Cumont (1868–1947). His best-known book was translated into English as *The Oriental Religions in Roman Paganism* (1911).

see it like a frieze in high relief against the background of the sky. Downstream, the cypresses of the "hut" closed the horizon. What admirable silence! A lovely girl in a nearby field was looking after sunflowers, all turned, like an imprisoned people, to the side the light would come from. She was cutting off the smallest flowers so that the biggest could grow further. "You have to leave only one at every stem," that young aristocrat said to me. I asked her for one of those cut flowers. On the path, along the river, a Spanish wood-cutter was pushing his oxen, which were dragging tree-trunks behind them. He was singing songs from his country at the top of his voice.

August 11

A visit to little old Benda* yesterday morning, in Carcassonne. I find him in the same furnished room he stumbled into when he had to leave Paris. What does he care! All he did, it seems to me, is hang the chromos with which his land-lord had beautified the room nearer to the ceiling, so as not to have them under his eyes. He's a sort of Spinoza. He is happy, he tells me, and enjoys a silence he has never known, writing his best books, feels miraculously young at seventy-six, at least as much as Gide*—that's what he said—he wears old clothes that a friend sent him from Paris and eats cans of food that the neighbors get for him (they took pity on him). And finally, to crown it all, he's rich, for they're going to publish one of his books in America: *The Ordeal of the Democracies*.[237] I hadn't been there for five minutes before he was already reading me his new work and his new plans of attack. He's after Gide, Valéry, Éluard, Giraudoux*—everybody. The only ones he spares are Roger Martin du Gard and Jules Romains. But Gide and Valéry are particularly irritating to him, and I can feel that he is slightly jeal-ous. "The status given to those people is inconceivable. That Gide and his *Journal*. Writing whatever comes into his head! What a method, and what pretentious-ness! What an idea. And Valéry? He has no consistency whatsoever, he contra-dicts himself freely and he doesn't care. An esthete. The worst of it is that people take him for a philosopher, and an intellectual to boot. It is astounding!" So Julien Benda is sharpening his little daggers against "those people." He'll get them all... He has taken all his manuscripts out of an old suitcase and reads me the strokes of which he is most proud. "What do you think of that?... And that?" I was able to get away around noon. He thinks he has not aged: "It's astonishing," he says to me amusingly. "This will have to stop!" But I noticed he has twitches on the left side of his face that would worry me, in his shoes. As for the war, he

---

[237] *La Grande épreuve des démocraties* was published in French by Éditions de la Maison Française in New York. In the next lines, Paul Éluard (1895–1952), first a Surrealist and then a Communist, is considered a major French poet; the novelist Roger Martin du Gard (1881–1958) won the Nobel Prize for Literature in 1937; Jules Romains (1885–1972), a novelist and playwright, is still read in France today: his play *Knock* is a comic classic and was turned into a film starring Louis Jouvet.

talks of it like a philosopher. His fellow Jews irritate him, too; he finds "simply incredible" their obsession with bringing everything back to themselves. "The war is greater than the Jewish question."

Incredible, inconceivable, astounding—these are his words, and words that probably depict him. The only real world is his world; as for the one in which he is obliged to live with us, he renders on it the judgments of a delegate of God, of an angel. But that angel is irritated, and his irritation gives away his fall among us, reveals him as human, too human, at least as much as all those he is getting ready to assail—his rivals, his colleagues.

Be that as it may, this old, little Jew, driven out of Paris, imperturbable in his garret and giving the final touches to a book he is calling *The Ordeal of the Democracies*, makes a rather fine image for these times.

August 15

Tell Them.[238] This is the title of the book of a certain Agapit, which a friend had recommended to me. A vain, naïve, artless book, but a rather good piece of testimony precisely for that reason. The author tells how he was wounded in May 1940, was taken prisoner, treated in German ambulances, had a foot amputated, and was freed. No doubt my friend wanted me to take the measure of our misfortune and our baseness, since there can be no account more candidly spineless than this one. So, have we fallen into that vile love for life at any price, that fear of everything, and even that anesthesia? Since the author has no combats to relate, he tells the most dramatic stories of the anesthetizing injections he had to undergo at each operation. If a book like this truly represents the thought of the "average Frenchman," this country might as well die and it would be no great loss. It is bad to love life if one loves it like a coward. Reading a book like this is enough to make one love the harshest, cruelest words of Nietzsche. And I abjure all pacifism if pacifism serves to make men so flabby and so weak. These are things that should be said publicly, perhaps. I will say them as soon as I can. I regret some of my writings. I had too much confidence in men and I did not sufficiently take account of their skill in debasing everything, in pulling everything one says down to their own low level.

But let's be fair. The cry of this whole book is: "Let us live! Live!" How did I get to the point where I found it so low? A last episode—rather fine, intended no doubt to illuminate the moral of the book—shows one of the repatriated prisoners more uneasy about leaving than happy. It's on the departure platform. He asks the German doctor:

"I don't have tuberculosis, right, Doctor? That's not why you're sending me back."

"No, no, my friend."

[238] *Dites-le-leur* by Jean-Jacques Agapit.

But this answer does not reassure him. He asks Agapit. He entreats him:

"Tell me, some people are sayin' the sickness is written on this paper in German. You, Monsieur, you know German, that's not tuberculosis written there, right?"

During this time, another prisoner, happy as a clam, is singing for all he's worth:

Marie-Madeleine has silk socks
Sox sox sox sox sox sox sox
She puts 'em on to lead her ox
'Erox rox rox rox rox rox rox.

That entreaty and song, equally pitiful, were surely heard. They are really the same cry: "Let us live! Live!"

The moaning of the wounded in 1914 moved me far more. What a contradiction I have fallen into! I accepted the groaning of the wounded in a victory. And I can't stand the groaning of the wounded in a defeat? I really need to clarify all that...[239]

A wounded soldier in 1914, unlike the wounded of 1940, thought he was a lucky man and hardly thought of pointing out his sacrifice. This is true. But wasn't that joy in a good wound also the sign of men happy to escape death and fighting? And haven't I cried "Ah, let us live! Live!" in my own way? So let us be tolerant.

I am no longer quite sure of my position. This much remains, however: men are not made for war, assuredly. But they are not made for servitude, either.

August 23

The effect of a word. "Relieving the prisoners." It covers the vilest blackmail. It took a Laval to find it.

In fact, 50,000 farmers who are prisoners will come back to France out of 1,250,000 prisoners[240]—against the delivery to Germany of 150,000 unskilled workers. So it's one for three. And one out of twenty-five. But the word was enough to stir up great hope and terrible nostalgia in the prison camps. The poor men are going to "languish" a bit more. Each one thinks he'll be freed, is surprised he hasn't been freed yet, and complains in his letters that France is doing

---

[239] In fact, I grieved for the dead in victory; I found the pride of the victors intolerable. I certainly have the right to find the vanity of the defeated intolerable. I never accepted the idea of being proud of taking part in an action where you were following orders, even despite yourself. I have never had anything but disgust for the boasting of veterans, the little benefits they draw from their title. One may have gone to war, but one cannot boast of it.—J.G.

[240] Historians today put the figure still higher. Prisoner "relief" (*la relève des prisonniers*) was Vichy's excuse for enforcing the Compulsory Work Service.

nothing for him: that is, three fellow workers have not yet given themselves up in his place. No one has any doubt that he will be the one to be liberated out of the twenty-five men suffering in the same shed. What new suffering, what hatred, what new jealousies. M. Laval is working for "French unity."

In Paris, people live in war; here, they live in a rotten world. The basest idiocy is king. Last night, the president of the Legion, the local pharmacist, went to every house—for the past two years he has been taking his revenge for having had no influence before—asking people to accompany him to the "War Memorial," where he would gather a bit of the "sacred earth" in a bag to send to Gergovie.[241] The same ceremony will take place in all the villages of France. I wanted to see this procession of heroes and I managed to pass by it on the road. It wasn't brilliant. Not many people. But the mayor was there, and his deputy mayor, and the schoolteacher, all Radical or Socialist activists two years ago,[242] along with the heads of local associations and a few local eminences. In total, fifty-odd men degraded by fear, self-interest, or vanity: the mayor does not want to miss his Legion of Honor; the schoolteacher is afraid of losing his position; the presidents of local associations are always proud of parading; this or that sick old man joined the procession for fear that the pharmacist might let him die the next time he has an attack. It is on fine sentiments like these that the new government is founded.

But the working people were not there. They keep their common sense and honor. Of those who were there, what they said gives cause for hope. One complained that he was forced to "get on the bread line." Another assured me that he'd recognized, in the ribbon that tied up the little bag, the garter of the president-pharmacist's wife. The deputy mayor, who was more serious, said that so many little bags from all the villages of France meant so many shovelfuls of earth on the corpse of the Republic, but . . . There were people around and he was unable to finish his thought.

August 31

(For the book of joy.) Two wide eyes, brilliantly blue, slightly protruding from a face slightly too wide and flat, frankly, honestly open, unblinking. Not daring in those eyes, but a kind of confidence so calm that they were illuminated by gentleness, so that he wondered afterward if they had been an offering or a challenge. He said some indifferent words to her, but while he was speaking, his glance projected so much light—on her alone—isolated her so well in the midst of all those others who were saying nothing, that she felt as if she were lifted out of herself. She, too, answered with indifferent words, and they parted as

---

[241] The site of a battle in 52 B.C.E. between the Gauls under Vercingetorix* and the Roman legions of Julius Caesar. For the pharmacist's "Legion," see note 157, p. 101.

[242] Despite its name, *Le Parti Radical* was a very moderate center-left party.

strangers. But from now on, both knew there had been that moment between them and they had been perfectly tuned to each other, although they were never to say it to each other and each of them had to grow old and die alone.

September 3

If I write nothing here, it's because outside of my work, my life in this village is completely empty. Here is probably the most considerable event, and it gives a good idea of social mores on this side of that famous Line. My barber is vice-president of the Legion. The day before yesterday, I show up in his shop in the morning for a haircut. He was busy and told me he would inform me as soon as he was free. I come back in the afternoon. Same answer. I've been waiting for two days and I finally got it. He longs to cut my head off but no longer wants to cut my hair. He's anticipating all the benefit he'll get from the insult he gave me by telling it to all the new Notables of the region. Better still, this evening I'll go to another barber; then he'll finally have every right to send the prefect or the gendarmes what they call here a "deenunce"—that is, an anonymous letter—to denounce a republican, a Communist like me, a man who still dares walk around the streets of the village dressed all in red (for it is true that for the past month, to spare my other clothes, I have dared to wear an old, red Breton fisherman's pea jacket). What audacity! What a provocation!

Legionnaires, *francisquans*,[243] Jesuits, finks, and informers—what a show! Why am I not in a good enough mood to find it funny?

September 6

(For the book of joy.) First day of the hunting season. He was coming back from that first hunt, drunk with fatigue, so stunned by the wind and sun that he had to go to bed right after lunch, but he also asked to be waked up in an hour, an hour and a half at the latest. He fell asleep like a stone. And at the time he had indicated, she came to wake him. She was happy. At last he belonged to her like a child, she felt. She watched him stretched out there on the couch as he had fallen. For one day, he was no longer that man consumed by ideas and books, always elsewhere, but a man who had returned to simplicity. That morning he had watched the sun rise, and ran after animals; he still smelled of all the scents of the scrub, thyme, rosemary... Then she gave him a thousand little kisses on the lips, the ears, and the eyes, and he regained awareness of his marvelous happiness at the same time as life itself.

September 8

The little I have done with my life I did out of fidelity, by holding fast to a promise I made in my twentieth year. I have lived like a dedicated man, committed

---

[243] Guéhenno is playing on "Franciscan" and *francisque*, the Vichy emblem (see note 6, p. xxxii).

to serving one single idea. And I will certainly remain faithful to it, but perhaps I have conceived of fidelity too narrowly. I have sometimes put it into practice the way one plays a part, always assiduously, always tense. If I had been more natural, it would have been more profound. My very diligence prevented me from recognizing the wonderful variety of life, from seizing all the occasions life offers; and it prevented me from acting generously, liberally, according to the circumstances. I considered only myself and did only those little things that the rule I had imposed on myself commanded. A deeper, more natural fidelity would have given me a transformational vision of the world. But the fear of betraying my idea locked me inside myself as in a prison. I brought everything back to my little rule, to my little problems. A stronger heart, less mistrustful of itself, would have shone forth far more. Perhaps I have been faithful to myself alone, not to an idea, not to Caliban. Truth must be served as truth, that is, as the common good, and not as one's own truth—that is, as the possession of one person.

But it seems to me I am finally making some progress and the "he" is ripening inside "me." Why should I be afraid? I'm sure I am not so very attached to myself. Why this surveillance? This continual tension? Wherever life may lead me, I know I will not betray myself or others. Isn't it time finally to accept myself as what I have become—a man of books, a seeker of wisdom? What reasons do I have to mistrust myself? I know I will do nothing out of self-interest. That "he" who is asking to live in me is much vaster than myself, deeply rooted inside me; it is the means to the greatest fidelity. It's up to him to speak from now on, much more than I; let him look at all of life and judge it. Let him lead me out of this little canton where I have been complaining. My revolt was not really revolt. Revolt is much finer, and all I have to do is follow it down whatever paths it wishes to lead me. It is time to set out in quest of discovery. I have no more time to lose.

The "he": the means of rejoining all the living, all the dead, all men yet to be born.

September 11

Enjoy life more, and to do that become "he."

Every work of art is "play," as the old poets used to say. It's always the "play" of Robin and Marion.[244] The question is how far to go. Every work of art is also a piece of testimony and a commitment. The cord that connects all that play to their mother, suffering, should never be cut. The danger in writing only for pleasure, in telling a story just to tell. If the puppets in our plays are broken or flayed alive, they have to bleed. Little Wilhelm dreams that his stage has collapsed: his

---

[244] *Le Jeu de Robin et de Marion*, a 13th-century play by Adam de la Halle, is the oldest surviving secular play in the French language. *"Jeu"* has all the meanings of the English "play" and "game."

David, his Goliath, King Saul, and Jezebel—everything is in pieces, and that makes a pool of blood.[245]

September 17

This morning I opened the window. Melodies of the Pergolesi I heard last night were still running through my head and I had a glimpse of brilliant red brocade. One of Giono's books was lying on my table and I thought of those gushing waters, those knotty, tense muscles. I re-read letters from the past and the same birds that were singing long ago began to sing in the cypress trees. Then I looked at the golden September day, beyond happiness, beyond suffering, and I felt life as it is, outside of us, without us, wonderful and indifferent, ripe, abundant, and sweet.

(For the book of joy.) He was walking to the cemetery. Deep inside himself, he had suddenly felt a great need to go there. He had to spend a few moments near the woman he had loved. A young woman passed him on the way. Her wooden-soled sandals clacked on the rising path. He watched the way the muscles of her calves moved. She had beautiful legs. He thought of how sweet it would be to speak to her, to walk next to her. He slowed down. But when she disappeared at a turn in the road and he was sure she couldn't hear him, he called her and blew her a kiss. And then he entered the cemetery. He remained seated on the grave for a long time, and sometimes he bent down and kissed the ground passionately. His teeth scratched on the granite. Every time he raised his head, he looked all around him to make sure no one could see him. No, he was really alone...He kissed the stone again. He walked back down to the village and it was only then that he suddenly felt the strangeness of what he had just done. He thought about what madmen we are when we're alone, as soon as others are no longer watching.

September 21

I spent three days in the mountains near Roquefort-de-Sault, and at least one of them in a marvelous silence all day, beyond this world—outside of time. I was following an old man, a forest warden, who was going out to keep watch over the wood-cutting. We spoke very little, concentrating on the effort of climbing in the "cuts." If he spoke to me, it was about his profession, about "his forest," as he said. He taught me to look at the trees, judge them, and evaluate their volume; he showed me their illnesses, their wounds, the ones that were of noble birth, the ones that had all the luck—good ground, good sun—the ones that were destined for greatness and beauty; and the ones that had too many branches, the ones gnawed by a canker, the stunted ones, the humiliated ones, those from

---

[245] An allusion to Goethe's 1796 novel *Wilhelm Meister's Apprenticeship*. The young hero has a puppet show at one point.

whom powerful neighbors had stolen water and light, those blasted by the fire of the sky, burnt from top to roots, or torn apart or shattered, and the luck in all that. The forest he looks after is not a National Forest; it belongs to a private individual, and he complained about his greed, and his haste.

"This forest," he told me, "is cleared too much already. What you see here—it all needs rest, at least twenty years. I'd like to leave it beautiful! At my age, you get me? But the boss can't see it. He never goes all the way up here. They cut too much, they're cutting too much wood. What can I do about it? Still got to spot 200 square meters this week. With pine trees like these, that'll make at least 900 trunks. It grieves me, understand? I resist as much as I can. Luckily the boss has a son and the son understands. Sometimes he comes here, he says, when it's his turn to be boss, in ten years, in fifteen years, those 900 trunks there, they'd give us a thousand cubic meters...But if I didn't put up so much resistance, it'd be like 'bald mountain' here. A forest shouldn't be the property of one man. It can only belong to the men who come after. A man grows too fast and a tree too slow."

Then he stopped near a young pine that was not yet as tall as a man and he showed me this year's growth, his hope, a little arrow as long as your hand, with a bud of needles at the end of it straining toward the light, greedy for the sun in which—when it becomes a branch—it will bathe in thirty or forty years, when this young pine attains the height of its neighbors and like them will attract lightning. For that's what is admirable about pine trees: each tries to grow higher than the other, the better to tempt the lightning.

We wandered all day, and all day I remained under the impression of those simple and great things of a world where man does not sow, where he does not have to sow, where he intervenes only to destroy. The old warden was worried. "The forest's gone mute," he explained. "I'm not deaf. It's the forest that doesn't sing any more. Look, we didn't meet any animals and you can't see any birds. Not a single thrush. Just a few little blue tits and wrens. I don't know what's wrong. Maybe it's because the forest's too thin."

Then he explained that you can't get lost in the forest (and I thought of Descartes' great image); with the streams, the rocks, the "cuts," you can always find your way. But it's bad up on the plateaus, the plateaus where one piece of grass looks like another piece of grass and you can go around in circles all day if you're caught in the fog.

When we got back to the village, we were back in the miseries of these times. Eleven men from Roquefort are prisoners in Germany. Nobody believes in that much-vaunted "prisoners' relief." These common-sense peasants have detected the blackmail and understand that since 50,000 men at best will be liberated out of 1,250,000, their sons won't be among the liberated. M. Laval will exploit "the relief" to his advantage, use it to buy a few clients and free the sons or brothers of those who support his treason.

September 25

New decrees on "the organization of workers." This whole unhappy country is no more than a camp of convicts.

September 26

The sadness of these past few days. Thursday we go back to the other prison. I'm leaving a sick old man here, and I'm sad at the idea of the impassable barrier there will be between us and him.

October 4

Back in Paris. Difficult trip. Paralysis is spreading to the limbs of Europe. Spent Wednesday night in the Toulouse railroad station, in Paris Thursday night, another station: Gare d'Austerlitz. We arrived after midnight (three hours late), and had to wait till 5 a.m. to go back home.

October 5

A young poet gave me the poems he wrote these past two years, 1941–42. This young poet, lost in old fables which speak to him only of himself, thinks he's Adonis or Narcissus. For two years he has not seen a face other than his own or heard a complaint other than his own. Oh, the deaf, blind, stupid, pitiless young! I fear the events themselves have burnt all the bridges between them and us. They are blasé, disappointed before they have really lived, full of sleep, and when they wake up, I think, rather cynical. In their eyes, we're just silly to have believed so strongly in justice and freedom. How will they even know what these words mean?

October 8

Decidedly, the "I" bothers me. It is a prison. I have something else to say than he.

October 9

No doubt we "ain't seen nothing yet." This is merely the beginning of our miseries. Everyone senses that this winter will be terrible. Famine and servitude. The workers are fleeing conscription. Our guests are frightened, victory is escaping them; they are organizing terror. I have seen hatred grow like a tree for two years. Now it is going to bear its fruit . . . and what fruit.

Vichy's new institution is "The School of Leaders." There are natural leaders and they will always find their place. But what are we to think of manufactured leaders? We can see all too well in what milieu Vichy will find them, among which sons of which self-important notables, solely preoccupied with consolidating and consecrating the injustice from which they benefit.

October 12

For the first time in two years my profession feels like a chore. I learned this morning that among the young people I'll be talking to this year, a fairly large number have been won over by the new order and "Collaboration," and two of them are informers for Doriot* and the PPF. Some of last year's students came to warn me and advise me to be prudent. But my profession excludes prudence. Probity alone is the rule. I can't say how painful it is for me to think that I'm going to be speaking to young informers. I hoped that the University, and my class, would always be preserved. But the servitude we are in must debase everything. Nothing was nobler or purer than those *khâgne* classes where fifty young people were seeking only truth, together. It was our "common cause" and my role was merely to watch, to sort out their dialogue and sometimes to help them. I will never succeed in showing myself to them as different from what I am; I cannot lie to them, and besides, I do not want to.

October 17

Things aren't going so badly after all, to judge by Goebbels'* article in this morning's *Das Reich*. "What are you complaining about?" he asks German civilians. So they are complaining. And he goes on: "Aren't you ashamed? The men at the front aren't complaining. They're happy to die. They know that blood fertilizes the soil."

French workers are avoiding conscription. So Laval has announced that he "will not tolerate any infringement of the freedom to work..."!

October 21

We had fun all morning, my students and I, with the dissociations and contradictions—those "leaps and capers"—of Montaigne. Did that give me a taste for play? At eleven I was free; the light was admirable and I walked toward the Seine. But it wasn't *I* who was walking. The idea came to me to look at things with the eyes of my friend Paulhan. And here's what I saw—things I wouldn't even have noticed on another day.

I saw the finest shirker of this war. He's a handsome, blond young man, some illegitimate child of Hitler's. He's a sailor on the *Lutèce*. The *Lutèce* is a large dinghy that has always been anchored between the Pont Neuf and the Pont des Arts, requisitioned two and a half years ago by the occupying authorities. I surprised the handsome, blond young man as he was coming out of sleep and dreams. He had dreamed of his friends who are sailing just below the surface, dead or alive, in the Sargasso Sea. He was coming out on deck. First I saw his hands on the top of the ladder on the copper bars, then his blond head, his eyes, surprised by the day, then his whole body, the body of a young Nordic god. He stretched in the sun and he began to wash down the *Lutèce* with a sponge and a dishtowel in his hands. For two years now, this has been his task every morning. The *Lutèce* gleams brightly in the sun.

On the Pont-Neuf, I saw a worker busy painting Henri IV's beard and scrubbing the bird droppings off it. At that height, he seemed a Lilliputian lost in Gulliver's miraculously long beard.

I contemplated a seed merchant's sign for a long time: *The Bold Rooster*. A rooster is placidly pecking away at the seeds in a lion's mane.

But the real wonder is a hunting horn on display in a curiosity shop on the Quai des Augustins. It's a glass horn, clearly a harmonic horn that strings out sounds along ten meters of translucent pipes. Gérard de Nerval* is, they say, the last one who knew how to play it.

The most important thing, my friend Paulhan would probably say to me, is to give things back their mystery in any way you can.

This unhappy country is no more than a reservation of convicts.

Laval spoke again last night, and I cannot say how painful it was to listen to that vulgar, base, greasy voice calling workers to servitude as if to a duty and a celebration.

All they're talking about in the papers is the coming American attack on Dakar. My friend B... points out to me that the Americans hardly need Dakar: the base at Freetown is much better. Wait and see.

October 25

Sometimes a phrase or a verse you've read a hundred times over with indifference stirs an extraordinary fervor in you. That's what happened to me yesterday when I read this hemistich by Lucretius:

...Noctes vigilare serenas.[246]

These words were enough to make me happy all evening. Those great, long, exalted nights you spend reading when you're twenty, on watch in the silence and darkness with all that great order of stars around you, that hope, that expectation, that awareness... And the finest moment is when, with the help of a kind of tired drunkenness, it seems to you that the order of the tranquil night has become the actual order of your mind, the light in its rank among the lights... The line in Lucretius was telling me all that:

...Noctes vigilare serenas.

And then the sirens howled out the air-raid warning.

Conversation with P... and M...: we agree that the return of the Republic seems assured, inevitable: it never seemed more beautiful, and the moronic traitors of Vichy are making it more beautiful every day. But P... tells us he's afraid that nothing has changed, and electoral politics will continue to preclude great projects and long-term plans. What is most necessary, he explains, what must be

---

[246] "To stay awake through clear nights." From Lucretius (99–55 B.C.E.), *De Rerum Natura* (*On the Nature of Things*).

established at any cost in the Republic (he is resigned to it)—and that, at least, is what our misfortunes should teach us—is a body which will assure the permanence of France, the continuity of its policies and its conscience. And no doubt he is right. But I'm not sure if he's not posing the question too narrowly. It is the life and permanence of Europe that we should be thinking of from now on. We must act so that each of the nations that compose it—particularly France—will be an active principle in Europe and give it everything it has to give. France will maintain, in Europe, the sense of liberty.

November 3

In the midst of this frightful silence in which we are obliged to live, ignorant of everything, where the mere attempt to learn something is almost considered a crime, deprived of the right merely to call into question the lies the newspapers try to impose on us every morning, I think of the efforts we make to think more or less clearly and to be "citizens." These efforts seem to me an absolute duty. Premature efforts, my friend B . . . says, to console me. But there are dark hours when I doubt that the time of being citizens will ever return. The degradation machine is running, and what an output it has! Perhaps men will soon have forgotten those fifty to a hundred years during which, thanks to some kind of miracle, they thought they could and should try to live in truth and clarity.

November 9

That joy we felt yesterday morning. The Americans had landed in North Africa. People who heard the news on the radio couldn't keep quiet; they phoned their friends:

"You know the news?"

"No."

"I can't tell you."

"Can't tell me *what*?"

"Listen to the radio at noon. This is huge! Huge!"

In actual fact Vichy itself had announced it and we had every right to repeat it. But the news was so loaded with happiness that it was surely dangerous to say again—forbidden.

The fact is of enormous consequence; it can change the rhythm of the war and speed up everything. The situation goes back to what it would have been without the treason of June '40. The Italian toad will soon be crushed.

Vichy is raging and organizing the defense of the Empire. "Honor demands it." All the leaders are spluttering at the same time: Pétain, Darlan, and Laval. Confusion reigns in Algeria and Morocco: the generals are arresting each other . . . In the latest news this morning, Algiers had asked for a suspension of combat, in other words: they were surrendering to the Americans, "to save women and children." But, says Vichy, make no mistake, it is understood that the fight goes on...What a dismal comedy!

During this time, Hitler was playing another game in Munich. He spoke to his *Parteigenossen*[247] for a full hour, doing his utmost to make them laugh, to reassure them, to persuade them they were in 1942 and not in 1918. He strutted around cheekily with his greasy, dull voice, and I heard the laughter of a hysterical woman right next to him. Naturally he went into a few rages. Then he banged on his lectern to accentuate his phrases; the rhythm quickened and at the height of his fit, a veritable drumroll accompanied his falsetto voice. I could hear the blows on the lectern. The crowd, in its turn, went into a trance...If he can see all that from the depths of his clouds, *unser Gott* must judge it a bit of a joke.

Sometimes we're tempted to think that our masters in Vichy are just acting and are actually making fun of Germany. But what rules out this hypothesis is that we would then have to suppose they were veritable saints. For how, unless they were saints, could they take on themselves all that opprobrium, as they have for two years? No, M. Laval is no saint and neither is Pétain.

They are merely two morons who believed in German victory and gave themselves up to Germany, and gave us up to Germany, too. So they use the grossest trickery with everybody in order not to reverse their decision, and to stay in power and gain one day at a time. True, it may seem strange that they vociferously announced they would defend Dakar and piled up all their troops there. The Americans wisely concluded that North Africa was undefended and easy to take; they took it, and our people in Vichy took the fall. They firmly believed in an attack on Dakar. It never occurred to them that the American troops massed in Liberia and Gibraltar could have another destination than Dakar. Our misfortune for the last three years, perhaps, boils down to this: not one of our soldiers or sailors was able to read a map. Only events and action could reveal to them the grandeur and strategic importance of our Empire.

November 11

The German army is panicked, runs to the Mediterranean, occupies all of France,[248] and the whole French Empire is entering the war. The inevitable cannot be avoided. The proof is there: the Armistice of June '40 was a stupid blunder as well as an act of treachery. All we gained was dishonor.

Pétain, who decidedly thinks only of himself, complains in an unbelievable radio address: "I thought," he says, "that (in June '40) I had lived through the darkest days of my life." It's really a question of *his* life! And now he is in despair

---

[247] Comrades in the (Nazi) Party; further on, *unser Gott* means "our God."

[248] In direct violation of the Armistice agreement, German forces occupied the Free Zone on this day. In the next paragraph, Guéhenno is quoting the first sentence of Pétain's November 10 radio address precisely, adding only a parenthesis.

at the very moment when all of France is beginning to have hope once again. Never has a chief of state been more ignorant about his people, or more deaf…If we had any doubt about it, today's events demonstrate that the pretended savior of June '40 was merely an ambitious old fool.

But we feel lost in something so vast that it is beyond our comprehension. At least we feel that from now on hope will grow as time goes by…

November 14

Vichy babbles away and has now become merely silly. The old fool clings to his shame and multiplies his orders, which no one is obeying anymore. (Telegram to Darlan: "I gave you the order to defend Algeria…I am ordering you…")

In order to pray better, one day Pascal forced himself to write down his prayer, to note all the moments of his meditation. Once he had written it down, he put it away in his papers. He did not publish it. It was an affair between God and him. Can one imagine turning over "The Mystery of Jesus" to advertising?

Luckily, the paper was not lost, and it is a great privilege for us to be able to read it, to watch Pascal at prayer. But he did not write this paper for us. It's the researchers of the 19th century who ferreted it out and published it; Havet was the first, I think. Port-Royal[249] knew that such personal prayers should not be published.

Some Christian writers today pray very differently. I'm thinking of Claudel, Péguy, and Charles du Bos[250]; their prayers are ostentatious and they even hope they'll be best-sellers. After André Gide had read *Le Mystère de Jésus*, he decided no work of Pascal's was more moving. He told himself that there was an emotional element in it that should not be neglected. Why shouldn't he leave his own *Mystère de Jésus* to posterity? And that was the *Numquid et tu.*[251] Everyone could see André Gide breathless with anguish and asking his readers: "Will I fall on my knees or won't I?" Frankly, what do we care?

The Genius of Christianity.—The Faith, too, has its history, and changes. Chateaubriand only restores, and claims to restore, one possible Catholicism.

"We are living," he writes, "at a time when a great deal of indulgence and compassion are needed. The generous youth of today are ready to throw themselves into the arms of whoever preaches the noble sentiments that accord so well with the sublime precepts of the Gospel, but they reject servile submission, and in their ardor to learn, they have *a taste for reason* remarkably greater than their age."

---

[249] Port-Royal des Champs was an ancient abbey not too far from Paris; in the 17th century, it became the center of the Jansenist stream of Catholic thought, which strongly influenced Pascal.

[250] A Catholic essayist and literary critic (1882–1939), author of *What Is Literature?*

[251] The title of Gide's work comes from the Vulgate Latin of John 7:52: "Art thou also of Galilee? Search, and look: for out of Galilee ariseth no prophet." For *The Genius of Christianity*, further on, see note 67, p. 32.

November 19

This line of Pétain's has been making the rounds: "I have more power than Louis XIV." Luckily, his radio addresses are getting shorter and shorter, but more and more stupid. All that remains is his vanity. "You have but one duty: obedience," he told us this evening. "You have but one country, which I incarnate: France." An unhappy incarnation! One is stupefied by the idiocy of statements like this. He's Ubu the King![252] Getting old always means a hardening of the main trait in one's character: this former colonel has grown old, hardened in his authoritarian vanity.

Be careful to choose the main trait in your character well, while there is still time, while your arteries still have some flexibility.

November 22

I find excellent advice for biographers in Valéry's new book *Bad Thoughts and Others* (p. 94). I should keep them in mind when I work on my Rousseau:

Those who have something great in them don't tie it down to their person. On the contrary. What is a person? A name, needs, habits, little absurdities, absences; someone who blows his nose, coughs, eats, snores, etc.; a plaything for women, a victim of heat and cold; an object of envy, antipathy, hatred, and ridicule... But the biographer watches out for these things and devotes himself to extracting from the greatness which signaled them to him that quantity of common pettiness and inevitable, universal miseries. He counts the socks, the mistresses, the silly things his subject has said. In short, he works in exact opposition to the man's goal: his vital force, in its totality, exerted itself against what life imposes of vile or monotonous similarities on all organisms, and against diversions or unproductive accidents to all minds. His illusion consists in thinking that what he seeks can engender or explain what the other man found or produces. But he is not wrong in the slightest about the taste of the public, which is all of us.

— No doubt, but the purest mind is carried by its body, it can be useful to know its history, and that history is not necessarily degrading. Last night I was re-reading the admirable preface-letter to Lamartine's "Poetic Reflections" (*Recueillements poétiques*). The mind appeared in it like the flower of a man who was wonderfully strong and well-balanced. And he would not be so great without that strength and that balance of the thing that carries him. A mind is always

---

[252] Guéhenno is quoting Pétain's November 19 radio address almost word for word. Ubu is the grotesque "hero" of Alfred Jarry's farcical, proto-Dadaist play *Ubu roi* (*Ubu the King*, 1896).

only the thought of a body. Pascal, Rousseau . . . Valéry, that cynic, knows it better than anybody, but sometimes he plays the angel.

Yet he is right about biographers. They should be careful not to degrade their subject, and not to please the public by losing themselves in kitchen accounts—the history of the body, its passions, and its needs.

Luckily M. Laval himself can feel his impotence: "I learned," he says, "That young men wanted to defend our empire. The government will not discourage them . . ." What determination in that turn of phrase!

All these traitors are giving us a rather dismal comedy. And now they're betraying each other. A question of habit! Yesterday Darlan, today Boisson.[253] Ubu is making repeated calls for obedience. "Get under my heel! Under my heel!"

November 25

I'm reading Claudel's odes. How ponderous! How obscure and confused![254]

"The clearer he is, the better we can see God," wrote Lamartine to his friend M. de Genoude. This is surely not Claudel's opinion.

December 1

Three weeks ago, Hitler was proclaiming that he would never touch Toulon, or the fleet, or the army of the Armistice. Was he afraid the fleet might escape to Algiers and there might be resistance in Toulon? His proclamation enabled him to occupy the rest of France as peacefully as possible. Now that the operation has been concluded, he declares that he is forced to occupy Toulon and enters it. The fleet, caught in the trap, has no other resource but to scuttle the ships. It would have done better not to give up the fight two years ago: there is no merit in being a dupe. But those Navy gentlemen did not like the English and did not want to fight at their side. France must now pay for their vanity and stupidity.

December 3

A storm this morning at the École Technique. All I had to do was recall Michelet's words and give a somewhat lively commentary on them: "What is difficult is not to rise in the world, but to remain oneself as one rises." Without enough consideration for them, perhaps, I told these young plebeians what traitors, what deserters they could become, unfaithful as one becomes through vanity, through cupidity, tempted as they would be to advance, to succeed—and to forget, the better to enjoy their new fortune. I asked them to think about the history of the 19th century, about its failure, about the deep-seated reasons for

[253] Pierre François Boisson (1894–1948) was the administrator of French colonies in Africa; he opposed an attempt by de Gaulle's Free French forces to land in Senegal, but made a turnaround in 1942 (like Darlan) and backed the Allies after they had taken North Africa.

[254] *Cinq grandes odes* (1910). Many readers do not share Guéhenno's reaction to these long poems; the translator of this diary is one of them.

that failure, about that history of continual desertion: for as they rose in society and became leaders, countless sons of the people deserted and betrayed it; the culture they acquired, which should have assured the deliverance of all, served only their own advancement; so that we reached the point where there were only two political parties everywhere in Europe: the party of those faithless deserters who had become leaders preoccupied with saving the privileges of their vanity, and the party of the masses from which they came, and which they betrayed. Fascism and communism. "Are you sure," I asked them, "that you are better than that, and you'll be more faithful than your elders?" And then, I reassured them, but I had said enough to give the traitors—if there are any among them—a bad conscience.

December 9

Read Gide's preface to Goethe's plays. Rather fine. But two or three times it appears that Gide, as he wrote, was thinking too much about himself. The idea of his own future glory never leaves him and it seems that he's taking care to gather, by himself, the arguments historians and critics might need to defend him later on. No doubt whatsoever that he thinks his life, at least as much as Goethe's, was "exemplary," and he makes his case. When he strives to justify Goethe's tran-scendent amorality, the "venerable little devil" denounced by Dumas *fils* in 1870[255]—his egoism, that quick way he had of using everything and everyone only to drop them a moment later—he is thinking of himself and of himself alone; he is worried about accusations leveled against him two years ago, in 1940, by the phony gentlemen of "French recovery and reform." And to cap it all, if he blames Goethe for having been too reasonable, if he shows his limits, takes him to task for having been able to love only light and deplores in him a certain horror of obscurity, he is still pleading for himself, and all that is addressed to future critics. We are supposed to understand that he was always all that Goethe had been, plus something else…What? Christian uneasiness. It pleases him that we can glimpse that little aigrette of divine fire above his death mask. It can rally Catholics to his fame, and they are no negligible part of the reading public.

December 16

The National Lottery is having more and more drawings, but people are get-ting tired of losing, so it is increasing its propaganda. A little while ago, a sort of story-book picture, an edifying poster in praise of Bernard Palissy* and persever-ance, could be seen on the walls of Paris. The same theme is reappearing these days, but this time it's Pasteur who is advising us to persevere and assuring us

---

[255] Alexandre Dumas (1824–1895), the son of the Alexandre Dumas (1802–1870) who wrote *The Count of Monte Cristo*, *The Three Musketeers*, etc. "Dumas *fils*," as he is usually called, was a successful playwright and novelist.

that we will end up by winning. This hijacking of virtue is the height of swindling, brilliant in its way. Never has the government in France been so vile and counted so heavily on people's stupidity.

More than once, Renan, while speaking about France, brings up the destiny of the Jewish people. It is the grandeur of its spiritual mission, he explains, that compromised the temporal power of Israel, and it seems to him that France runs the same risk. Never does he clearly choose between her spiritual mission and her temporal power, and that uncertainty in his thought enabled the forgers of Action Française to draw him to themselves and claim him as their master. If you listen to them, you would think he was only preoccupied with the temporal power of France and advocated only base realism. Now, he never accepts the idea of increasing France's force to the detriment of its spirit. Besides, these last years have proven that the relation between the temporal and spiritual realms was not quite what he thought. The temporal power of France was only compromised by its timidity, its fear, its care for a good pot roast. If France dies, it will be the wealthy who will have killed it. France would have been stronger if her faith had been stronger and she continued to accept the risks of her mission in Europe. Not all peoples are the same. None is, more than France, a spirit, a thought: for a people like that, giving up its dreams means to die completely, even in the temporal realm.

December 26

Christmas: I'm listening to a fragment of Berlioz' *L'Enfance du Christ* on the radio: the flight to Egypt. The great, terribly supple phrase, repeated ten times, speaks insistently of a shelter, a refuge where there must be a sanctuary for the thought that will save us, while waiting for its time to come. But it seems that today there is no longer any refuge, no longer any Egypt.

December 27

Propaganda blares news into our ears from morning to night, but we're no better informed; we know nothing. What's the state of public opinion in Germany? Oh, if only we could be sure that they were suffering a great deal, dying in great numbers on the Russian front! Sure that the women of Germany have no more tears to shed. Sure that they're on the verge of revolt. For only the excess of all those misfortunes can give us hope; it has come to this!

We know nothing. Only, Goebbels' articles in *Das Reich* grow more somber every week. I read them with curiosity. Last week's article is a consolation, a frenzied, desperate hymn to death. Let German mothers rejoice: death fulfills heroes. *Die Vollendeten.*[256] This is the title of his article about those who have already died. He speaks of them with a sort of envy. They died in their first

---

[256] "The fulfilled, the completed."

enthusiasm, without any doubts, in certainty. They are already in the light, whereas those who are still living are only *Suchenden*—seekers in the dark, in difficulty, doubt, compromise, enigmas, and duties. The next article will be a call to death, which delivers us. It is clear that Goebbels is not exactly cheery. Death has drawn closer to his people and to him. He's in a fit of peculiarly German depression, a sad pleasure in blood and death. Wagner.

1943

January 9

We're back from Montolieu. Grandfather died January 1, in the morning. The Germans had occupied the village on December 30. He had already lost consciousness. He won't have known. Now they're going to move into his house, no doubt. In what state will we find it when we return? It's all happening as if every bit of former happiness had to be destroyed. But the trees will remain, and the fountain between its high cypress trees, the terrace over the river, the whole horizon, and the whole sky. I'll always have enough to remember it by.

January 12

I certainly won't generalize; and I hope all young people in France do not resemble some of the ones I come across in Louis-le-Grand.[257] A *khâgne* class always was populated by hypercritical young intellectuals, and it is a bad environment for faith and energy. Yet never had I felt such flabbiness and inertia in front of me. Except for a few of them, they're all following current events with the most terrifying indifference. The mind of this country is deeply sick. Is it the influence of a few masterly actors—Gide,* Giono,* Montherlant*? Every one of these young intellectuals has never thought so much about himself alone, his happiness, his joy, his career—and with such pettiness, such servility. When you talk to them of freedom or honor, they just get embarrassed. They rub their noses and lower their heads, deaf, fearing nothing so much as to be asked to do something, however little. For the past few weeks, I had the feeling they have been still more inert. Last night I had to read them the official notice according to which "French law, confirmed by the German authorities" gives them a student exemption from requisition and deportation.[258] I tried to get them to

---

[257] One of the great Paris lycées, with a tradition of sending students to the elite schools of higher education (*Grandes Écoles*) and universities in France.

[258] Guéhenno is not talking about deportation to concentration camps here, but about the Compulsory Work Service (see note 7, p. 32). After the war, this confusion between the two very different "deportations" delayed understanding of what happened to roughly 76,000 Jews who were deported from France, only 2,000 of whom survived.

understand that they were enjoying a great privilege, and a privilege must be earned; that it was impossible for them not to feel it, when all of France was no more than a reserve of convict labor; that they should hold on to the tension that suffering keeps alive inside themselves, and if they did anything less than that, later on they might be judged as not even having deserved the honor of deportation . . . All I did was embarrass them. They remained silent. I asked them to tell me what they thought. Then one of them, more naïve and vain than the others, answered that they didn't have the impression of enjoying a privilege, that they weren't ditch-diggers, didn't know how to work with their hands, that this ignorance was their only protection, and besides, the work of those who were "requisitioned" wasn't all that hard, and finally—the idiot—that if *they* weren't being deported, it was perhaps because they were feared.

I write these things down with great sadness: this country would be ready for servitude if its young intellectuals resigned themselves so easily to the misery of others. And then, I think I can see all too easily how the spirit can die. The kind of fever that used to animate the great University classes has already fallen spectacularly.[259] In the freedom of former years, great choices were offered to these young people, and that was enough to give some of them a certain impulsion, a certain anxiety and nobility. Now they don't even know what great choice they could make. Most of their teachers no longer dare talk about it. Discussion is forbidden. Just one kind of propaganda is permitted—nay, encouraged: the propaganda of obedience and submission. One must think "Marshally." I am not saying that this is already succeeding with most of them. They listen to that no more than to anything else. They remain wary. But what degradation, already, in three years! They are now in a period of sleep, as if dead to all ideas. When they become total fools, the authorities will assemble them, flatter their vanity, give them khaki, gray, or black uniforms, and march them off to glory—to idiocy! And to top it all off, they will soon be quite proud of marching in step so well. That's the story of the new Germany. Twenty years, ten years are enough to produce a nation of morons.

January 18

A conjuncture I've thought about for a long time is becoming more likely every day. Nazi Germany is lost. But what if it went over to Bolshevism and gave itself to Russia. What would happen? Would the war continue between Anglo-Saxon capitalism and the European Soviets, and then what choice would we have to make, we French?

He is dead and will not have seen, as he wished so ardently, the end of this fight. A few hours before he fell on the stairs—and it is that fall which led to his death—he wrote me, and it was to advise me, since he knew I was sick, to hold

---

[259] The post-secondary *khâgne* classes in the lycées were considered to be part of the University.

out, to be *curious* enough to wait for the end of all this, and deliverance. For two days I watched him dying, struggling. He didn't hear the Germans singing in the street under his window. It seemed that he couldn't die. His old heart was resisting. Very early Saturday morning, the fits became more frequent. I was next to him, powerless, so totally useless. Then suddenly the sad, hoarse ringing of foreign bugles sounded in the nearby barracks and heralded, to me alone, his last day. And our curiosity seemed vain to me, and I wondered if we were giving too much of ourselves over to current events: as tremendous as they may be, that is not where our real life lies. I was full of doubt, full of the words of the old sages: what will be is what was; we must live every moment as if it were the moment of our death, and it is only under that condition that we can have some soundness of judgment and see things as they are. But is that wisdom or abdication?

January 27

I decided to go see a doctor, and here we are: "Actiphos and sympathyl" turn out to be more powerful than all the books of the greatest sages—Plato, Marcus Aurelius, the Gospel, and Montaigne, whom I had been studiously reading for months...Perhaps I am going to begin to look at the world with all the love it deserves once again, and live with the gods, as the Greeks say: μζήνθεοιζ. It is because I am breathing better. O Sympathyl! O Actiphos!...

Admirable pages in Saint-Exupéry's* new book: *Pilote de guerre* ("Flight to Arras"), p. 140:

> The injustice that goes with the defeat is that the defeat seems to make the victims guilty...Life always breaks apart ready-made expressions. Defeat can prove to be the only way to resurrection, despite its ugliness. I know very well that to create a tree, a seed is condemned to rot. The first act of resistance, if it comes too late, is always a loser. But it is the awakening of resistance. A tree can come out of it as if from a seed.
>
> France has played her role. It consisted in volunteering to be crushed, since the world was arbitrating without collaborating or fighting, and seeing herself buried for a while in silence. When an attack is launched, there are necessarily men at its head. These men almost always die. But in order for there to be an attack, the first men must die.
>
> This role is the one that prevailed, since we agreed, without any illusions, to oppose one soldier to three soldiers and our farmers to workers. I refuse to be judged on the ugliness of the debacle. Will we judge the man who has agreed to burn in full flight by his swelling flesh? He, too, will grow ugly.

The occupying authorities distractedly let this book appear. But its very success woke up the authorities and they have just pulped it.

January 27

Stalingrad delivered.[260] Rostov threatened. Tripoli taken. Roosevelt and Churchill meet in Casablanca and decide to continue the war until the "unconditional surrender" of Germany, Italy, and Japan.

June 1940: "If the hazard of a battle, that is, a particular cause, destroyed a state, there was a general cause which made that state inevitably perish through one battle: in a word, the principal momentum carries all particular accidents along with it" (Montesquieu, *Causes of the Grandeur and Decadence of the Romans*).

The obligations of my profession made me re-read the three volumes by Abbé Bremond* on pure poetry these past few days. The argument they provoked was one of our entertainments during the mid-20s, between the two wars. With what delight did we endlessly cogitate about them. So, poetry was a "mystery." Bremond had said so—derisively. A mystery! You never can get to the bottom of a word like that. Everyone could write his article and earn his sustenance. Old Boileau* said only "*A je ne sais quoi*," which is much less moving, but was enough for him and also for Racine and La Fontaine... But a mystery! All right-thinking esthetes went into raptures. And that would have been merely amusing if it hadn't been one of the innumerable signs of the mental flabbiness into which the country's elite was slipping, feeling life only as a source of pleasure, savoring it like a piece of candy, getting drunk on words (mystery! mystery!), and losing its taste for truth in favor of its taste for vagueness.

When France was in good health, Voltaire was writing: "A mystery was never an explanation." And losing himself in the ineffable did not seem to him the noblest use of his mind.

Never had poetry been talked about so much and never were there fewer poets. They sought the ultimate: pure poetry. That rage for purity was still merely a form of escape, a kind of desertion. Thus we lived in mortal silence. All the best could do was to remain silent. Hugo, Lamartine,* Vigny* himself, in their time, did not fear impurity so much. For them, poetry was not beyond life. It was life itself, the life of all of us, only felt more intensely, known more intensely, deeper and transfigured.

The crisis of poetry is the crisis of the world. It did not only affect France. It concerns all of Europe. When Europe begins to take hope again, when it finds its order again, it will find poets again to sing it.

---

[260] The Russians had already liberated most of the city by late January, but the final surrender of what was left of the German Sixth Army actually took place on February 2. It was a decisive turning point in the war. Germany had lost at least 500,000 of its best troops, and the Soviets took over 100,000 prisoners.

January 30

Hitler has been in power for exactly ten years. But the chatterbox has been silent on this anniversary. Goering and Goebbels* spoke in his place. Goering imitated him as best he could. But not everyone who wants to scream screams well. His screams lack rhythm and vanish into emptiness. The whole speech was directed against Russia. About England, hardly a word. "England has not understood Europe." That is, Germany. This moderation is strange. What can it be hiding?

Yet England had just played a good trick on him. He was to speak at eleven. An English squadron flew in. They had to sound the air-raid sirens and take shelter in the cellars. Finally at noon, all the dignitaries of the Nazi Party and all the generals were able to come back up from the basement and Goering gave his speech. He screamed as much as he could, till he was out of breath, but there was not one single round of applause. No doubt those were the instructions. Applause is reserved for the Führer. It was ceremonious and sad. In the evening, Goebbels gave an uninspired reading of a proclamation from the Führer. "In this war there will be neither victors nor vanquished, but only," he said, "survivors and peoples that have been eliminated." He, too, denounced only Bolshevism. Perhaps a vague attempt and a last hope to rally England and America to "the crusade."

February 1

Yesterday afternoon at A...'s, G..., M..., F..., and L... were there. I had not been in the midst of so many men of letters for four years, and I could immediately feel my solitude among them. Those cultivated, murmuring voices, so unnatural, irritate me. And then, in these salon conversations, there is what is said, and that's what everyone agrees about. But there is also all that is not said—so much weightier and more important. We spoke about France, and we seemed to agree. But no, for them France is not a people, not human beings. This people, those men... they scorn them, or fear them. Nationalists, not patriots. "France alone"[261]—that is their France! Miserly petty-bourgeois, they think of France as their own little pile of money, not as an idea or a sense of justice to be extended to everyone. They no longer see what connection she can have with the rest of the world, with the rest of mankind. They, too, are afraid of Bolshevism. They are full of the past: they think only of pleasure and consumption, not action. France is dead in their hearts; she has no future.

In the course of the conversation, I hear curious things about the Marshal. L... tells how Lyautey* was surprised that he wanted to enter an institution (the Académie Française) where "he would meet that loathsome Pétain." F... tells how that same Pétain, as soon as he saw the way free when Lyautey died in 1934,

---

[261] The watchword of those who thought they did not have to choose between the Allies and Nazi Germany.

took lessons in politics every morning. A...and G...were his masters—the same men he made his ministers in 1940. Premeditation?

February 6

The piercing eyes of a man of letters preoccupied by his reputation: whether he's leafing through a book or a newspaper, eager to find his way instantly in the confusion of the page, he can always see and recognize his name like a sun.

N...tells me about his Chinese and Indochinese friends—what European civilization means to them, what they bring with them when they return to their country. Very little. A few images. The Boul' Mich,[262] the lights of bars and dance halls. And above all the idea of a "new violence." Nothing else. Of the broad mass of European people, of its wisdom, of European humanism, they know nothing, have seen nothing. Rarely have they had the opportunity of entering a European family, to become familiar with its order, its gravity, all that which would actually enable them to find themselves and find the unity of mankind. (Pearl Buck* constructed all her books on that great intuition. For there is only one man in the world, one destiny, and the unity of that destiny sweeps away all differences, all exotic strangeness.)

But it is as if they came here only to find an authorization to "practice," in turn, that new brutality of a Europe in which, moreover, they only see a sort of America.

At bottom, Abbé Bremond's books were merely edifying manuals for the decomposed Christians of the 20th century, a kind of *Genius of Christianity*. From Bossuet* to Chateaubriand,* the fall was already steep. But from Chateaubriand to Bremond! It's because the Catholic conscience, ever more flabby, can no longer bear any demands. From now on, the path to God must be the very path of one's pleasures. A priest has reached the point where he tries to catch souls any way he can. Unable to make virtue interesting, he describes vice as its anguished absence, and if he exalts saintliness, it has to be in relation to sin. With his flock, who don't read the *Imitation* very much but rather Baudelaire, Verlaine, and Claudel,*[263] it is advisable to persuade them that the pleasure they find in those writers is a foretaste of celestial delights. And so poor poets riddled with sins become, with modern apologetics, marvelously edifying characters and virtually fathers of the new church.

---

[262] Familiar short form of Boulevard Saint-Michel, which goes through the heart of the Latin Quarter.

[263] Guéhenno is probably referring to the translation of the medieval *Imitation of Christ* by Lamennais, a 19th-century revolutionary Catholic (1782–1854). Paul Verlaine (1844–1896), while a magnificent lyric poet, was a hopeless alcoholic, and the great Charles Baudelaire (1821–1867) died of syphilis.

February 7

I have only lived and been worth something through a passion, by the remembrance of an offense I had undergone early in the dawn of my life when I was beginning to think and gain the capacity to judge things and men—through the fever for justice which that offense put into my heart. But what will I be worth now that the passion has died down despite myself, from the mere fact of age, and also from my having moved into the comfortable middle class and security. One should be able to grow older and define an order—precisely that order which my youth demanded, in which the offense would be abolished—but the definition would have to be so large that it would extend beyond myself, beyond my puny life and my passion, and one would have to feel that my "Caliban" was man himself, all men. I feel I need to make a last effort. There is a deeper order than the one I have never been able to think through. The smallest star twinkling in the sky has its sun, undergoes its influence, obeys it, and owes it its life, its movement, and its beauty. So it goes for our thoughts . . .

February 12

Never did the Republic dare frankly to teach the Republic. Perhaps it died for that reason. The bourgeoisie only became "republican" to continue to hold the levers of power. It never stopped "resisting," as M. Guizot* resisted. It never stopped fearing equality[264] and had no desire to exalt, in the lower orders, the right to hope that was inscribed in the law itself. On the contrary, it had no desire either to remind them that the law of the Republic must be a tough law; it cared too much about keeping its comforts for itself and preserving its own flabbiness. And thus the sense of liberty under law was lost. The civic ethic taught in the schools had something facile and silly about it—a conformism without enthusiasm or faith. If Rousseau was taught in the lycées, it was his feeling for nature, for the lake, the periwinkle.[265] Little or none of his *Social Contract, Discourse on Inequality,* or *Civil Religion.* As for socialism, it was forbidden to say a word about it: Saint-Simon, Fourier, Proudhon,* Marx, Sorel,* and Jaurès* are only names for most Frenchmen. Their political consciousness of this subject is as ill-informed as can be. Socialism has its partisans and its enemies, equally fanatical. But for most, it's only a word—a myth—in whose name they may soon cut each other's throats without understanding very much, and their very ignorance will make them cruel. That is the result of fear. Lucid, courageous instruction would have accustomed them to the idea, showed them its various aspects, and prepared the form it could take in France.

---

[264] We recall that "Liberty, Equality, Fraternity" (*Liberté, égalité, fraternité*) was the motto of the abolished French Republic. It still is the motto of France.

[265] This flower appears in a lyrical episode in Book 6 of his *Confessions.*

February 22

The deportation is continuing,[266] each day more methodical and better organized. They're taking a census of all young men between the ages of twenty and thirty, under the surveillance of the occupying authority. For the past week, they stand on line in the town halls to register as convict labor. With appalling, but henceforth inevitable docility. If there had been a climate of resistance, if every government department had been an accomplice in sabotaging the orders, the Germans would have needed armies of policemen to assemble the trains of convicts. But in the present situation, brave men have almost no means of escape, without papers, identity cards, or ration cards. This whole country is now nothing but a fearful mass of protoplasm. No thought intervenes anywhere. How will we climb out of this shame and degradation?

At least all young people now feel the same offense, and those young intellectuals who were still so indifferent a month ago are growing tougher now. Will they eventually understand. In his notebooks, Barrès* quotes this phrase of Renan's* to Déroulède[267]: "Young man, young man, France is dying: do not disturb its death-throes."

This was around 1885—already! I must confess this to myself: I can find neither pleasure nor honor in thinking of France, nothing but an immense sadness. I have to think beyond her, to find truth and joy again.

The Line of Demarcation has been eliminated. At last! But luckily, it is too late for us to be won over by such kindness. Nobody is fooled. The troops who guarded the line have better things to do in Russia. That's all. *Bon voyage!*

(To the German I pass by on the street.) I don't know exactly what I feel when I'm near you. I don't hate you, I don't hate you anymore. I know you will never be my master. I pretend not to see you. I act as if you did not exist. I promised myself never to talk to you. I understand your language, but if you talk to me, I raise my arms in the air and act like someone who doesn't understand. And yet the other day on the Place du Châtelet, you walked up to me: you were wandering around like any lost little soldier, looking for Notre-Dame cathedral. So I condescended to understand you, and with a gesture, without saying a word, I pointed to the towers rising in the sky on the other side of the river, staring you in the face. You felt stupid, you blushed, and I was glad. It has come to this.

What do you think you look like with your green uniform on our streets, in our public squares? A soldier in Paris, in France, is blue, or dark red. You're too buttoned up. And those gentleman's gloves you wear? You're far too proper. And what about your dagger? And your revolver? A gloved executioner. And your

---

[266] Again, Guéhenno is not talking about deportation to concentration camps.

[267] Paul Déroulède (1846–1914), a right-wing nationalist poet, songwriter, playwright, and activist.

boots? How many pairs of shoes could be cut out of them for people who now go barefoot.[268]

I do not hate you. I don't know how to hate. When you get into the Metro we squeeze together to make room for you. You are the Untouchable. I lower my head a bit so you won't see where my eyes are going, to deprive you of the joy of an exchange of glances. There you are in the midst of us, like an object, in a circle of cold silence. I can see you from top to bottom in your uniform that's a bit crumpled and pretty well worn at the knees and elbows by now, and in your middle, over your belly-button, on your belt, a badge with the inscription that I always decipher with the same surprise: *Gott mit uns* . . . I must be dreaming: *Gott mit uns!* I consider curiously what kind of God is with you. A most peculiar God. Is he still there when you're in the firing squad? Was he there when you pinned a white paper heart on the chests of my friends so as to aim better? For you do like a job well done. But do you understand that I can't look at you? For after all, what if you were the one who did that? And what if I were to recognize that little flame in your eyes which enables you to shoot so well in a firing squad? There aren't so many of you in Paris, and 670 Parisians have already been shot by firing squads. Counting 10 per squad, that makes 6,700 executioners. How do I know you're not one of them?

I tell myself that you probably come in all kinds, as we do. There are some very low kinds of you. There are those officers one meets around the Madeleine and the Opera in their fine linen greatcoats, with their vain, high caps, that look of proud stupidity on their faces, and those nickel-plated daggers joggling around their bottoms. Then there are your busy little females—those mailwomen or telephone operators who look like Valkyries: one can sense their vanity and emptiness. The other day on the Place de la Concorde in front of the Ministry of the Navy I stopped to watch the sentries—those unchanging puppets who have stood there on each side of the door for more than two years, without drinking, eating, or sleeping, like the symbol of your deadly, mechanical order right in the middle of Paris. I was looking at them for a while as they pivoted like marionettes. But one tires of the Nuremberg clock, and I was leaving, full of disgust, when, oh, what a trick of fate! I unintentionally bumped into someone as I turned around. I apologized. I raised my eyes. Whom did I see before me? One of those telephone operator Valkyries, red with fury, foaming at the mouth, ready to call over the guard for the offense she had suffered. But my apologies had disconcerted her. She got a grip on herself, and said triumphantly: *Ach!* . . . *So* . . . (*Ah!* . . . *Really!* . . .) I was truly sorry for my apologies.

But you are not all of that kind. I see you every Wednesday as I go to work, out on the square in front of my office. What lawful looting are you there for, every

---

[268] We recall that Guéhenno's father worked in a shoe factory and his mother stitched leather at home.

week? When I arrive around eight, your vehicles are already parked under the trees along the sidewalk. The work detail is in the neighboring factories, to get the merchandise. Only a few men are guarding the carts and horses. I sit down on a bench a bit further on, waiting for my office to open. Most of them are farmers, reservists, a few very young people, too, but misshapen and puny. Among them, a sort of dwarf with his pants dragging over the ground; he seems to be the squad scapegoat. They chat away but I'm sitting too far off to hear them. They have a look of sadness and nostalgia that encourages me to look at them. It isn't the dwarf who interests me most. It's an old man who has been in the line of vehicles exactly at the level of my bench every week for at least six months. Such is the regularity of their service. I look attentively at his worn-out jacket, pants, and boots. He stands at the head of the team of horses, leaning against the beam. He seems so alone, so resigned, so distressed. *Zu Befehl*, as I hear him shout, clicking his heels every time a Feldwebel talks to him.[269] *Zu Befehl* forever. He smokes a porcelain pipe, like a legendary German. The dwarf sometimes comes over to him, but he doesn't keep him for long. He only has one comrade. His comrade through exile and war, for all the many years they've been roaming together across the roads of Europe from east to west and west to east, through rain and shine, dust and snow, for all the years that both of them have been marching without knowing why, *Zu Befehl, Zu Befehl*, his comrade is a horse, the horse on the left of the team, an old black horse who has also endured countless miseries and victories. Every Wednesday I see them exchanging tokens of affection. The old horse pulls on his yoke until he can touch his companion with his muzzle, nibbles gently at his shoulder, so that finally the old soldier turns around and rubs the nostrils of the happy animal with his thick fingers. Each of them has met his soul-mate...

This old man, reduced to himself and this friendship for his horse over the long, dreary stretches of war and exile, is the one who helps me to think of you with some pity still, and to consider you as men. He and I are probably almost the same age, and I think of our common history—lost Europeans vainly striving, for forty years now, to reconcile the demands of our honor and our hunger. It seems as if the hunger of some can only be satisfied by the gluttony of others, that the honor of some must always come at the price of the debasement of others. That is not true. But really, old man, go home, just go home...

March 10

Of all the oracles of Antiquity, Ammon is the most famous. Leclant* explains the reason to me. Its name made a convenient ending a verse in hexameter: *Corniger Ammon*. That dactyl and spondee did more for its fame than the value of its prophecies.

---

[269] *Zu Befehl*: "Yes, sir!" Feldwebel: sergeant.

March 11

Politician and political leader. We call "political leaders" the politicians who think the way we do, "politicians" the ones who don't.[270]

March 12

For the very first time in twenty years, I can feel a certain discord between my students and me. I feel truly hurt because of it; in the midst of these young people, I feel alone and old. It's the effect of the times, of this disaster in which we live. Even my faith, my hope—all that which inside me resists and says "no"— embarrasses them, irritates them. Is it their instinct of self-preservation, a will to happiness at any price? Are they telling themselves that they must make terms with the disaster, willy-nilly? Everything I tell them in the exercise of my profession that evokes another time, another courage, another France, seems vain eloquence to them. The faith in freedom that moved the men of the 19th century must be a mere illusion since it all ended up in this servitude they are subjected to today. They have a kind of vital interest in scorning everything they lack, and, they think, they will continue to lack. It's the same break between generations that took place in 1852.[271] But I would still like to believe that this time the break is not definitive, no more than the defeat that caused it.

Fascism, Hitlerism—ideologies of disaster: peoples, still more than individuals, make a virtue out of necessity.

At least these young people are right not to indulge in fine words but want to wring the neck of democratic eloquence.[272] May the ordeal we are going through help us better to love truth! I wonder if, for my part, I did not too often love phantoms, my own pipe dreams. My merit was not great. It is harder to see and love men as they are. May democracy not only be a great idea of our minds, but a patient effort to get men to live in justice and freedom—men who, after all, each taken separately, may not care so much about one or the other. We will never think enough how hard democratic law must be, and its application, difficult.

The bourgeoisie is tired of thinking; is it deserting or resigning? It hardly matters. Thought emigrates when it is served badly. There is a great sound of wings in the poor outskirts of the cities around the masses, who had always been silent and desolate. Hope has changed nests.

March 13

Why I keep this diary? To remember, and to put a bit of order inside me, inside my life. Through discipline, the way one does exercises. But it would be

---

[270] Word-play in the French: *un politique* is (or may be) favorable, but *un politicien* is not.

[271] When Napoleon III took power, ending the Second Republic and beginning the Second Empire.

[272] Alluding to a line in Verlaine's "*Art Poétique*" that tells the poet to "take eloquence and wring its neck."

unfortunate if I contented myself with these notes, these disjointed fragments with no rhythm to them. All this cannot make a book. A great book is a rhythm that imposes itself on the reader: the reader necessarily adopts the rhythm without even realizing it, the way one follows a companion's steps. May I just once write a book that leads the way. A diary hardly says anything but where one is coming from, and it is where one is going that is important, where one wants to go, and that can only be said in books, works one has reflected on, composed through our will.

Anthology.—Translate Whitman's wonderful poem: "A Word Out of the Sea." How he learned to sing on the banks of Paumanok when he was a child by listening to a bird calling its vanished mate day and night, while the bass voice of the sea repeated, to all its waves, death, death...

March 20

He is just to the side of me: there, under my rostrum, constantly under my eyes, and at the slightest word I say that seems to evoke everything he knows I love—everything that he hopes has been definitively abolished—I see him smile and take notes. He has made himself a collection of all my words that seem suspect to him and perhaps good to report, all my blasphemies against the new order. He is the informer, protected in his stupidity and insolence by the little insignia he wears on the left lapel of his jacket—the *francisque* of the Marshal. And I can't say I take no account of his presence. I am subjected to his smiles, his surveillance. In other times, I would have sent him to the back of the room long ago. But no, he wouldn't even have smiled. He would have demanded explanations if he wished, if we had not agreed, and everything would have been done simply and frankly. But armed with his *francisque*, today he plays the generous one and explains to his classmates that he holds me at his discretion. This imbecile may think he can get me dismissed whenever he wants and the worst of it is, he has some reason to think so. Behind me, hanging on the wall in a golden frame, the portrait of the Marshal authorizes and protects this stupidity and this cowardice.

All the same, M...(the name of my informer) has gotten nowhere with his smiles. He doesn't dare denounce me and he is furious at not daring to do it. Clearly, it seems inconceivable to him that in the third year of the new era I can still blaspheme abundantly, as I do. Six or seven of his classmates (out of forty-seven) are as shocked as he is by what I say, but show it less. But this dull, violent opposition creates a kind of heaviness in the class. The other day, I ironically suggested that we give up analyzing texts that are too loaded with questions and too heavy with thought. Thus we would avoid friction and we'd all be more comfortable together. We could spend our time examining the various forms of the sonnet, a-b-b-a...and create agreement between us in a vacuum. Perhaps we're at the point where young Frenchmen can no longer hear about France without a sort of shame. It has happened before. Under the Second Empire, education had become completely formal in this way.

— But I have awakened, it seems to me, whatever ardor remains in these fifty young men, and the informer and his confederates seem to have lost, for the moment. In despite of everything, we will continue to talk to each other like free men for some time to come.

March 29

The atmosphere of my class in Louis-le-Grand has changed completely— cleansed, purified. I was right to ask the question bluntly. From now on, neither the students nor I will accept being subjected to the censorship and surveillance of the informers. But I had to make a fuss in order to keep our freedom. Ah, how well do I know by now how the mind can die! Six or seven snitches were enough to maintain a climate of fear. One would have thought I was compromising everyone in the class by speaking the way I spoke. I could no longer feel any give and take. The most beautiful texts left them indifferent. The silence was fright-ful. But now everybody is beginning to think and come to life again. The profes-sion of teacher, the most human of all professions, can only be exercised well in freedom and I would end up by resigning if this government of imbeciles were to last.

Reading notes. Lamartine: *Le Lac.*

The poem is born from a sensation, a circumstance: the poet's despair when, a year later, he finds himself in the same places where he had known his greatest happiness. Life is fleeing, time is fleeing, etc. ... His emotion is made of the con-trast between the happy time of the past and the wretched time of today. His genius is to have had the idea, to translate this contrast, of using those two rhythms that clash inside the poem: one elegiac and somber, the other lively and joyful. The clash of the two rhythms is the most exact expression of his pain, his shock: "Jealous time, can it be ..." (*Temps jaloux, se peut-il...*)

He had first, after the song of "Elvire,"[273] written two rather flabby stanzas which commented on his past happiness and served as a transition, but he real-ized that the most violent opposition would be more beautiful and he crossed them out.

"Close to the cherished waves ..." (*Près des flots chéris...*) Hypallage, say the pedants. And they are right. But here we can confirm how a poet is stronger, in a way, than the language that has been transmitted to him, with its tropes and figures, its conventional ornaments. He renews even the old-fashioned turns of phrase. *Flots chéris* is the simplest, most direct, and most natural expression. It

---

[273] "To Elvire" ("*A Elvire*") is another of Lamartine's poems in the same collection as *Le Lac* (*Méditations poétiques*). Further on, Guéhenno uses the technical word "Hypallage," a rhetorical term to describe an inversion of the relation between two words.

is exact, almost a bit familiar, although it is obtained by the artificial application of the rules of poetic language. A trope, hypallage if you will. But actually the very principle that led the ancient poets to create that figure is found again here. There is a transferal of words, transferal of epithets only because there is a transferal of feelings. Thus in *amica silentia lunae*...[274] The whole landscape seems to Lamartine as if permeated by his love. An interior landscape. Hypallage becomes silly when it is used didactically and theoretically.

That shock, that clash of rhythms, that cry and that song from the heart, all together—I imagine that is what struck young readers in 1820, male and female alike. From then on we have trouble finding it again through the thicket of commentaries. A man spoke and his words were marvelously melodious without ever losing their truth. More remarkable still, he attained that truth and that simplicity while using the language he had received—the most faded, artificial, fabricated, lying language, the horrible pseudo-classical language. But his heart was stronger, and imposed its own movement on the poem, restoring a moving purity to words worn out by the tribe of versifiers.

The eloquence of the heart was regained. Perhaps Lamartine, like all orators, occasionally said a little more than he thought. And even here. The last stanzas are a bit wordy. The young men of 1820 didn't notice. But real truth is more discreet and more humble.

March 30

Reading notes. Benjamin Constant*: *Adolphe.*

The singularity of this story of a *roué* converted to humanity. The new, extremely serious tone of this novel after the erotic novels of the 18th century, all those treaties on seduction, all those eulogies for infidelity, from the *Mémoires du Comte de D...* by Duclos to Laclos' *Liaisons Dangereuses*.[275] An utterly new feeling for the gravity of love, the tragic grandeur of the human couple. Delphine, Corinne, and Adolphe teach the same probity. It is like a new duty between people who from then on are no longer only committed to themselves and recognize nothing to appeal to and no other support but the love they promised each other. A whole new code would follow from that.

"The great question in life," wrote Benjamin Constant, "is the pain one causes, and the most ingenious metaphysics cannot justify the man who broke the heart that loved him."

(The progress of this idea through the 19th century. Vigny. His poem *La Maison du Berger* ["The Shepherd's Home."] The "divine sin" of Eve.)

---

[274] "The friendly, silent moon..." From Virgil's *Aeneid*, Book II, line 255.

[275] *Les Confessions du comte de *** (1742) is a libertine novel by Charles Pinot Duclos (1704–1772); *Les Liaisons Dangereuses*, the 1782 epistolary novel by Pierre Choderlos de Laclos (1741–1803), is generally considered to be the summit of the genre.

April 2

How strange it was, that shop my friend Bouché* and I went to this after-noon. They make globes there. They're everywhere, hanging from the ceiling, piled up in corners. Bouché explains that he always needs one of these globes within arm's reach. He's the man who knows most about the problems of air transport, and his profession gives him new habits of thought. Far more authen-tically than Paul Morand,* he is constantly thinking in function of "the whole world." He distinguishes three ages in the history of mankind. There was the early age of the Mediterranean—that was the first age. The second one was the age of the Atlantic. The third he talks about will be the second age of the Mediterranean and the glacial Arctic Ocean, when the poles of the most impor-tant exchanges will be Soviet Siberia and the United States, and planes flying 25,000 meters high in the ether will cross it in a few minutes.

April 3

With the Dominicans. In their monastery, on the sixth floor of a big building on Rue de la Tour-Maubourg. I had dinner with them. One of them, a recently freed prisoner, tells us about the martyrdom of Russian prisoners in Germany. One thousand seven hundred to two thousand five hundred died of suffering, cold, and hunger in a camp near his in January '42. His story was horrible. I give up attempting to transcribe it. The Russian government supposedly does not care about its citizens who are prisoners, as Stalin's orders are never to surrender (?)...

These monks, all things considered, seemed happy to me and I envied them.

My naïve surprise when I discovered among them someone from my part of the country, the son of the Serrands from Billé. I dream a little, thinking I could be in his place. The others are everything we might be, "possibly us" rather than "like us."

April 5

The Marshal has spoken: what greatness of heart and mind. "You must show," he said to the young men deported to Germany, "by your actions, by your words, by the quality of your work, by your spirit of initiative and invention, the genius of our race... My thoughts will not leave you on the way and in the places of your new surroundings; act so that that I may be proud of you." What ability to distance himself: the old idiot brings everything back to himself. "New surroundings"[276]—what a stroke of inspiration!

The Renault factories in Billancourt were bombed yesterday at two o'clock. A few bombs fell near the Longchamp racetrack, where there were anti-aircraft guns. They quickly gathered the dead, the wreckage of men and wounded, and

---

[276] Pétain's radio address of April 4, 1943, is quoted quite precisely in this entry.

rang the bell for the start of the first race. The die was cast. Didn't they have to honor the bets of the survivors and the dead, learn whether Vulcan or Almanzor would win?...This little fact is a fairly good measure of the extent of our degradation. The betting offices are eternal. This morning the papers publish "racing results" along with the list of victims.

April 15

Sometimes I pride myself on not liking to believe. It would be closer to the truth to say that I would like to think better and I know one has to believe as little as possible in order to think as much as possible. But I am a pious animal, and my whole life is that of a man of faith.

I get along as well with the Dominicans as I get along badly with habitual Catholics, the bourgeois of Sunday mass and their priests. I like people to think intensely whatever they may think. What I can't stand is that flabbiness of thought in which some people wallow, knowing all too well what it earns them. They hope to win on all fronts and really want to have great careers on earth and in heaven.

I want a man to be committed by his whole thought, and to know he is committed. The Dominicans and I are in harmony because of a certain taste for rigor, a desire for total commitment that seems to us the only means to achieve greatness.

The other day Vaillant* and I were talking about that monk's life we both lead. His, still more than mine. I told him that if we had been born sixty years earlier, we would have become priests the way we became professors: schoolteachers are now recruited from the same milieu in which you used to meet parish priests fifty years ago, and after all, a chance meeting could have made us monks today in a monastery just as we are now university professors. He protested. The love of truth, he explained, would always have shown us the way. I would like to be sure of that. What is true for someone like Renan may not be true for us. An incredible strength of mind is needed to conceive and seek the truth against the milieu in which one has grown up, the influences one has been subjected to, the facilities of habit and happiness, against the current, despite all opposition.

April 19

The contemporary school of history is living on a false idea of time. I see it confirmed once again as I read the new, very fine book by Lucien Febvre* on *The Problem of Unbelief in the 16th Century: The Religion of Rabelais*. Time isn't past, as the historians think: it passes. It is an indefinite duration, and comes out of the depths of the past but tends toward an unfathomable future. And for the thought of a man among men, like Rabelais, Montaigne, and Descartes, why should we insist that it be brought back only to the past and even to the present. It is above all of men like this that it is true to say they are valuable as much for their premonitions and their dreams as for their memories. For them, the future is no less real than the past.

M. Lucien Febvre calls this an anachronism and accuses us of wanting to make the past up to date. We don't think so. But is it really so difficult to think of history as a movement? The aspect of history that speaks to our emotions—for example in those exemplary lives—is entirely in this movement. History doesn't stop any more than time does. So yes, show us Rabelais and Descartes caught up in the past despite themselves, encumbered by the mistakes of their era. That is just. But also show them to us as they move, with an invincible will, toward another truth that they present. The tragedy of someone like Descartes is to have been both a Rosicrucian and the author of *Regulae ad directionem ingenii*.[277] Nothing like contemplating a tragedy like that to reawaken confidence and energy in us.

That affected fear of anachronism—I'm not saying this for M. Lucien Febvre, who seems to have written this book only out of a polemical instinct, against Abel Lefranc—all too often hides hypocritical designs. They only wish to slow time down. They are actually afraid of the future, and only wish to confine us to the past. Without intending to, M. Lucien Febvre justifies the enterprise of another critic, M. Plattard, so preoccupied with proving to us that Rabelais was only an entertainer and never claimed to think.

April 20

Almost every day a new measure is taken that is actually of limited scope, but can win over a few Frenchmen. Today they're announcing that the prisoners will be sent off for a holiday at Easter. Naturally this measure only affects a few thousand men,[278] and these prisoners, these delegates for propaganda, will be chosen (and how carefully!) from the most submissive, spineless ones. But this piece of news is enough to sow confusion in public opinion! Vichy is nothing but a vast effort to rot the very fiber of the French people. As if the revolting, degrading habit of servitude were not enough to destroy the soul of this country.

April 27

Did I note here the visit I received last winter from a young man, J. H...? He had read Dabit's* journal and wanted to consult me because I had been Dabit's friend. He's a long boy with a long face. He told me his life story: he was raised and still lived in a home for the poor where his mother is a cleaning woman. Nowhere are there more wretched people per square meter. He felt that every-

---

[277] *Rules for the Direction of the Mind.* Further on, Abel Lefranc was a scholar who had presented Rabelais as an atheist; Febvre's book, which explores how people really thought and practiced religion in the 16th century, is a refutation of this theory.

[278] We recall that the Germans took well over 1.5 million French prisoners in May and June of 1940.

thing he had seen there had left its mark on him. For the moment, he was a clerk in the tax office, but he dreamed of doing something else, he didn't know what. Clearly, I had before me a new Dabit, a boy whose experience of life, quasi-monstrous for his age, would soon oblige to bear witness, an artist who was beginning to be smothered by what he had to say. For a long time, he spoke to me about the "home" and about his mother, with a tenderness I found admirable.

Three months ago, he returned. He had changed jobs. He was a clerk in a bookstore, and happy. He was living among books. What luck! He was running a lending library in a Passy bookstore. In short, he was a director of consciences, advising people what to read. He had some amusing experiences. Thanks to him, white Russian émigrés, the rich bourgeois of Auteuil, and all the bookstore's customers were going to know a literature they would never have known, Malraux*, Aragon...[279]

And then, one March evening, a phone call. J. H...announced he was being deported to Germany. I received a first letter almost immediately...He's working in Belzig, in the Berlin area. "I'm on the night shift," he wrote, "in an explosives factory along with workers who used to be a pork-butcher, a commercial artist, a student. (For my mother, I'm doing secretarial work.) The reality is, behind the carts with shovel in hand. 'Strength through joy.' Night work makes you lose the notion of time, you find yourself on an unlit road following an invisible leader who reminds us of his existence from time to time, as we are worried. When day comes, Belzig appears to our tired eyes between two pine woods, its baroque belfry the color of time. Our shacks are scattered over a field where the sacrificed sprouting trees cheer you up like the vegetation in a cemetery. All we can hear is the songs of the Ukrainians locked up not far away; and yet the *lag*[280] is on the edge of the road, but the whole area around it is deserted. Old German women and young guys who've lost their childish faces, wounded men from the USSR, and a few soldiers on furlough look at us in the streets of the little town, without a word or anything in their eyes that might break through our loneliness."

Yesterday afternoon a new letter: "When this letter goes off I won't have eaten for eighty hours, sick from not having the taste to eat anything, fortunately in bed with drunken visions..."

The idea came to me to go see his old mother at the home before answering the boy. It's near the Porte d'Ivry, in those neighborhoods that stretch out toward

---

[279] Apart from their literary status—André Malraux was an important novelist, Louis Aragon (1897–1982) a major poet and a novelist—the two were on the far-Left politically. (Malraux changed; Aragon, a leading Communist, did not.)

[280] Short for *Lager*: camp in German. Officers were imprisoned in an *Oflag*, ordinary soldiers in a *Stalag*, and deported Jews, *Résistants*, and other "undesirables" in a *Konzentrationslager*—concentration camp.

the outskirts of Paris through long streets bordered by cement walls. The "home" is a huge building, gray and silent, with dirty windows.

Madame H...wasn't there when I got there. For a long time I walked back and forth on the sidewalk across the street, waiting for her. For a long time I looked at this refuge of miserable people passing through it. The windows all seemed like blind windows. Just one was sparkling, on the third floor, with carefully pleated curtains. Weary of the sight, I walked in to talk with Madame H...'s fellow workers in their white aprons. I told them why I was there and that I did not know Madame H...but I knew her boy. Did she hear from him? How was he?

"Yes, she heard from him on this very day. Of course he was OK. Besides, he wouldn't say he wasn't, you understand..."

But Mme H...still did not return. I left a note and went away. And then on the way back, I found an old woman wearing a white apron. She had a long face and pale gray eyes. "Are you Mme H..."?

She was. We walked back to the home, talking about her son. "Oh," she said to me, "this is all I needed in my old age! I've had a lot of hard knocks, Monsieur. Oh! He loves his mother." She wasn't crying. But every word twisted her face. "He was really pampered in the home, you know. That's where I brought him up...for twenty-two years. Well, he tells me he's not unhappy...He's organizing a library for his pals...For him, books are everything, it's the only thing that interests him...Literature."

We had reached the home again. We walked by the other women, who marveled at our meeting as if it were a miracle. We walked up the gray stairs of this poor man's barracks. "We'll go to his room. Oh lord, it's not a palace...But it's his room. You can write him and say you saw it."

She opened a door, and there it was. In front of me was the sparkling window with yellow curtains. The room was small, meticulously neat, all shining, the bed ready. There was just one picture on the wall, a reproduction of a wounded lioness. An animal that would like to leap again, with its mouth twisted in suffering, stretching out, its body pierced with arrows. I said: "A very nice picture!"

"Yes, he likes it. He sees all kinds of things in it."

And Mme H...had me read all Jean's letters. Belzig! This is Jean H...'s first novel: Belzig! The prettiest village in the world. It's a land of lakes, woods, and meadows. Spring is admirable there, in fact. Berlin is not far off. They go there on excursions, like tourists, you know. Nothing is lacking in Belzig. There are even two movie theaters—everything, actually. J...is sure he'll see Paris in the newsreels. He'll see places he knows again. His work is not tiring. He's a secretary. And then, unbelievable but true, in Belzig he ran into three friends from school, three friends from Estienne. All kinds of luck. His friends called him "Zazou" because of his kazoo.

"And you know him, Monsieur," Mme H...says. "If tells me that's the way it is, then that's the way it is, he's not saying that to console me. You know him...Of course he's telling nothing but the truth...His kazoo. He wanted to take it with him. To play it for friends. He's so funny..."

She looks at me with a strange intensity and the tone of her words is the tone of someone who's asking but at the same time forbidding you from contradicting her.

I left. Mme H...walked me to the street. She wanted to show me her school, in passing. She's the one who's in charge of keeping the kindergarten of the home clean. "You'll tell him you saw it. He'll be really happy." I promised.

In the street I looked at the window with yellow curtains one more time. It shone in the middle of the gray façade, like a sign of all that a loving heart can do. Belzig! Belzig!

May 8

Tunis, Bizerte, and all North Africa have been liberated.

May 17

I had a visit from Nathanaël.[281] Nathanaël has proliferated for the last fifty years. He has become a whole species among young French intellectuals and the history of this proliferation would be no more, I fear, than the history of our abdication.

Nathanaël is pleasant, delicate, and chlorotic. He is increasingly malnourished. All the "fruits of the earth" are terribly regulated. There is a card for all pleasures, even for the most vulgar, even for bread.

What will you do with your master's precepts? The whole world is forbidden to you, with all its pleasures. "Assume as much humanity as possible," Gide wrote—meaning, in a happy world, and more simply put: enjoy. But really! Nothing is left to assume except suffering. Nathanaël is utterly disconcerted and has no idea what to do in a world full of distress. Nathanaël turns up his nose at that world. He has lost all appetite and has only his fine soul in reserve. He is devouring himself with a small noise: the noise of a mouse in a little box.

"You understand," Nathanaël said to me, "we have the thoughts one has at our age. We would like to be happy. We think about ourselves a great deal."

"But you are not alone."

Nathanaël is proud of his solitude and his chlorosis. That vanity is his last resource.

"But our problem is ourselves, of life inside us, of the wound it makes in us."

I pitied Nathanaël. He was grave. He was trying to find his thought and his words. A kind of shame was holding him back. Finally:

"The only problem is the problem of man alone."

---

[281] The name of the character to whom Gide's 1897 prose poem *Les Nourritures terrestres* (*The Fruits of the Earth*) is addressed; his teacher Ménalque advises Nathanaël to exalt sensuality and freedom but despise family ties, convention, and social responsibility.

And his eyes shone. He was pleased with his aphorism. I confessed that I defined man to myself in quite another way.

"Nathanaël," I added, "while you cogitate endlessly on your solitude, aren't you afraid that other people are preparing a life for you that you don't want and making a prison for you where you won't even have the right to be alone anymore? Alone, as you believe yourself to be. But one is never alone. The idea of our solitude is an utterly abstract idea, and a rather vain one, perhaps. Real solitude, the solitude people suffer from, is itself only a product of our society, the result of its disorder. Don't be too hasty and call this a paradox. Most of the problems of your man alone are decided by society. When it is in good health, the connections of each one of us to all the others are multiplied and enriched. When it is in bad health, we're confined inside ourselves. But that solitude is nothing but a misfortune. There is no reason to be proud of it and one should wish to get over it."

Nathanaël smiled at me. He found me completely ridiculous.

"But," he said, "we can no longer believe the way you believe. We seek only the truth inside ourselves, where we are free."

"Nathanaël, I'm afraid we will never agree. Truth is not that little inner, personal thing any more than freedom is merely the freedom of our dreams and our whims. If we want to know what freedom is, let us rather think of the freedom of others, not of ours own. It is not a healthy habit of mind to think in relation to oneself. We are not alone, Nathanaël. We are not alone, or, if solitude there be, let us not turn it into a refuge. Are they free, are they alone, all the men of your age who this very morning, perhaps, left for Germany . . .?" But Nathanaël does not have a soul that can think about things like that.

May 18

"Servitude debases men so much they begin to love it." (Vauvenargues.*)

May 24

There are only two principles, two systems of government in the world. One plays on the courage and intelligence of men and exalts them; the other plays on their cowardice and foolishness, and exploits them. One is democracy, the other, tyranny. Since foolishness is quick and intelligence is slow, the tyrant can always win at first, but he always loses in the long run. So let us have confidence.

Playing on the foolishness and cowardice of men only makes them more foolish and more cowardly. It's a wonder they end up correcting their mistake.

One can only conjecture how tyrants, so convinced of the common foolishness and the common cowardice of men, get their confidence in themselves, in their own wisdom. This is the essential contradiction of authoritarian politicians. Why should the "leaders" escape the common definition, why should they be better than their troops? The day comes when they die from their foolishness and their pride.

The contradiction of democratic politicians is that since they are betting on our intelligence and our courage, they must still never forget that we may be lacking in those virtues at any given moment. In order to last, democracy must be both confident and distrustful, both optimistic and pessimistic. A difficult balance to strike, but all great things are difficult and rare.

June 1

To preserve one's own freedom in a world of slaves. This is the whole political agenda of many people—and to crown it all they think they're some kind of hero. But it is only the politics of Narcissus. Freedom is other people's freedom. In a world of slaves, a real man feels like a slave. He can't bear living in it. I think of the words of Saint-Just*: "The day I am convinced that it is impossible to give the French people mores which are gentle, energetic, and sensitive, but inexorable toward tyranny and injustice, I will stab myself."

Thus the greatest moral and political force will always belong to *the man who asks nothing for himself*, and Narcissus is, fortunately, condemned to impotence. He always ends up by drowning himself in his fountain. It makes a few rings on the water.

A strange silence for the past two weeks. We have no more news at all. The RAF has not made one single raid on Germany. Is this the time of the decisive concentration of forces? And will they succeed? Sometimes we have a terrible feeling of dread.

June 12

All young men in the classes of '40–'42 have to leave for Germany on July 1. The panic of a crushed anthill. Some are thinking of crossing the border into Spain. Others of hiding in the mountains, in Savoy, or in the Massif Central. But most will resign themselves to it and leave. Many are already talking about the difficulties they will cause their parents if they flee... It's nobody's fault—and everybody's, the fault of common cowardice: it is getting harder and harder for someone who wants to hide. Those who have not yet left are grateful for the ordeals and suffering of those who have. The families of the men who are already drafted hope the draft will be general. Why would they help those who remain to have the courage their own young men lacked. I would venture to bet we'll see associations of STO veterans[282] and ex-prisoners after the war. The one who submitted to servitude for the longest time will take the prize. Whoever was most submissive will be entitled to the largest pension. What can vanity not

---

[282] We recall that the STO (Service du Travail Obligatoire) was the Compulsory Work Service in German factories.

accomplish: I see many young intellectuals gladly making up their minds to leave, so long as they're not quite subjected to the common fate. "Scientists" supposedly feel consoled at the idea that they'll be employed in laboratories, "literary people" as interpreters or office-workers. It would all be for the best if they were appointed staff sergeant in regiments of slaves.

One can't help seeing all this, and there is nothing happy about it.

The Allies have taken Pantelleria.[283]

June 20

"Everyone must be the king of himself." (King David.)

June 21

All Europe continues to wait.

"France alone." What vainglorious foolishness! France has no other future than Europe and the will to make its principle and its faith prevail.

June 22

Vichy is pushing its propaganda. Taking advantage of the feeling of helplessness the quasi-inactivity of the Allies for the past month has given us, it is spreading the rumor that we're on the verge of a new reversal of alliances. Hitler and Stalin are supposedly getting together to throw the Anglo-Saxons out of Europe. Such a conjuncture, if it came to pass, would put the final touches on the destruction of the conscience of France. To have some certainty in this confused fight, one should only judge by a few principles and not let oneself be moved by contingent facts. But we have to live in this chaos; it is not enough to judge it.

Montolieu, July 20

On vacation, after a month of exhausting work. Correcting papers. Exams— assembly line work. In two weeks, I examined 490 candidates at the oral,[284] five of them going by under my nose every hour without leaving me a minute's respite. I was exhausted. But perhaps the ordeal was salutary and instructive. I learned again, if I had ever forgotten, what it's like to spend your whole life earning a living; that is the condition of many men and it is terrible.

---

[283] Heavy bombing (by "the Tuskegee Airmen," among others) made it easy for British Commandos and U.S. Rangers to invade this island near Sicily on June 10.

[284] There is always an oral component to important nation-wide examinations in France, like the Baccalauréat at the end of secondary school and the competitive entrance exams to the government-sponsored *Grandes Écoles* like the École Normale Supérieure or the École Nationale d'Administration (ENA) that trains future executives and government ministers.

During that time, tremendous events had burst onto the scene and I had neither time nor energy to rejoice. The invasion of Sicily. A German offensive toward
Belogorod, but a Russian counter-offensive around Orel first, and then along the
whole front. It is, says Churchill, "the beginning of the end," but the end can
be long.

The village is drying in the sun. It has not rained for three months. The
drought reduced the crops to nothing. People are talking about famine, but each
one is still eating, behind his locked door. "Foreigners" like us are the only ones
who are really unhappy. The peasants on the surrounding farms aren't quite sure
what to think: Vichy's regulations irritate them, but all the same, when you can
sell an egg for six francs and a wild rabbit trapped in your neighbor's field for
sixty, things are going great.

July 25

Mussolini has resigned.

General Badoglio* has become head of the government, no doubt to do the
various Marshals' jobs and soon hand over his country to Germany. Ordinary
people in the village are rejoicing, but the low comedy continues. A notorious
Pétainist, just yesterday a great admirer of Mussolini, is running around on
the village square shouting to everyone who goes by, "Hey, how about those
Macaronis?" All the traitors are getting ready to betray again. Victory is not
far off.

I would like to be in Paris, with my friends, the better to share my joy. It is
mild out and one would think it was September, harvest time. A thin fog is
hanging over the valley. The sky, low and overcast, traps all noises. I can hear all
the birds singing in the bushes of the wood on the other side of the stream. But
they are singing for the Eternal.

If events develop a bit quickly, I'll go back to Paris.

July 27

The truest pleasure one can give to a human being with some nobility is to
give him the feeling that he is needed. There is without a doubt no greater charity
than to seem to need someone else's charity. On the contrary, nothing is crueler
than to impose on someone the feeling that he is useless, that he's good for
nothing, that he is absolutely not needed and he is nothing but a burden on the
earth and on men.

B... — He belongs, as I do, to that species of writer whose wealth and poverty,
both, is to have lived a somewhat singular life, to have a biography. Our patron
saint, for all of us, the extreme example, is Rousseau. The risk we run is to become
overly attached to our singularity; what we then write has only the value of an
anecdote. The problem is no different for us than for any writer: to succeed in
dominating that strange experience and bring it back—however strange it may

be—to the common law, integrate it into the human condition. Rousseau is so great only because he drew lessons from his life that are valuable for everybody: the *Discourse on Inequality* and the *Social Contract*.

August 2

A curious letter from B....He's worried: the rumor was circulating in Paris toward July 20, he explains, that I was "relieved of [my] duties and a decision on [my] subsequent administrative fate is to be made within three months." We shall see. It's a sign of the times. I don't want to worry about it. The end, the real end, is drawing near. And I always thought that the last year would not be without problems for me. If this is serious, I'll surely find other ways of earning a living for us.

August 8

No news from the Ministry of Education. But the same rumor has come back to me from another source. Let us wait.

Life is very difficult here, and in order to eat you have to be a poacher and a killer. I spent yesterday morning hunting with a ferret. It's stupid, cruel, and quickly becomes boring. You send out the dogs so that they hem in the rabbits, you put nets over the holes, and in there you put the ferret, a vile little beast with a rat's face. And you wait, crouching in the thicket, without moving or breathing, with your ear to the hole. The ferret's little bell is lost in the deep earth. All of a sudden the growling of a fight and the rabbit jumps, twisting, into the net. All you have to do now is knock it out. The ferret at the edge of the hole shows its silly, cruel face. I don't want to talk about the things that go wrong. Sometimes the rabbit lets itself be bled, or what is stranger, gets itself "scratched": its head between two stones, it presents only its back to the ferret. The ferret sucks, scratches, doesn't come back. Yesterday that happened twice to us. My companion finally got it to come back by banging on the stones at the rim of the hole for a long time. But we were really concerned. What if the ferret got lost, fell into some ravine, or "counter-ferreted," that is, got stuck between the bottom of the burrow and the dead rabbit. A ferret, these days, sells for 1,200 francs.

August 22

Roquefort-de-Sault.—I'm spending a great deal of time on what the people here call the "Campanat." It's a kind of natural belvedere on top of which they installed a bell to toll death knells and sound the alarm. It is also, unfortunately, a garbage dump. In the evening, everybody goes by to lower their pants or raise their petticoats. And the only sanitation service is the flies, the chickens, and the sun. And yet I found a refuge there, a shaded rock I sit on, sheltered from the wind. I re-read *Robinson Crusoe* or Van Gogh's *Correspondence*. Immediately below me there is the chaotic, sordid life of the village, but all around, in the distance, the simple, great order of the mountains and the forest, and the sight distracts me. Pigs are eating in the farmyards with their trotters in their tubs, and at the doorstep of the houses, hens are scratching around in the dung. It's threshing time. The men are seated in the shady side of the threshing field, relaxing with their elbows on their knees. But suddenly it all swings into action, everything gets organized as in a Breugel painting. It becomes a work circle. In front of a rich house, they're threshing with oxen. A young boy swings the sheaves into a drum with his pitchfork; the women, white scarves on their heads, shake out the straw. The men bind it and take it away. Poor people thresh with a flail at the end of a pole. At the edge of the village, two men, father and son, threshed with a pole for four days, "doing by themselves," as they say, "all the work alone." I sensed a tragedy, or misfortunes. The two men are alone; the women are dead. The worst of it is, they hate each other, can't talk to each other, and work away without saying a word. Once the sheaves are threshed and the straw is picked up, they sweep up the meager harvest on the threshing fields without losing a grain.

Oh, to know how to find the principle, the right expression for all that! The all-seeing gaze of a Balzac or a Tolstoy.

I turn my eyes away from the village and look beyond it. All the sounds carry in the calm air. A rooster crows. A reaper in a meadow is sharpening his scythe, women are digging potatoes. Children are pilfering an orchard. On the slopes of the mountain I can make out the fields, so narrow they look like ribbons divided to infinity. The conditions of life make life. Here they encourage greed and shameful quarrels. Each can think only about himself. It is written into the very earth. The laws and the conditions of life must be changed. Here, order begins only above the village, above men, where nature has remained the master and has not had to bear division and parceling out, and seems to maintain for us all her virgin forests and pasturages. It all became sordid everywhere men could climb up, fix limits, set up markers, and proclaim: "This is mine alone."[285] I think of laws that would organize generosity and exchange the way the laws that we are subjected to organize greed. I dream of a deeper order so that life may no longer be this mold on the side of a huge rock.

It is society that saves man. The marvel, the miracle is to have interested these economical ants, despite everything, in a general system, in great vague things they hardly understand: France, freedom, honor. A few conversations I had with the people of this countryside were quite astonishing from this point of view, and, all in all, rather comforting. It is not hard to get them to understand that the general interest is the real country of man. But that vague thing does

---

[285] Guéhenno is echoing the passage that opens Part II in Rousseau's *Discourse on the Origin of Inequality* (1755): the invention of private property, the basis both of inequality and society itself. Guéhenno changes it slightly, for emphasis: "mine *alone*."

not yet have enough vital force inside them and costs them still more sacrifices than it brings joys.

September 1

Sometimes a great surge of hope elates us—at the news of other people's misfortunes. Hamburg razed to the ground, 40,000 families in Milan homeless, Nuremberg destroyed, the whole population of Berlin in flight...Now that's really something. And we call for more ruins, more miseries still. They alone can bring us closer to deliverance.

After all, peoples are responsible for their misfortunes, too, and it is just and necessary for their cure that Italy and Germany should expiate the vain stupidity they have been intoxicated with for the past twenty years. They have to confirm for themselves that decidedly, nationalism does not pay. It is a pleasure to consider that from now on the most notorious idiots and the most hideous torturers in Italy, so proud of their uniforms only yesterday, are burning their black shirts in their fireplaces, terrified, taking care to make even the ashes disappear.

In this village, there were twenty-three prisoners. Three have returned on account of "prisoner relief." But ten young men have been deported on account of "compulsory work" and there are now thirty prisoners. *Vive le Maréchal!*

September 3

Art for art's sake. A silly invention of decadence, of an era when artists, along with all other men, lost the sense of the universal and became makers of trinkets, specialists in a little profession, and brought everything down to that level. Great poets never posed such questions. But they built their tragedies, their novels and cathedrals to respond to their time, to their world. All great works are works for the occasion. This one makes a fan or a mirror for his mistress, but that one makes a shining cross that will open the way to the next crusade. Another recites the first prayer to a new God. Yet another explains our new anxiety to us. A poet is not a specialist. Everything is his domain. He wants to say everything, every time. Everything rings out in his work and in each part of his work. And that is what creates the strange harmony between all the great works of one era. The occasion commands them. The greatest artist is simply the one who seizes it in all its complexity, the one who sees and hears more than others. Balzac, Hugo...

September 8

Italy has surrendered.

Wuthering Heights.—What French mania is revealed in this title, chosen by the first translator: "The Lover" (*L'Amant*). Lacretelle translates *Hautes plaintes* ("High Lamentations"), the work of an academic peasant. I prefer *Les Hauts de*

Hurlevent[286] of I don't know which translator: it is darker, better suited to the text of the novel.

September 10

I've just spent a few days in the company of an admirable young lad, a staunch individualist, someone who is the best that contemporary capitalist education can achieve: instinctively generous but reserved and delicate, distant, marvelously polite, tender but very intelligent and careful about his tenderness, always distrustful of his heart, and aristocratic. We debated endlessly last night, on the terrace, while it was raining stars. The future worries him. Communism. The sole question for him is preserving a certain nobility which seems to him inseparable from the cult of the individual, and freedom—his freedom. He thinks he has no prejudices at all, yet he seems to me full of them: a prisoner of his habits, of an order from which he profits—quite unconsciously—and of his happiness. Equality is horrifying to him. I observe that it's easy, for him. He says, "I'm not giving other people the right to care for me. It's fine for them to enjoy the same happiness as I do, but I am not ready in the slightest to sacrifice myself for the happiness of the greatest number and I will not accept a regime that imposes a law on me which I find odious, with no recourse and with no hope. An instinct, however fine and generous it may be, does not have the same value as a thought."

At one point, I think, we got to the heart of the argument. I was telling him about those accounts of my life I'm writing now under the title of *Changer la vie*.[287] I told him what a "Communist" I was, by my origins, my youth, almost all my memories, but what an "Aristo" books had almost made of me, how uncertain I was about the usefulness of that great striving for intelligence and culture that had filled my life, destroyed passions in me, disciplined the instincts and perhaps weakened the simple sense of fairness. "I am no longer quite sure," I told him, "which is better: life or consciousness, the energy of one or the clarity of the other."

Then he noisily blew smoke out of his pipe.

"But that would be the end of intelligence."

"No. But merely the end of intellectualist games, perhaps."

"But those games, that detour, are quite necessary. Man seems to me an abominable animal. God knows where his instinct alone would lead him."

"We are losing our way. The contemporary bourgeoisie lost itself in this 'detour,' as you say. It's not a detour, it's a labyrinth and they find great pleasure

---

[286] Literally "Wind-howl Heights"; it has been the usual French translation of the title for some time.

[287] "Changing Life." See, among other entries, July 17, 1940, and note 25, p. 8.

in losing themselves in it. They never take the straight path, the best path, the one men walk on."

"You're talking of intelligence as an instinct? Instinct alone plunges straight ahead. Intelligence scours around in the bushes."

And this very young boy obliged me to become aware of my incorrigible optimism. I mumbled, for myself:

"Yes, the intelligence of dilettantes, but not the intelligence of humanity. The mind."

And that's when he said:

"An instinct, however fine and generous it may be, does not have the same value as a thought. And thought is prudent and slow."

"But the mind is quick. And you have to realize that all the people who are suffering are in a bit of a hurry and can't accept the idea of lingering in that detour. The mind emigrates elsewhere when it is ill served in that detour; I'm not sure it isn't abandoning that bourgeoisie, so proud of its culture, to fly to people about whom we'd say—quickly and rashly—that they don't think, they only have instincts. Intelligence is an instinct, too, but we are stuffed with intellectualism. It's as if, having possessed words for so long, intellectuals had reduced the things they name to their own use. Freedom, for example, is only intellectual freedom for them—the freedom of intellectuals. We must think of the other people's freedom as much as our own. We can only be free among free men."

"And the Soviets seem to you to guarantee that freedom? What is the value of their system of representation? A system of barely opened doors, so that decisions can finally be made only by a few individuals who have shown their credentials many times."

"I don't know. But one difference between the Soviets and our parliaments appears rather clear to me. The law, the mores and prejudices were such in our countries that in a deliberative assembly there were four intellectuals—real or sham, and more often sham than real—compared to one what I would call 'thingist.' In a soviet made up of factory delegates or peasants, the proportion is reversed, I imagine. I will not decide where the intelligence is better represented..."

"Intelligence is general; it's not a specialist."

The discussion died out. A cloud on the horizon was rising in the clear night, occasionally striped by crossbars that lit it up in a new way each time...

September 11

A speech by Hitler. Very short. Not quite fifteen minutes. The morose voice of a gloomy, concentrated man.

What I owe to that Christian air in which I grew up: the feeling that just one thing is necessary. But it almost made me lose all pride. My mother's dismal humility. The atmosphere of defeat in the house. The one necessary thing is a struggle.

September 21

It's done. They're not relieving me of my functions, no: they're "demoting" me. They're sending me back to the job I used to do twenty years ago. These are wretched little persecutions and I would be ashamed if I suffered from them. I am full of disgust and scorn.

Paris, October 4

We've been back here since October 1. A difficult journey. Our train hit a bomb near Argenton. (It was the 17th attack in two weeks, in this region where thousands of "deserters" from the Work Service have taken to the maquis.) But the train was going slowly and we got out of it without much harm done.

Here two air-raid warnings a day is routine. The planes rumble in the night as they did three years ago. But they aren't the same. Then they were going toward London. Now that's where they're coming from.

The petty persecution is continuing. They appointed me to a position that was abolished two years ago . . . Let's see what happens next.

October 5

Goebbels, speaking as a delegate from the Eternal, proffers mysterious menaces: "Neither English trees," he says, "nor American trees will be able to grow toward the sky. We will stop them." This is, at least, what we can read in *L'Oeuvre*. What does he mean? But I suppose he can thank a misprint or a bad translation for having made him appear to speak like a prophet just this once.

October 6

An invisible little paragraph in this morning's paper announces that fifty Communists have been shot. Two years ago, news like that would be printed in poster-size characters. In the meantime, they keep on shooting a few patriots every day. They do it without saying so. Now they're changing tactics once more. These announcements in small print, they think, will be read by patriots and will scare them without arousing horror in the general public.

H . . ., back from Germany, from Belzig, came to see me. He developed heart problems from pushing those carts in the Belzig explosives factory and almost died. I would like to write his story down, but it is absolutely impossible. He spoke as if in a dream, without raising his eyes, and the horrors he was relating seemed unreal. He landed in a transit camp near Berlin. For four days and four nights, amidst thousands of "pals" like him, he waited to learn where he would be sent. The loudspeaker spewed out names without stopping. He couldn't sleep, had to be ready when his name was called. If not you'd run the risk of waiting for still more days and nights. The loudspeaker ordered you to go stand in front of this or that panel, #1 or #2 or #3. There company managers would come, evaluate you, look you up and down, feel your biceps and calves, and either take you or leave you, according to what they thought. You were lucky if you were taken by a craftsman with his own little shop.

He left with a team for Belzig. An old factory admirably camouflaged in the woods. When they came into the building where they were to sleep, they saw a coffin for the first man who ... The administration had planned everything ... He worked at loading and pushing carts with three little deported Ukrainian girls between thirteen and fifteen years old. They gave them soup twice a day. And that was all. Impossible to live without the packages. The Russians didn't get any. Each Frenchman, spontaneously, had adopted and fed a child ... The fear was Potsdam, the third floor of the little palace of Potsdam where the Gestapo had set up its services; you were sent there at the slightest suspicion of sabotage ... The prisoners, locked up by the dozen in each cell, were absolutely naked and slept on the cement, packed one against the other ... For two hours he told me his story like that, looking slightly crazy, and I don't know what to believe out of all he told me. Sometimes a little light: in the hospital the nurses treated them "better than mothers." Good as well as evil is done mechanically, according to regulations. Nothing in Germany, he told me, has a face anymore, neither the streets nor the men. And perhaps all of Europe will be like that tomorrow.

October 9

Vildrac* and Dunois* were arrested Thursday.

I haven't gone out these last, infinitely dreary days. I walk through the streets without curiosity, wondering why I should keep on living. Sleeping is my only pleasure: it means not living. The wonderful thing is that I can always sleep—and without dreaming, like an animal. Last night I sank down into sleep as into death, with great pleasure. But this morning the phone wakes me up. It's a young madman shouting his plans to me, absolutely heedless of wiretapping: he wants to see me as soon as possible to found an internationalist review that will make fun of German censorship. And his frenzy makes me realize the extent of my despair.

October 10

I leafed through the notebooks that have made up this diary for four years, and it's a rather depressing ordeal, just right for stripping me of all illusions about the unity of a human being, and my being. So many contradictions! How events and circumstances bowl us over and drive us this way or that! How our kingdom is of this world, whether we like it or not! And how much we are subjected to the confusion of this kingdom!

Nonetheless, I will continue this diary. May it help me to give myself a bit of internal order. Or let it bear witness to my mistakes.

October 11

"Yesterday was one of those beautiful sunless days that you say resemble that beautiful blind woman with whom Philip the Second was in love." Yesterday reminded me of that precious sentence of Balzac's[288] and the fine letter that follows it. We crossed the Bois de Boulogne, from the Muette to the footbridge of Saint-Cloud. One would need the ample forms of long ago to relate that silence and that peace. "Peace was universal, from the highest regions of the air to the surface of the earth…" A soft, light fog filtered the light and enveloped the bushes and trees. Not a leaf was stirring. The trees have not yet turned yellow. Only a few sycamores foretold the fires and fatal destruction of autumn. We met no one except two little old ladies, who—for what reason?—were picking horse chestnuts. The Seine was a great shimmering mirror. Along the banks a few men were fishing, strangely silent. The war was Lord knew where. In front of the Rothschild estate where the Kriegsmarine had set up its headquarters, two blue soldiers were standing guard, but they themselves had forgotten their orders and rules, and like real human beings, seemed to be talking about things back home.

The ragman has changed his song. I hear him singing in the street:

C'mon you housewives with old clothes
Don't you throw 'em in the ashcan
Here I am, here comes the ragman

They say 160 people have been shot last week in the prison of Fresnes, and 50 in the Santé.

October 18

I think of my friend Dabit. The other day, Blanzac,* Mauriac,* and I went for a walk along the Quai de Jemmapes, just to see the Hôtel du Nord again,[289] as sordid as ever with its dark windows and leprous façade. Mauriac pointed out that all that remained of the writing was the word *maison*. A "house" indeed.

Since then, I've re-read a few books by Dabit and I think again of the questions he used to ask me in his sing-song voice, when he would bring them to me hot off the press. He apologized for writing and publishing "such sad things."

"Say, that exists, too, doesn't it?" he would murmur. "And after all, it has to be said?"

He was full of envy for Giono who only had to talk about water, wind, and sun and all the joys of the earth.

"It's not our fault, right?" he would continue. "That, too, exists and it has to be told, it has to be told. But how can one make beautiful books from that filth?"

---

[288] Guez de Balzac, not the novelist (see note 128, p. 71).

[289] The classic film *Hôtel du Nord*, based on Dabit's novel of the same name, had come out some five years earlier.

And almost always, as we went from one misery to another, we would come back to talking about the war. About the war he'd fought in, and kept its anguish inside him, as if he had never cleansed himself of the greenish, infected muck he had slogged through on the days of attack around Verdun.

"You can't feel it," he would say. "But it never left us. And it's coming back, it's coming back. I'm sure of it. Tell me, what should we do?"

For him, death resolved the question.

October 23

The Russians have taken back Dniepropetrovsk.

I explain things to little children and I have them recite their lessons—that's my new profession.

Tityre, tu patulae recubans...[290]

Notice the alliterations, gentlemen. Tity, tu patu? Tity. Tutu. It's magnificent.

No, I do seriously try to find ways of amusing them and adapting to them.

A young man came to see me. New style. Brilliant white sweater. Mountain jacket under the raincoat. Cleated shoes. He sets down his Tyrolean bag at his feet before making his confession to me: he wanted to see me because his friends, my former students, but also de Man,* Alexis Carrel,* and Father Maydieu[291] told him that he always spoke as if he were a disciple of mine. "And yet," he tells me, "I've read nothing of yours, nothing but a few articles, perhaps... The general himself must march in step with his troops. You did say that one day." I answer that that is indeed quite possible. "Well then, I'm going to tell you my story now, tell you my plans, I'd like to know what you think of them. You'll even tell me what you think of my language, because I don't know if it's any good. If it's weak, that's because my thought is weak, too."

He says this very quickly, very much at ease, like a man who chatters away and asks questions at a pause between two parts of his chatter. Deep down, he knows where he's going, and I can feel that in reality he has no need of my advice.

Then he tells me he was originally a Marxist. His mother was an embroiderer. The depression of 1929 and the change in fashion abolished her trade, and he knows how humiliating it is to go stamp an unemployment card every week. She kept him in the lycée despite everything. And then he was at the École des Cadres d'Uriage, before it was recently dissolved.[292] There was both good and bad there, but a huge

---

[290] The beginning of the first Eclogue in Virgil's *Bucolics*: *Tityrus, tu patulae recubans sub tegmine fagi* ("You, Tityrus, reclining under the cover of a beech tree...").

[291] Father Jean-Augustin Maydieu (1900–1955) was an early member of the Resistance; Carrel and de Man were not—to say the least (see the *Biographical Dictionary*).

[292] A national school founded in 1940 to train the future elite of Pétain's *Révolution Nationale*; it became increasingly critical of Vichy and was shut down by Laval* in January 1943. Many of its members entered the Resistance. The school is the ancestor of the present École Nationale d'Administration (ENA), which still trains the political and economic elite of France.

amount of good will. He is still a Marxist as far as the economy is concerned. But his last years taught him that nothing can be done and all is lost if men do not recover the sense of their equality. The question is to know how to protect, in the communist society he desires, the values of freedom. The government dispersed his classmates, but they decided to live like a religious order lost in the mass of humanity. This "order" has been formed. They have no illusions; they know that "victory" itself will only lead to chaos. How to save what must be saved? Meanwhile, of course, they are working underground. Should they enter the Communist Party or do their work at its side? They are still hesitating on this point.

I had to tell him I was still less optimistic than he was, that he didn't realize the strength of political parties, which—in a rather low way perhaps, but honestly—only take account of the way things really are. I told him I admired his friends' enterprise but doubted its effectiveness; the word "order" is a fine word, but it might be no more than that, and spirituality will be suspect from now on, for it served as a cover for so many swindles over the past fifty years—and still more for the last three, under the reign of Vichy. I told him a language which is too "spiritual" is often merely hypocritical and dishonest, and there were, for example, no worse enemies of a communist economy than all those who for the past three years have had nothing but the word "community" on their lips;[293] for my part, I felt condemned to solitude and I didn't see any other duty for us but to keep a few true words alive through the chaos, the master words, so that they might continue their work when men begin to think once again.

He left with his pack on his back, for what work, for what persecutions? There was nobility in his eyes and on his face . . .

October 26

I'm re-reading Vigny's admirable *Daphné*. Few books are as relevant today. The words of that young "monk" who came to see me the other day are hardly different from what the disciples of Libanius might have said to each other toward the end of the Greco-Roman world.[294]

October 27

Lusseyran,* Besnier, and Février from Louis-le-Grand have been arrested.

November 3

The Germans are shooting hostages or people who have been convicted, every day in Fresnes. V . . . says the same admirable scene takes place every morning.

---

[293] Instead of representative democracy, Pétain advocated a society of "organic communities" ruled from the top. Unions, however, were illegal.

[294] Libanius is a major character in Vigny's posthumously published novel (1912), set in late antiquity; the novel ends with a plea for an apology to the Jewish people for the persecutions inflicted on them by the Christians.

The order goes from cell to cell, through the gutters, the toilet pipes, the water pipes: "Six o'clock for cell thirty-two." And at the appointed time, the whole prison begins to sing the *Marseillaise* or "The Song of Departure."[295] The prisoners have broken all the windows so the victims can hear their farewell song as they cross the prison yard. The Germans have forbidden all singing. They are going to make examples, torture, and execute. Uselessly. The prison continues to sing.

The thought of things like that should never leave us.

The Russians have arrived before Kherson; they've occupied Perekop. From now on, the Germans in Crimea are isolated.

November 13

Abel and his little darlings[296] have done their work well. It is clear that all year I will be able to do nothing more than my job. I have the duties of a novice and everything my colleagues did not want. Seventeen hours of classes per week instead of six, and I have the greatest difficulty in finding a tone suitable for the little children I now have in my charge. After three weeks, I'm already crushed by fatigue and I can't take it anymore. Will I even be able to go on with this diary?

There is no more France, there are only isolated Frenchmen whose only relations with each other, almost, are secret relations, dangerous and forbidden, and that in itself will make it very hard to make any general judgment on this country in the years to come. Every Frenchman, without any assistance, without anything to inspire him, confined to his prison, no longer has the worth he used to have all alone. And it's true that some have become accustomed to servitude, already so long, so old, and they're just waiting for the end, any end. But countless, too, are those who are on the watch, and if I noted down the names and adventures of those I know there would be no end to it—if there were no danger in that for them. For we've reached the point where I can very well write down all our shame here without compromising anyone, but I have to keep for myself, only in my memory, even the names of those who, secretly and silently, are saving our honor.

The dream of St. Jerome. He was too fond of pagan books, orators, and poets. One night he saw himself dead and called before his judge and he shouted to defend himself: "I am a Christian! I am a Christian!" And he heard the judge answering him: "No, you are lying. You are a Ciceronian, not a Christian: there is your treasure, there, too, is your heart." From then on, he wanted to recognize nothing but the Gospel. "I set out to read the holy books," he said, "with as much passion as I had for reading human books."

---

[295] *Le Chant du départ*, a revolutionary war song dating from 1794, became an anthem of the Resistance.

[296] Abel Bonnard,* Minister of Education. His homosexuality was a frequent target of underground satire.

How many "Ciceronians" there are among us! But we have the excuse that the book in which we will discover the new Word has not been written.

November 14

"You didn't recognize me?" he triumphs. He has changed his face, cut off his mustache, grew sideburns and an unruly mop of hair, put on glasses, discarded the leather jacket he used to wear, and put on a raincoat. He tells me his story. "Thirty-nine months in a concentration camp. Imprisoned by Daladier* from December 1939 on.[297] Prison, camps, and then I was released. Funny, but that's the way it was: a pal of mine from the camp who got me released, a 'Christian' who'd been locked up for not wanting to hand in information about men who could be deported for 'prisoner relief.' A strange guy, a little craftsman who made watchcases. One year he made 100,000 francs, but he realized it was the same year he'd made three men work who were working alongside him. So he didn't want the 100,000 francs and pooled his business. He told me he found that in the Gospel, but I couldn't believe him. But now, I've seen it. It's huge: there are two factories, one in Valence, the other in Besançon, and then a farm they bought with the profits, 400 acres in the Vercors,[298] where they hid guys from the factories who were supposed to go to Germany. He knew people in Vichy, he was released and he got me released right after. Like he told me. Wasn't more than four days after I was released, they came back to lock me up again. But I was way off the road, if you see what I mean. I'm directing the communal farm. Eight hundred meters up. With a lookout checking the valley and the whole road coming up from the plain. The gendarmes know what's going on. I'm the only guy up there who knows something about working the soil. I went to Paris when I was fifteen, but before, I worked on the farm with my father. All the other guys are watch-makers. Can you imagine. But it works! It works! We work and we argue, the Christians and us. There's one hour of education every day. On Sundays, mass on one side and me on the other, I explain Marxism to my buddies . . ."

I listened to him for a long time. It was so very evident that this man had no self-interest whatsoever and that not for a moment did he have the feeling of his own superior nature, which was, however, glaringly obvious.

---

[297] We can guess he was a member of the Communist Party, illegal in France from September 1939 (when Daladier was prime minister) until the end of the war.

[298] This mountain range in southeastern France became a center for Resistance fighters, who were decimated by German forces there in June 1944 with the help of the French Militia. Created by Vichy in January 1943 and headed by Joseph Darnand,* at its height the *Milice* numbered about 30,000 armed and uniformed men with a homegrown program for the Nazification of France. While it was used mainly to fight the Resistance and root out Jews, the Militia also assassinated some well-known progressive figures of the Third Republic. Many militiamen fled to Germany in August 1944, often with their families.

A recruitment poster for the Service d'Ordre Légionnaire (SOL), the ancestor of the
French Militia, which hunted down *Résistants* and Jews. The "21 points" in the
program of this militant arm of the French Legion are *against* republican democracy
(called "anarchy") and *for* "discipline"; *against* "Jewish leprosy," *for* "French purity";
etc. *Author's Collection.*

November 17

The young students going to work in the mines to avoid going to Germany
have a strange experience: they are hired on and hidden by patriotic managers,
but I doubt the experience teaches them everything it could. Acquired prejudices
are the strongest. One of the students I saw recently (M...), a *Normalien*, specializing in Egyptology, is for the moment head of a logging squad in a forest
above Grenoble. First he worked on the assembly line in a factory for two months,
in Grenoble itself. Fifty-four hours a week of exhausting work surrounded by
infernal noise. It still horrified him as he told me about it, but he only brings
everything back to himself. Having lived among men who didn't think and whose
work exhausted them so much they couldn't have thought even if they wanted
to, had only puffed up his feeling of his own superiority. And he was proud of
having held out. He felt nothing but scorn for his companions at work, decried
their lack of awareness, their coarseness, and proclaimed them unworthy of

BEKANNTMACHUNG | **AVIS**

1. Der Kapitänleutnant **Henri Louis Honoré COMTE D'ESTIENNES D'ORVES**, französischer Staatsangehöriger, geb. am 5. Juni 1901 in Verrières,

2. der Handelsvertreter **Maurice Charles Émile BARLIER**, französischer Staatsangehöriger, geb. am 9. September 1905 in St. Dié,

3. der Kaufmann **Jan Louis-Guilleaume DOORNIK**, holländischer Staatsangehöriger, geb. am 26 Juni 1905 in Paris,

sind wegen Spionage zum Tode verurteilt und heute erschossen worden.

Paris, den 29. August 1941.

Der Militärbefehlshaber in Frankreich.

1. Le lieutenant de vaisseau **Henri Louis Honoré COMTE D'ESTIENNES D'ORVES**, Français, né le 5 juin 1901 à Verrières,

2. l'agent commercial **Maurice Charles Émile BARLIER**, Français, né le 9 septembre 1905 à St-Dié,

3. le commerçant **Jan Louis-Guilleaume DOORNIK**, Hollandais, né le 26 juin 1905 à Paris,

ont été condamnés à mort à cause d'espionnage. Ils ont été fusillés aujourd'hui.

Paris, le 29 Août 1941.

Der Militärbefehlshaber in Frankreich.

The Germans posted this announcement in the Metro and elsewhere, informing the public that "three men were condemned to death for espionage. They were shot today." The first man listed, d'Estienne d'Orves, is a hero of the Resistance. *Author's Collection.*

doing anything different from what they did. At the end of two months, the boss, whom he hadn't heard from since he hired him, suddenly asked him to dinner one evening and promoted him to head logger. Now he commands a team of twenty loggers in the forest. They work like mad, he says, and quickly earn money that they spend even more quickly by getting blind drunk as soon as they've finished their job. In a few weeks he'll go back down to the factory, but this time it will be to run the assembly line and organize the "Bedaux system."[299] The boss can count on him, his intelligence and his toughness. If the war left him the time, he would make him his associate and his son-in-law.

My young intellectual finds all this perfectly natural.

He thinks he's born to command, and in any case not for those servile tasks that are, on the contrary, so precisely suited to the men he met. I question him about the future; the prospect of Communist rule worries him. What would it do with him? With the Egyptologist he wants to be? (For one must grant him this: he has remained faithful to all his passions of a young *Normalien* and a seeker of truth.) He takes society as a fact: there have to be all those forced laborers in

[299] A way of speeding up the assembly line by timing each task and paying more for faster work.

A 1942 Vichy anti-communist propaganda poster. A young working-class thug, political leaflets under his arm, knife and half-drunk bottle of wine under his belt, writes graffiti on the wall ("[Let's have] Soviets everywhere") while a dog urinates against it. The text reads, "Different ways of dirtying things up . . . Same result!" The Communists became active in the Resistance after Hitler invaded the USSR in June 1941. Vichy and the Nazis claimed they *were* the Resistance. *Photo courtesy of Jean-Kely Paulhan.*

order for there to be an Egyptologist. The old system, as empirical as it was, seems to him rather good on the whole, since it distinguished between the intelligent people and the idiots and was not wrong in his case, picked him out and made him an Egyptologist. I ask him if he is quite sure that all the idiots and drunkards among whom he is living for now were really born idiots and drunkards . . .

The Russians are at Jitomir and continue to advance toward Poland.

November 28

I don't have the time to keep this diary. I run from one task to another. Truly "plagued by children and young people." I counted: I see close to 300 pupils every week. I had to change and reschedule the hours. On Thursday, for the sixth hour of classes, I was to meet the young ladies who are candidates for

A Vichy poster recruiting Frenchmen to work in German factories: "Hard times are over! Papa's earning money in Germany!" When propaganda failed to attract enough volunteers to meet the needs of their war effort, the Nazis demanded a Service du Travail Obligatoire (Compulsory Work Service). In September 1942, Vichy complied by drafting men between eighteen and fifty and unmarried women from twenty-one to thirty-five. *Library of Congress LC-DIG-ds-03288.*

the *Agrégation*.[300] But I was literally stammering with fatigue. I put the hour off till Wednesday. It will be at my fourth hour: the students have a few more chances to have something to devour.

I'm reading a little book the Dominicans sent me: *France, A Country for Missionaries?* It would seem that the de-Christianization of France has gone so far that from now on, in order to bring the bulk of the French population back into the faith, priests should proceed as they do in Cambodia or Chad. This or that neighborhood around the outskirts of Paris is as "pagan" as a large Ubangi village. In years gone by, when I believed so strongly in reason and had so much

---

[300] See note 14 in the *Translator's Introduction*, p. xv.

confidence in man, admissions of defeat like the figures and graphs published in this little book would only have made me rejoice. Today they worry me somewhat. Not that I am moved by the declamations of these "missionaries," or that I believe, as they do, that all working class morality has been lost because the workers no longer go to mass. Christianity was dying: if it is now completely dead, perhaps it is only hypocrisy that has died. But it must be said that nothing has yet replaced that great order in people's souls, that path of prayers and dreams that Christianity gave to souls when it was strong and influential. At any rate, there can be no question of restoring or resuscitating it. The authors of this little book wonder vainly about the reasons for this de-Christianization: they are unable to recognize them, or do not want to. It's because we can no longer believe what they ask us to believe. But what can we, what should we, believe?

Moreover, their conclusions are full of doubts. They write: "If we don't create missions for workers with no religion and no culture, others will do so; and they will soon have a culture and a religion, too ... Please God that it won't be too far from that of Christ ..."

So missions of the new faith must be organized.

Professional Readings. This is the book they put in the hands of all the children in technical and professional schools. The whole thing should be changed. Everything is brought back to the profession. The readings they've selected teach the child the definition of a potter, a miner, a pastry-maker, a mechanic, a shopkeeper, a shepherd, a nurseryman, a servant—"devoted" of course—a driver, a rag-dealer, a lifeguard, a gold-miner and a young movie-star ...! What foolishness. You couldn't do better if you wanted to train convicts and shackle everybody to his chain. Nothing to remind each one of these future drudges what, perhaps, a whole man is and should be. And no doubt one must teach the duties of the trade. But one earns a living, one should earn a living, only to live better. You don't spend your whole life in the factory, on the assembly line. Man has to be educated for the whole of his life and given a direction for his dreams. It should also be a principle of education above all to teach everyone everything he would normally get to know the least in the prison of his family, professional, and national habits. It's in secondary schools rather than in vocational schools that it would be a good idea to teach the greatness and servitude of the trades. There is no paradox in this.

Vichy has been in crisis for the past few weeks. We're just beginning to get a vague idea of what's happening. The Marshal, preoccupied as he is with clearing his name, had prepared an address in which he asked, not the Council of Ministers, but the former parliament to name his heir and successor. Laval naturally forbade its publication. And since then, the old Tartuffe has been sulking in his hotel, refusing to sign any decree. Laval is spreading the rumor that he's sick, but the old man walks around his estate to show the population that he is quite alive and in good health. He threatened to hand in his resignation, but cannot do so, since his address did not appear in the *Journal Officiel* and the old constitutional decree is still law. If he resigned, the Council of Ministers would install Laval in his place.

As far as one can see, if the trick had worked, it was to place all responsibility for what Vichy has done for two years onto Laval, and the old man—exonerated, parliamentary and republican—would be helped again by the senators and deputies who handed France over to Germany three years ago. As they are eager to recover some power themselves, he would become, against de Gaulle and the Committee of National Liberation in Algiers, a kind of Giraud* with seven stars on his cap: the French bourgeoisie would be reconciled to him, and the English and Americans, who knows, might agree to deal with him.

Massive, continuous bombing of Berlin. Horror is reaching its height.

December 3

This evening on Boulevard Saint-Michel as night was falling, we suddenly heard the *Marseillaise*. It was prisoners being taken in police wagons to Fresnes or the Santé. A few people on the sidewalk barely stopped to watch them go by. It's true that night was already protecting us, but the black-uniformed police were watching. I hope the people were at least clenching their fists in their pockets.

This week at school I put my Applied Science students through a curious test: I had them read Madame de Staël's *De l'Allemagne*.[301] As they have absolutely no sense of history, to them this seemed like pure provocation on my part. They understood nothing of that dithyrambic encomium of Germany and could not conceive of it being so different from what it is today. So I asked them to compare the France of 1943 to the France of 1810, and I felt that they were deeply moved.

It is an honor for France that at the very time when Napoleon, betraying and confiscating our Revolution, was trying to enslave Germany and Europe, a French writer should have written this praise of a foreign people: in the name of the Revolution itself, she recognized different peoples in their singularity and greatness, and gave us the principle of a European federation.

The problem remains the same today. The miseries of our country may throw us back into some kind of base nationalism, but the very spirit of the country will command us to work at constructing Europe and making a place in it for Germany.

This week I recommended reading Jacques Rivière,* *The German*. After Madame de Staël's dithyramb, it's something to make them a bit more flexible.

---

[301] *On Germany* (1810), an important work for French literature, as it gave France a sense of the early Romantic Movement and the work of Goethe and Schiller.

Germany, the belly of Europe. Always led by its belly. That's the source of its contradictions. Its heart used to inspire it, but at other times its bile, its hunger, and its colic. Intellectualism has its advantages. Our desire for clarity.

"So many heroes, so many idiots," Montaigne thought as he watched his contemporaries, no doubt. Montaigne or d'Aubigné*? The hero or the sage? Which one is an exemplary human being? Both of them. I cannot choose. The time we live in is such that one needs the courage of d'Aubigné to save the ideas of Montaigne.

I'm trying to explain the "charm" of La Fontaine to myself. Chamfort* speaks of the variety of tones he uses, and he is right. But there is good reason, it seems to me, to consider the variation in each one of his tones. A fable is actually, as Chamfort said, sometimes a tragedy, sometimes a comedy, sometimes an ode, and sometimes an epic poem. But the tone is never completely clear-cut, never quite pure. We're always in a parody of the tone being used. "While my brow, like a Caucasus mountain peak..." The rhymes *pareil* and *soleil* sound like Malherbe,*[302] but too much so. We're in the tone of an ode, but it is only to make fun of it. And it's that dissonance modifying each one of his tones that enables him to pass from one to the other without a break. Thus the fable gains its unity amidst the greatest diversity. All these "genres" are treated with the same irony. That irony is his base. The mind, always wonderfully present, watches and enjoys the spectacle. I think of that poetic couple Claudel talks about: Animus and Anima.[303] In the *Fables* Animus is the one who leads, always.

B...brings me news of some of my students, his friends, who are in the maquis.

The worst of servitude is that it shuts us inside ourselves whether we will or no. Never have we thought so much about each other, but it's a sad sweetness: it's always from cell to cell and our affection and our imaginations are never equal to people's unhappiness despite our best efforts. Oh, what soliloquies! We never stop telling ourselves what our reasons are for living, but we do not really live. Endless, obstinate, exhausting cogitation. Sometimes it seems to us we're close to madness and we're going to unlearn speech and even thought. But what joy when the visit of a friend reveals that everything that must continue is continuing, assures us that we are not yet the monologuing, rebellious madman we fear we have become, and suddenly re-creates around us our liberty, and our country.

---

[302] In "The Oak and the Reed" ("*Le Chêne et le Roseau*") in La Fontaine's *Fables* (1688), the oak boasts: *Cependant que mon front au Caucase pareil/Non content d'arrêter les rayons du soleil/Brave la tempête* ("While my brow, like a Caucasus mountain peak/Not content to stop the rays of the sun/Braves the tempest").

[303] Roughly, the mind and the soul, in a little parable Paul Claudel invented in 1925 to illustrate his poetic theory.

We talked for a long time in the night as we walked along the iron fences of the Luxembourg Gardens.

I promised to write him in his maquis. But didn't we say it all by recognizing together that everything we had served and loved still deserved our service and our love? Every word after that seems vain. Nothing is worth that deep commitment we had made long ago; we will never agree to turn our backs on it. The counterfeiters who have been talking about revolution for the past four years in order to avoid it in reality never understood what it is. A revolution for them is only a cabinet reshuffle in a ministry through which they can temporarily grab a position, honors, and profits. But the real Revolution is nothing but the constancy of our love. It throws everything into question all the time, because everything can be perverted and degraded at any time. If we think about it, it really has no object except to maintain and save everything—everything, that is, man—and his freedom, which is nothing but his honor and the means of his progress.

December 11

Often in the afternoon, in the almost lightless corridors of the Metro at the Châtelet station, a young beggar indulges in the same innocent provocation and continues to ply the same little trade. Solidly seated on a folding chair against the wall, with his white cane lying on the ground in front of him to mark the boundaries of his refuge, and a false pride on his face with chin uplifted and empty eyes condemned never to see, he plays a martial tune on his accordion, without stopping: the *Marseillaise*. He has put a silly little flag on his instrument and sports a blue-white-and-red rosette whose ribbons drag to the ground. The coins rain into his cap. Everyone thinks he is being revenged by this blind man and saves himself from shame through this charity—all too cheaply. He profits from the black market all day long. He had one of those ideas that make great fortunes: he feels protected by his infirmity and tells himself that they won't dare shut him up. In fact the Germans do pass by indifferently. Sometimes, one of them may even push delicacy to the point of making his little offering to this image of France: he gives him back twenty *sous* that he stole from him.

December 12

I'm doing my time at hard labor and I'm so tired I can't even keep this diary.

December 25

A new hypocritical address from the old Tartuffe: "Listen to a man who is there only for you and who loves you like a father... I beg of you..." Two years ago he was "ordering" us to obey without thinking, without catching our breaths. What a fiasco, from that "I order" to "I beg of you"! That, at least, is to the honor of France.

December 28

This time everything shows that the battles of our deliverance are imminent: we feel a strange impatience, a kind of warmth in the head and heart. Last night, it seemed to me that it was about to happen this morning. Servitude is so heavy that we don't even think of the terrible ordeals this country is about to endure. Freedom is on the other side of a barrier of fire, but everyone is ready to cross it.

December 31

A long air-raid warning toward noon. Hundreds of planes over Paris. Impossible to see them, though the sky was very clear.

In the evening we learn that towns just outside Paris were hit.

1944

Yesterday evening toward five o'clock, the last sun of the year was admirable. I was sorry to have gone and shut myself in at A...'s. A bunch of old gentlemen whose benign, ambiguous remarks could hardly hide their terror. All those gentlemen were chuckling, murmuring, putting on their last airs and graces as they drank a last cup of maté! But their ears were ringing; for somewhere in the world, people were talking about them and their death.

I'm holding an issue of the *Journal des Volontaires* in my hands. It's one of the newspapers of the maquis. No Resistance newspaper takes a higher tone. It's put out by a few young men and comes out every week on forty stenciled pages.[304]

One of the pages of their editorial, with the rather romantic title "We of the Maquis," makes us touch the depths of France's misery.

The cry of these young men makes us ashamed and fearful: in order to save their youth and the country, their only resource is to hide in the depths of the woods. They write: "You don't inherit your father's honor the way you inherit his government bonds...We are the sons of the heroes of Verdun, but there are no more heroes of Verdun. Some are mixed into the earth for which they died; others walk around our streets behind the standards of the legionnaires,[305] wearing berets and displaying all their decorations, seeming to say to anyone looking at them: 'We have gained the right to be cowards.' But the pale face of the France that has not been soiled asks each one of us: 'What about you?' We can only erase dishonor by an overabundance of honor and sacrifice."

I think of the old revolutionary song:

---

[304] Hundreds of underground newspapers were published under the Occupation, most stenciled but some actually printed, with circulations over 100,000—this despite strict rationing of paper and savage repression: those caught working for a Resistance journal were executed or deported to concentration camps. See notes 2 and 3, p. xxxi.

[305] For the Legion, see note 157, p. 101. Further on, the "old revolutionary song" was written in 1800 for the celebration of the French Revolution.

The sons are greater than their fathers
And the fathers are not jealous at all.

It is well known that fathers and sons have never gotten along. But the health and strength of a country is, however, only the result of a certain understanding and emulation between them about the greatness of the country. Oh, these French boys, how well I understand their anger! But I would like to warn them. There never were heroes at Verdun. There were only men who held out, with fear and humility—with honor, too, because that's how they were, because they had to and could not do otherwise. In fact, France's illness began, perhaps, when there was so much talk of heroes, when the naïve dignity of the combatants changed into the self-interested vanity of veterans. The inflated words dispensed them from having solid thoughts. There were too many medals, too many ribbons, too many parades—too many pensions, too, a little degrading commerce in vanity. — But I would like to tell these boys they are not as alone as they think. How can we convince them that the anguish all of us feel is the same anguish? All they feel is everything they miss: our country. How could they imagine the sorrow men of our age feel at the idea that we might indeed miss our country forever as we have known it, as we experienced it, as we live on air and light? We can only die with some degree of calm if we know that they are assured of living in a country capable of nourishing their bodies and minds. We must transmit the tradition from us to them. The cause of fathers and sons is a common cause: it is the same honor of the same country.

No, dear children, you are not alone. I read your manifesto again: "This people," you say, "never accepted treason or defeat." That's when you are speaking the truth, and you know it very well. You are the avant-garde of this people, not some lost, isolated sentinel.

But it had to happen: they can feel only the exaltation of that artificial, moving solitude in which they must live. In what tones do they cry out: "We have said no to the lies and we are brothers because we said no. On one hand there is 'doing one's duty,' social conformism, facility, obedience…On the other, risk, and the leap into the unknown. We have chosen. We have chosen to be outlaws…You can breathe better in the maquis: you're not stifled by equivocation. Today all of that France which made us what we are is asking us to make it, once more, what it once was: a free country, peopled by free men. That day will come, but for it to come, each of us must accept ahead of time, from the bottom of his heart, that he will never see it."

Dear boys ready for death, with their red scarves in the wind! In their difficult lives, they have regained the true idea of freedom. They have re-learned that it can only exist when one is ready to die for it. They have taken with them the highest idea of France. But how can we reconcile them to all they left behind, to misery and even shame, to the suffering and humiliation which sickens them.

Freedom is still more difficult, children. It is not intoxication or detachment, but the deepest kind of commitment. The soul has to pull the painful, soiled body after it and save it with itself. "Outlaws." Don't be intoxicated by the word. Think, rather, that you are the law itself, the one that is not written, the one that, since it isn't written, cannot have misprints, the one that no sly devil, no powerful man can ever profit from, the one that is above transitory laws, above the hazards of history, the one that needs no interpretation, but is perfectly obvious to the heart. It is the law that a people does not transgress, even when those who claim to speak in its name betray it. A people cannot transgress that law because it cannot give up being; but it *is*, and nothing can stand against its being. You bear inside you the very law of France, while treason has left it without laws. You have learned, again, what liberty was when it was great, and voluntary. But what can one do, what can one tell you so that you learn again as well, in your forests, the sweetness of its fraternity. Only on that condition will all of us, together, be strong and invincible. Our individual revolts and fits of anger, however elevated they may be, would not suffice to save us. The life of a great country is only the tradition of a hope, and that hope must be living and vast, but the tradition must be firm and solid. Nothing will be accomplished without love.

January 7

I'm looking through that maquis paper again. These young patriots fear nothing so much as seeming to be nationalists. And that is, no doubt, one of their most moving qualities. They don't want their suffering to make them lose their reason and reduce the idea they have of the nation.

An evident wish, too, not to submit to propaganda. Allusions, often severe, to English policies and strategy. They seem to be just as free as far as communism is concerned: at the back of the issue they publish some fine "selected pages" from Berdyaev's book: *The New Middle Ages.*[306]

All of this is intelligent, but with an overly critical and restless cast of mind. They always keep their distance. Some of the young editors of this journal have read, I fear, too much of M. Gide.* Youth is, in them, no more than the romanticism of a critical mind (Anarchy). They would have more to gain by seeking what might put them in tune with all that is young in the world today. "French boys, the most intelligent of all," Henri Franck used to say.[307] But that very intelligence makes duty more difficult for them. They know very well what they don't want to be, but don't feel what they want to be, nor what they could be at this fateful time for Europe. Intellectual French youth must get over its Gide-ism and find

[306] Nicolas Berdyaev (1874–1948) was a Russian "Christian existentialist" who broke with Marxism in the name of freedom and religious faith.

[307] Franck (1888–1912) was a *Normalien* of Guéhenno's generation. A committed socialist and a poet, he died when he was twenty-four.

the movement of history once again. Can't they realize that to be young like Ménalque or Nathanaël[308] means to be terribly old? That quest for pleasures, that meticulous, assiduous sensual enjoyment presupposes a private income, a trust fund; it reveals the end of a race.

January 10

Another boy from the maquis came to see me. There were close to twenty of them in a chateau in the Vercors. Two hundred Germans led by a dozen French militiamen surrounded the chateau.[309] Luckily the boys had cleared off. Thinking they were hiding inside, the Germans set fire to the chateau; everything burned. An STO evader who had hidden in the attic succeeded in fleeing through the flames, killing two Germans.[310]

He told me about the evenings around the fire, talking about revolution. He lived through four wonderful months, he told me. Yet I can feel in him as much despair as exaltation. It is because they lack a common faith. There are Gaullist maquis, Communist maquis, Giraudist* maquis. Such is the confusion that the Giraudists imagine they are obeying Marshal Pétain. No republican instinct anywhere. And often, he explains, the pre-fascist mentality of youth camps. The camp is as good as its "leader." And most of the leaders are merely young officers with no doctrine, or still infected with the poisons of Action Française.

January 14

A man is sometimes a soldier by order, but he is always an officer by choice, and consequently it is conceivable that a young monarchist could have been a soldier in the armies of the Republic despite himself; but what are we to think of those royalist cadets and students headed for the *Grandes Écoles* who chose to make a career there?[311] How could the armies of the nation be strong when the men who commanded them placed their vanity in standing apart from the nation, quite determined at heart not to submit to what Rousseau called "the general will," that is, the will of the republican majority they despised. What dignity could there be in the lives of so many counterfeiters and liars—generals who for the past twenty years would read Maurras' *Action Française*, learning to conspire against the Republic, while scheming in the offices of the ministries to get a piece of braid or a star more on their caps and a raise in pay. Probity and honor would have commanded them to exercise another profession. If "the general will" disgusted them and they did not agree with it, why did they not resign? Or

---

[308] In Gide's *Les Nourritures terrestres* (*The Fruits of the Earth*); see note 281, p. 207.

[309] For the Militia, see note 298, p. 223.

[310] For the STO, see note 7, p. xxxii.

[311] For the *Grandes Écoles*, see note 257, p. 188, and note 284, p. 210. Also see note 312 below.

rather—for it was, when they enlisted, inscribed in the law—why did they pledge to serve it? But they had already begun to lie when they enlisted; they had no problem turning traitor. Their lives have been nothing but one long lie, one long act of treason. Moreover, it's the treason of men who were often uncultured and stupid, incapable of real political reflection, monarchists or fascists only through snobbery and vanity. Good or bad mathematicians when they were preparing for Saint-Cyr or the École Polytechnique or Navale,[312] they reduced their magnificent profession to nothing more than poor, soulless technique; for these accountants and garrison bureaucrats, our national holiday of July 14 had meaning only in the year it brought them an appointment to the Legion of Honor and 200 francs a year to add to their pay. It is certainly true that many of these lost souls found themselves again when France was in danger and did all that duty required. Nonetheless, that spirit of revolt so common among the officers had never stopped undermining the army's strength in peacetime, and when the real test came, it deprived the army of all national fervor and offensive energy.

The one club that has been authorized at the École Normale for the past three years has been the Catholic Circle. Students wanted to start another, which they called "Philosophical," and they came to see me to ask if I would give a lecture one evening. I gave my promise. I was to talk (we had agreed to avoid any topic that might be too burningly relevant) about the problem of literary creation. But the boys, full of embarrassment, came to inform me that the Director of the School was banning the lecture. I was thought to be "too visible."

February 5

Giraudoux* is dead. As bad luck would have it, I had talked about him unkindly that morning. In the evening, a phone call from Blanzat* informed me of his death, and I was full of sorrow and regret. Of the feeling of my stupidity, too. Rarely have I been so rudely reminded of the indulgence we should all have.

These times make us hard and demanding. In my heart of hearts, I blamed him for his hesitations in 1941; they seemed to me a kind of infidelity to himself. And for his prudence, his cleverness, his personal business negotiations with the Occupying Authorities, his apparent submission, for continuing to pursue his career as a man of letters and being unable to keep quiet, for being one of the entertainers of our servitude as much as any other little braggart on the literary scene, for having filled the silence of a subjugated Paris with his name. I resented him for that fête he gave to all the incorrigible snobs—*Sodom and Gomorra,* that useless piece of chatter, an anachronistic spectacle, a cowardly piece of entertainment

---

[312] Saint-Cyr is the French equivalent of West Point. The École Polytechnique, like the École Normale Supérieure and the École Nationale d'Administration (ENA), is a *Grande École*; it produces officers (or business executives or scientists). The École Navale, of course, trains naval officers.

which seemed to authorize cowardice.[313] I probably didn't say anything so severe, but I denounced his precious dandy esthetic, his games, his artifices, and I actually think I concluded with spiteful anger that besides, a country always has the poets it deserves.

And yet he was crossing "the shallow stream" with his nonchalant steps as if he weren't paying attention to it. He was still walking with his head high, slightly turned to one side. He stepped over it without seeing it. He died. I know my severity was unfair and stupid. Whereas he was indulgence itself because he was intelligence itself. I remain with the memory of my idiotic anger and I will have no way of asking his forgiveness.

I had known him during the other war, in October 1914. He was wounded, under treatment in the hospital in Fougères where I was convalescing myself. The registrar of the École Normale had asked me to visit him. I walked into the ward filled with a hundred soldiers, wounded like him. I saw him as soon as I got to the door, sitting on his bed, wearing the obligatory white gown, a man with a long face, a monocle in his eye, reading. I walked up to him. "Giraudoux?" I asked. It was Giraudoux, of course. Even war had not been able to reduce him to the common measure, distract him from that will for elegance which had made him a poet in 1905. I am sure there was not another sergeant like him in the whole French army. I remained in Fougères for two weeks or so. He wanted to re-read Stendhal; I brought him *The Red and the Black* and *The Charterhouse of Parma* in ugly cheap editions, all I owned.

France was lucky, from '20 to '40, to have the poet it deserved. All the grace, all the kindness, the joy, all the humanity it was capable of—it was up to this tall, non-chalant, amiable boy to show them that and tell it to the world. He came from the heart of the nation, like Voiture,* like La Fontaine, like Marivaux,* like Nerval, like his friend Charles-Louis Philippe.* He was simple, as they had been simple, despite appearances. He meditated, as his country did, while force was spluttering all over a confused Europe. He had the honor of reminding men who had lost their way of the true path, by means of a few beautiful images. *Siegfried* and *Tiger at the Gates* are his claim to fame, and France's claim, too: the condemnation of moronic heroes, the conspiracy of stupid fates, and protests against pointless deaths. And if France, at the moment when it was tested and had to organize its own propaganda, found nothing to combat Goebbels but this peaceful poet, there is probably no more striking proof of its purity, its innocence, and unfortunately of its innocuousness.

Yesterday I ran to his funeral between two classes. It was an imposing ceremony, but solemn and cold. Have we even forgotten how to weep, in our servitude?

---

[313] The play was produced in October 1943 and was a smash hit in Paris. In the next paragraph, "the shallow stream" is death: Guéhenno is quoting a line of Mallarmé: *Un peu profond ruisseau calomnié la mort* (literally "A shallow maligned stream death").

France could not be there to mourn her poet. Large gatherings of Frenchmen are forbidden. Only a few theater people, men of letters, and socialites were gathered there, a few friends, too, and a few women who had loved him. I searched vainly among the people there for the characters of his plays, the nice Frenchmen of *Intermezzo*. Yet he would, no doubt, have been pleased to see the choirmaster on the platform, utterly provincial, thrashing about like a buffoon, unfolding like an accordion and undulating like the sea, the better to show his choir the movements of the music. And how fine-looking and grave they were, those two masters of ceremony standing on either side of the catafalque in a big black capes with their three-cornered hats at their fingertips—the same for centuries, ever since they watched over the body of Jean de la Fontaine.

February 14

Death once again, another head heavily sinking into a pillow, closed over its secret: *The Secret*. V…'s old "Aunt Rose,"[314] so intelligent and astute. "Now we're at the same point," my old friend said to me. "Nothing left to cover either of us. From now on the ax will fall on us." One should adjust one's thoughts more to that.

February 18

C…, one of my students three years ago. A boy of wonderful purity. A Christian. A philosopher. Even then, he wanted to leave for England. His family held him back. He took to the maquis with his brother, February 20 of last year, when the occupying Authority registered his class. "You don't let yourself be registered as a forced laborer." First he tried to get to Algeria,[315] but did not succeed. In March, he was in the French Alps. In a camp, 2,000 meters up. "Since then," he told me, "I have appreciated many things," and he told me of their life, with its admirable fraternity, comrades so different from him, their devotion; the struggle against the snow and the cold, the war with the Italians and then with the Gestapo; and the informers. He became the leader of an irregular force and then of a camp. Four of his comrades were executed. Others tortured with a "potato masher" or repeatedly half-drowned in a bathtub. "So," he explains, "you understand, I had to give orders…I was responsible for the life of 150 men." He went back down to the plain; he's in Paris for a few days. He asks me questions, he wants to know if the French are worthy of the suffering that his comrades are taking on for them, if they're really worth the sacrifice. He has been here for three days: and he's tired of being regarded somewhat ironically as a "hero" by his friends of a year ago who are still tranquilly pursuing their "dear studies" in

---

[314] Undoubtedly the aunt of Guéhenno's oldest friend, André Vaillant.*

[315] The Allied invasion of North Africa in November 1942 brought France's colony Algeria into the Allied camp.

the Sorbonne, or having to justify himself to the bourgeois as if he were a "bandit." They are used to servitude; can most of them even understand what simple courage and honor are anymore?

I question him in my turn. The maquis lacks weapons. Weapons were dropped by parachute only a few times. It seems that England and America do not want to arm revolutionary bands. They are beginning to see what the debate will be tomorrow. There are three distinct forces: the AS (Armée Secrète), organized and armed by the Anglo-Americans, tightly linked to the British Intelligence Service; the FTP (*Francs-Tireurs et Partisans*), Communists who've had weapons and experience in underground action for a long time and who call their own tune in complete independence; and finally the MUR (*Mouvements Unis de la Résistance*), ready for sacrifice and wanting to save France's autonomy; but with no doctrine and few weapons, it may well be crushed between the AS and the FTP.[316]

February 26

Marot's preface to the *Roman de la Rose*.[317] The Queen of Sheba wanted to test the wisdom of King Solomon. "She took two roses, of which one came naturally from the tree, and the other through simulation: for she had made it, in a sophisticated way and through her art, so that it well resembled the natural Rose, so subtly was it crafted. 'Here,' she said, 'are two roses before your pacific Majesty presented, of which one truly is natural, but the other not. And yet, tell me, Sire, which is the natural Rose, show it me with your finger.' Solomon, that seer, had various honey-flies brought in, thinking and considering by the knowledge he had of all natural things that the said flies, according to the property they possess, would go incontinent to the natural Rose, not to the sophisticated: for such celestial birdlets, pleasant and mellific, desire and hunger for sweet flowers above all things. Through which he showed the Queen the true Rose, discerning it from the other which was made of scents that counterfeited nature."

A fine story...We lack the swarm that would guide us to the true Rose, like King Solomon. The spirit of King Solomon is in us, but also the spirit of the Queen of Sheba, the Egyptian. We are amused by our own sophistication, our own counterfeits, and we can't distinguish between them and the real thing anymore. Then the time comes when we realize that we have killed the "celestial birdlets."

---

[316] In actual fact, the MUR resulted from the union of three Resistance groups, one of which was the FTP. It was eventually transformed into the Conseil National de la Résistance (CNR) which united all the various groups in the Resistance.

[317] Clément Marot (1496–1544) is a poet renowned for his lightness and clarity. The *Roman de la Rose* (*Romance of the Rose*) is a poem written some three centuries before he was born.

February 29

A boy from the maquis has written me about his life:

"After the village you have to walk for two more hours…suddenly you discover the camp: men in bizarre costumes. A kitchen sheltered by corrugated iron, near which hangs a cow that has been cut to pieces. The wash is cooking on three stones…Something between a military encampment and a gypsy camp. But there is pure air circulating through all of this; there is no other rule here but our honor. Here are free men. When they are asked why they're here, the answer is sometimes slow to come and badly formulated and yet it is always the same. In truth, very few have reflected on their decision. Simply, it was inconceivable for them to go elsewhere. To leave for Germany was a humiliation to which, given their character, they could not be subjected, a defeat rejected out of hand by their sense of honor.

"As for us, we had pondered that admirable page where Jünger,[318] before a flock of French prisoners guarded by a sentinel, remembers the resolution he made never to surrender because any surrender would inflict a wound on the deepest source of his being. We did not want a second surrender. As it would have been performed in the middle of peacetime, it would have led to a still more terrible collapse than the first one. Our 'no' preserves the *capacity* to set forth the liberating acts of tomorrow. It is the refusal of a failure that would weigh on us forever.

"The camps have given another value to our refusal. Nothing is negative in our actions anymore. *We are conscientious objectors who want to be soldiers.* Now all those who had taken to the mountain only to hide out have left, so as not to be subjected to winter. Most STO evaders are not in the camps. They are in that vague "maquis" which means anything at all. In the camps, there are no evaders to be found now, but volunteers. The distance that separates those two words gives the measure of the evolution that has occurred over six months. Whoever has lived for two days in a camp understands it. We live here cut off from all the joys, all the conveniences of the world—in shacks, blinded by smoke, with a little hay to sleep on and sometimes nothing. Food supplies, uncertain. Equipment, precarious. Entitled to nothing, not even one's bread. In truth, never have French troops known such destitution. The same will unifies these men, comes from the same suffering. We think of *Man's Fate*.[319] They are "relatives of torture victims' and sometimes have been tortured themselves. This one's father was killed by a firing squad, that one's an Alsatian, another is a Jew, and many spent time in prison. A seemingly heterogeneous army, but welded together by persecution and suffering far more than any discipline could."

---

[318] Ernst Jünger (1895–1998) was a German author who often wrote about war, sometimes glorifying it. Here the incident seems to come from the First World War.

[319] *La Condition humaine* (1933), a novel by André Malraux* about the Chinese Revolution; the revolutionary hero, Kyo, is burned alive at the end. Further on, we recall that Alsace was annexed by Germany under the Armistice Agreement; Alsatian men were drafted into Hitler's army, as they were now considered to be German.

And he writes:

"The camps are very different from one another. Sometimes a camp is native to the spot: a schoolteacher or a mailman with a strong personality or who was 'in politics' before the war took to the mountains, taking along some young people of the region with them. Sometimes the camp was created out of nothing on whatever basis—military, religious, industrial—and the recruits are varied . . . But whatever the camp may be, you're entering a separate world which has its own structure, its hierarchy, its myths, its own unconscious, a world in which the break with legal frameworks has allowed the resurgence of an ancient legacy one might have thought buried forever—a feudal world in which you possess a region rather than a rank, where the vassal measures his strength by the number of his men and sometimes thinks he has become a suzerain, where men obey through a sort of allegiance bizarrely mixed with constraint, where justice is rendered outside of codes and laws, utterly given over to human evaluation."

And he explains that that's where the danger lies, and what creates an urgent need for education in these camps: "For the schoolteacher or the officer or the boss persists in considering the camp that depends on him as his thing, his possession, his 'cohort.' If each man remains on his own threshold of this strange, varied world, how can they forge a coherent army?" The problem is, it is unclear if these men should be considered as "soldiers" or as "partisans." My correspondent wants them to be treated as partisans. Some officers thought they had simply changed troops. They got out of the dilemma with a word: "Liberation Army." But these men are much more than an army. The "liberation" they want is also Revolution. There, you can see "an exceptional milieu in which French patriotism might recapture its grandeur and its revolutionary efficiency."

Actually—and the last pages of this letter fill me with the same anguish I had already felt when I read the *Journal des Volontaires*—these young men feel their isolation cruelly. The miseries of servitude. These camps of free men are prisons themselves: reflection turns into bitterness and revolt. He goes on:

"They know that their pals in nice, sheltered situations consider them dupes or madmen. So why should they sacrifice themselves? Why, if they weren't also revolutionaries . . . But the abandonment in which a great part of the country has left them, the disappointments after the promises, the brutal repudiation of the fraternity of the nations who are fighting the war—all that forms a climate in which a kind of skepticism is dominant, sometimes ironic, sometimes stubborn. The general feeling is that the great problems will be solved over their heads, and they are merely numbers thrown into an inevitable combat. Just one thing remains intact: their faith in the probity and intransigent fidelity of General de Gaulle. Let that be their homage to him. He cannot receive purer homage, more marked by anguish and hope. But the very faculty of belief seems gravely affected. Fascism is born from despair, but is there not still time to give a meaning to all that, to give hope again to the best part of this people, to deepen the reason for its combat and its life? I can hear my comrades singing, as if in reply, the song of the Thälmann Battalion[320]:

> Far off is our land
> But ready we stand
> We're fighting and winning for you:
> Freedom!

"O far-off homeland...My comrades, partisans, are we really outcasts? O homeland so close now, so alive among us..."

The morning paper announces that thirteen of these "bandits" have been disposed of.

March 3

I'm reading Malraux's *La Lutte avec l'ange* ("Wrestling with the Angel")...It is no more than a prologue. But this prologue is often admirable. I can easily see all the criticisms that may be leveled at these pages, too brilliant, too strained; a technique more suitable for a film than a novel; a bit of bluff, some inflated passages, a too obvious quest for effect and a pose that is slightly irritating when you think about it. But the striving for greatness is everywhere manifest, too. More exactly a striving to think and speak on a scale equal to this time, equal to the events in which we are caught and by which most of us are simply crushed. Malraux will at least have the honor of having published, during the war, perhaps the only book that is not an anachronism. He published it in Geneva, in Switzerland, on the only free land that remains, as a free man should.

It seems that when the novel has been completed, it will evoke the history of these past forty years. Malraux continues his meditation on the human condition. We do not, he and I, look to the same men to define it for us. The men he looks to think too much; thought is their mania; they lose themselves in it. Beyond the human condition, and, through an excess of pride, rather inclined, I fear, to judge as lacking all those who are not capable, as they are, of incredible endless cogitations.

March 4

What I wrote yesterday is not quite correct. In the prisoners' camp in Chartres, Malraux "looks at thousands of shades in the uneasy light of dawn" and he thinks: "This is man" (p. 25).

---

[320] One of the battalions in the International Brigades, which volunteered to fight against the fascists in the Spanish Civil War. The battalion was named after a German Communist leader who was later murdered in Buchenwald. The song the *maquisards* sing in French was originally in German (*Freiheit* ["Freedom"]) and used to be fairly well known in the English words that follow.

He adds:

> I thought I knew more than my culture because I had encountered mil-
> itant crowds with a faith, religious or political. Now I know that an
> intellectual is not only the man for whom books are necessary, but any
> man who is committed to an idea, however elementary it may be, and
> this idea gives order to his life. As for the men around me, they have
> been living from day to day for thousands of years.

Obsessed by this question: what is man, he is there in this camp before "the
original matter" and what he sees fills him with despair, rather than with scorn.
Nevertheless, it seems that there are two species of men, for him: men—and
they are those unconscious shades—and intellectuals.

His experience as an adventurer and his travels make the answer more difficult for him. He has too many memories and they have too many colors in his
mind. In some of the most interesting pages of his book, he explains that the
new science of ethnology has complicated the problem far more than history
did. All too true: a simple, fairly attentive visit to the Museum of Man[321]—I ver-
ified this just the day before yesterday—makes it hard to believe in a constant,
eternal man. How can one reduce so many strange ways of living to one, unique
law? Malraux loses himself in his memories.

At one point (pp. 78 and 107), he shows us, perhaps, his deepest faith. To all
lovers of mystery, all too tempted to confuse "the knowledge of man with that
of his secrets" and who, to the question "What is man?" would quickly answer
"What he hides," Malraux seems ready to answer: "No, he is what he does."

Like a theme, all through the book, the thought returns that man is the only
being who knows that he must die. Malraux takes this definition for his own.
But it is Voltaire's. (In fact I remember quoting and commenting on it in an
article on Voltaire.) This being the case, man struggles to escape that knowledge,
that awareness. But everything brings him back to it. He flees himself because
he can find in himself, if he dwells on it, only the continuous work of death. It
governs his will, his action, and his destiny. And that is no less true for "men"
than for "intellectuals."

The real merit of Malraux is to incite emulation. Many writers, no doubt,
would like to do what he tried to do, not what he did. I know that as for myself,
I will always do less. But I would like to do more to answer that question of questions he asks—but simply and modestly, while remaining truthful and natural.
An unfortunate taste for the sublime all too often makes him get lost in shams,
sham illuminations and sham darkness.

[321] See note 114, p. 60.

March 10

We are still waiting. We are well aware that the Anglo-Saxons can't wage this war just to save us, but to win it, and they can only try to land in France if they are sure of succeeding; we know a failure would be the most frightful disaster and the Germans, relieved from the threat in the West, would throw all their reserves into Russia and perhaps... But we can't hold on to such wise reflections very long. There is too much misery. We think of the men in the prisons, in the maquis. The soul of this country would be completely undone if this were to last for a long time to come.

March 13

Yesterday in Germany it was "Heroes' Day." I listened to the sermons and propaganda on the radio. Glory, like everything else in that country, is strictly controlled. It is turned on like a faucet. Each came in for his exact amount of praise: the tank-drivers, the aviators, the sailors in submarines, the ones who were burned alive, shot down from the sky, drowned. That whole people is locked into a colossal lie as if in prison and sings and bawls as in a Wagnerian chorus. But this time the grand sorcerer did not dare speak. In 1942, this day had given him the occasion for his finest trances: he was prophesying the death of Bolshevism, the coming advent of a Germanic peace which would last no less than a thousand years. Now he keeps quiet. Because, no doubt, like all sorcerers, he needs people to believe him in order to pull off his tricks; he needs to be believed and knows that he is believed no longer. From now on his word is powerless. His lie is collapsing with the cities of Germany, and when the dust falls, the fires go out and all the fanfares of heroism fall silent again, the poor German "Michel" will recognize the truth all around him: a great desert.

March 21

I don't know if the story is true, but if it is, it manifests an utterly new feeling for the greatness of life: they say that up to this very day, the rule in Russia, contrary to what was done always and everywhere, has been to engage only the oldest men in combat, men thirty-five to forty years old, those who have already lived enough to be able to die. The youngest remain on the other side of the Urals where they train, held in reserve for the last battles, for the victory. Meanwhile, they want them to live.

March 24

Every day we learn of new horrors. Young STO evaders were hanged in Nîmes and various villages of the Midi (seventeen in Nîmes). The farms suspected of feeding the maquis burnt, the farmers shot. Huge round-ups in Paris. Mass deportation,[322] with the help of the new Minister of Labor and National Solidarity, Déat.

March 25

Saw C...again. There is now a sort of frenzy in him. "We do not despair," he says to me. "But if this lasts two more months, we'll all be dead." More than fifty out of the original hundred have been arrested over the last three weeks, and no one knows what became of most of them. He speaks to me of Malraux, of Chen, the hero of *Man's Fate*, who seemed so strange and impenetrable when he read it for the first time six years ago: Chen now holds no secrets for him. The round-ups on the boulevards, in the Metro, make everything terribly difficult and slow. He walks twenty, thirty kilometers every day. He saw one of his classmates again, a philosopher. A young Jew. He has not gone out since February 25 of last year. He lives hidden in a little house in the suburbs. His hair comes down to his shoulders. He reads Spinoza and Kant. He is ashamed and fearful.

Many former *khâgneux* and *Normaliens* in the Resistance. But few from the École Polytechnique, it seems. Why?

I'll recopy this admirable letter from the maquis to the prisoners:

"Prisoners, friends, here is a short fraternal message from captives who resemble you, who feel very close to you and have as much hope in you as in themselves. We are the people of the maquis, the volunteers of 1943 who took to the hills to respond to forced labor by an act of war. Now we are hunted down as "outlaws" and "terrorists" by the Nazis, aided and abetted by the traitors in Vichy's militia. We are captives, like you. Our thirst for freedom and the struggle for that freedom made us raise our flag in a circle of ground which is certainly not ours, on a mountainside or a piece of forest; but inside that circle, we are shut in. Here in the heart of the woods, we have set up a camp and prepare for combat. We live as citizens who are conscious and proud of having thrown their refusal into the balance of the war; but the rounds of our sentries keeping watch at the edges of the forest remind us every two hours that we are encircled by oppression and a threat hovers over us. We are reminded that our citadel of honor is as small and vulnerable as it is proud, and a hail of bullets may be our evening sleep.

"When, from our high slopes, we see the mists rising from the valley and at the first shadows of night we watch the lights turn on in the windows of villages where we never go, like you, we feel nostalgic for the world down below, for a garden, a road, and a roof. And when, at dawn, we take the loaves of bread out of

---

[322] Again, Guéhenno is talking about shipping Frenchmen to Germany to work in factories (the STO); see note 7, p. xxxii. In the next entry, Chen is not exactly the hero of Malraux's novel, although he is a major character: increasingly attracted by death, he dies in a suicide attack on Chiang Kai-shek.

the boarded-up cache near the crossroads—bread from a baker we may never see—we feel cut off from the world and its warmth. There are Sundays frozen with sadness, when we walk along the side of a path like a wall, seeking, without admitting it to ourselves, a way out, an end to our interminable wait. And when the sentry prevents us from entering the café of the hamlet where they say there's such a beautiful girl, all along that invisible wall inside us we have your captive's heart. And then, in the evening, when the mess kits are washed and the pot of that morning's coffee is blackening on the big hearth, we squeeze together in a circle near the flames and the woods can hear, rising from our chalet, the sad tune of your *Peat Bog Soldiers*: it has become our song. You would be moved to tears if you could guess with what manly tenderness our thoughts go out to you as we chant the lines that give a rhythm to your sorrow:

> We are the peat bog soldiers
> We're marching with our spades
> To the bog...

"And if you could hear how our chorus is changed into a roar of passionate hope at the last stanza:

> One day we shall rise, rejoicing
> Homeland dear
> You're mine at last.

"You would understand that we have become your brothers, for we have voluntarily shared your redemptive suffering and have, like you, changed the word *liberty* into a reality, throbbing with desire and life.

"Rejected by the community, we've had the time, like you, to think about the second-rate men and the mistakes that led us to this disaster. And as you must have done, we have vowed to work to reconstruct a strong, free country that will use its strength in service of a just peace. Like you, we are cut off from life, which went on without us, and like you, we have been forgotten. You may have been betrayed once. We were betrayed twice: delivered as slaves to the enemy by a vile bourgeoisie of Pharisees in debt to the Collaboration, which ensures its order and the conservation of its wealth, we were betrayed a second time by our elders, those career officers of twenty-five or forty-five who should have welcomed us like a blessing from heaven, volunteers to be trained, brothers to be protected...That bureaucratic pseudo-elite, the worthy image of a dying bourgeoisie, stayed in their supply offices, deaf to our appeals, as insensible to the call of duty as to that of fraternity. Left to ourselves, we have learned to command and obey without them; we have lived and thought without them and against them. Declared outlaws for having wanted to remain worthy, we spontaneously created free communities in our mountains. Thus we had to conceive and cobble together a new society. And through that break and that new beginning, we became revolutionaries, not in words and armchairs, but in our acts and in our flesh.

"You, who have suffered more and thought more deeply, surely you will precede us on the road to that indispensable Revolution which alone will enable us to reconstruct a pacified, rationally organized society.

"Brothers in today's redemption and tomorrow's Revolution, we would like to remain so in the fight to come. Even if they are pathetically few in number, our submachine guns and carbines give us a different soul from yours. Unlike you, we have the privilege of preparing ourselves for the liberating fight ahead. At the decisive moment, we hope to take the enemy from the rear at the same time as the army of French Africa strikes from the front. It would give us joy if at the same time you over there in Germany could provoke the sudden paralysis of their huge, exhausted machine through a vast refusal to obey. At that time, in that crucible of dying Germany where 25 million slaves suddenly fraternize together to free themselves, we would like you to be the catalyst of French forces. We would like the cry of "liberty or death" to rise from French throats first, and for the new, free Europe to be born under that sign. What glory that would be! Could France dream of a greater victory? All Europe is waiting for your signal and the example of your courage. A great conquest is opening before you. We are with you."

April 14

I have the mock-up of a special number of the *Journal des Volontaires*. Actually, the men who composed it have finally given up on publishing it: "A question of timeliness," they say. They themselves do not dare publish this testimony of their isolation and despair.

The whole paper is a protest against Vichy's odious propaganda which denounces them as terrorists and bandits—and the worst of it is that it is having some effect on public opinion. They had left for the maquis thinking they were merely the avant-garde of the armies of liberation, and now they must see that the mass of the nation, reserved and wary, is not following them. They themselves explain very well that this country of logicians and lawyers has a hard time realizing that "order is not necessarily identical to legality." It was enough for someone like Darnand to call his gangs of assassins "forces to maintain law and order" for the petty bourgeois to scratch their heads and actually distrust those "bandits" who are their sons and brothers: we've actually reached the point where these young "volunteers," who are saving the honor of us all, have to justify themselves, argue their case, and prove their common honesty.

How can we be surprised at their bitterness, even surprised they're saying something like this to us: if this propaganda has some effect on you, isn't it because you have a bad conscience and you don't dare face reality? Because you're afraid to join us, it's convenient for you to believe that the men of the maquis, your boys, are actually disreputable men. The love of security and what remains of comfort makes you distrust those who are fighting for you. The disagreement between the maquis and the plain is the disagreement between men who fight and men who don't. If German propaganda works, it's because it uses the deep difference in mentalities that separates a man in peacetime from a man at war. We are asking neither for charity nor support. We are only asking that all French people enter the war at our sides and join us in the fight: then we will be brothers once again.

"You have forgotten the war," they cry to us. "We are waging it." And that is indeed the difference between them and us. It's not true that we have forgotten the war, nor that we can forget it. But it is true that many of us are only capable of being subjected to it and slavery can become a habit; we have even found entertainers to keep up the habit, and when misery goes on for too long it can reduce even the best to think only of themselves. The men in the maquis, all together, are following a great dream and living it out, seriously. They are living with their weapons in their hands, like men who are *already free*.

I shall recopy this admirable page:

> Our law is the law of war . . . We denounce all those who accuse us, out of selfishness or fear, all those who have an equal fear of the truth and the night and all those who are afraid of words, acts, and arms. It is not that great fear of right-thinking people[323] which will save the French. It is not order, security, and thrift that will restore courage to a people that has lost it. In all fairness to the Germans, it must be said that they understood this. If they favored Marshal Pétain's "Moral Order," it is because they knew it was the best way of undermining the vitality of France. But we won't let ourselves be fooled twice by the same tricks. We now know the meaning of the words they use to try to put an end to our action today: Morality (bourgeois morality), education (Nazi education), order (financial order), and security (of financial capital). We know that today we are fighting for our freedom, and a country that is not free has neither morality nor values. This is why all men today who give in to the blackmail of fear are betraying the destiny of France. If you play the Germans' game in the name of order, you may have an easy conscience, but you should not be surprised if one fine day you meet up with a bullet, for if your consciences do not know your country's mission, those who took up arms for it are not obliged judge you by anything else but your actions.

[323] Guéhenno's correspondent writes "*grande peur des bienpensants*," the title of a violently anti-bourgeois essay (1931) by Georges Bernanos.*

Other articles relate the history of the maquis. Not all who refuse to serve in the STO are the same. The *maquisards* are particularly eager not to be confused with those petty-bourgeois "work-dodgers" who, through fear of work, found shelter in the country "at an aunt's house or on one of Daddy's farms." Many left to hide out, they explain, when conscription to the STO began in February 1943:

> But very soon it appeared that there are two ways of hiding, one of cowards looking for a burrow and the other of partisans looking for a thicket, the better to fire at the path. More than two thirds of them left in quest of a burrow, and they always found it. Those who remained had passed the first selection. Then instruction, discipline, tiring sentinel duties, and supply fatigues eliminated one part of that group. Alarms, counter-alarms, forced marches, dispersions, and attacks by units of mobile gendarmes, Italians, and Germans sent away many more. The lack of weapons and the length of the wait discouraged some excellent men. The facilities of city life and M. Laval's* amnesty tempted still others who were beginning to get bored. A highly selective entrance examination! Our July numbers fell in a proportion of six to one. It is a stroke of luck that we are very pleased about. We have done our duty. Our life was a school for character, screening out false values. The rabbit-skinned fighters went back to their families. Now we are alone, among soldiers, among true soldiers, since we are all volunteers... Having joined the maquis to save ourselves, we are staying here voluntarily. We feel connected to all the volunteers of our history and particularly to those young sans-culottes, the volunteers of '92...[324]

Some of these boys have lived through a singular adventure. Young bourgeois or petty-bourgeois, my pupils of two or three years ago, candidates for a *Grande École*, aspiring to become masters in a society which, after all, did not seem so bad to them, their "generosity," their love for France and spirit of revolt led them to the maquis. At first they were merely patriots. But they discovered Revolution. They realized that if their families, if the French bourgeoisie, has defended France so badly it is because it thinks only of its money. From then on, the cause of France and the cause of the Revolution appeared to them the same cause. Money must be suppressed to save France, and the country can only be well served by revolutionaries.

Terrorists—nothing in them is frightening but their purity. Let it frighten cowards and traitors; that is only just. The purity of the great snow plateaus, woods where all the trees grow straight up, the limestone plains that the wind

---

[324] 1792, when the first armies of the Republic—non-noble, thus "sans-culottes"—defended France against invasion.

whips through like a flame. The purity of those deserts where the soul springs forward. France went on a retreat there with them and found the sense of her greatness once again.

April 19

Noisy-le-Sec bombed.

April 20

Porte de la Chapelle bombed.

At the same time the sirens were going off, the first bombs were falling. There was no time to get to an air-raid shelter. We stayed in our fragile house with all the windows open, and had no other recourse but to watch the show. Magnificent, but rather frightening. Man is astonishingly powerful and stupid.

April 30

Quite obviously the showdown is approaching. What can we do? There is a chance all my friends and I will be picked up and put in some concentration camp. Vainly, up to now, have we looked for ways of hiding out together. It is not easy. The family and the profession hold us back. There is still time, however, but where can we go and be sure of going toward freedom? Where will the landing be made and the action get under way?

The day before yesterday during an air-raid warning, in the schoolyard of the Lycée Buffon,[325] I was listening to the conversations of the pupils. And it was hardly reassuring, when we consider that children merely repeat what they hear in their families. Always the same fear, the same rot. They're trembling. They distrust everybody—Germans, English, or Russians—and all they think about is "getting through" without harm, as if all the great mass of this country cared about was to live at all costs. But what people really lives otherwise than through a minority, through a few men who inspire it and lead it? That minority has now been forced into silence. Only traitors and cowards are talking. Hence that impression of flabbiness one gets from public opinion. But in fact, there is no public opinion, and if you think about it, after all, that sort of inertia which the masses of ordinary people, so malleable, are opposing to the propaganda that surrounds us is a good sign of the instinctive dignity of the country.

May 10

It's the dogs' turn now. They've announced that all dogs over 45 centimeters at the shoulder will be requisitioned. I measured Malik immediately. He's only 43 centimeters tall: he won't be deported. What luck!

---

[325] We recall that Guéhenno was demoted to teaching the lowest grades at this fairly prestigious secondary school. They would be middle school classes today.

Katie's beau
Drew the number fo'[326]

I don't know what to do. The path of wisdom would no doubt be to leave and go into hiding. Twenty thousand suspects, they say, are to be arrested at the first hours of the landing. The Militia, too, is supposed to have drawn up a list of hostages. But then, I can't leave my class, my lycée. Everyone follows the facile path of little duties.

May 20

The air-raid sirens sounded for a long time this morning. After a few days of bad weather, the sky has grown very pure. The planes themselves were invisible, but we were surrounded by their noise, and as a few of them—the fighter planes, no doubt—were diving from a great altitude, thin white streaks would form and float forward, delicate as threads on a piece of cloth. The people were at their windows, rather happy to watch. The calm of the last days had made us fear that everything might be put off again. The morning was magnificent. A mother pigeon on the branch of a locust tree was feeding her little ones. A prelude... to what massacre?...We heard this evening that the military camps at Orly and Villacoublay were destroyed.

May 21

Re-read Nietzsche's *Ecce Homo*. What grandeur. But what excessiveness.

"I cannot stand this race," he used to say of his fellow Germans. "It has no sense of nuance... It doesn't even know how to walk!" But he doesn't know how to walk either. Zarathustra's step is no more assured than Parsifal's.[327] It's the same gigantism.

Neither Montaigne nor La Rochefoucauld* nor Voltaire, who are sources of inspiration for him, needed to go mad in order to be great. It is from them that he learned to despise all the systems that try to make us ashamed of our being. But precisely, man was enough for them: limiting themselves quite gladly to the confines of the human condition, they did not take new pride in it. They were good psychologists, but did not think themselves supermen for all of that. And if they denounced the proud humility of the Christians who tell themselves such a lovely tale of their eternal destiny, it was not to fall into another kind of pride. All idealism is prideful, and pride is always idealistic. They did not play God, did

---

[326] *Lou galan de la Katin/A tirat le numero cin.* Guéhenno is quoting a Provençal jingle by Joseph Rouzoul (1875–1955).

[327] Referring to Nietzsche's *Thus Spake Zarathustra* (see note 61, p. 29), while Parsifal refers to the Germanic and Wagnerian hero. Further on, *fatum* means Fate. In Virgil's *Aeneid*, the hero's *fatum* is his pre-ordained destiny: to found Rome.

not claim to be a follower of Dionysus any more than of the Crucified One. None of them thought himself destined by some kind of *fatum* to operate some kind of transmutation of values. In their eyes, human values were only values of convenience and usage. Of long, long usage. They are established, clarified, and purified through thousands of trials and errors. Everybody works at it and collaborates. Man will end up by being man; this hope is enough. And madness begins, for individuals and peoples, when they claim the privilege of some kind of super-humanity.

May 27

Constant air-raid warnings. Yesterday and the day before, I taught for fifteen minutes out of four hours of classes. All the competitive entrance exams have been postponed *sine die*.[328] But the hypocritical administration is keeping all the schools open.

A few weeks ago a new weekly came out: *Germinal*, where all the traitors and cretins of "socialism" immediately gathered.[329] The height of shamelessness: they wanted to cover their enterprise with the name of my poor friend Dabit,* and began publishing his book as a serial: *L'Hôtel du Nord*. When you don't have a living soul behind you, you'd better mobilize the dead. A note from Beatrice Appia, Dabit's widow, explained to me a few days later that of course all this was being done against her will and against that of Dabit's mother; courageously, the two women were suing *Germinal* and the publisher Denoël, which had sold the paper the rights to Dabit's novel. The summary judgment was to suspend publication immediately, but *Germinal* is appealing the decision, to gain time. The affair came before the court yesterday. I listened to the arguments. The publisher's lawyer, a kind of hypocritical worm, waving *Germinal* in the air, asked what anyone could possibly blame this paper for, so pure and printed in such difficult times on such fine paper. "Say it all," cried this Tartuffe to his opponent, Dabit's lawyer. "Everyone must tell the whole truth." Oh, how edifying it was! *Germinal*, to gain another week, asked for a postponement (what remains to be published of the novel would make up two or three episodes) on the pretext that its lawyer was only able to consult the case file rather belatedly. Dabit's lawyer said, quite skillfully, all he could without giving himself up to the Gestapo. But what no doubt carried the day, what decided the trial, was justice, forced to be mute— what no one could say but everyone would have liked to shout. At the end, the presiding magistrate, more courageous than one might have expected, demanded that the publication of the novel be suspended while the decision was pending.

---

[328] *Sine die:* without a setting a date for future action.

[329] That is, "National Socialism"—Nazism. The weekly usurped the name of a great 1885 novel by Émile Zola about the suffering and rebellion of miners. *Germinal*'s co-founders are named below: Paul Rives (1895–1967) was first a socialist, then drew close to the National Socialists.

Déat* and Rives are obviously going to make use of everything they can this week, but in vain, I hope.

May 29

A torrent of stupidity. Two movie actors had put on *Andromaque*[330] in the Édouard VII Theater. Their interpretation of the play seemed immoral. *Andromaque* has been banned. This morning, the newspapers are publishing the following note: "The French Militia is concerned about the intellectual protection of France as well as public morality. That is why the regional head of the French Militia for the Paris region notified the Prefect of Police that it was going to oppose the production of the scandalous play by Messieurs Jean Marais and Alain Cuny now playing at the Édouard VII Theater. The Prefect of Police issued a decree immediately banning the play."

Constant air-raid warnings. Five or six a day. The planes remain invisible most of the time. Nothing but a dull rumbling in the bright sky. The railroad stations around Paris have been destroyed one after the other. From now on we are more or less isolated.

May 30

Last night a rehearsal of Sartre's new play, *No Exit*. It is very clever and well done. But what's the good of those infernal evocations? When I'm confronted with them I feel stupidly virtuous. I should take care: perhaps I am more stupid than virtuous...What bothers me is that the author never adheres to what he says; the horrors he depicts are never quite horrible because he is not horrified himself. At no point was I moved. Just literature.

Who will get us out of this swamp? M. Gide put all writers on guard against fine sentiments. They only make for bad literature, according to him.[331] But cultivating bad sentiments can be very "literary," too, and matter for other clichés...Watching Sartre's play, I feel myself one of those "prey for paradise" that he despises. Those who are "prey for hell" can't hold my interest for long. I am disgusted by the falsely cynical, provocative ravings of irresponsible people.

Without even thinking about it, a true writer always writes for my salvation, for the salvation of something inside me. He himself seeks the path to my salvation and forces me to accompany him for a while down this road, toward his light. All the rest is fashion and amateurism.

I noted some falsely allusive elements in the first scenes. You would think they're in a prison cell in Fresnes or the Santé, and the audience is ready to marvel at the

---

[330] *Andromache* (1667), one of Jean Racine's classic tragedies in verse. Further on, Jean Marais and Alain Cuny were famous actors of stage and screen.

[331] Gide's aphorism *C'est avec de bons sentiments qu'on fait de la mauvaise littérature* (literally "It is with good sentiments that one makes bad literature") is still quoted in France.

author's courage. But we quickly realize that this is only one more lie, as the "no exit" is only the hell of a ménage à trois, of a man and two women (one of whom is a lesbian) vying for their turn to sleep together. The dreary games of servitude.

N…came to see me. As I told him I had come across Annamite Waffen SS troops,[332] he tells me the stories of several of his fellow countrymen to justify them. They are peasants from the heart of Laos whom he sometimes runs into at the Ministry of the Colonies. Five years ago, a photographer on the village square showed them photographs. They, too, wanted to have their portrait taken. The photographer asked them, for all payment, to press their soot-covered thumbs on a white paper which was, he said, a promise to pay him when he came by again. A few days later, soldiers arrived with the white papers. Forty thousand peasants were brought to France in this way. Since then, they have lived in mines and factories depending on the hazards of the disaster and servitude. The ones N…runs into clean the offices. Never has the ministry been so clean. But their boss isn't satisfied and treats them badly: "What the hell did you come here for?" he asks them. They don't know French and can't answer. When their work is done, they dream of their plows, play cards, or fight with each other. They no longer belong to any world, N…tells me, and they are pitiful to behold. One of them came to see N…the other day and told him: "You understand, Monsieur, we know very well that everyone has to die. But to die here, like this…I wouldn't want to die a ridiculous death." And N…had a hard time stopping him from volunteering for the Waffen SS.

June 3

Yesterday Paulhan* took us to Luna Park. If a world can be judged by the pleasures it gives itself, the one we live in is frightful. You go in through a vast corridor between distorting mirrors where everyone can see himself alternately as a dwarf or giant, fat as a barrel or thin as a wire. After which, unsure of what you are, you are ready for all the "attractions"…I give up describing them. Many are just invitations to exercise one's skill or one's strength. Some invention is displayed in the choice of objects on which you exert them. We were walking along among the games of balls or rings, when suddenly here is what we saw: on a bed, hardly covered by a sheet, a woman just about naked; she was watching us approach; she had the look of an animal; she lies there all day. Above her was a target; the most skillful players, by throwing a ball, knock over the bed and the woman with it. That's what you can see in Paris, in 1944. Luckily, this infernal paradise was almost empty: a few prostitutes looking for customers, a few young toughs frantically breaking plates, and above all German soldiers and NCOs in quest of new reasons to commit suicide made up the whole public. No more than fifty people in all.

---

[332] The Waffen SS was the fighting wing of the SS (see note 230, p. 164); it eventually took in "non-Aryan" volunteers from other nations, despite the concern for "racial purity" in the SS, which was even more fanatical than in other Hitlerian organizations.

Members of the French militia herd off young men suspected of being in the Resistance—probably to their death. *Bundesarchiv, Bild 146-1989-107-24.*

As we were leaving, the woman left her bed, got dressed, and crossed the area, dancing a bawdy jig. We could see she is a poor idiot. I couldn't say if that lessened our disgust or added to it. To cheer us up again, Paulhan took us to the zoological garden nearby to see animals and children.

June 4

A visit from D..., a former student. A very intelligent boy, but incapable of doing anything but philosophizing. He is uneasy, thinks of going into hiding, but has scruples about it. I reassure him. Then, completely calm now, he explains that psychoanalysis will save humanity. All one has to do is psychoanalyze the German people, the Japanese people and all peoples led astray by an inferiority complex. And peace will reign among men of good will.

June 6

Robin* and Duval* call me around 8 a.m. The landing has begun.

June 10

Our anguish has changed shape. I no longer feel joy as I did on Tuesday. I was overcome by gratitude, by feeling all that thousands of young men were suffering for us at that very moment—and for things that, to a man with some nobility,

A smiling French volunteer leaves Paris to fight for the Nazis. He has chalked *Waffen SS Français* and "Heil Hitler" on his suitcase. The possibility of a Franco-French civil war comes up repeatedly in this diary. *Bundesarchiv, Bild 101III-Apfel-017-30.*

seem in a sense to be self-evident, cannot even be contested: freedom and honor. That is how ignominious this world is. Three years ago, Hitler was boasting of instituting his "order" for at least a thousand years. A thousand years? The prophecy of a moronic genius. But it's true, if he had pulled it off, servitude could last thirty years, fifty years, our whole lives and that of our children.

After the anguish of servitude, now the anxiety of combat. I unfolded the maps of the hikes I took in days gone by. I know all the villages where they're fighting: Langrume, Saint-Aubin, Arromanches, Saint-Honorine. We used to rush out there at Whitsunday [333] every year to see if the open sea was still there and re-learn a certain ample way of breathing. Freedom is perhaps no more than a certain fullness of breathing, the continuous awareness of a vast space around us

---

[333] The seventh Sunday after Easter.

where our dreams, our energies, and our desires can unfurl—the right to be one-self. Do thousands of men have to die to rescue such simple, obvious things?

The weather is bad and it's making the landings more difficult. Never have I looked at a barometer so anxiously...

June 12

One thing is certain: France can no longer put an end to its misfortunes alone and when our freedom and honor are regained, we will owe it to those young men who have come from England, America, and Canada, from the ends of the earth, to fight and mingle their blood with that of the young Frenchmen whom nothing could enslave. Thus history is made, and the man of tomorrow, for whom the freedom of all men on earth will be a common cause.

Strange rumors are going around which reveal, at least, our hope. Resistance forces, they say, have re-established the Republic in Auvergne from now on. A battalion of the 1st French regiment has joined the maquis. Parachuted Canadian officers are supposedly directing the movement...

The barometer is climbing. Continuous air-raid warnings last night.

Walks in Paris with Blanzat yesterday afternoon. The Germans are growing rare. The ones we come across around the Opera no longer have that look of boastful idlers they had just a few months ago. They are busy and gloomy. Parisians are restraining their joy.

June 20

Bad weather for the past ten days. Terribly violent combats in Normandy. Ridiculous impatience. No other resource than to try to lose myself in my Rousseau. I don't succeed very well.

June 22

We are beginning to have a few more precise pieces of information about what happened and is happening in Auvergne, in the Massif Central. The Resistance rose up too soon and the repression is appalling.

Oradour-sur-Glane. That was the pretty name of a little village near Limoges. A German officer was killed there some two weeks ago. They razed the village and machine-gunned the assembled population until no one was breathing or screaming anymore.[334]

Like a fool, I told this story to Jean Blanzat. I did not know Oradour was right near Bellac. Poor Jean is beside himself with anxiety. He's thinking of his little boy whom he sent to his parents, near Bellac.

---

[334] The June 10 massacre at Oradour was even worse than Guéhenno's summary: after killing the men, the SS locked all the women and children in the church, burned it down, and shot anyone who tried to get out. The site has been turned into a national monument.

The reason for England's victory, the victory of September 1940, which will probably appear in history as the Marne of this war, was a tiny technical invention.[335] That's what my friend Bouché* told me.

In May 1940, it had become clear that English fighter planes were inferior to German fighter planes. The losses were appalling. The German planes had a ceiling 800 meters above the English and they could climb much faster. The cause of this inferiority was, it seems, in the *pitch* of the English propellers. Consequently, the government very reasonably refused to engage its planes in the Battle of France in June and lose them. But they feverishly set to work. They tried an experiment. They changed the pitch of the propellers of a squadron of Spitfires. It was ready for the first days of August. In the first dogfight between the RAF and the Luftwaffe, the Germans lost four times as many planes as the English. The Spitfires could climb much faster and had a ceiling 2,100 hundred meters above the Focke-Wulfs. By September, all English fighter planes had been transformed and Hitler's armies could not cross the Channel. Those who know call that German defeat *the pitch panic*.

I'm working on my Rousseau. I could easily write 1,200 or 1,800 pages with everything we know about his life in them, but I doubt if I'll ever be able to write the hundred pages that would bring to light and resuscitate the driving intuition of his work. Scholars get out of their predicament and their impotence through erudition. What strikes me above all is the hazardous nature of the document I'm working on. I'm up to 1754 in Jean-Jacques' life. The gossip of his contemporaries—Grimm, d'Holbach, Madame d'Epinay—has preserved the memory of two or three facts in his social life: he dines at Mademoiselle Quirault's, he has a falling-out with d'Holbach. And that's what I'm going to recount at length, the year 1754, because I possess all I need to do so, because it may be amusing, because I have to fill up the time...But what do we know of his deeper life, his relationship with Thérèse in that year, the progress of his illness,[336] of his dreams, his thinking? All that will take up a few lines in my narrative. What is important remains shrouded in darkness. But that darkness gave birth to the *Discourse on Inequality*. What would I not give to walk with J-J through the woods of Saint-Germain again, to go back along all the paths of his thought with him and find the living intuition that guided him. All I'll be able to do is analyze the results, the finished *Discourse*, all done, like a dead, cold thing. History is almost always just footnotes. I would have to find the very movement of creation and be

[335] The Battle of the Marne ended the first German offensive in World War I. The "victory of September 1940" refers to the Battle of Britain, when the Luftwaffe tried to annihilate English cities by bombing them out of existence. The Germans stopped when their planes were shot down in great numbers.

[336] Thérèse Levasseur, a seamstress, was Rousseau's life partner and bore him five children, whom he gave away to a foundling home. He often complained of his "illness" and eventually died of it; however, its exact nature remains unknown.

Rousseau to tell the story of Rousseau. Every great artist is only a great intuition, and that intuition has the character of eternity, has a value outside of time. Something eternal that had always been obscurely felt, but never seen or said, is seized in a moment of time by a man who is himself destined to die. In order not to fail this man, one would have to write his history in eternity.

St. John's Day, June 24

It is less tiring to lose oneself than to seek oneself. As I work on my Rousseau I'm afraid of taking the easy way out. This immense labor would only have meaning if it were an occasion for critical self-examination.

I said goodbye to the girls of the Collège Sévigné.[337] When the principal asked me to teach classes that prepare them for the *Agrégation*,[338] she was showing her sympathy for me and wanted to protest against the harassment to which I was being subjected. I accepted and I don't regret it, although the fatigue of those classes added to that of my stupid duties at Buffon. It's the only slightly intelligent thing I will have done this year. And yet these were quite vocational classes, and their subject rather narrow: the first six books of the *Fables* of La Fontaine and Fénelon's *Telemachus*. Before leaving these girls, I wanted to speak to them more freely, for once, about literature, about what one can find in it, about the admirable profession that they would exercise if they wished and that was mine, too, a profession which enables one to live almost continually with greatness. A profession that reveals wonders. I put them on their guard against the excess of technical knowledge—pedantry, that way of degrading everything, which has destroyed so many teachers; and then, too, because I can sense that they are more Gidian than they should be, against that amateur mentality which degrades everything by reducing all books to mere occasions for our pleasure, so that we think we've said it all when we say that we "love" or "do not like" Montaigne or Pascal, Hugo or Baudelaire. Learning to read means learning to listen to that witness who always bears witness for us in some way, and in recognizing a tragedy which is always in some way our tragedy.

True writers, all of them, write for our salvation, or, if that formulation seems too lofty, for the salvation of something inside us, each according to his powers, his genius, according to the intuition he had of the world. One saves our lightness of spirit. Another teaches us insecurity and risk, both necessary. Another, difficult loyalty. All of them bring us back to some source in our deeper lives. Giving them a "close reading" should be nothing other than following with them the path of those returns, recognizing those fundamental intuitions. There is no

---

[337] *Collège* then meant secondary school; in France today it would mean middle school. Further on, François Fénelon (1651–1715) was an archbishop and classic French writer; *Les Aventures de Télémaque* (1699) is his most famous work.

[338] See note 14 in the *Translator's Introduction*, p. xv.

quest more exciting than this exploration, this recognition through the confused forest of a work, in the noise of phrases and words, beyond all the chatter—the quest for the idea that led a man, for the deep song that was unique to him and made him live. Nothing is more apt to make us men.

June 25

Inadequate. To feel oneself inadequate. No form of sadness is worse, and life does not leave us with a greater regret. To feel, to know that one lacks sensitivity and heart, that one often could not rise to the occasion and was not up to the contact with someone; ungrateful, unworthy even of one's happiness, of one's luck...Oh, be quiet!...There is no cure for these thoughts.

Faced by our common misfortune, I feel my inadequacy today. Let it save us, let it save me and enable me to last and to live, and not console me. "The Inadequate Heart"—a good title for a novel on the human condition. But I would like to be able to suffer better, as I would to enjoy things better and love better.

A petty dialectic, the dialectic of victory and defeat. I'm afraid the resentment at our servitude for these past four years has locked me into ideas that are too narrow. I sense that to think through what is now happening one would have to leave that confined atmosphere. Let me not be lacking in the tenderness necessary to see friends and even enemies clearly, in the terrible ordeal they are undergoing.

Freedom is rising. It is a wind blowing in from Normandy, still gently. But it will blow harder and harder, purifying the air and expanding our hearts.

I want to read everything Hemingway wrote.

A Farewell to Arms. It's a wonderfully tender book, full of silences and secrets. There is, no doubt, no more triumphant response to the horror and stupidity of the world than a certain goodness of spirit. That goodness is invincible. As I read I was full of memories, and I had all too many reasons to be deeply upset by it. I knew another Catherine Barkley.[339] When will I say my own farewell to arms? For five years now I've felt like a mobilized soldier and those are bad conditions in which to think clearly.

June 26

"It is not enough to reveal, the revelation must also be whole, and clear; there is a kind of obscurity that one might define as *The Affectation of the Great Masters.* It is a veil which they delight in drawing between the people and nature...Let us hasten to popularize science and 'philosophy.' If we want the *philosophes* to lead and progress, let us bring the people to the point the *philosophes* are at in their investigations." (Diderot, *On the Interpretation of Nature*, 40 [*De l'Interprétation de la nature, Pensée XL*].)

---

[339] The main female character in Hemingway's novel.

June 28

Philippe Henriot assassinated.[340] He was not worthy of such a death. I was listening to his editorial just last night. In all fairness, it must be said that Vichy, hypocrisy, and treason finally found their voice in him: a solid, scornful, somewhat nasal voice. (It is rather remarkable that vain people often talk through the nose, no doubt because they listen to themselves talk and are delighted by the nasal echo their words produce in their brain.) He was justifying himself last night, proclaiming that he had never denounced anyone, on the contrary, and if there was blood between him and his enemies, they alone had shed it. Fear or premonition.

I'm sorry to see such grand deaths for such little men. It would be better to condemn them to live with a sign around their necks.

What was the sincerity of a man like Philippe Henriot made of? He was the very type of those bourgeois terrified by all the deepest wishes of their country as they have appeared for the last twenty years. They could see themselves losing everything if their country got the better of them: their religion and their homeland, which they did not distinguish from their power and their fortune. To remain what they were, they had no other recourse than to betray their country and they betrayed it with the deepest sincerity.

July 5

The greatest life has only a few great moments, often set far apart from one another. The ones in which a man seems lifted up by what he was born to say or do. There are long intervals of total calm. I see this in the case of Rousseau himself. Those intervals are what are hardest to recount. One gets out of it through anecdotes. But how to bring out, beneath the story of so many trivial events, the guiding intuition that secretly continues to lead its own life? It should be felt as a basso profundo under the ornaments of those trivial events which then seem to make up the whole song.

We've been getting together with a few friends every two weeks, to conquer that silence in which we are imprisoned. Each one brings what he knows or thinks he knows. Yesterday Zay killed in his cell,[341] shootings of hostages and STO evaders, burned villages and reprisals of all kinds. But I think what touched me the most yesterday was the story that B...told about the show put on by the "propaganda" of Vichy the other day: English and American prisoners insulted and covered with spittle by women and men carefully mustered to do just that.

---

[340] Phillipe Henriot (1889–1944), a recurrent voice on Vichy radio from 1940 on, was appointed Minister of Information and Propaganda in January 1944. His violent attacks on de Gaulle and the Resistance were notorious.

[341] Jean Zay (1904–1944), like Léon Blum,* had two things against him in the eyes of the far Right: he was Minister of Education in the Popular Front government (1936–1939) and he was Jewish, frequently denounced as "the Jew Jean Zay" in the daily press during the Occupation. He was assassinated by the French Militia. In the next sentence, B...is almost certainly Blanzat.

So many vile efforts to fool the world about the true feelings of France. It was amusing to hear B...tell of one of the insulters being followed and seriously beaten up. But that, no one will ever know.

Blanzat has given me a novel to read by a new writer, Peyrefitte; he's having a big argument with Mauriac* about him. It's called *Les Amitiés particulières*,[342] and it's the story of the loves of two adolescents brought up by priests. The book is merciless, ironic, and dry. One thinks of Laclos and Stendhal, and it is sometimes very strong. A certain charm is lacking, however, that charm which always justifies youth, whatever it may do. A very great painter, it seems to me, always finds a way of justifying and getting us to excuse what he paints, even monsters. M. Peyrefitte's hatred, like his analysis, is too meticulous. Nonetheless, his book poses important questions. What a condemnation of institutions run by priests. The reason is, they talk too much about love there. It is reassuring to see that education in our lycées, so dry on the surface, has something good about it. It avoids the confusions of the reign of the heart. It only claims to develop the intelligence, not the soul, and the only virtue it recommends is probity. And that is fine. It only touches the soul indirectly. Which is better than touching it directly in a heavy-handed way, at the risk of offending or deforming it. The soul develops by itself and it is not a good idea to talk to it too much about itself. It should be left to its silence and its secret; only work around it with discretion, like a good gardener, to make sure everything around it is neat and clean. Honest and true.

July 13

We live with just one thought. Time is long and short, both. Every minute goes by with infinite slowness, but the days with an incredible rapidity. Forty days have already gone by since the landing, and it seems as if it were yesterday. The ferocious battle is still indecisive. That battle is all we can think about. We have to wait for 9:30 at night. No electricity during the day so we can learn that one army or the other has advanced or retreated a few hundred meters at the price of horrifying losses...

July 18

I wanted to write a sort of sequel to my *Caliban Speaks*[343]: "New Notebooks from Caliban" for 1944. I can't manage to do it. Caliban himself does not grow older. His anger is renewed with the generations. But I have grown older: not that I'm already so old that when I say "I have lived," I'm tempted to see the evidence in it that after all, one can live. I still feel inequality as a deep offense. I know that

---

[342] Published in 1943, this is Roger Peyrefitte's (1907–2000) best-known novel. It deals with the homoerotic love of two adolescents. Translated into English as *Special Friendships* (1950). Further on, for Laclos, see note 275, p. 201.

[343] See the *Translator's Introduction*, pp. xv–xvi.

the great mass of people still cannot really live. But my anger has grown old inside me. I re-read my little book of twenty years ago. There is a tone in it I am not capable of reproducing today. Have I become used to the misery of others?

And yet Caliban's appeal could be so strong, if only I had the heart for it, if I could make him speak today not only from my own meager experience (and the youth of my heart, as I did twenty years ago), but truly from his own, and according to his spirit. The dubious battle in which he has been engaged for thirty years—sometimes fighting and sometimes submitting—in which he is sometimes duped, led astray by the lies of his latest tyrants and struggling against himself, his mistakes, his servitude, his degradation, his defeats; but speak also of his martyrdom, his victory, and that light which grows invincibly within him in the very midst of combat, the certitude of being right, hope and dignity for all—what matter for meditation. And all that the ordeal itself has taught him: freedom is everyone's cause and you lose it if you claim you're saving it only for yourself. My freedom is the freedom of others and man is never alone, he is all the relations he has with other people; his nobility is in the nobility of those relations and there is a greatness of participation: the fullness of my being and my joy can only be acquired by the fullness of being of others and their joy. The common soul must be strong and rich enough to feed those who are most in need, those whom the injustice of nature has deprived the most, so that they may regain confidence and hope nonetheless.

July 20

For the past few days there has again been a rumor of a coming armistice between the Germans and the Russians—negotiations in Sweden. The stock market was catastrophic yesterday, all the stocks were plummeting. That, at least, is rather amusing. I'm sure these rumors are silly, and in fact stirred up by German propaganda to take our hope away. But from time to time, we can't avoid feeling a dull fear. What if that happened? Last night M . . . amusingly brought up what the situation would be: the new combinations, the Communists denouncing to the Collaborators all those who've "held out their hand" to them for three years. Nothing is more frightful than the fact that these reversals cannot be totally excluded: they are not absolutely implausible and a rumor like this can easily exist: nothing reveals more how everything we love depends on a game, on chance. And boys are dying during this time.

News comes in of a few of my former students who took to the maquis. Boulanger was killed. Jean Bruneau, who was taken prisoner, was saved from death. He is sentenced to hard labor. Domenach[344] sends me a card from Dordogne: "I know," he says, "that you haven't forgotten me."

---

[344] Jean-Marie Domenach (1922–1997) became a well-known politically active intellectual, editor of the respected left-wing monthly *Esprit*.

July 22

An attempt on Hitler's life. Failed. During the night, he spoke to his people to show that he was really still alive. How sorry I am not to have heard him. But the papers have published the translation of his speech: the bomb exploded two meters away from him and all he got was a few scratches. A striking confirmation of the great designs Providence has for him. So he will continue to thank his creator with a clear conscience.

Strange how a man in such an exceptional situation still can speak only in clichés. But on second thought, it says a lot about him and about the kind of greatness he possesses. False greatness. The greatness of a tyrant is not peculiar to him; it is constructed by and from the foolishness of those over whom he tyrannizes. The only divination he has is the stupidity and cowardice of men. In fact clichés must be his whole language, founding and maintaining his power. Insincerity and inauthenticity are the very conditions of his reign over a mass that is servile and consequently insincere and inauthentic itself. Master and slaves in perfect harmony in the same nothingness.

Yesterday evening I got Berlin on the radio at the very moment they were having deported workers take the mike one after the other: a Frenchman, a Czech, a Dane, a Serb, a Croat...all of whom were spouting the same pitch, expressing in bad German their "deep satisfaction that the Führer was still living for the happiness of Europe." A monstrous scenario of servitude, while in every country in the West and even in Germany there was not one single household where hope had not quivered for a moment. Oh, how the eyes of the slaves were shining today: the attack failed, true, but the beast will die, that is certain. Truth outstrips the imagination and never, perhaps, has a man's death awakened so deep a desire. Luckily, men grow weary and take their revenge for being treated like idiots. Then they won't rest until the moron they had promoted to their head disappears. They begin to think again, and that's enough to finish the moron off.

July 30

Every night German propaganda resuscitates Henriot. It could find no one to serve it so well. He was absolutely irreplaceable. So at exactly 10:15 every night, he has to grumble out one of his old editorials and call us back to our duties as "Europeans." He's the company ghost, a colleague who must worry, I imagine, de Beauplan, Paquis, and all his surviving comrades,[345] when they hear him growling

---

[345] Robert de Beauplan (1882–1951) and Jean Hérold-Paquis (1912–1945) were pro-Nazi propagandists. De Beauplan hoped for German victory and wrote military analyses predicting it in a daily newspaper until the Allies were actually just outside Paris; Hérold-Paquis ended his radio commentaries with "England, like Carthage, will be destroyed." After the Liberation, Hérold-Paquis was tried for treason and executed; de Beauplan's sentence was commuted to life.

in the studios of Radio Paris. It is rather comforting that German propaganda is reduced to mobilizing phantoms. But *Je Suis Partout* is worried[346]: it seems that the records are wearing out at a frighteningly rapid rate, and if some new technical discovery does not save it, this "great voice that is saving France" will soon be decidedly extinguished.

I think of the wife and children of this man. Do they listen every evening?

August 9

We are not living well. We are getting thinner. A kilo of butter costs a thousand francs. A kilo of peas, forty francs. And then, you have to find them. But we hardly think of these miseries. We only think of one thing: the return of freedom.

The night before last, an extraordinary speech on Radio Paris by a "German soldier"—a soldier with glasses, without a doubt, and several PhDs. He warned us against appearances, against the naïve victory bulletins of the Allies. The truth is that this war is "undulatory." We're at the end of the second undulation and at the beginning of the third. The first undulation (1939–41) ended with a German victory, the second (1941–44) with an English victory and the third, the last, will end in six months by a German victory. That is the reality, hidden behind appearances. The new German weapons, which are still secret, will be the means of this victory.

What is still more curious is that poor Déat is trying his best to spin out the same yarns. His article this morning explains that the robot-planes, the V-1, are the soldiers of *L'An II*, Year II of the European Revolution."[347] The attempt to assassinate Hitler opened another phase of the war. The miracle of Hitler's escape is a sign of other miracles to come.

As a "conscripted civilian," I stood guard from six to midnight in front of a grocery (just about empty moreover, it seemed to me?). My companion worked for a saddle-maker. We sat down on a bench in front of the store and for six hours I listened to him tell me his story.

Nothing is as awful as diving into people's lives like that. He spoke to me quite innocently. Father of a large family and someone who likes to fish is the sum of his duties and pleasures. He lives on the Rue de l'Égalité in one of those big buildings where Paris piles up its rabble. He now earns 550 francs a week. He doesn't like the Germans. He occupied Germany in 1920, in the Ruhr, but he didn't even want to see them, not even the "skirts." He didn't shoot anybody,

---

[346] *Je Suis Partout* (*I Am Everywhere*) was a virulently anti-Semitic, pro-Nazi weekly (see note 226, p. 161); Robert Brasillach* was its editor-in-chief. Further on, the "great voice that is saving France" was the phrase used by the press to describe Philippe Henriot.

[347] Year II: 1793, when the new French Republic mobilized its armies and expanded their operations. See the end of note 225, p. 159.

either. But those guys, we got to know them. He's French. "Everybody in their own home." His neighbor to the right on the same floor owes him twenty-seven francs. His neighbor to the left is much more honest, but he really goes too far: he has eleven kids, that neighbor. "You know, Monsieur, that's just not reasonable. And the doctor told his wife she'd have fourteen. Eleven. Me, I didn't believe him, you don't see 'em, there are kids everywhere. Three in the sanatorium they tell me. So René, I says to myself, you, you gotta stop right there. Four, that's reasonable."

He is rather pleased with himself, with his wisdom. He has a married sister. She didn't have any children. A piece of luck! So she and her husband can live a life of pleasure. Before the war, they bought a motorcycle with a sidecar. Well, what with the money they spent at the garage and taking it out on Sundays, they didn't have any more money than he did. As for him, on Sundays he goes fishing. He informs me how deep you have to fish to get bleaks, big roaches and little ones. He'd rather fish for the little ones. They bite faster. It's fun.

Around eight o'clock, three of his children arrived. Two little boys and a girl, ragged, pathetic, frighteningly thin. They wanted to see their father stand guard. It would be something to remember. The father authorized them to go back home by taking the long way round, Rue de la Délivrance. A walk before bedtime. They smile a poor smile and when they leave they give me their little hands to shake.

It's my companion's turn to ask me questions, and when he has a few of my wretched little secrets, to encourage me. Prudently he asks me what I think of the Marshal, and of Russia. He didn't believe the Marshal could be an old crook. But he feels that the Russians must not be as unhappy as he is told, and they must love their country since they defend it so well. He's a Catholic, but he's not going to pick up the priest's robe and kiss it. You have your dignity, you understand. But children have to believe in something because otherwise they become criminals. Before the war, he has to tell me just to be honest, it's true, he let himself be dragged in by the PSF.[348] He paid his dues, but they slipped the money back to him when no one was looking. And then, their youth organization gave him a rabbit from time to time. "So I says to myself, René, you're not wrong. What'm I supposed to do with four kids and the 950 francs I made a month. Since I couldn't support my kids. I didn't do anything dishonest, Monsieur. You agree?" I didn't have the courage to deny it. I even assured him he was right. Night fell around ten o'clock. At midnight we walked back together to the police station, following our orders. He was happy. The time had gone by quickly. Not counting that we're supposed to have earned ten francs an hour. Just to talk, that's not such bad pay. And then, we told each other a lot of stuff. Like at confession, he said.

---

[348] PSF: Parti Social Français, the largest nationalist, far-Right party in France during the '30s.

What a luxury freedom is. My freedom.

I feel myself full of questions. What is the way to revive freedom in these dead souls? You don't make grafts on dead trees. It's better to replant the forest...

August 13

This week and Easter week are the two most important weeks of the year. We've had magnificent days, worthy of the return of freedom. We wait, all we do is wait, in an impatience that the absence of news increases still more. But it is returning, it is coming, impossible even to walk out of the house. All the Metros have stopped running. I vainly try to work, to read. Artillery or bombs rumble on the horizon almost continuously. Paris is at stake in this battle and everybody can feel it.

The day before yesterday the radio announced the death of Saint-Exupéry,* who had gone over to the rebellion and was shot down during a night flight in the Midi. This morning it announces that Drieu la Rochelle,* whose job for the last four years is well known, tried to commit suicide and failed. Two facts that take the measure of today's France.

The time is drawing near when scores will be settled and we'll "give back his person" to that ambitious old fool who imposed his gift on us for four years.[349] A great gift: the seven stars of a marshal on the uniform of a convict. All we felt was the uniform, which he and his party had thrown over our backs.

Voltaire, annotating the *Social Contract*, says of Rousseau: "He was mad enough to believe that his books would make revolutions." Yes: and that's exactly what interests us about him. And then, was he so wrong?

I'm making slow progress in the second volume and I'm often tempted to give up. I lose myself in the infinite details of his life. Without enough inner strength to find the movement of the modern revolution inside him at every instant.

August 14

The same German soldier who warned us against appearances last week resumed his sermon last night. This learned doctor has learned that the French distrusted "German heaviness": now he plays on the light side, strains for jokes, and gets nowhere. Among other stories he hoped were brilliant, he told us he had consulted all the most famous astrologists in Paris this week. All of them read German victory in the stars. Just one refused to talk: he had made the same reading, but he was a Gaullist... After which he discussed at length the nice name, "with a pinch of kindliness in it," that we gave them this time around: not the *Boches* anymore, as in 1914, but the *Fridolins*. That's supposed to be the sign of a lasting love between France and Germany.

[349] In his broadcast of June 17, 1940, Pétain said, "I am making France the gift of my person."

They're beginning to sing again as they march by in the streets to prove their unshakeable confidence to us...The last show.

August 18

The munitions depots are blowing up around Paris. They'll have left by tomorrow.

August 20

Slightly less nervous than I was over the last few days, I can take a few notes here. All Paris was expecting the Americans to arrive the night before last. Nobody came. Yesterday was feverish. One neighborhood doesn't know what's happening in the next. Phone calls, uncertain and vague, are all the information we can get. The Resistance was in firefights here and there. At the Hôtel de Ville[350] and Place de la République. Last night the Germans finished blowing up their depots and set fire to the big flour mills in Pantin. The night was calm and today an extraordinary silence reigns. The fever in the streets seems to have fallen. No news of an American advance. Not a plane in the sky. Everything is mysterious. Rumors are flying. In particular, the rumor of an armistice so that the German troops can evacuate Paris...But no, as I write these lines—it is four o'clock—I can hear machine-gun fire in the streets again.

7:30.—Police loudspeakers are indeed announcing an armistice. On Rue de Belleville, people are just waiting to sing for joy. Everybody's in the street. A German car speeds by despite the steep climb. People run into the alleyways. The Germans, in their car, are no less scared than we are.

Yesterday morning on Rue Manin, on the bridge, I had noticed two German sentries who had seemed quite bold to me. Only an idiot could have placed them where they were, completely in the open. It is not possible that the two men couldn't have felt the danger. With their grenades in their belt, their submachine guns in their hands, they were terrified, waiting for an inevitable death—the passerby with an indifferent air who would fire a revolver at them through his pocket almost at point blank range. In flashes of consciousness, they were thinking of their Saxony, their Thüringen, their wives, their children, their fields. What were they doing there on Rue Manin, in the middle of that crowd which neither hated nor loved them and yet thought only of killing them? In the evening, toward eight o'clock, they are dead. I am incapable of rejoicing; decidedly, I do not have the soul of a warrior. But neither can I forget all the crimes of these stupid army valets for the past five years. All my heart is with those boys of Paris who are fighting almost without weapons, and my pity is reserved for them.

I'm not even sure I'm happy with the armistice that was signed this afternoon, either. My friend D...calls to describe a scene he saw a little while ago on Avenue

---

[350] The city hall of Paris.

de l'Opéra. A German half-track came across a Resistance vehicle. The Germans were the first to wave a white handkerchief. Both of them stopped, negotiated, then went their way, while the crowd cheered. Those bravos bother me.

The truth, I think, is that the country can use and find its whole soul again only in an honest fight that circumstances are still preventing. But servitude is going to end.

Night of August 21

The situation is still the same. A prodigious night, black and silent. The Germans finished blowing up their munitions depots, setting off the last fireworks of their defeat. Nothing but tree branches whipping around in the garden. Then, around 2 a.m., a heavy rainstorm. But we can't sleep and everybody is staying up like me. I can feel Paris in the darkness, Paris mute, Paris snuffed out for four years. But Paris that used to shine and will shine again, for the light and joy of the world. Paris is waiting; our servitude is coming to an end.

Freedom is returning. We don't know where it is, but it is all around us in the night. It is approaching with the armies. We feel an immense gratitude. It is a very deep joy to verify that what we always thought about man is true. We could not break our chains alone. But all free men finally swung into movement, and they are coming. We were not wrong when we whispered to each other in our prison: Courage. Hold fast. Let our minds, at least, remain free. For all men who are worth something, liberty is a common cause, and it is the love they have for it that makes them brothers. We lost a battle for liberty but it is not defeated and all our brothers will revenge us. How sweet it is to see that fraternity.

Big words are true words. That's what we learned in our ordeals. One's hand trembles again in writing them. They live with our lives, with our blood. We know it. The blood necessary for their lives, for the lives of the sacred things they stand for, was never lacking.

August 22

The truce (in fact asked for by the Germans) was naturally broken as soon as it was proclaimed. The town halls of each arrondissement and the ministries were occupied by the FFI [351] and Vichy vanished like a puff of smoke. The Germans no longer control life in Paris. They only hold the points where they have dug in. There is fighting all over. Place de la République, Place du Panthéon, on the Île de la Cité, and in front of the Senate. The newspapers of liberty have reappeared, and among them the papers that were underground just yesterday: *Combat, Libération, Défense de la France,* etc.

---

[351] FFI: Forces Françaises de l'Intérieur, the military force created in January 1944 from the unification of the main Resistance groups. It was commanded by General Marie Pierre Koenig, who had joined de Gaulle's Free French in London.

I vainly tried to get to the other side of the Seine this afternoon. I would have liked to meet Blanzat and Duval. I ran into barricades in the neighborhood of Les Halles.[352] German tanks were patrolling. As I was going to cross Boulevard Sébastopol, one of them fired thirty-odd meters ahead of me, decapitating a woman and ripping a man's stomach open. In the little streets fifty meters from there, as strange as it seems, people were sitting in their doorways chatting. Curiosity and joy are strongest.

August 23

They're fighting all over Paris this morning. The Resistance had occupied the Grand Palais and the Germans attacked and set fire to it.

A long argument on the phone with my friend Blanzat. He is not, he explains, "in tune" with what seems to him no more than a useless fight. All these combats in Paris to give us the illusion that we owe our freedom to ourselves alone when it is so clear that we owe it to others, to the armies that are on the way; it seems to him this fighting is vain, dishonest, and a waste of lives. But perhaps a people needs such illusions. And it is psychologically and morally useful for it to believe that it owes nothing to anyone but itself. The life of an idea—of liberty—cannot be the same in the masses and in critical brains like my friend Blanzat's or mine. And the history of peoples is made of such illusions. We know very well that the storming of the Bastille was not the Revolution. But it was necessary for the Bastille to be stormed for the idea of the Revolution to live in the French masses for centuries. In the masses…And in the most critical minds. For what do we not owe, we ourselves, to the passion of others? Our ideas, far more than we think, live from the blood that they naïvely, generously shed, and Blanzat himself would never have had such a deep, critical sense of freedom, if freedom had not first inspired the unthinking enthusiasm of simple, generous crowds. But, he observes, these street battles don't come from the crowd at all, but only from a minority who wants them and engages in them. That is true; but there is no doubt, too, that this minority is in a sense delegated by the crowd and represents what is best in it.

Morning, August 24

American radio was announcing yesterday that the FFI had liberated Paris, and this morning that General Leclerc entered the city at the head of his army.[353] But they can't fool us.

---

[352] This huge, mostly wholesale food market was located in the heart of Paris until 1971, when it was torn down to make way for an underground shopping mall and a commuter train station.

[353] One of the few officers to join General de Gaulle in London, Philippe Leclerc de Hauteclocque (1902–1947) then fought in Africa, landed in Normandy at the head of a Free French armored division in General Patton's 3rd Army, and accepted the surrender of the German garrison in Paris on August 25, 1944, in the Gare Montparnasse.

What is the meaning of these lies? Whose interests are they serving? It isn't even good propaganda. The truth is far greater. The truth is, Paris is no longer accepting German control: it has given itself free institutions, and that simple affirmation is being paid for every minute with a great deal of blood. They're fighting at this very moment on the Île de la Cité, on Rue Manin, at the Porte des Lilas, everywhere. They're building barricades that they don't have the weapons to hold.

August 25

Yesterday evening around 9:00 they were still building barricades on Boulevard Sérurier. They were chopping down the plane trees at the street corners. I came back home around ten. Friends call me, saying they can see huge fireworks over the Hôtel de Ville, with red and blue rockets answering them in the south and west. It was the signal. The first tanks of Leclerc's army had just rolled up to Notre-Dame. And then all the bells of all the churches rang in the night, drowning out the rumbling of the big guns.

Freedom—France is beginning again.

BIOGRAPHICAL DICTIONARY

Abetz, Otto (1903–1958). Hitler's ambassador to Vichy France. He was a lifelong lover of French culture—cleansed of all anti-Nazi or Jewish elements: the long list of books banned from 1940–1944 (called *La Liste Otto* in his honor) included works by Freud, Jung, Heinrich Heine, Thomas Mann, André Malraux, Louis Aragon, Max Jacob…and, after 1941, American authors.

d'Aubigné, Théodore-Agrippa (1552–1630). A poet and a Protestant fighter in the religious wars of the 16th century between Catholics and Protestants. His work can be found in most anthologies of French poetry. In the April 11, 1941, entry here, he refers both to winter (*labeur* also means plowing) and old age.

Badoglio, Pietro (1871–1956). Field Marshal Badoglio was instrumental in Mussolini's downfall and then in arranging an armistice with the Allies (signed on September 3, 1943).

Barrès, Maurice (1862–1923). An influential and prolific journalist, novelist, and politician, known for *le culte du moi* ("The Cult of the Self"). He was nationalistic and anti-Semitic.

Benda, Julien (1867–1956). A cultural critic and novelist. He was Jewish, which explains some of the notes about him in this diary. His 1927 book *La Trahison des clercs* (*The Treason of the Intellectuals*) was read and discussed for decades.

Bergery, Gaston (1892–1974). A politician who moved from the anti-fascist Left to the pro-fascist Right, an ambassador under Vichy. He was tried for treason after the Liberation and acquitted. He remained an ardent Pétainist until his death.

Bernanos, Georges (1888–1948). A distinguished Catholic writer whose novels are still read today; three of them were turned into movies by some of France's finest filmmakers.

Blanzat, Jean (1906–1977). First a schoolteacher, then an author and editor. He was a good friend of Guéhenno's and a member of the Resistance group in the Museum of Man (*le groupe du Musée de l'Homme*), one of the earliest networks created in France. He was also a founder of L'Éducation Populaire (Education for the People) just after the war.

Blum, Léon (1872–1950). A political leader on the moderate Left, three times head of the French government, and the author of a dozen books. He was hated by the Right for two reasons: he had headed the Popular Front—the Socialist-centrist-Communist coalition that governed France in 1936–1937—and he was Jewish. He was arrested and imprisoned by French authorities in 1940, put on trial in 1942 (embarrassing Vichy with his speeches against Collaboration), and deported to Buchenwald in 1943.

Boileau, Nicolas (1636–1711). The poet who was also the main theoretician of 17th-century French classicism, a movement that included Racine, Corneille, Molière, and La Fontaine.

Bonald, Louis-Gabriel-Ambroise, Vicomte de (1754–1840). A royalist Catholic thinker and one of the harshest critics of the French Revolution, the Declaration of the Rights of Man, and the very principle of equality.

Bonnard, Abel (1883–1968). Minister of Education under Vichy. He was sentenced to death in absentia for collaboration with the enemy in 1945 and died years later in Franco Spain.

Bossuet, Jacques-Bénigne (1627–1704). A bishop whose sermons and other writings are classics of French prose.

Bouché, Henri (1893–1970). One of Guéhenno's closest friends. An anti-fascist intellectual with a passion for planes (a decorated pilot in World War I), he had a distinguished career in civil aviation and was a Vice-President of Air France from 1932 to 1938.

Bousquet, Joë (1897–1950). A poet much admired by major French poets and writers.

Boylesve, René (pen name of René Tardiveau) (1867–1926). A novelist and critic famous then, forgotten now.

Brasillach, Robert (1909–1945). A novelist, poet, essayist, and critic (especially of the cinema) as well as former student in the École Normale Supérieure. He is mostly known today for his active engagement in the far Right (Action Française, then fascism). His wartime journalism supported the Nazi cause and the deportation of the Jews. He was tried for treason after the Liberation of France and executed despite pleas for clemency from leading writers and intellectuals.

Breitscheid, Rudolf (1874–1944). A German politician and an elected delegate to the Reichstag during the pre-Hitler Weimar Republic who was deported to Buchenwald.

Bremond, Henri (1865–1933). A Jesuit who left the Order in 1904 and the author of nearly thirty books of literary history, theory, and criticism. His *La Poésie pure* appeared in 1926.

Buck, Pearl (1892–1973). An American writer whose novels—particularly *The Good Earth*, a Pulitzer Prize–winning bestseller—won her the Nobel Prize for Literature in 1936 for their descriptions of Chinese peasant life.

Caillard, Christian (1899–1985). A minor painter.

Carrel, Alexis (1873–1944). A Nobel Prize winner for medicine in 1912 who later joined Doriot's fascist Parti Populaire Français (PPF). He was a notorious collaborator with the Vichy regime—though perhaps less "notorious" at the time when Guéhenno's visitor refers to him.

Céline, Louis-Ferdinand (1894–1961). One of the most innovative and important French novelists of the 20th century. He was also a wildly anti-Semitic, pro-Nazi propagandist who was convicted for collaboration with the enemy in 1950 and amnestied a year later.

Chamfort, Sébastien-Roch Nicolas de (1741–1794). Known for his witty, often disabused aphorisms, collected in his *Maximes*... the year after his death.

Chateaubriand, François-René de (1768–1848). A prose writer and precursor of Romanticism. *Mémoires d'Outre-Tombe* (*Memoirs from Beyond the Grave*), published posthumously in 1848, is his best known work today.

Chénier, André (1762–1794). A major poet who was guillotined as a royalist.

Claudel, Paul (1868–1955). A major poet and dramatist whose plays are still staged in France. A devout Catholic and a conservative, he first applauded Pétain—actually writing a poem in his praise—but was soon disgusted by Vichy's collaboration with Nazi Germany.

Clémenceau, Georges (1841–1929). Prime Minister of France during the First World War.

Comte, Auguste (1798–1857). Founder of positivism. He wished to apply scientific method and data-gathering to the social sciences. He coined the term *sociologie*.

Constant, Benjamin (1767–1830). A writer, essayist, and politician. His 1816 novel *Adolphe* is still read today.

Dabit, Eugène (1898–1936). A "proletarian writer." His 1929 novel *Hôtel du Nord* was turned into the classic 1938 film directed by Marcel Carné, starring Louis Jouvet and Arletty.

Daladier, Édouard (1884–1970). As head of the French government in 1939–1940, he approved changes undermining laws benefiting working people that had been passed by the Popular Front. He resigned in March 1940, but not before he signed the disastrous Munich agreement, along with Chamberlain, Hitler, and Mussolini, to "appease" Nazi Germany. Nevertheless, he was arrested by Vichy as a leader of the Republic and eventually deported by the Nazis.

Danton, Georges-Jacques (1759–1794). An influential orator and leader during the French Revolution, his saying *Il nous faut de l'audace, toujours de l'audace!* ("We must be daring, always daring!") is still famous. He was the first chairman of the Committee of Public Safety, which administered the Reign of Terror, but he grew too moderate for it and was guillotined.

Darlan, François (1881–1942). Admiral Darlan was second only to Pétain in the Vichy government from February 1941 to April 1942, when Germany insisted that he be replaced. He urged close military collaboration with the Nazis, but they preferred Laval. In December 1942, Darlan was assassinated by a member of the Resistance in Algeria after the Allies had invaded.

Darnand, Joseph (1897–1945). After a long history in far-right groups (Action Française [see note 19, p. 6] and the Cagoule [see note 117, p. 62]), he founded the Service d'Ordre Légionnaire (SOL), a paramilitary organization supporting Vichy; it became the Militia in 1943 (see note 298, p. 223). Darnand was named Vichy's Secretary for the Maintenance of Order in 1944. He later joined the Waffen SS, fled to Germany in August 1944, and was executed for treason in France in October 1945.

Déat, Marcel (1894–1955). Like Guéhenno, a man of modest origins who succeeded in getting into the elite École Normale Supérieure (hence *Normalien* in Guéhenno's commentary). A socialist until 1933, he then became enthusiastic about the National-Socialists (Nazis), founded a political party to the right of Pétain, and became Vichy's Minister of Labor in 1944. Sentenced to death *in absentia* at the Liberation of France, he died in an Italian monastery.

Doriot, Jacques (1898–1945). A Communist politician of working-class origin who became a fascist. He founded the Parti Populaire Français (PPF) in 1936, and his newspaper *Le Cri du peuple* took the name of a 19th-century revolutionary journal. He also helped create a unit of French volunteers in the German army and fought with them on the Russian front. After D-Day he fled to Germany, where he was eventually shot and killed by an Allied plane.

Drieu la Rochelle, Pierre (1893–1945). A well-known novelist, essayist, and poet. A "prophet" of French doom and decadence, he was an ardent fascist and wrote of his hopes for the New Nazi Order in Europe. He committed suicide after the Liberation of France.

Dubreuil, Hyacinthe (1883–1971). A labor union leader, activist, thinker, and author of many books. He published *La Chevalerie du travail* ("The French Knights of Labor") in 1941.

Duhamel, Georges (1884–1966). A prolific novelist, critic, and playwright. His work was banned during the Occupation.

Dunois, Amédée (pseudonym of Amédée Catonné) (1878–1945). A left-wing union activist who edited an underground newspaper. He was deported in 1944 and died in Bergen-Belsen.

Duval, Jean (1896–1957). An old friend of Guéhenno's, and an academic, critic, and *Normalien* like him. He joined the first active Resistance group in Paris at the start of the Occupation and was awarded the Médaille de la Résistance and the Legion of Honor after the war.

Febvre, Lucien (1878–1956). A specialist in 16th century France and one of the most influential French historians of the 20th century. He was among the principal founders of the École des Annales, the study of history from the bottom up.

Gide, André (1869–1951). The most famous French novelist of his time. He also wrote essays, autobiographical writings, and his well-known *Journal*.

Giono, Jean (1895–1970). A novelist, essayist, and short-story writer whose work was deeply rooted in his native Provence. A number of his novels have been turned into films.

Giraud, Henri (1879–1949). For a time, General Giraud led one current of the anti-German French. A favorite of U.S. diplomacy, he distrusted de Gaulle and only withdrew his support from Pétain in 1943, despite his nationalism.

Giraudoux, Jean (1882–1944). A novelist (*Siegfried et le Limousin,* 1922) and dramatist whose plays, known for their "poetic" quality, were produced in many countries. *The Madwoman of Chaillot* (1943) and *Tiger at the Gates*, a 1955 adaptation of *La guerre de Troie n'aura pas lieu* (1935), also translated as *The Trojan War Will Not Take Place*, were acclaimed in the United States. He also pursued a diplomatic career.

Goebbels, Joseph (1897–1945). As Hitler's Minister of Propaganda from 1933 to 1945, he was the most important political figure in Nazi Germany after Hitler (and ultimately in charge of all publishing in occupied France).

Fanatically devoted to the Führer and violently anti-Semitic, his oratory incited Germans to violence before the war and to fight to the bitter end during the conflict. After Hitler committed suicide in his bunker in May 1945, Goebbels followed him, along with his wife and his six children, whom he killed or had killed.

Goy, Jean (1892–1944). A prominent politician, head of a right-wing veterans' organization, and Deputy from a small center-right party. He was an early apologist for Hitler.

Grenier, Jean (1898–1971). A philosopher and author of over fifty books. He was first the teacher and then the friend of Albert Camus.

Groethuysen, Bernard (1880–1946). An eminent intellectual historian and philosopher who left Germany in protest at the rise of Nazism, settled in Paris in 1932 and became French.

Guizot, François (1787–1874). A conservative statesman and historian who had a long political career. *Enrichissez-vous!* ("Get rich!") is the phrase for which he is most remembered, a pronouncement he was supposed to have made when he was head of the government.

Halévy, Daniel (1872–1962). Guéhenno dedicated his first book to this eminent French historian.

Hervé, Pierre (1913–1993). A former student of Guéhenno's who became a high-ranking member of the Resistance. A Communist deputy after the liberation of France and an editor of *L'Humanité*, he was expelled from the Party in 1956 and finally became a left-wing Gaullist.

Hilferding, Rudolf (1877–1941). A prominent German socialist. Arrested by the Gestapo and imprisoned in the Prison de la Santé in Paris, he is thought to have committed suicide in his cell.

Jaurès, Jean (1859–1914). A socialist leader, philosopher and historian, and founder of *L'Humanité*, the newspaper that later became the official organ of the French Communist Party. When Guéhenno was sixteen, he heard Jaurès address the striking factory-workers in Fougères and was deeply moved. Jaurès was assassinated on the eve of World War I because of his pacifist views. Streets in many French towns (including Paris) bear his name.

La Rochefoucauld (1613–1680). A classic French *moraliste*—that is, someone who reflects, often with irony, on human behavior. His *Maximes* (1665–1678) are known for their witty, often disabused observations on human nature.

Lamartine, Alphonse de (1790–1869). One of the French Romantic poets. *Le Lac* ("The Lake") is his best-known poem.

Langevin, Paul (1872–1946). A world-class physicist and a left-wing anti-fascist. He was arrested on October 30, 1940.

Laval, Pierre (1883–1945). Pétain's Prime Minister except for one short period (December 1940–April 1942). He came to personify the policy of Collaboration. "I want a German victory," he declared publicly in June 1942. Unlike Pétain, he was widely hated in France, as he was held responsible for the Compulsory Work Service (see note 7, p. xxxi) and other unpopular measures. He was executed for treason at the Liberation of the country.

Leclant, Jean (1920–2011). An eminent Egyptologist. His wife's parents were neighbors of Guéhenno's in Fougères.

Leconte de Lisle, Charles-Marie René (1818–1894). Probably the best-known poet in the "Parnassian" movement.

Lhote, André (1885–1962). Painter, sculptor, and writer on modern art, especially Cubism.

Lusseyran, Jacques (1924–1971). A student of Guéhenno's who was inspired by him. At seventeen, he founded a Resistance group and later organized distribution of Resistance propaganda in trains. Arrested by the Gestapo in 1943, he was deported to Buchenwald. His autobiography (1953) was translated into English as *And There Was Light* (1998).

Lyautey, Hubert (1854–1934). A general in France's wars of colonial expansion in North Africa and Madagascar. He served briefly as Minister of War during World War I and was promoted to Marshal in 1931. He was active in French pro-fascist organizations during his later years.

Malherbe, François de (1555–1628). A poet who saw his task as purifying French diction and versification. He is often considered as the first theorist of 17th-century French classicism.

Malraux, André (1901–1976). A writer and art historian., *La Condition humaine* (*Man's Fate*, 1933) is his most famous novel, and *The Voices of Silence* (1951) is his best known essay on art. He was President de Gaulle's Minister of Culture from 1959 to 1969.

Man, Henri de (1885–1953). A right-wing Belgian socialist thinker later accused of collaboration. (The speaker is surely not referring to his now more famous nephew Paul, a literary theorist.)

Marivaux, Pierre Carlet de Chamblain de (1688–1763). A classic playwright and novelist. His plays are known for their delicacy of dialogue and feeling and are still performed today, especially in France.

Martel, Thierry de (1875–1940). A great neurosurgeon. As Guéhenno says, he committed suicide as the Germans entered Paris.

Mauriac, François (1885–1970). A distinguished Catholic novelist and a member of what came to be called the Intellectual Resistance. He won the Nobel Prize for literature in 1952.

Maurras, Charles (1868–1952). An influential right-wing writer, intensely nationalist, anti-democratic, and anti-Semitic. A leading figure in the monarchist movement Action Française and an enthusiastic collaborator (famously describing Pétain in power as "a divine surprise"), he was sentenced to life imprisonment at the Liberation of France.

Mesnil, Jacques (pseudonym of Jean-Jacques Dwelshauvers) (1872–1940). An art historian and journalist who published in France (e.g., in *Europe*, which Guéhenno edited), in Belgium (his birthplace), and in Italy. He was first a committed anarchist and then an anti-Stalinist Communist.

Michelet, Jules (1798–1874). A historian who was also a great writer. Some of his works are still read and studied in France and elsewhere. Guéhenno's first book, *L'Évangile éternel* (*The Eternal Gospel*, 1927), was a study of Michelet.

Mirabeau, Honoré-Gabriel Riqueti, comte de (1749–1791). A great orator in the National Assembly, the governing body of France during the revolutionary period. He was a moderate, who died before the radicals came to power and the Reign of Terror began.

Montherlant, Henry de (1895–1972). A writer whose plays are still performed in France. Some of his novels are still read, too.

Morand, Paul (1888–1976). A prolific novelist, short-story writer, travel writer, and chronicler.

Nerval, Gérard de (1808–1855). A great, esoteric, mad poet. He committed suicide by hanging himself from a lamppost.

Palissy, Bernard (1509–1590). A distinguished ceramist who was also an agronomist, scientist, lecturer, and writer on scientific subjects.

Paulhan, Jean (1884–1968). A critic and writer. He helped found the underground left-wing literary review *Les Lettres Françaises* in 1942. Before, during, and after the War, he was a highly respected, influential figure in Gallimard (then and now the main quality publishing house in France) and in its literary magazine, the *Nouvelle Revue Française* (NRF).

Péguy, Charles (1873–1914). A writer, philosopher, poet, and essayist who died in World War I. He was a mystical Catholic nationalist who wanted a war with Germany to get back Alsace and Lorraine, which had been annexed by

Prussia after it defeated France in 1871. When Guéhenno says one "cannot think [of him] today without great sadness," he may also be alluding to Péguy's loathing for anti-Semitism.

Philippe, Charles-Louis (1874–1909). A writer of "populist" novels relating the lives of working-class people, employees of modest means. *Bubu de Montparnasse* (1901) is his best-known work.

Pourrat, Henri (1887–1959). An extremely prolific novelist and ethnologist, popular at the time, who specialized in French rural life. He collected folk tales from Auvergne.

Proudhon, Pierre-Joseph (1809–1865). A libertarian socialist. *What Is Property?* (1840) is his most famous work. (His answer: "Property is theft!")

Pucheu, Pierre (1899–1944). Like Guéhenno (and Déat), he was of working class origin and rose in society through the École Normale. As Vichy's Minister of the Interior—the ministry responsible for maintaining order in France—he created the "Special Sections" to try and quickly execute "terrorists" (members of the Resistance). He himself was the first member of the Vichy government to be executed by the Free French.

Renan, Ernest (1823–1892). A philosopher and historian often cited by Guéhenno. He wrote *La Réforme intellectuelle et morale* in 1871, after another French defeat at the hands of Germany (or more precisely, Prussia) in the Franco-Prussian War.

Reynaud, Paul (1878–1966). In June 1940, he was prime minister of France (*Président du Conseil*) and held two ministries besides. His radio address of June 13, 1940, recognized the terrible military disaster but said "the democracies" are strong and can still come to the rescue of France. He resigned on June 16 and was replaced by Pétain.

Rivet, Paul (1876–1958). A doctor, anthropologist, and ethnologist who founded the *Musée de l'Homme* (Museum of Man). His open letter attacking Pétain in July 1940 foreshadowed his commitment to the active Resistance. The network he formed in the museum was one of the first in France. Many of its early members were arrested and either executed or sent to concentration camps.

Rivière, Jacques (1886–1925). A critic, writer, and editor-in-chief of the *Nouvelle Review Française* (*NRF*) from 1919 on. *The German* (*L'Allemand*, 1918) was a reflective memoir of his experience as a prisoner of war.

Robespierre, Maximilien Marie de (1758–1794). The principal leader of the Jacobins, the group in power during the radical phase of the French Revolution. An advocate of a "pure" republic, he was instrumental in waging a "Reign of

Terror" against its enemies by guillotining them. He was guillotined in his turn, without trial, in 1794.

Robin, Armand (1912–1961). A poet, translator, and political and cultural journalist. He was a student of Guéhenno's.

Saint-Exupéry, Antoine de (1900–1944). Though most famous in the United States as the author of *Le Petit Prince* (1943), his novels won a number of literary prizes in France, and *Wind, Sand, and Stars* (*Terre des hommes*) won the American National Book Award in 1939. A pilot in the Free French Air Force, he died on a reconnaissance mission in 1944.

Saint-Just, Louis Antoine de (1767–1794). A young, eloquent defender of Robespierre and the radical republic of the Jacobins. He was guillotined along with them when they fell from power.

Sainte-Beuve, Charles Augustin (1804–1869). Perhaps the foremost French critic of the 19th century.

Sarraut, Albert (1872–1962). Often a government minister, he stepped down as head of the government in June 1936 to make way for Léon Blum and the Popular Front. His brother Maurice (1913–1943), a Senator and newspaper editor, was assassinated by the *Milice* (see note 298, p. 223).

Sorel, Georges (1847–1922). A political philosopher and the theoretician of "revolutionary syndicalism"—confederations of labor unions, which would replace capitalism. He probably did more than anyone to introduce Marxism to France. *Réflexions sur la violence* (*Reflections on Violence*, 1908, with many subsequent re-editions) is his most famous work.

Strauss, David Friedrich (1808–1874). Called "a German Renan." Like Renan, he wrote a "Life of Jesus" (*Das Leben Jesu kritisch bearbeitet*, 1835–1836), scandalous at the time, which tried to distinguish myth from fact. During the Franco-Prussian War, he wrote an open letter to Renan (1870) inviting him to reflect on the causes of the war. Their public exchange became part of the history of thought in both countries.

Stülpnagel, General Otto von (1878–1948). The commander of German occupation forces in France until he resigned early in 1942. Accused of war crimes (ordering the execution of hostages, etc.), he committed suicide in a French prison.

Supervielle, Jules (1884–1960). A much-admired poet and novelist whose poems are classical in form, deceptively simple, but convey a modernist sense of anxiety and loneliness. His work often shows a tendency to fantasy and a certain playfulness that has charmed contemporary readers.

Tagore, Rabindranath (1861–1941). An Indian poet, artist, philosopher, musician, and the first non-European to win the Nobel Prize for Literature (1912).

Talleyrand (full name: Charles-Maurice de Talleyrand-Périgord) (1754–1838). One of the most famous diplomats of all time. He served five radically different French régimes.

Vaillant, André (1890–1977). A lifelong friend of Guéhenno's. After the war, they lived in the same building on Rue Pierre Nicole in the Latin Quarter for years. A professor in the greatest universities of France, he was the author of a five-volume grammar of the Slavic languages.

Valéry, Paul (1871–1945). A major poet and essayist. All anthologies of French poetry contain a hefty selection of his poetry, and a university as well as many schools in France bear his name. Guéhenno first refers to one of his poems—actually the book for a cantata (*Ébauche d'un serpent*)—and later to a book of his essays (*Mélanges*).

Vauvenargues, Marquis de (1715–1747). A *moraliste*—that is, someone who reflects, often with irony, on human behavior—and literary critic. A friend of Voltaire's, he is known today mainly for his aphorisms.

Vercingetorix (ca. 82–46 B.C.E.). The head of the Arverni tribe, in Auvergne, the region where Guéhenno had been sent with his class after the German invasion. Vercingetorix led the Gauls—the Celtic people whom the French traditionally think of as their ancestors—in a revolt against the Roman Empire but was eventually defeated, taken to Rome, and executed.

Vigny, Alfred de (1797–1863). One of the French Romantic poets. He was also a playwright and a novelist. Proust particularly admired his poem *La Maison du berger* ("The Shepherd's Home").

Vildrac, Charles (pseudonym of Charles Messager) (1882–1971). A left-wing poet. His work was included in *L'Honneur des poètes*, an underground anthology of Resistance poetry published by Éditions de Minuit in 1943.

Villon, François (1431–1463). One of the greatest French poets.

Voiture, Vincent (1597–1648). A poet known for his light verse and elegant letters, much admired in the 17th and 18th centuries.

Weygand, Maxime (1867–1965). A World War I veteran and Commander-in-Chief of the French Armies in the last month of the Battle of France in 1940. He was instrumental in the decision to give up the fight and sign the Armistice with Germany. He became Pétain's Minister of Defense in the Vichy government.

Appendix

CHARLES DE GAULLE:
"THE CALL OF JUNE 18"

NOTE: Not only was Guéhenno stirred when he heard Charles de Gaulle's radio address of June 18, 1940, but many of his own thoughts recorded in this diary echo de Gaulle's analysis of the situation, knowingly or not. Moreover, as this brief speech is now a classic and one version of it is posted all over France every June, it seems useful to include the full text here in English. In French, it is the *Appel du 18 juin*, usually translated as "The Appeal of 18 June," but it is far more a *call* than an appeal. This translation is based on the official text (found, among many other places, on http://www.charles-de-gaulle.org/pages/l-homme/dossiers-thematiques/1940-1944-la-seconde-guerre-mondiale/l-appel-du-18-juin/documents/l-appel-du-18-juin-1940.php). De Gaulle's address was not recorded on June 18, so the text that has passed into history may not be the precise words Guéhenno heard on the radio: There is some evidence that the second line was eliminated at the request of the English War Cabinet.

—D.B.

The leaders who have been at the head of French armed forces for many years have formed a government.

This government, alleging the defeat of our armies, has contacted the enemy to put an end to the fighting.

Certainly, we were—we are—overwhelmed by the enemy's mechanical force, on land and in the air.

Infinitely more than their number, it is Germany's tanks, planes, and tactics that have pushed us back. It is the tanks, the planes, and the tactics of the Germans which surprised our leaders so much that it brought them to the situation they are in today.

But has the last word been said? Must all hope vanish? Is our defeat definitive? No!

Believe me: I know whereof I speak, and I am telling you that nothing is lost for France. The same means that have defeated us can one day bring us victory.

For France is not alone! She is not alone! She is not alone! She has a vast Empire behind her. She can join forces with the British Empire, which holds the sea and is continuing the fight. She can, like England, make unrestricted use of the immense industrial power of the United States.

This war is not limited to the unhappy territory of our country. This war has not been decided by the battle of France. This war is a world war. All our mistakes, all our delays, all our suffering do not alter the fact that there are, in this universe, all the means necessary to crush our enemies one day. Struck down today by mechanical force, we can win by superior mechanical force in the future. That is where the world's destiny lies.

I, General de Gaulle, now in London, call on the French officers and soldiers now in British territory or who may come here with or without their weapons, I call on the engineers and workers in the arms industry who are in British territory or who may come here, to contact me.

Whatever may happen, the flame of French resistance must not and will not go out.

Tomorrow I will speak on London radio, as I have today.

INDEX